WITHDRAWN

ADVANCES IN CLINICAL COGNITIVE SCIENCE

ADVANCES IN
Clinical Cognitive Science

Formal Modeling of Processes and Symptoms

EDITED BY
RICHARD W.J. NEUFELD

AMERICAN PSYCHOLOGICAL ASSOCIATION
WASHINGTON, DC

Published by
American Psychological Association
750 First Street, NE
Washington, DC 20002
www.apa.org

To order
APA Order Department
P.O. Box 92984
Washington, DC 20090-2984
Tel: (800) 374-2721
Direct: (202) 336-5510
Fax: (202) 336-5502
TDD/TTY: (202) 336-6123
Online: www.apa.org/books/
E-mail: order@apa.org

In the U.K., Europe, Africa, and the Middle East, copies may be ordered from
American Psychological Association
3 Henrietta Street
Covent Garden, London
WC2E 8LU England

Typeset in Goudy by World Composition Services, Inc., Sterling, VA

Printer: Edwards Brothers, Ann Arbor, MI
Cover Designer: Berg Design, Albany, NY
Technical/Production Editor: Harriet Kaplan

The opinions and statements published are the responsibility of the authors, and such opinions and statements do not necessarily represent the policies of the American Psychological Association.

Library of Congress Cataloging-in-Publication Data

Advances in clinical cognitive science : formal modeling of processes and symptoms / edited by Richard W. J. Neufeld.—1st ed.
    p. ; cm.
Includes bibliographical references and index.
ISBN-13: 978-1-59147-784-6
ISBN-10: 1-59147-784-0
1. Psychology, Pathological. 2. Cognitive science. I. Neufeld, Richard W. J.
[DNLM: 1. Cognition Disorders—diagnosis. 2. Clinical Medicine—methods. 3. Cognition. 4. Cognitive Science—methods. 5. Models, Theoretical. WM 204 A244 2007]

RC454.4.A38 2007
616.89075—dc22   2006023460

British Library Cataloguing-in-Publication Data
A CIP record is available from the British Library.

Printed in the United States of America
First Edition

CONTENTS

CONTRIBUTORS

William H. Batchelder, Department of Cognitive Science, University of California, Irvine

Kristine Boksman, Department of Psychology, Hotel Dieu Hospital, Kingston, Ontario, Canada

Jerome R. Busemeyer, Department of Psychological and Brain Sciences, Indiana University, Bloomington

Jeffrey R. Carter, Mme Vanier Children's Services, London, Ontario, Canada

Richard A. Chechile, Department of Psychology, Tufts University, Medford, MA

J. Vincent Filoteo, Department of Psychiatry, University of California, San Diego

Leonard George, Department of Psychology, Capilano College, North Vancouver, British Columbia, Canada

Rachel A. Heath, School of Psychology, University of Newcastle, Callaghan, New South Wales, Australia

Elaine M. Heiby, Department of Psychology, University of Hawaii at Manoa

Ralph E. Hoffman, Department of Psychiatry, School of Medicine, Yale University, New Haven, CT

Jennifer Jetté, Forensic Adolescent Program, Calgary Health Region, Calgary, Alberta, Canada

John K. Kruschke, Department of Psychological and Brain Sciences, Indiana University, Bloomington

Lawrence R. Levy, Department of Psychology, William Osler Health Centre, Brampton, Ontario, Canada

W. Todd Maddox, Institute for Neuroscience, University of Texas, Austin

Richard M. McFall, Department of Psychological and Brain Sciences, Indiana University, Bloomington

Thomas H. McGlashan, Yale Psychiatric Institute, Yale–New Haven Psychiatric Hospital, New Haven, CT

Richard W. J. Neufeld, Department of Psychology, University of Western Ontario, London, Ontario, Canada

Robert M. Nosofsky, Department of Psychological and Brain Sciences, Indiana University, Bloomington

Ian S. Pagano, Cancer Research Center of Hawaii, Honolulu

David M. Riefer, Department of Psychology, California State University, San Bernardino

Julie C. Stout, Department of Psychological and Brain Sciences, Indiana University, Bloomington

James T. Townsend, Cognitive Modeling Program, Department of Psychological and Brain Sciences, Indiana University, Bloomington

Teresa A. Treat, Department of Psychology, Yale University, New Haven, CT

Elizabeth S. Veinott, Department of Psychological and Brain Sciences, Indiana University, Bloomington

Richard J. Viken, Department of Psychology, Indiana University, Bloomington

David Vollick, Department of Psychology, University of Western Ontario, London, Ontario, Canada

Shirley S. Wang, Department of Psychology, Yale University, New Haven, CT

Eldad Yechiam, Behavioral Sciences Area, Faculty of Industrial Engineering and Management, Technion–Israel Institute of Technology, Technion City, Haifa, Israel

ACKNOWLEDGMENTS

It has been a fortunate fact in the modern history of physical science that the scientist constructing a new theoretical system has nearly always found that the mathematics he required for his system had already been worked out by pure mathematicians for their own amusement.
> —Braithwaite (1968, p. 48)[1]

Acknowledged are analogous labors of love engaged in by mathematical behavioral scientists, whose fruits may be realized in part through advances in clinical science and assessment. I thank Jim Townsend and Robert Gardner, for the edifying conversations on mathematical modeling and statistical issues, and Lorrie Lefebvre, for her conscientious help with clerical aspects of producing this volume. Thanks are extended as well to Lansing Hays and Ron Teeter of the American Psychological Association Books Department for suggesting the volume to its editor and for support throughout the book's development phase, respectively.

The most important acknowledgment is that of the participation of patients and clients, whose provision of cognitive performance samples has contributed to the body of clinical science knowledge and progress toward the ultimate goal of improving assessment and intervention for themselves and others.

---

[1] From *Scientific Explanation: A Study of the Function of Theory, Probability and Law in Science*, by R. B. Braithwaite, 1968, Cambridge, England: Cambridge University Press.

ADVANCES IN CLINICAL COGNITIVE SCIENCE

INTRODUCTION

RICHARD W. J. NEUFELD

This volume is designed to showcase fertile clinical applications of contemporary quantitative cognitive science. Contributions are from cognitive scientists who have formally modeled clinically relevant aspects of cognitive functioning or cognition-related symptoms among special populations and clinical scientists who have adapted techniques of quantitative cognitive science to advance their clinical research and assessment. Each addressed disorder or symptom is listed in the *Diagnostic and Statistical Manual of Mental Disorders* (American Psychiatric Association, 2000).

The contributions for the most part detail findings from specific clinical samples, but the methods are intended to have general application. Ways in which readers can apply the expounded techniques to similar problems in their own research, and potentially in clinical practice, are made apparent. Descriptions of results from productive applications are intended to motivate engagement of the associated methods. Exposition of the latter, along with provision or citation of supporting resource material, are designed to facilitate understanding and implementation of the methods.

The target audience includes those doing research on cognitive faculties in clinical populations or the cognitive neuroscience thereof. It includes as well those pursuing the development of cognitive assessment instruments or routinely engaged in the assessment of clients' cognitive efficiency. Often,

3

the reader will be one who is not indisposed to mathematical developments but who nevertheless desires a rigorous exposition of promising formal methods that is less austere than usually is the case in so-called "high-level" technical sources.

OVERVIEW

In his status check on mathematical psychology as of the mid-1970s, William K. Estes (1975) wrote, "A fertile interaction between measurement theory and research seems more likely to evolve when a measurement model is part and parcel of a theory developed for the interpretation of a process" (p. 273). Shortly thereafter, Paul Meehl (1978), in lamenting the slow progress of so-called "soft psychology," and Richard McFall and James Townsend, in their 1998 update, noted that in older disciplines, notably physics, measurement is prescribed by substantive theory itself rather than entailing an exercise in measure selection from an off-the-shelf array. Estes, in the above inventory of successes and challenges, observed that many instances of empirical data processing are accompanied by a tacit promise to eventually supply the theoretical infrastructure needed for rigorous interpretation, a promise seldom fulfilled. R. Duncan Luce (1997), in enumerating lingering issues in mathematical psychology, pointed to the continuing artificial and detrimental rift between mathematical psychology (substantive formal theory development, typically directed to a specific problem or content domain) and psychometrics (data structure theory and analysis, typically transcending content domains) that contrasts economics' productive interlacing of mathematical economics and econometrics (see also chap. 2, this volume). On this note, in a recent high-profile article bemoaning a shortage of quantitatively trained psychologists (Clay, 2005), opportunities in the areas of measurement and statistics were extolled, but completely missing was any mention of mathematical psychology's potential to inspire graduate students to develop quantitatively grounded theory or, to this end, its provision of workshops on contemporary developments (e.g., Myung, Forster, & Browne, 2000; Wagenmakers & Waldorp, 2006; also, workshops routinely given at meetings of the Society for Chaos Theory in Psychology and the Life Sciences). As for regard in the broader scientific community, it should not go unnoticed that the latest Nobel Prize to come psychology's way (in 2002) was for none other than work firmly entrenched in the mathematical psychology of predictive judgments. Clinical cognitive science and assessment arguably are uniquely poised to benefit from inroads of formal theory and methodology and even to provide fertile ground in their own right for progress in quantitative cognitive science.

The chapters in this volume exemplify clinically significant returns on the investment of subjecting sometimes-formidable problems to quantitative modeling. Otherwise obscured avenues of data collection, analysis, and interpretation are disclosed, and clinically significant inferences regarding underlying sources of cognitive functions and symptomatology are unveiled. Performance levels that are superficially similar by conventional analyses are shown to emanate from offsetting latent processes that turn out to be separable via formally contrived measurement tools (e.g., chaps. 1 and 2). Identified is the multicomponent complexity of certain routinely used measures—for example, of judgment, selection, and choice—along with rigorous methods for estimating the integrity of those components (see chaps. 3 and 4). Embedding data processing and interpretation in formal theory furthermore demonstrably conveys resolution of enigmas attending conventional scoring of neuropsychological test batteries (e.g., chap. 1). Potent methods for capturing subjective relations among disorder-significant items are shown to educe intractable distortions that ramify to memory and categorization processes (chap. 6). The construct of automatic-controlled processing, invoked routinely in clinical studies, is dissected into discrete components whose mathematical grounding yields quantitative signatures of their status (chap. 7). New explanations of clinically important phenomena (e.g., prominent symptoms) are forthcoming, and seemingly disparate phenomena become unified via a single explanatory process (chap. 8). Also offered up are penetrating numerical diagnostics that indicate the nature of multivariable dynamical systems governing disordered affect (chap. 9). Methods of mediating group-level findings on symptom-relevant cognitive performance to individual group members are shown to be viable (chap. 5).

Quantitatively formulated latent mechanisms of the presence or absence of statistical interactions entailing diagnostic groups and testing conditions, essential to informed interpretation (Busemeyer, 1980), are made available by formal process models (chaps. 1, 2, and 5). Cognitive-science-principled, model-guided paradigms and accompanying platforms of interpretation in principle are at the disposal of electrophysiologists of cognitive neurocircuitry (e.g., functional magnetic resonance imaging [fMRI], magnetoencephalography, electroencephalography, etc.).

Intervention stands to be guided by an improved mapping of targets for cognitive–behavioral rehabilitation, and for pharmacological regimens whose efficacy ostensibly includes cognitive efficiency. Analogous to neurosurgical navigation based on high-resolution fMRI or magnetoencephalography, navigation of cognitive behavior therapy has access to gold standard assessment of the perceptual organization of clinically significant content and hence to related memory and categorization processes (chap. 6).

Potential contributions from quantitative clinical cognitive science to progress in quantitative cognitive science at large can be by-products of successful responses to challenges *sui generis* to the clinical domain. Adaptations and extensions of extant models of cognitive performance deviations attending clinical disorder provide an opportunity for what Busemeyer and Wang (2000) termed the *generalization testing* of model validity. Models that accommodate performance abnormalities are preferred to those that do not or that are strained to do so.

Furthermore, individual differences represent model-exogenous noise to formal cognitive science but are focal to clinical assessment. Coherence of model performance at the group and individual levels, impelled by clinical exigencies, is an extension of the above generalization testing for selection among competing models.

Models can be excessively complex or overparameterized, with the theoretical significance of their parameters being poorly understood (Luce, 1997). Substantive meaning of model parameters, however, can accumulate through their association with measures, psychometric or otherwise, linked to pathognomonic, prognostic, or etiological entities (Carter, Neufeld, & Benn, 1998). Other contributions from the clinical field should become apparent as the frontiers of application continue to recede.

Before leaving this topic, it should be mentioned that contributions to formal cognitive science from the clinical setting ideally will go beyond those of supporting roles. Clinical applications in principle can motivate and figure directly into model construction *ab initio* by raising rare perspectives on cognitive phenomena and angles on empirical testing. Unique necessities can be the mother of otherwise-unrealized mathematical invention (Kline, 1980). If clinical cognitive science acquits itself admirably in its give and take with the broader field, it does so with some travail.

CHALLENGES TO FORMAL CLINICAL COGNITIVE SCIENCE, AND AVENUES OF RESOLUTION

The Hilbert-like enumeration of unresolved problems and targets for mathematical psychology, supplied by Estes (1975) and Luce (1997), is undiminished when it comes to the arena of clinical science and assessment. The list of thorny issues continues to entail, among others, effective methods of model testing and competing model selection; parameter interpretation; individual differences in model structure and parameter values; intractability of the inherently dynamical nature of processes under study; managing model-exogenous noise in empirical data; and coping with the epistemic status of hypothetical structures, which amidst their demonstrable utility (see above) are nonetheless latent and unobservable. Because of their salience in clinical implementations, emphasis below is placed on the related issues of individual differences and model-exogenous noise.

Just what constitutes noise, or variation in data not addressed by the specified model? First, note that a random feature is directly built into some models, hence their name, *stochastic models*. These models "recognize" as fundamental to the makeup of their target phenomena an element of unpredictability, analogous to Brownian motion in physics (Evans, Hastings, & Peacock, 2000; Luce, 1986; Townsend & Ashby, 1983). Most of the treatments in this volume entail models of this nature (exceptions being developments in chaps. 8 and 9). Such models of course may differ in the minuteness of variation that is expressly incorporated; one modeler's noise is another's subject matter, depending on the processes being targeted for study (Gilden, 2001; Shavelson & Webb, 1991). Furthermore, genuine noise may have substantive significance in its own right. When characterizing fluctuation in affect, it may signify adaptive spontaneity in responding to environmental contingencies (chap. 9).

This said, variation in empirical observations defensibly lying beyond a model's staked-out territory must be addressed. If not, attempts at empirical fit may inevitably end up in a slough of despond as they are overwhelmed by extraneous sources of variation. A conventional solution is to intensively study an individual participant by administering a large number of trials—sometimes into the thousands and oft-times across multiple testing sessions. This tactic of course attenuates the noise in noisy data by exploiting the principle "error tends to cancel." Selected reports in this volume exemplify the intensive study of one person at a time and the potent inferences that can result from estimation of participant-specific model properties (chaps. 3 and 4).

Depending on the cognitive task requirements, however, sufficient testing for stability of estimation may be unworkable owing to clinically indigenous constraints, including distressed states of participants (although test-taking tedium seems not to have fazed proponents of some extremely long but routinely used psychometric tests). When obtaining the necessary complement of trials at the level of the individual is infeasible, aggregation across participants within a diagnostic group is indicated.

Such aggregation, however, incurs the well-known hazard of conflating systematic individual differences within the data amalgam subjected to modeling. Modeling now stands to address what amounts to being a statistical artifact comprising an aggregate that is unrepresentative of any of its constituents. There are several lines of defense against this pitfall, cogently illustrated throughout this volume.

One of these lines of defense is to carry out preliminary analyses on the candidate data profiles so as to rule out heterogeneity that would contraindicate their being folded into one another. For example, a chi-square contingency test may be applied to good advantage where the data comprise frequencies and can be arrayed into a Participant × Response

Category matrix (chap. 1). Where the data format that is to be subjected to modeling is other than frequencies, Tukey's (1949) test for nonadditivity may serve a similar purpose in identifying significant heterogeneity in data protocols. Likewise, ascertaining requisite data homogeneity may be achieved through selective adaptations of coefficient alpha applied to data profiles of individuals within the sample (chap. 7), or where individual data points are to be aggregated, through application of selected Kolmogorov–Smirnov tests to their distribution (chap. 5). Another tactic entails the use of profile-analytic procedures, including the familiar method of principal-components analysis, or singular-value decomposition (and their extensions), to isolate systematically differing clusters of task performance. Such isolation may be followed up with aggregation within those clusters (Carter et al., 1998).

Alternatively, Monte Carlo simulations may be used to establish that model properties recovered from aggregate data faithfully reproduce population values (see chap. 2, this volume; Riefer, Knapp, Batchelder, Bamber, & Manifold, 2002).

Even without consistent differences in ensembles of data nested within the aggregate, it is possible to meaningfully implement what otherwise would be regarded as model-exogenous noise into an expanded model. Provision for indeterminacy now is extended beyond the performance model proper (i.e., stochastic model with fixed parameters, above) to variation in model expression within a given data assembly. Performance model parameters, for example, can be deemed as randomly distributed across participants. In any case, distributions of parameter values make for stochastic mixture models. Among other advantages, ushered in is a principled assault on at least some of the dispersion in performance (*overdispersion*) beyond that embedded in the basic performance model (chap. 1). Also introduced is a potent method of estimating the mean population parameter values of the performance model (population parameter mapping; see chap. 2), along with their probability distributions and related significance tests. Moreover, exploiting Bayesian statistical methods, a natural outgrowth of mixture models, improves prediction of individual task performance beyond that available from classical parameter estimates (e.g., maximum likelihood and moment-matching estimates; see chap. 5).

VALIDITY STATUS OF MODELS AND THEIR PARAMETERS

Models presented in this volume are accompanied by varying amounts and types of evidence bearing on construct validity (Cronbach & Meehl, 1955). *Construct validity* here pertains to the interpretation of model properties, which often are parameters, and the organization of model components, which often are constituent processes represented by the parameters or in which the parameters participate (e.g., stimulus encoding, memory search, assimilation of encoded stimulus properties, response selection, etc.). When it comes to varying stages of development, we are reminded of Cronbach and Meehl's (1955) observation that construct validation is an ongoing process. We are reminded as well that evidence from multiple and unexpected sources can enter into the case for construct validity.

One such source includes observations from clinical applications themselves. For example, values of model parameters (e.g., elevated sensitivity to reward for successful choices; chap. 3) should conform to clinical characterizations of participants (e.g., cocaine abusers). Thus, results from the present clinical implementations become part of the corpus of evidence bearing on model (property) validity, potentially to be added to the collective validity credentials that preceded such implementations.

Persuasive support for the substantive significance of model parameters notably includes their selective sensitivity to affiliated experimental factors (e.g., chaps. 1 and 2). Other sources involve coherence with documented neurophysiology of disorders under study (chaps. 3, 4, and 8). Still others entail the position and operation of model parameters in a formal deductive system (Braithwaite, 1968), whereby meaning is endowed by the system's structure, including roles assigned to the complement of other parameters. A formal theoretical apparatus also enables the unveiling of substantively significant mathematical properties of model elements—properties that can affirm with the backing of precise derivations the claimed understanding of the elements (Neufeld, in press). This form of support obviously is a province of formal models.

Model-based estimates of cognitive functions, moreover, arguably are more valid in key ways than are estimates that rely exclusively on experimental procedures, as follows. The suggestion has been made that in contrast to tapping targeted faculties through modeling methodology, the targeted faculties may well be studied and measured more directly and simply by isolating them according to function-specific discrete tasks. Extricating the operations of interest from the global task in which they typically are set, however, may violate their makeup relative to what it might be within a context of collateral operations. To illustrate, estimating the integrity of stimulus encoding subserving stimulus processing with respect to memory-held information is predicated on the intact assemblage of both the encoding and memory-scanning requirements. Estimating the nature and status of the encoding process stipulates effective modeling of its architecture and parameters, specifically as encoding operates in the service of memory search.

In certain instances, it is a stretch to envision how certain elements of cognitive performance might even exist outside the intact processing system. Examples include the anchoring of response selections in accumulated information about advisability of alternatives (e.g., chaps. 3 and 4). The same could be said about sensitivity to positive versus negative outcomes attending decision and choice (chap. 3). It also is less cumbersome, and conceivably less costly, to estimate process parameters from a single well-designed task than to obtain multiple scores from a battery of tasks, each addressed to its own designated process (cf. Broga & Neufeld, 1981).

Precedent for concepts being inextricably bound up with the phenomena to which they contribute readily come to the fore in older disciplines. As Flanagan (1991) stated,

> In physics, there are many explanatory constructs, electrons for example, which cannot be measured independently of the observable situations in which they figure explanatorily. What vindicates the explanatory use of such constructs is the fact that, given everything else we know about nature, electrons best explain the observable processes in a wide array of experimental tests, and lead to successful predictions. (p. 380)

Finally, definitions of inferred variables are tightly constrained in formal models by virtue of their quantitative format. Their specificity, lent in part by the formal system in which they operate, exposes them to more rigorous testing and refutation than otherwise would be the case (Staddon, 1984, 1991).

THE ULTIMATE CONSUMER

A sort of mission statement for the present anthology is that it should endow the pursuit of information, ultimately destined for use with individuals who have problems in living (i.e., clinical clients), with the latest applicable advances in cognitive science and associated measurement. Deviations in model properties accompanying disturbances in principle present themselves as potential targets for intervention; model properties whose status remains intact point to functions apparently spared. The upshot is an individualized, cognitive-science-principled profile of strengths and weaknesses. This same assessment method comes into play in monitoring the effectiveness of intervention it initially helped to deploy. Demands on the client to provide cognitive performance samples in principle can be lightened through Bayesian methodology (Batchelder, 1998; Neufeld, Carter, Boksman, Jetté, & Vollick, 2002). Techniques overlapping with those monitoring client progress moreover are available to evaluate cognitive aspects of the efficacy of entire treatment regimens (Neufeld, in press).

More indirectly, but harboring no less benefit, model-based cognitive assessment has the potential to inform and evaluate pharmacological interventions. Neurocircuitry, as monitored by fMRI or other technology, can be activated by paradigms embedding processes identified as disorder affected (e.g., with the aid of parametrically homogeneous samples; Neufeld et al., 2002). Pharmacological agents ideally can target the associated neurocircuitry (e.g., glutamitergic or dopaminergic systems). The very cognitive assessment tools used to guide pharmacological interventions in turn can be used to evaluate success of the latter with respect to cognitive efficiency. Suffice it to say that creative applications toward client benefit may take multiple routes, the reader undoubtedly having envisioned several others.

MATHEMATICAL AND COMPUTATIONAL TOOLS

Mathematics involved in model development tend to go beyond the usual sequence of introductory calculus and linear algebra. In addition, an appreciation of discrete and continuous stochastic distributions is essential to implementations of stochastic models. Such appreciation, however, usually is acquired in an introductory statistics course as well as courses in research design and analysis that are part of most graduate psychology program curricula.

The reader therefore may selectively access one or more of the following sources in order to buttress his or her understanding of certain parts of the expositions presented here, to adapt existing models to new instantiations, or to develop new versions altogether. The glossary of technical terms, located at the back of this volume, should help. These sources of course may productively augment collaborations with colleagues who may have extensive quantitative training. The sources listed below are presented partly out of personal familiarity, with the full recognition that favorite and possibly better alternatives may be preferred.

For a refresher on basic calculus, including some first principles, the venerable *Quantitative Methods in Psychology*, by Lewis (1960), offers a highly accessible presentation; so does Dowling's (1980) *Theory and Problems of Mathematics for Economists*, part of Schaum's Outline Series in Economics, which includes linear algebra and several other relevant topics (albeit without much in the way of first principles). Spiegel's (1963) *Theory and Problems of Advanced Calculus* and, for certain problems involving continuous stochastic distributions, *Theory and Problems of Laplace Transforms* (Spiegel, 1965), both from Schaum's Outline Series in Mathematics, may prove useful, along with Hildebrand's (1986) *Advanced Calculus for Applications*. Helpful aids include *The HarperCollins Dictionary of Mathematics*, by Borowski and

Borwein (1989); *Statistical Distributions*, by Evans et al. (2000); and *A Dictionary and Bibliography of Discrete Distributions*, by Patil and Joshi (1968).

For exposition of Bayesian methods, the reader may consult O'Hagan and Forster's (2004) volume, *Bayesian Inference*, in Kendall's Library of Statistics series, or Berger's (1985) *Statistical Decision Theory and Bayesian Analysis*. Finally, informative treatments of stochastic modeling include Ross's (1996) *Stochastic Processes*, Townsend and Ashby's (1983) *Stochastic Modeling of Elementary Psychological Processes* (with an extremely helpful exposition of mathematical essentials), Luce's (1986) *Response Times: Their Role in Inferring Elementary Mental Organization*, and Wickens's (1982) *Models for Behavior: Stochastic Processes in Psychology*.

Because of the nature of mathematical modeling, entailing as it does problem- or content-specific developments, readily applicable software is less available than is the case for routine computations and analyses. There are, of course, exceptions, as with the widely used methodology of multinomial processing tree (MPT) modeling (see chap. 1, this volume) and Townsend and colleagues' factorial technology for discerning processing system structure capacity and process-termination criteria (referred to in chap. 7, this volume).

On the other hand, symbolic-manipulation computer algebra programs (e.g., Waterloo MAPLE), highly suited to assist the modeling enterprise, have been growing more user friendly. It is interesting that a few mathematical preliminaries sometimes can smooth the way even when applying symbolic-manipulation programs. Occasionally, computational logjams can be dislodged through feeding to the program certain command modifications that can be as simple as rigorously rearranging the order of mathematical operations. Similarly, simple operations can sometimes substantially reduce total computing time. In some instances, a routine can be "helped along" by providing it with interim derivations to which it seems "blind." Moreover, extracting the full complement of information latent in computational output depends on mathematical insight. Also, exploiting computational power, whether it be from symbolic or numerical manipulation programs (e.g., MATLAB), to expose the outworking of a well-developed mathematical model presupposes a certain understanding of the model's composition (Luce, 1997).

As a bonus to possessing mathematical tools that equip the owner for modeling endeavors, options for tapping otherwise overlooked reserves of information are increased. For example, inferences about the dynamics of cognitive performance lodged in the more granular properties of data can be exploited through commensurately detailed analyses (Townsend, 1990). The potential upshot can be meta-analyses of published or archived data that are substantively richer than those available from standard effect size and related calculations.

THE CONTRIBUTIONS

The contributions to this book address a variety of disorders, with methods of study and assessment tailored to focal problems. The contributions are united in their exemplary use of quantitative methods to obtain information not otherwise available or available only suboptimally.

The first two chapters, by Batchelder and Riefer and by Chechile, are devoted to MPT modeling of memory performance. This topic reasonably occupies two chapters because of the relative prominence of this methodology in clinical science and assessment and its power for identifying stages of memory that are spared, and those that are affected, with disorder. The chapters are complementary. For example, Batchelder and Riefer supply formalisms that are strategic to the mathematical groundwork for MPT modeling, and Chechile presents a unique method of parameter estimation and significance testing. Within the MPT modeling environment, different paradigms are used to study memory in schizophrenia and other disorders (chap. 1) and developmental dyslexia (chap. 2). On the face of it, memory performance has a rather immediate relation to the symptomatology of developmental dyslexia and a more indirect relation to that of schizophrenia (be it paranoid or nonparanoid, or so-called "positive" vs. "negative"; e.g., Nicholson & Neufeld, 1993). Regardless, individually estimated MPT modeling parameter values are found to be correlated with clinically meaningful variables. In each treatment, construct validity for the interpretation of model parameters is established before they are used to explore abnormality. In particular, parameters are observed to be selectively sensitive to experimental treatments targeting the specific stages of memory the parameters purportedly express.

Turning to the related domain of decisional and perceptual processes, chapter 3, by Yechiam, Veinott, Busemeyer, and Stout, begins by describing pilot exploration of model parameters and the predictive efficacy of competing decision-model structures. Results are used to guide the examination of decision processes among patients with Parkinson's disease and Huntington's disease and cocaine abusers. Problems in living arise when future events are ignored or misconstrued. By their mathematically informed analysis of performance on a prototypical gambling task, these authors are able to isolate reasons for such difficulties among each of the respective groups. The reasons involve balance of attention to successive gains versus losses, acquisition of optimal-response information, and compliance of responding with the available information as updated across trials. The modeled sources of difficulty, in turn, are coherent with known neurophysiology of the respective disorders.

In chapter 4, Maddox and Filoteo invoke generalized recognition theory (Ashby & Townsend, 1986), a multidimensional extension of signal detection theory (e.g., Green & Swets, 1966), to study deviations in the learning of variously complex stimulus categorization rules. The included rules arguably encompass classificatory principles fundamental to daily handling of multifaceted stimuli. Mathematically principled tools once more break down global categorization performance into components that are either spared or affected with well-charted neurophysiological damage. Strategies of stimulus classification and consistency in their use are separated out among amnesic patients and Huntington's and Parkinson's disease patients. The technique of *minimal titration* parsimoniously releases hypothesis-related model properties while clamping the remainder. In addition, a normative model depicting objectively optimal performance provides a benchmark to which descriptive models, corresponding to actual performance, can be examined for the degree and nature of departure among the studied groups.

The presentation in chapter 5 by Neufeld et al. capitalizes on pre-existing identification of deficit among schizophrenia participants in a component of information processing that subserves collateral functions. The deficit entails delayed encrypting of presenting stimulation into a cognitive format that facilitates the operations of so-called "short-term" working memory. A specific stochastic model parameter of the stimulus-encoding process has been singled out as the source of delay, with support for this formulation emanating from divergent sources of behavioral data and alternate quantitative (neuroconnectionist) levels of analysis. The parameterized processing deviation has been deemed to ramify to clinically significant variables, including thought-form disorder and compromised stress negotiation. Using Bayesian procedures, group-level findings on encoding performance are mediated to individual participants, which ushers in model testing on individual performance data, completing model testing on group data.

Treat et al. show in chapter 6 how current methods of multidimensional scaling can rigorously tap perceptual organization of clinically significant stimuli (those bearing on eating disorders and sexual aggression). Perceptual organization in turn feeds into memory and item classification processes. This chapter integrates the quantitative expressions of these three domains, making for an extensive account of problem-domain cognition. The rigorous assessment of perceptual organization presented here holds the promise of serving as a sort of high-resolution guidance system for deploying cognitive treatment interventions.

If automatic-controlled processing (a certain representation of which dates all the way back to Hylan, 1903) is perhaps the most ubiquitous multicomponent construct in clinical cognitive science, then its constituent component of processing capacity may be the most commonly invoked concept in the field. Described by Neufeld, Townsend, and Jetté in chapter 7 is a mathematically established definition and measure of processing capacity. This index is elemental to signatures of capacity properties of investigated processing systems. The presented indexes provide the diagnostic power and dynamic processing detail over intervals of cognitive task transaction, necessary for embarking on an unambiguous determination of capacity characteristics, and their changes across examined groups. The method is used to characterize anxiety-prone individuals' visual-search capacity and its pattern of deployment over a visual array as well as memory-search capacity among paranoid schizophrenia patients. In the former instance, a benchmark of optimal capacity deployment once more is provided by a normative model, against which the descriptive models of both less and more anxiety-prone groups are compared.

Addressing clinical symptoms directly, computational modeling, with its computer simulation of perceptual and cognitive neurocircuitry, is used effectively in chapter 8 by Hoffman and McGlashan to manufacture salient aspects of schizophrenia (auditory hallucinations). Many signs and symptoms of psychopathology have been mimicked to date using computerized neural networks to represent what might be called the "computational nervous system." The present work is exemplary in its modeling of the neurophysiological footprints of abnormalities in developmental milestones that accord with established findings for schizophrenia. Results from theoretically prescribed perturbations of neuroconnectionist architecture persuasively converge with related speech-perception data and observed patterns of synaptic elimination.

Using techniques spawned by nonlinear dynamical systems theory (chaos-theoretic methods), in chapter 9, Heath, Heiby, and Pagano analyze the variation that takes place in mood over an extended measurement period. Methods are adapted to the limitations of repeated measurements from human participants, specifically limited observation sample size and ordinal data properties. Described methods distinguish between normal and pathological mood variation using deterministic–chaotic and Gaussian–stochastic–noise markers. It is intriguing that normal variation is more proximal to the latter, a result that is considered to express a greater degree of adaptive spontaneity in response to environmental exigencies. The report bespeaks groundbreaking, almost futuristic, but decidedly rigorous time-series-endowed directions of clinical assessment of mood and other disorders. Apropos of cognition, observe that in the literature on the topic, affect has a close tie to cognitive processes and, like neuroconnectionist modeling, the behavioral science home of nonlinear dynamical systems modeling is squarely in the field of cognitive science (including perception, psychophysics, and information processing).

As a final observation, note that embedded in these contributions is a general quantitative toolbox. The particular instantiations with selected clinical problems and data by and large are cases in point.

REFERENCES

American Psychiatric Association. (2000). *Diagnostic and statistical manual of mental disorders* (4th ed., text revision). Washington, DC: Author.

Ashby, F. G., & Townsend, J. T. (1986). Varieties of perceptual independence. *Psychological Review, 93,* 154–179.

Batchelder, W. H. (1998). Multinomial processing tree models and psychological assessment. *Psychological Assessment, 10,* 331–344.

Berger, J. O. (1985). *Statistical decision theory and Bayesian analysis* (2nd ed.). New York: Springer Publishing Company.

Borowski, E. J., & Borwein, J. M. (1989). *The HarperCollins dictionary of mathematics* (2nd ed.). New York: HarperCollins.

Braithwaite, R. B. (1968). *Scientific explanation.* Cambridge, England: Cambridge University Press.

Broga, M. I., & Neufeld, R. W. J. (1981). Multivariate cognitive performance levels and response styles among paranoid and nonparanoid schizophrenics. *Journal of Abnormal Psychology, 90,* 495–509.

Busemeyer, J. R. (1980). Importance of measurement theory, error theory, and experimental design for testing the significance of interactions. *Psychological Bulletin, 88,* 237–244.

Busemeyer, J. R., & Wang, Y. (2000). Model comparisons and model selections based on generalization test methodology. *Journal of Mathematical Psychology, 44,* 171–189.

Carter, J. R., Neufeld, R. W. J., & Benn, K. D. (1998). Application of process models in assessment psychology: Potential assets and challenges. *Psychological Assessment, 10,* 379–395.

Clay, R. (2005, September). Too few in quantitative psychology. *Monitor on Psychology, 36,* 26–28.

Cronbach, L. J., & Meehl, P. E. (1955). Construct validity in psychological tests. *Psychological Bulletin, 52,* 281–302.

Dowling, E. T. (1980). *Outline of theory and problems of mathematics for economists.* New York: McGraw-Hill.

Estes, W. K. (1975). Some targets for mathematical psychology. *Journal of Mathematical Psychology, 12,* 263–282.

Evans, M., Hastings, N., & Peacock, B. (2000). *Statistical distributions* (3rd ed.). New York: Wiley.

Flanagan, O. (1991). *Science of the mind* (2nd ed.). Cambridge, MA: MIT Press.

Gilden, D. L. (2001). Cognitive emissions of 1/f noise. *Psychological Review, 108,* 33–56.

Green, D. M., & Swets, J. A. (1966). *A treatment of the theoretical and empirical fundamentals of signal detection.* Oxford, England: Wiley.

Hildebrand, F. E. (1986). *Advanced calculus for applications* (2nd ed.). Englewood Cliffs, NJ: Prentice Hall.

Hylan, J. P. (1903). The distribution of attention, I. *Psychological Review, 10,* 373–403.

Kline, M. (1980). *Mathematics: The loss of certainty.* Oxford, England: Oxford University Press.

Lewis, D. (1960). *Quantitative methods in psychology.* New York: McGraw-Hill.

Luce, R. D. (1986). *Response times: Their role in inferring elementary mental organization.* New York: Oxford University Press.

Luce, R. D. (1997). Several unresolved conceptual problems of mathematical psychology. *Journal of Mathematical Psychology, 41,* 79–88.

McFall, R. M., & Townsend, J. T. (1998). Foundations of psychological assessment: Implications for cognitive assessment in clinical science. *Psychological Assessment, 10,* 316–330.

Meehl, P. E. (1978). Theoretical risks and tabular asterisks: Sir Karl, Sir Ronald, and the slow progress of soft psychology. *Journal of Consulting and Clinical Psychology, 46,* 806–843.

Myung, I. J., Forster, M. R., & Browne, M. W. (Eds.). (2000). Model selection [Special issue]. *Journal of Mathematical Psychology, 44*(1–2).

Neufeld, R. W. J. (in press). Composition and uses of formal clinical cognitive science. In W. Spaulding & J. Poland (Eds.), *Nebraska Symposium on Motivation: Vol. 52. Modeling complex systems: Motivation, cognition and social processes.* Lincoln: University of Nebraska Press.

Neufeld, R. W. J., Carter, J. R., Boksman, K., Jetté, J., & Vollick, D. (2002). Application of stochastic modelling to group and individual differences in cognitive functioning. *Psychological Assessment, 14,* 279–298.

Nicholson, I. R., & Neufeld, R. W. J. (1993). Classification of the schizophrenias according to symptomatology: A two-factor model. *Journal of Abnormal Psychology, 102,* 259–270.

O'Hagan, A., & Forster, J. (2004). *Kendall's advanced theory of statistics: Vol. 2B. Bayesian inference* (2nd ed.). New York: Oxford University Press.

Patil, G. G., & Joshi, S. W. (1968). *A dictionary and bibliography of discrete distributions.* New York: Hafner.

Riefer, D. M., Knapp, B., Batchelder, W. H., Bamber, D., & Manifold, V. (2002). Cognitive psychometrics: Assessing storage and retrieval deficits in special populations. *Psychological Assessment, 14,* 184–201.

Ross, S. M. (1996). *Stochastic processes* (2nd ed.). New York: Wiley.

Shavelson, R. J., & Webb, N. M. (1991). *Generalizability theory: A primer.* Newbury Park, CA: Sage.

Spiegel, M. R. (1963). *Theory and problems of advanced calculus*. New York: McGraw-Hill.

Spiegel, M. R. (1965). *Theory and problems of Laplace transforms*. New York: McGraw-Hill.

Staddon, J. E. R. (1984). Social learning theory and the dynamics of interaction. *Psychological Review, 91,* 502–507.

Staddon, J. E. R. (1991). Review of Klein & Mowrer's (1989) "The distemper of learning . . ." *Contemporary Psychology, 36,* 506–507.

Townsend, J. T. (1990). Truth and consequences of ordinal differences in statistical distributions: Toward a theory of hierarchical inference. *Psychological Bulletin, 108,* 551–567.

Townsend, J. T., & Ashby, F. G. (1983). *Stochastic modelling of elementary psychological processes*. Cambridge, England: Cambridge University Press.

Tukey, J. W. (1949). One degree of freedom for non-additivity. *Biometrics, 5,* 232–242.

Wagenmakers, E., & Waldorp, L. (2006). (Eds.). Model selection [Special issue]. *Journal of Mathematical Psychology, 50*(2).

Wickens, T. D. (1982). *Models for behavior: Stochastic processes in psychology*. San Francisco: Freeman.

1

USING MULTINOMIAL PROCESSING TREE MODELS TO MEASURE COGNITIVE DEFICITS IN CLINICAL POPULATIONS

WILLIAM H. BATCHELDER AND DAVID M. RIEFER

Multinomial processing tree (MPT) models are a well-studied class of mathematical models that can be used as measurement tools to study cognitive processes. They are structurally simple statistical models that can be expressed as tree diagrams, with cognitive processes represented as parameters of the model. Estimates of the values of the parameters provide insight into the separate contributions of different cognitive factors. This can be of great help to researchers trying to develop theoretical explanations for various cognitive phenomena. Many MPT models have been developed by experimental psychologists to study a wide range of theoretical issues, and

We are grateful for the help of Jared Smith in some of the points developed in the "Individual Differences in Multinomial Processing Tree Modeling" section. William H. Batchelder acknowledges the support of National Science Foundation Grant SES-0136115 to A. K. Romney and William H. Batchelder, coprincipal investigators, and Grant IIRG-03-6262 from the Alzheimer's Association to William H. Batchelder and E. Batchelder, coprincipal investigators.

19

Batchelder and Riefer (1999) provided a review of these many experimental applications.

A recent trend in this field is the use of MPT modeling to study cognitive deficits in clinical populations. In this application, the parameter estimates from the model provide information about which cognitive factors differ between clinical groups and their controls. An overview by Batchelder (1998) offers the most general treatment of this approach, and examples can also be found in Batchelder, Chosak-Reiter, Shankle, and Dick (1997) and Riefer, Knapp, Batchelder, Bamber, and Manifold (2002), as well as a number of additional examples discussed in the section of this chapter titled "Applications of Multinomial Processing Tree Modeling to Clinical Populations." As Batchelder (1998) described, applying MPT modeling to the study of clinical populations raises a number of methodological issues and potential problems, the most notable of which is the problem of individual differences. Experimental work with MPT models typically involves pooling data across participants and computing parameter estimates for the grouped data. Individual differences are often ignored in this type of work. In contrast, with groups from clinical populations, within-group individual differences are likely to be present. In these cases, it is important to have methods of detecting individual differences and, if they are present, to have options for dealing with them.

Many articles have described the statistical properties of MPT models (e.g., Baldi & Batchelder, 2003; Batchelder & Riefer, 1990, 1999; Hu & Batchelder, 1994; Knapp & Batchelder, 2004; Riefer & Batchelder, 1988; Riefer et al., 2002), but only a few have addressed the issue of individual differences in any detail (e.g., Batchelder, 1998; Klauer, 2006; Riefer & Batchelder, 1991b). Thus, as clinical applications of MPT modeling become more popular, the time seems right for a general discussion of these issues. The rest of this chapter is organized as follows. First, we give a brief overview of the formal structure of MPT models. Next, we provide a comprehensive review of the different applications of this type of modeling to clinical populations in a variety of experimental paradigms. We then present a detailed discussion regarding how MPT models can be used to study clinical populations in cases where there are participant and/or item differences. In particular, we show how to test for individual differences within a clinical group, and we outline some of the options for addressing these differences if they exist. Last, we offer specific suggestions for researchers who wish to study clinical groups with MPT models.

BRIEF REVIEW OF MULTINOMIAL PROCESSING TREE MODELS

MPT models are developed for experimental paradigms that lead to categorical data; namely, where the responses of participants in an experiment can be described in terms of frequency counts in a set of disjoint and exhaustive response categories. In a typical experimental application, each of N participants makes a response to each of a set of M items (possibly on each of a series of trials). The data usually come from pooling responses over participants and items (however, in the section titled "Individual Differences in Multinomial Processing Tree Modeling" we look at the case of individual differences in great detail). Therefore, if there are K categories, C_1, C_2, ..., C_K, the pooled data consist of frequency counts, F_1, F_2, ..., F_K, where $\sum_{k=1}^{K} F_k = N \cdot M$.

The values of the parameters of an MPT model measure the capacities to perform various cognitive skills that are postulated to underlie the processes involved in response production. For example, in a simple memory experiment, one might have a model that defines parameters for the capacity to attend to presented items, θ_1, to store items in memory, θ_2, and to retrieve items from memory, θ_3. More generally, each parameter θ_s of an MPT model represents the probability that a particular processing event occurs at an appropriate point during processing and, correspondingly, $1 - \theta_s$ represents the probability that the processing event fails to occur at that point. From a statistical perspective, the parameters are latent (unobserved) variables in an MPT model that combine probabilistically to generate the manifest (observed) category frequencies. Because the parameters refer to probabilities of latent cognitive events, they take values in the interval (0,1).

Basically, each MPT model postulates that observed categories result from processing branches (or paths) consisting of a sequence of latent occurrences or nonoccurrences of hypothetical processing events. Each occurrence or nonoccurrence is quantified, respectively, by a corresponding θ_s or $1 - \theta_s$. Each such branch in the tree can be viewed as a sequence of processing links, and the probability that a particular branch occurs during processing is the product of the parametric probabilities that appear on the links that make up that branch. Following our earlier example, suppose a model has a branch in which a participant attends to an item, stores it in memory, and fails to retrieve it. This branch would have the probability $\theta_1\theta_2(1 - \theta_3)$, and if it occurred, then the participant would fail to recall the item. In MPT models, it is possible that several branches can lead to the same observed category; for example, a branch in which a participant fails to attend to an item would have the probability $1 - \theta_1$, and it would lead to a recall failure as well.

The probabilistic assumptions of an MPT model are expressed in a special binary tree structure. These trees are described in detail with examples given by Batchelder (1998) and Batchelder and Riefer (1999). Examples in this volume include the pair-clustering model of this chapter (Figure 1.1) and the storage-retrieval model by Chechile (see chap. 2, this volume,

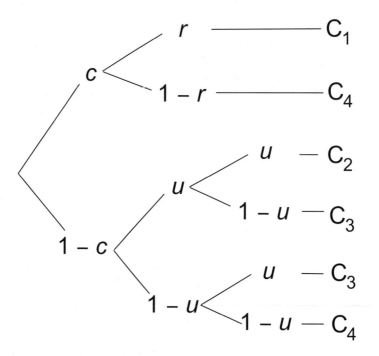

Figure 1.1. A multinomial processing tree diagram for the pair-clustering model.

Figures 2.1 and 2.2). Any MPT model postulates a set of S parameters to explain the distribution of category counts over K categories. The model defines a probability distribution over the categories for each of its parameter values $\theta = (\theta_1, \theta_2, ..., \theta_S)$ in the parameter space Θ, where $\Theta = (0,1)^S$. Specifically, let

$$\Lambda_K = \{\mathbf{p} = (p_1, p_2, ..., p_K) | p_k > 0, \sum p_k = 1\} \qquad (1.1)$$

be the set of all possible probability distributions over the K observable categories. Then an MPT model specifies a function that determines, for each $\theta \epsilon \Theta$, a single member of Λ_K, denoted by $\langle p_k(\theta) \rangle_{k=1}^K$. In general, the tree structure implies a special form of the $p_k(\theta)$ given by

$$p_k(\theta) = \sum_{i=1}^{I_k} \Pr(B_{ik}; \theta), \qquad (1.2)$$

where $\Pr(B_{ik}; \theta)$ is the probability of the ith out of I_k branches (or paths) leading to category C_k. Further, the probabilistic rules illustrated earlier in the example lead to a general expression for the branch probabilities given by

$$\Pr(B_{ik}; \theta) = \prod_{s=1}^{S} \theta_s^{a_{iks}} (1 - \theta_s)^{b_{iks}}, \qquad (1.3)$$

where a_{iks} and b_{iks} are nonnegative integers. The summation sign in Equation 1.2 shows how branch probabilities are combined when more than one branch of the tree terminates in any particular category, and the probability of any branch is just the product of terms of the form θ_s and $1 - \theta_s$ corresponding to the links on that branch. Thus, a_{iks} and b_{iks} are integers representing the number of times θ_s and $1 - \theta_s$, respectively, appear on links on branch B_{ik}.

Under the assumption that observations are independently and identically distributed (i.i.d.), and given the earlier assumption that each of N participants responds to M items, then the category counts have a multinomial distribution given by

$$\Pr(F_1, F_2, \ldots, F_K) = (N \cdot M)! \prod_{k=1}^{K} \frac{p_k^{F_k}(\boldsymbol{\theta})}{F_k!}. \qquad (1.4)$$

Equation 1.4 is a parameterized multinomial distribution, and given data in the form of category counts it is possible to infer facts about the unknown (latent) parameters of the model. Any of the major approaches to statistical inference, including both classical (frequentist) and Bayesian methods, can be used to analyze MPT models; however, in this chapter we stress only classical approaches based on the likelihood function because they are most familiar to psychological researchers.

In using an MPT model to measure (estimate) uniquely the parameters of the model, it is necessary that the model be identified. An MPT model is identified in case different parameter vectors in Θ always lead to different probability distributions over the categories; that is, the function from the model parameter space, Θ, into the category probabilities, Λ_K, is one to one. Identification of an MPT model allows recovery of unique estimates of the parameters for each set of category frequencies, which is a crucial aspect of any measurement method. Agresti (2002); Bishop, Fienberg, and Holland (1975); and Read and Cressie (1988) are good sources of the classical statistical theory of parameterized multinomial models, and Batchelder and Riefer (1999), Hu and Batchelder (1994), and Riefer and Batchelder (1988) have discussed this theory in regard to MPT models.

There are several sources of software for analyzing MPT models that are free and Web accessible, including software developed by Xiangen Hu and described by Hu and Phillips (1999; see http://irvin.psyc.memphis.edu/gpt/). Hu's software enables an investigator to represent the model as a specific set of equations like Equations 1.2 and 1.3. Then one can enter one or more sets of categorical data for the model and perform point estimation and confidence-interval estimation of the parameters, conduct goodness-of-fit tests, and test hypotheses about the model's parameters both within one group and between groups. Hu's software also enables the investigator to simulate data from a model, where the possibility that different participants may have different parameter values is allowed (see the "Individual Differences in Multinomial Processing Tree Modeling" section). These simulations allow one to obtain point and confidence interval estimates when the sample size is not large enough to use asymptotic methods based on the likelihood function. Other software packages include AppleTree for Macintosh computers by Rothkegel (1999) and HMMTree by Klauer (2006; see http://www.psychologie.uni-freiburg.de/Members/stahl/HMMTree).

APPLICATIONS OF MULTINOMIAL PROCESSING TREE MODELING TO CLINICAL POPULATIONS

Multinomial Processing Tree Models for Measuring Storage and Retrieval

Storage and retrieval are cognitive processes that are fundamental components of human memory. In our laboratory (Batchelder & Riefer, 1980, 1986), we have developed and tested a model for separately measuring storage and retrieval that uses a pair-clustering paradigm, in which the study list contains pairs of words from semantic categories (e.g., *dog, horse*). People attempt to memorize the list and then freely recall as many words as they can in any order. Recall of each category pair can be tabulated into one of four mutually exclusive recall events: (a) C_1, both items recalled consecutively; (b) C_2, both items recalled, but not consecutively; (c) C_3, one and only one item recalled; and (d) C_4, neither item recalled. The pair-clustering model assumes that these recall events are a function of three cognitive processes, represented as parameters of the model. Parameter c is the probability that the two category items are clustered and that the cluster is stored in memory at the time of test. Parameter r is the conditional probability that a cluster is retrieved from memory, given that it is stored. Parameter u is the probability that a single item is stored and retrieved, given that it was not clustered. Basically, parameters c and r constitute the model's measures of storage and retrieval, respectively, whereas u is an ancillary parameter that combines both storage and retrieval processes.

According to the model, successful cluster storage and retrieval result in both items of the pair being recalled consecutively (C_1). If a pair is clustered and stored in memory but not retrieved, with the probability $c(1 - r)$, then neither item is recalled (C_4). And if a pair is not stored in memory as a cluster, with probability $1 - c$, then each item in the pair can be stored and retrieved independently (with probability u for each item). Thus, category C_2 represents the event that both items are recalled, but not consecutively (an approximation discussed in Batchelder & Riefer, 1986, 1999), and category C_3 represents the case that exactly one of the two items is recalled. Notice that failure to recall a category pair (C_4) can result from either a failure of storage, $(1 - c)(1 - u)^2$, or a failure of retrieval, $c(1 - r)$. From the above equations, separate estimates for parameters c, r, and u can be derived from the frequencies over the four recall categories. These assumptions are represented in the tree diagram in Figure 1.1.

The exact equations expressing the recall events as a function of the model's parameters can be derived directly from the tree in Figure 1.1. These equations can be written in the form of Equations 1.2 and 1.3 as

$$
\begin{aligned}
\Pr(C_1) &= cr \\
\Pr(C_2) &= (1 - c)u^2 \\
\Pr(C_3) &= (1 - c)\, u(1 - u) + (1 - c)(1 - u)u \\
\Pr(C_4) &= c(1 - r) + (1 - c)(1 - u)^2.
\end{aligned}
\tag{1.5}
$$

The validity of the pair-clustering model has been established through its successful application to a range of storage-retrieval issues in human memory, including the effects of spacing, providing category cues at recall, retroactive inhibition, presentation rate, and part-list cueing (for a review, see Batchelder & Riefer, 1999). However, it can also be used to examine memory deficits in different participant populations. For example, Riefer and Batchelder (1991a) used the model to show that memory deficits exhibited by elderly adults are due more to problems with retrieving information from memory than with the storage of information. More recently, Riefer et al. (2002) used the pair-clustering model to examine storage and retrieval deficits in two well-studied clinical populations: (a) schizophrenics and (b) alcoholics with organic brain damage. A great deal of research on both schizophrenics and organic alcoholics has shown that both groups suffer memory problems compared with normal control individuals. One issue addressed by theorists in this area is whether these deficits are mainly due to problems with storage or retrieval, but, as Riefer et al. pointed out, research and theorizing on this issue are mixed and inconclusive. A number of empirical measures have been used in an attempt to disentangle the separate contributions of storage and retrieval factors in clinical populations, including the contrast between recall and recognition, cued recall of semantic clusters, incidental learning tasks, and forgetting rates. These measures have often produced conflicting results, and thus there is no theoretical consensus on the storage–retrieval locus of these memory deficits, with some theorists concluding that the problem is mainly one of storage and others that the problem lies with retrieval.

It is under these circumstances that formal modeling can help clarify these theoretical issues by providing a more direct measure of the underlying cognitive processes in question. Each group in Riefer et al.'s (2002) study memorized a list of 20 category pairs over six study–test trials, and the pair-clustering model was used to estimate the storage and retrieval parameters for both groups. Riefer et al. concluded that the schizophrenics had both storage and retrieval deficits compared with the control group. However, the deficit was stronger for retrieval, occurring on early trials and continuing throughout the later trials as well. In contrast, the differences in storage between the schizophrenics and the control participants were not as pronounced and became statistically significant only on the later trials. A similar pattern occurred for the organic alcoholics, with retrieval deficits being stronger than storage deficits and occurring on earlier trials. What was particularly striking about the organic alcoholics was their performance across the six study–test trials. Prior research has shown that alcoholics with organic brain damage often exhibit minimal improvement in their recall of a list of words even after multiple presentations of that list. Riefer et al.'s modeling analysis revealed that this deficit is due to problems with retrieval, not storage. Although the organic alcoholics showed modest improvement in their storage of clusters over trials, their ability to retrieve clusters was low and lacked improvement across the six list presentations.

Another example of an MPT model for measuring storage and retrieval is that of Chechile, described in chapter 2 of this volume. Chechile's model has been used to explore the storage–retrieval bases of a wide variety of memory phenomena, including the serial position curve, interference effects, state-dependent memory, and others (for a review, see Chechile, 2004). However, as demonstrated in chapter 2, it can also be used to examine deficits of storage or retrieval processes in clinical populations. Chechile's application of the model to children with developmental dyslexia suggests that children who are poor readers have poorer storage but better retrieval than average readers, a pattern of results that was not evident in the standard empirical analysis of the data.

Modeling the Results of Neuropsychological Test Batteries

Understanding the cognitive deficits in the early stages of Alzheimer's disease (AD) and other forms of dementia is crucial is any attempt to diagnose these afflictions. One assessment device that has been used toward this end is the neuropsychological test battery of the Consortium to Establish a Registry for Alzheimer's Disease (CERAD; Morris et al., 1989), which incorporates many basic tests of cognitive abilities. However, these measures may be limited in their ability to detect the early stages of these diseases. Moreover, without a substantive model it is difficult to establish which specific cognitive processes exhibit deficits in these clinical groups. To explore the usefulness of mathematical modeling in the assessment of AD, Batchelder, Chosak-Reiter, et al. (1997) developed an MPT model based on the free-recall task of the CERAD. In this task, individuals attempt to memorize and recall a list of 10 words across three separate study–test presentations. The model itself is based on earlier Markov learning models (see Greeno & Bjork, 1973) that assume that memorized items can be in one of three levels of storage: (a) an unstored state; (b) an intermediate state, where items are weakly stored and retrieval may be difficult; and (c) a long-term memory state, where storage is stronger and retrieval is more likely. The model contains four parameters that describe the transitions among the states and the probability of retrieval from each state. The data categories for the model consist of the 8 (2^3) possible patterns of recall success or failure across the three test trials, and the MPT model derives the probabilities of these categories as a function of the four parameters of the model.

Batchelder, Chosak-Reiter, et al. (1997) analyzed data collected by the University of California at Irvine Alzheimer's Disease Research Center to form groups consisting of individuals diagnosed with AD, those diagnosed with vascular dementia (VD), and a control group of age- and education-matched nondemented individuals. Each of the two clinical groups consisted of four subgroups that differed in the severity of the disease, ranging from very mild to severe as measured by the Mini-Mental State Exam (Folstein, Folstein, & McHugh, 1975). The important result was that the model's analysis was able to differentiate between clinical groups even when standard empirical analyses did not. For example, the model was able to reveal significant differences between the very mild AD and VD groups compared with the control group, even when these clinical groups had virtually the same levels of overall recall performance over the three study–test trials. In particular, the AD group showed storage deficits compared with the VD group, but these were compensated by retrieval advantages for the AD group.

Another test that has been used to assess cognitive capacity in AD patients, in addition to the neuropsychological tests from the CERAD, is the Boston Naming Test (Kaplan, Goodglass, & Weintraub, 1983). This test consists of a series of line drawings of familiar objects, and individuals are asked to provide the name for each object. Chosak-Reiter (2000) developed and tested an MPT model that is capable of measuring underlying cognitive processes in this task. She applied the model to AD patients and individuals with cerebrovascular dementia, plus a comparable control group. Like Batchelder, Chosak-Reiter, et al.'s (1997) study, Chosak-Reiter's model was able to differentiate between very mild levels of AD and cerebrovascular dementia compared with the control group.

Source Monitoring

Source monitoring is a popular experimental task in cognitive psychology in which items are presented from multiple sources, and individuals must keep track of, or monitor, the correct source for each item (M. K. Johnson, Hashtroudi, & Lindsay, 1993). In a typical source-monitoring experiment, participants study a list of items coming from two sources (e.g., List 1 vs. List 2, or pictures vs. words). On a final recognition test, they are shown previously presented items plus new distractors and are asked to indicate which items are from Source A, which are from Source B, and which are new distracters. Because there are three possible responses to three types of items, the pattern of correct and incorrect identifications can be arranged in a 3 × 3 data table, which provides a rich set of data for formal modeling. In our lab, we have developed and tested an MPT model (Batchelder & Riefer, 1990) that is capable of taking source-monitoring data and deriving estimates of two underlying cognitive capacities: (a) the ability to detect whether an item was an old item (item detection) and (b) the ability to discriminate the source of detected items (source discrimination). In addition, the model is able to estimate the biases used to respond when the items are not detected or are detected but not discriminated.

In our original application of this model, we tested it by applying it to a series of previously published studies. One of these studies was conducted by Harvey (1985), who examined schizophrenics in a variation of source monitoring called *reality monitoring*. In a reality-monitoring task, people must discriminate between external items that are presented from an outside source and internal items that they generate themselves. Harvey and others have speculated that the thought disorders associated with schizophrenia may be the result of deficits in reality monitoring. To test this, Harvey presented a list of words in a source-monitoring task to schizophrenics and normal control participants. In a mixed list, half of the time the participants had to say the words out loud (external), and the other half of the time they just had to think of the word (internal). The final memory test required participants to indicate whether a word had been spoken aloud or thought. Using traditional empirical measures, Harvey observed very poor source discrimination for thought-disordered schizophrenics compared with normal control individuals or schizophrenics without thought disorders. Batchelder and Riefer (1990) reanalyzed Harvey's data using their source-monitoring model, which revealed essentially the same pattern of results as Harvey observed. What was interesting about the model's analysis, however, was that the source-discrimination parameter for the thought-disordered schizophrenics was so low that source-memory performance was essentially at chance levels (i.e., a value of the source-discrimination parameter equal to zero).

More recently, additional applications of MPT models for source monitoring to schizophrenics have been conducted by Keefe and associates (Keefe, Arnold, Bayen, & Harvey, 1999; Keefe, Arnold, Bayen, McEvoy, & Wilson, 2002). The Harvey (1985) study demonstrated that schizophrenics have trouble differentiating between internal and external sources of information. Keefe et al. (1999) explored whether this source-monitoring deficit also extended to external versus external, as well as to internal versus internal, source discriminations. Using a modification of the original Batchelder–Riefer (1990) model, Keefe et al. (1999) found that schizophrenics exhibited deficits in source discrimination for all of the source comparisons. This is an important result, because it indicates that the problems that schizophrenics have with source monitoring are more far reaching than the reality-monitoring deficits demonstrated by Harvey. In a related study, Aleman, Böcker, Hijman, de Haan, and Kahn (2003) found no significant difference in the item-detection parameters of the model between schizophrenics who exhibit hallucinations and those who do not.

Keefe et al. (1999) also explored another issue relevant to source monitoring: the role of response bias. In a source-monitoring task, people must identify old versus new items and assign them to different sources. Response bias can play an important role in this process, because people may have a tendency to favor their responses toward one source over another or have a tendency to exhibit a large number of false identifications to new items (Riefer, Hu, & Batchelder, 1994). One of the advantages of formal mathematical models of source monitoring is that they are capable of separately measuring, and thus factoring out, the various response biases inherent in this task. This is an especially important issue when examining clinical populations, because it can reasonably be expected that clinical patients may operate under response biases that are different than the ones used by normal control participants. Keefe et al. (1999) observed that schizophrenics in their study did in fact have significantly different response biases than controls. Specifically, they found that when the schizophrenics could not remember the correct source of information, they exhibited a bias toward guessing that the information came from an external source, even when it actually came from an internal source (see also Nieznanski, 2005).

Although most of the clinical applications of source-monitoring models have been conducted with schizophrenics, a few studies have applied them to other clinical populations. For example, Batchelder and Riefer (1990) also analyzed a study by Harvey (1985) that examined source memory in manic patients, and Schmitter-Edgecombe, Marks, Wright, and Ventura (2004) used MPT modeling to study source-monitoring deficits in people with severe closed-head injury. Similarly, von Hecker and Meiser (2005) used an MPT model for multiple source dimensions to examine source memory in depressed college students. They observed no source-memory differences between depressed and nondepressed students for relevant stimulus dimensions but found that depressed students actually exhibited superior source memory for irrelevant source dimensions. The authors contended that these results were inconsistent with a capacity-reduction explanation of depression and instead supported the hypothesis that depression leads to a "defocused" mode of attention in which attentional resources are widely distributed across all stimulus dimensions.

Another interesting application of the source-monitoring model comes from a study by Simons et al. (2002), who examined source-monitoring deficits in patients with semantic (or frontotemporal) dementia. Unlike prior applications of the source-monitoring model, which examined group data, Simons et al. (2002) derived parameter estimates for each patient individually. The model's analysis showed that most patients with semantic dementia did not exhibit any deficits compared with control participants on either item detection or source discrimination. An exception to this came from 3 patients with the highest level of impairment, who showed deficits in item detection. Because parameter estimates were calculated for each patient individually, Simons et al. were able to examine the correlations between the model's parameters and other diagnostic variables. For example, the value of the source-discrimination parameter was positively correlated with performance on a neuropsychological battery of frontal lobe tests. In contrast, source discrimination was uncorrelated with the volume of loss in the hippocampus of each patient.

Process Dissociation

An experimental paradigm closely related to source monitoring is the *process-dissociation procedure* (Jacoby, 1991, 1998). In this task, participants are presented with items from two lists, A and B, and are then presented with items from List A, List B, and new items on a memory test. Memory is tested in one of two ways. In the *inclusion* task, participants are required to say "yes" to items from either List A or List B and to say "no" to new distractors. In the *exclusion* task they are asked to say "yes" only to List B items but to say "no" to List A items as well as new items. The theory and model behind process dissociation are that responding to items is a function of two cognitive processes: recollection and familiarity. Recollection is represented by parameter R in the model and happens when an item is consciously remembered. Familiarity is represented by parameter F and happens when recollection fails but the item still seems familiar through automatic or unconscious processes. Thus, for inclusion trials, the probability of saying "yes" can occur either through recollection or familiarity, with the probability

$$\Pr(\text{yes/old}) = R + (1 - R)F. \tag{1.6}$$

However, if a participant makes an error by saying "yes" to a List A item on the exclusion trial, that occurs when the item is not recollected but seems familiar anyway, with the probability

$$\Pr(\text{yes/old}) = (1 - R)F. \qquad (1.7)$$

These two equations are in the form of Equations 1.2 and 1.3 and can be used to estimate the values of R and F. In fact, it is easy to show that Equations 1.6 and 1.7 arise from a very simple MPT model. Jacoby (1991) interpreted R as a measure of conscious processing and F as a measure of automatic or unconscious processing. Some theorists (e.g., Curran & Hintzman, 1995; Erdfelder & Buchner, 1998) have criticized the core assumptions behind Equations 1.6 and 1.7, including the assumption of independence between the process represented by R and F. One important criticism stems from the fact that the exclusion and inclusion tasks each have a substantially different number of items requiring a "yes" response. For this reason, Buchner, Erdfelder, and Vaterrodt-Plunnecke (1995), as well as others, have developed more complex MPT models that expand on Equations 1.6 and 1.7 to include differential response biases for the two tasks. Bellezza (2003) also developed a series of MPT models to explore the relationship between process dissociation and source monitoring.

Process-dissociation models based on Equations 1.6 and 1.7 have been used to examine a wide variety of issues (for a review, see Yonelinas, 2002), including applications to clinical populations. Probably the most common clinical application has been in the study of conscious and automatic processes in patients with various forms of amnesia. A common research finding is that patients with amnesia exhibit cognitive deficits through explicit or direct tests of their memory, but they show little or no memory impairment on implicit or indirect memory tests. A number of studies using the process-dissociation model have shown that this is because patients with amnesia show deficits in conscious processing but not in automatic processing (e.g., Bastin et al., 2004; Hay, Moscovitch, & Levine, 2002). However, Yonelinas, Kroll, Dobbins, Lazzara, and Knight (1998) warned that such conclusions are suspect when the false-alarm rates differ between groups, which may happen when clinical groups are compared with normal control individuals. They reanalyzed the results from a number of studies using a modified version of the process-dissociation model that incorporates signal detection procedures to measure and correct for response bias. They concluded that although amnesiacs showed large deficits in recollection compared with control participants, they also showed smaller but reliable deficits in automatic processing. In addition to the study of clinical amnesia, the process-dissociation model has been used to examine other clinical groups, including schizophrenics (Kazes et al., 1999; Linscott & Knight, 2001, 2004); patients with AD (Adam, Van der Linden, Collette, Lemauvais, & Salmon, 2005; Kessels, Feijen, & Postma, 2005; Knight, 1998; Koivisto, Portin, Seinelä, & Rinne, 1998; J. A. Smith & Knight, 2002); and individuals with developmental dyslexia (McDougall, Borowsky, MacKinnon, & Hymel, 2005), acute distress disorder (Moulds & Bryant, 2004), epilepsy (Del Vecchio, Nei, Sperling, & Tracy, 2004), depression (Jermann, Van der Linden, Adam, Ceschi, & Perroud, 2005), multiple sclerosis (Seinelä, Hämäläinen, Koivisto, & Ruutianen, 2002), and Parkinson's disease (Hay et al., 2002).

INDIVIDUAL DIFFERENCES IN MULTINOMIAL PROCESSING TREE MODELING

It is clear from the above review that MPT modeling is becoming more frequent as a means for assessing clinical populations. However, most MPT models in the literature were originally developed for basic theoretical (as opposed to applied) research. Thus, the most common application of MPT models has been to standard experimental paradigms in which several groups of participants are each exposed to a set of items (Batchelder & Riefer, 1999). In a typical experimental application, the participants are drawn from an approximately homogeneous group, such as college students taking introductory psychology. In turn, the items are drawn from a homogeneous set defined by narrow ranges on such variables as word length, frequency of occurrence, and concreteness ratings. Differences between groups are generally traced to differences in the experimenter-controlled manipulations that define each group rather than systematic differences between the participants in the groups. Consequently, it has become standard practice to pool observations within a group over items and, except in cases where each participant provides many observations, to also pool the data over participants. When such aggregation is done, each group is treated (approximately) as providing a large set of i.i.d. observations that fall into the categories of the MPT model. In this case, inferential statistics for the model are not plagued by small sample sizes. However, despite efforts to achieve item and participant homogeneity, sometimes there remain reasons to be concerned with pooling over participants in experimental studies using MPT models (e.g., Batchelder & Riefer, 1999; J. B. Smith & Batchelder, 2003).

When using MPT models to assess differences in cognitive abilities among special populations, concerns about item and participant homogeneity not only are different than those in experimental studies but also can be even more severe (for a detailed analysis of these differences, see Batchelder, 1998). Unlike a typical experimental study, in a study involving special populations each group is defined by properties of the participants, such as age range; clinical classification in the *Diagnostic and Statistical Manual of Mental Disorders* (American Psychiatric Association, 2000); or neuropsychological tests such as the Mini-Mental State Exam, which is used to indicate levels of dementia. It is a necessary consequence of creating groups from special populations that there will be within-group variation on the classificatory variables used to define the groups. Important covariates are also likely, such as level of education, gender, and ethnicity, any of which may contribute to within-group differences even if they are not part of the classification criteria for defining groups. Because there are several sources of within-group variation with special populations, it is therefore not enough simply to apply an MPT model to the pooled data to draw conclusions about group differences. It is also necessary to examine the data for within-group differences and provide some statistical analyses that control for them.

One way to assess within-group variability is to determine whether the conclusions based on the pooled data are robust in simulations where the parameters underlying the observations are allowed to vary from participant to participant. This method was used in Riefer et al.'s (2002) study, discussed earlier, in which groups of schizophrenics and organic alcoholics were compared with appropriate control groups. The pair-clustering MPT model in Equation 1.5 was used to analyze the data to see if there were between-group differences in storage and retrieval capacities. First, the data within each group were pooled over both items and participants and analyzed in the usual way using Hu's software, which includes a simulation option to examine the possible effects of individual differences within a group. The procedure involves simulating and analyzing many sets of data, where the parameter values vary from participant to participant by drawing them from beta distributions. The *beta distribution* is a flexible family of parametric distributions useful for modeling individual differences on the interval (0,1) (Evans, Hastings, & Peacock, 2000).

To illustrate, let θ_s be one of the parameters in an MPT model, and assume that participants' values of θ_s are drawn i.i.d. from the beta distribution given by

$$g(\theta_s; \tau_{1,s}, \tau_{2,s}) = \frac{\Gamma(\tau_{1,s} + \tau_{2,s})}{\Gamma(\tau_{1,s})\,\Gamma(\tau_{2,s})}\, \theta_s^{\tau_{1,s}-1}\,(1 - \theta_s)^{\tau_{2,s}-1}, \qquad (1.8)$$

where the two parameters of the beta distribution, $\tau_{1,s}$ and $\tau_{2,s}$, are in a parameter space Φ consisting of pairs of positive numbers, that is, $(\tau_{1,s}, \tau_{2,s}) \in \Phi = (0, \infty)^2$, and $\Gamma(.)$ is the well-known gamma function (e.g., Evans et al., 2000). In the following equations, we use the facts that for the beta distribution in Equation 1.8, the mean is given by

$$E(\theta_s) = \frac{\tau_{1,s}}{(\tau_{1,s} + \tau_{2,s})} \qquad (1.9)$$

and the variance is given by

$$Var(\theta_s) = \frac{E(\theta_s)[1 - E(\theta_s)]}{(\tau_{1,s} + \tau_{2,s} + 1)}. \qquad (1.10)$$

The analysis using Hu's program is done with the constraint that the mean of each parameter's distribution is matched to its maximum likelihood estimate (MLE) on the basis of the pooled data, and the variance is set to a "moderate" value on the basis of prior studies of the pair-clustering model in Riefer and Batchelder (1991b). For each of the many data sets simulated in this way, the software enables one to conduct the same series of hypothesis tests and goodness-of-fit measures that were done with the pooled data from the experiment. In this way, one can see which scientific conclusions based on the pooled data are supported by the simulations.

In the case of Riefer et al. (2002), it was shown that despite changes in the actual values of some of the statistics, the main statistical inferences from the analyses based on the pooled data remained essentially unchanged with the simulated data. Because the scientific conclusions were unchanged when moderate amounts of parameter heterogeneity were introduced into the data, it was argued that the approximations based on the original pooling of the data over participants were not misleading. However, there are two problems with the simulation approach viewed as a general way to deal with individual differences in MPT model analyses. First, the simulation option requires one to inject a fixed amount of parameter variability across participants, but unfortunately, there is no way to know a priori just how much variation in parameters is needed to match the within-group variation in latent parameters likely to be present in the data. Second, unlike the result in Riefer et al. (2002), the statistical inferences made from the simulated data might not have matched the inferences made by pooling the data over participants. In this case, one would not be able to draw any conclusions from the analyses of the pooled data without some additional procedure.

In this section, we provide several approaches to handle the problem of individual differences. First, we describe a test for the presence of individual differences in the participants that can be applied to the raw category frequencies. We then discuss three procedures for dealing with individual differences if they are present. The first of these provides a way to analyze the variation in the individuals' frequency count vectors to suggest a level of variance to use in the simulation approach. The second approach involves analyzing each participant's data separately with an MPT model. This method must deal with small sample sizes for each participant, and this means that the parameters estimated for each partici-pant may be quite variable. However, the approach provides display methods that allow one to see trends across participant's in each group. Finally, we discuss an approach, called *hierarchical modeling*, that actually models individual differences within an MPT model. This enables one to analyze the pooled data with an MPT model that incorporates individual differ-ences directly.

Testing for Individual Differences

It is possible to develop a straightforward test on the raw category frequencies to see if there are individual differences within a group. Suppose that each of N participants makes a response to each of M items. Also assume that each response is classified into exactly one of K categories, $C = \{C_1, C_2, \ldots, C_K\}$. Let $X_{ij} = k$ if the category of the response of participant i to item j is C_k, for $i = 1, 2, \ldots, N$; $j = 1, 2, \ldots, M$; and $k = 1, 2, \ldots, K$. These participant-item response random variables can be arrayed in a matrix, $\mathbf{X} = (X_{ij})_{N \times M}$. We assume that the X_{ij} are mutually stochastically independent; however, they may not be identically distributed. The independence assumption states that for any realization of $\mathbf{X}$ given by $(X_{ij})_{N \times M} = (x_{ij})_{N \times M}$,

$$\Pr[(X_{ij})_{N \times M} = (x_{ij})_{N \times M}] = \prod_{i=1}^{N} \prod_{j=1}^{M} \Pr(X_{ij} = x_{ij}). \qquad (1.11)$$

The data for the participants can be arrayed in an $N \times K$ contingency table, where the ikth entry, $F_{i,k}$, is the number of times that participant i's response was in category k, that is, the number of times $X_{ij} = k$. The hypothesis that there are no individual differences is equivalent to the assumption that the $N \times K$ contingency table exhibits independence, and one method for testing this is the well-known chi-square test (e.g., Hays, 1981; Moore & McCabe, 1999). The test statistic compares the observed values in the table against the expected values under the independence assumption. The expected values are given by $E(F_{i,k}) = \dfrac{M \cdot F_k}{N \cdot M} = F_k/N$, where $F_k = \sum\limits_{i=1}^{N} F_{i,k}$, and the test statistic is given by

$$X^2 = \sum_{i=1}^{N} \sum_{k=1}^{K} \frac{\left(F_{i,k} - F_k/N\right)^2}{F_k/N}. \qquad (1.12)$$

Under the independence hypothesis, which in this case states that there are no participant differences in the use of categories, X^2 has an approximate chi-square distribution with degrees of freedom given by $df = (N - 1) \cdot (K - 1)$.

If the value of X^2 falls well into the upper tail of the chi-square distribution with the above degrees of freedom, then the identically distributed assumption can be rejected, and this means that there are significant amounts of individual differences in the data. For X^2 to approximate a chi-square distribution, there must be sufficient numbers of observations in the

EXHIBIT 1.1
Value of the Statistic X^2 Computed for Each Learning Trial for Participants
With Schizophrenia in Riefer et al. (2002)

Trial 1	Trial 2	Trial 3	Trial 4	Trial 5	Trial 6
123.1	172.5	259.4	307.2	306.6	310.7

contingency table. In most statistics texts, a rule of thumb is offered for when it is reasonably accurate to use the chi-square distribution to test for independence in an $R \times C$ contingency table. For example, Moore and McCabe (1999, chap. 9) stated that the chi-square statistic can be used if the average count per category is five or more and each category has at least one count. Because there are M items and K categories, a necessary condition to use the chi-square distribution is that $M/K \geq 5$. If this condition is not satisfied, or if there are zero cells, one can use a nonparametric permutation test called the *Fischer exact test* that can be applied to sparse contingency tables to test for independence (e.g., Agresti, 2002; Hays, 1981).

To illustrate the chi-square test, consider the experiment discussed earlier that was reported by Riefer et al. (2002) in which schizophrenics were compared with suitable control individuals. We applied the test in Equation 1.12 to each of the six trials of the group of schizophrenics. There were 20 items per participant and 4 categories, so the average count per category was 5, satisfying one of the conditions for the use of the chi-square test. There were 29 participants, so the test had 84 degrees of freedom. The values of X^2 are reported in Exhibit 1.1 for each trial. Because the critical value for this test at the $p = .01$ level is 117.4, we can comfortably reject the hypothesis of no individual differences in the participants, and in fact the evidence for participant heterogeneity is seen to increase over the first few trials. This increase is likely due to the different learning rates of the participants as well as differences in storage and retrieval capacities. The data in Exhibit 1.1 suggest that the step of pooling over participants in analyzing the data with the pair-clustering model is questionable, and in the case of this study the subsequent analysis using the simulation approach discussed earlier in this section was crucial in justifying the conclusions drawn from the pooled data.

Calibrating Hu's Simulation Subroutine

When the test in Equation 1.12 rejects the hypothesis of participant homogeneity, it is possible that a more general hypothesis holds, namely, that each individual's frequency counts come from the so-called *Dirichlet–multinomial (D-M) distribution* (N. L. Johnson & Kotz, 1969; Mosimann,

1962), also called the *compound multinomial distribution*. In this section, we describe the D-M distribution and show that we can use it to suggest values of the variances in the beta distribution to use in applying Hu's simulation option.

In the context of a Bayesian approach, the Dirichlet distribution is often used as a prior distribution for the category probability vector $\mathbf{p} = (p_k)_{1 \times K}$, an approach that Chechile uses in chapter 2 of this volume. In our application, we regard the Dirichlet distribution as a model of how the category probabilities vary from participant to participant. For the Dirichlet distribution, the probability of any pattern of probabilities for a participant is given by

$$\Pr[\mathbf{p} = (p_k)_{1 \times K}] = \frac{\Gamma(\alpha)}{\displaystyle\prod_{k=1}^{K} \Gamma(\alpha_k)} \prod_{k=1}^{K} p_k^{\alpha_k - 1}, \qquad (1.13)$$

where the parameters of the Dirichlet distribution satisfy $\alpha_k > 0$ for $k = 1, 2, \ldots, K$, and $\alpha = \sum \alpha_k$. Actually, it is easy to see that the beta distribution in Equation 1.8 is a special case of the Dirichlet distribution in Equation 1.13 for $K = 2$.

The D-M distribution combines the Dirichlet distribution with the multinomial distribution. In particular, if we assume that the N participants' probabilities, $\mathbf{p}_i = (p_{i,k})_{1 \times K}$, are i.i.d. from a Dirichlet distribution, and that the N category frequency count vectors, $F_i = \langle F_{i,k} \rangle_{k=1}^{K}$, are independent and multinomially distributed with the sampled probabilities, then it follows that the N count vectors are i.i.d. from the D-M distribution given by

$$\Pr(\mathbf{F} = \langle F_k \rangle_{k=1}^{K}) = \frac{M!}{\displaystyle\prod_{k=1}^{K} F_k!} \frac{\Gamma(\alpha)}{\Gamma(\alpha + M)} \prod_{k=1}^{K} \frac{\Gamma(\alpha_k + F_k)}{\Gamma(\alpha_k)}, \qquad (1.14)$$

and this distribution has K parameters, the α_k, instead of the $(K-1)$ category probability parameters in Equation 1.1 for the multinomial distribution.

The D-M distribution has category means given by $E(F_k) = M\alpha_k / \alpha E(F_k)$ and variances (Mosimann, 1962):

$$Var(F_k) = \frac{E(F_k)[M - E(F_k)]}{M} \cdot \frac{(M + \alpha)}{(1 + \alpha)}. \qquad (1.15)$$

Recall that from the multinomial distribution, the variance of the counts in any category k is given by $\dfrac{E(F_k)[M - E(F_k)]}{M}$. Equation 1.15 shows that the D-M distribution predicts that the variances of the category counts have greater dispersion than expected from the multinomial distribution, and this overdispersion is measured by the right-hand-most factor in the equation.

It is useful to fit the D-M distribution to the category frequencies of the participants, because the result can suggest values of the variances of the beta distribution to use in the simulation option of Hu's software. One way to obtain estimates for the parameters of the D-M distribution is to maximize a likelihood function based on Equation 1.14. This approach requires access to computational software and is described in Batchelder and Smith (2003). For many purposes, a simple method-of-moments approach to estimation is to use the category means from the data and estimate α by solving Equation 1.15. The estimate $\tilde{\alpha}$ is related to the overall amount of variance in the underlying category probabilities in the sense that the variance is a decreasing function of α. Our suggestion for calibrating the simulation routine for any parameter θ_s is to equate the MLE $\hat{\theta}$ to the mean of the beta in Equation 1.9 and estimate the denominator of Equation 1.10 by $\tau_{1,s} + \tau_{2,s} = 2 \cdot \tilde{\alpha}/K$. This suggestion is based on the reasonable assumption that parameter variability is approximately proportional to category probability variability, so each parameter in the beta is approximately $\tilde{\alpha}/K$.

Assessing Individual Participants

Another approach for examining participant differences is to estimate parameters for each person individually. To illustrate this approach, we will use the pair-clustering model in Equation 1.5 to analyze the data separately for each participant in the schizophrenic and control groups from Riefer et al.'s (2002) study. As mentioned earlier, Riefer et al. used only combined data aggregated over the 29 schizophrenic and 25 control participants. In this demonstration, we illustrate how it is possible to assess storage and retrieval for each individual participant as well.

Using MPT models to measure individuals' cognitive capacities raises a number of special methodological concerns. One important consideration is the minimum number of data observations needed for stable parameter estimation. For the pair-clustering model, Riefer and Batchelder (1991b) conducted computer simulations on this issue and recommended that 100 observations are generally sufficient for accurate parameter estimates. In experimental studies, when data are usually aggregated across participants in each group, achieving 100 or more data observations is a simple matter. In fact, 10 participants each recalling 10 category pairs would be sufficient. However, when the goal is the assessment of storage and retrieval for a single participant, it is not feasible to record data over 100 or more category pairs from one list in a single session. Instead, it would be necessary to present the participant with multiple lists over many test sessions. In the case of Riefer et al.'s (2002) data set, however, participants memorized only a single list of 20 category pairs—a sample size much too small for producing stable estimates. Fortunately, each participant memorized this list over a series of study–test trials. By tabulating responses over multiple trials, it should be possible to gain larger sample sizes for more accurate parameter estimation. Of course, combining responses over trials is not optimal, because it can be assumed that parameter values change somewhat across trials. To minimize this factor, we decided for the purpose of this demonstration to combine data over Trials 3, 4, and 5. Performance across these three trials was relatively stable for both parameters c and r in each group. This created 60 data observations per participant—still fairly small for general purposes but a sample size that should be reasonably sufficient for this demonstration.

We used Hu's software to compute the MLEs of c and r for each schizophrenic and control participant in Riefer et al.'s (2002) study. For 12 of the 29 schizophrenic participants and 9 of the 25 control participants, the estimate of r was 1.00. These cases violated an inequality constraint of the model described by Batchelder and Riefer (1986, p. 134), suggesting that the model is not appropriate for these participants, perhaps because of the small sample size. For the purposes of this demonstration, we excluded these individuals from the analyses presented below.

Figure 1.2 shows, in the form of a scatter plot, the values of c and r for the 17 schizophrenic participants and 16 control participants with parameter values within the unit interval. A quick glance at Figure 1.2 reveals, not surprisingly, that there is a wide range of storage and retrieval estimates across both groups. However, it is also easy to see that the schizophrenic group's performance is generally poorer than that of the control group— and that this deficit is especially pronounced for the retrieval parameter r. As indicated above, it is also possible to estimate the standard deviation for each parameter value using the closed-form solutions from Batchelder and Riefer (1986). These standard deviations can be useful, for example, in computing confidence intervals for each individual's parameter values. There is not enough space in Figure 1.2 to show these standard deviations for all individuals, but we have included them for one member of each group as an illustration.

With parameter estimates for each individual, we can evaluate the performance for the two groups using more traditional statistical analyses. For example, t tests reveal a significant difference between the schizophrenic and the control participants for parameter r, $t(31) = 3.91$, $p < .001$, whereas the difference for parameter c just failed to reach statistical significance at the .05 level, $t(31) = 1.96$, $p = .06$. The observation that differences in retrieval are stronger than those for storage is consistent with Riefer et al.'s (2002) analysis, using the pooled data. However, unlike in Riefer et al.'s analysis, because we have parameter estimates for each individual we can

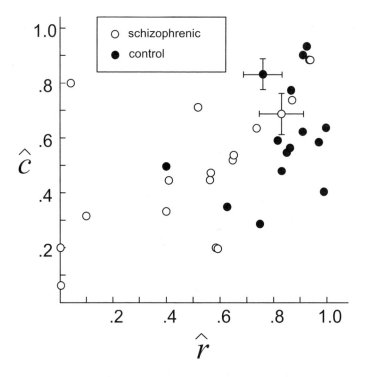

Figure 1.2. Estimates for parameters *c* and *r* for the schizophrenic and control participants from Riefer et al.'s (2002) study.

compute measures of effect size for these differences. We don't know of a useful way to define such measures for MPT models when data are pooled across groups, but they are easy to calculate with parameter estimates for each participant. The effect size is $\omega^2 = .30$ for parameter *r* and $\omega^2 = .08$ for parameter *c*, indicating stronger differences for retrieval than for storage.

It is also possible to compute the correlation between *c* and *r* depicted in Figure 1.2. This correlation is .57, indicating that individuals with strong storage capacity also tend to have strong retrieval capacity. In addition to determining whether parameters are correlated with each other, an advantage of computing parameter estimates for each individual is that one can also see whether the parameters are correlated with other measures, such as age or severity of clinical dysfunction. Unfortunately, such data are unavailable for Riefer et al.'s (2002) study, but an excellent example of this technique can be found in Simons et al.'s (2002) study on source monitoring, described earlier. By computing estimates of the source-discrimination parameter for each patient, they were able to examine the correlations between source memory and a battery of different diagnostic tests.

Hierarchical Multinomial Processing Tree Models

Another way to handle individual differences is to structure the MPT model to incorporate them. One natural approach is to postulate a *hierarchical model*. Such models have only recently begun to appear in cognitive modeling (e.g., Rouder & Lu, 2005), but for many years they have been standard in classical data analysis models. For example, they can be seen in random-effects models in analysis of variance, where the levels of an experimental factor are thought to be sampled from some distribution. In addition, they constitute an especially popular form of modeling data in Bayesian statistics (e.g., Gelman, Carlin, Stern, & Rubin, 2004; Gill, 2002). In this section, we discuss hierarchical modeling from a classical perspective to make it more accessible to psychologists; however, future work on hierarchical MPT models will almost certainly use modern Bayesian computational approaches. (For a Bayesian approach to individual differences in memory search in schizophrenia, see chap. 5, this volume.)

In cognitive modeling, a sample of observations typically is thought to be i.i.d. governed by a particular distribution from a parametric family of distributions. One of the main uses of hierarchical modeling is to handle cases where the variance of a sample of observations is larger than it would be if it were governed by a fixed distribution. This situation is called *overdispersion*, and hierarchical models retain the distribution family and explain the overdispersion by postulating variation in the parameters across the observations. In fact, the D-M model in Equation 1.14 can be viewed as a hierarchical model in the sense that each participant's category counts are governed by a multinomial distribution whose underlying category probability parameters are drawn independently across participants from a Dirichlet distribution.

Parametric hierarchical models can be explained by comparing them to standard parametric models. To be precise, a standard parametric model assumes that the data sample is characterized by the observations of a sequence of i.i.d. random variables (possibly vectors) $\mathbf{X}_1$, $\mathbf{X}_2$, ..., $\mathbf{X}_N$, where each of the $\mathbf{X}_i$ is marginally distributed as a random variable $\mathbf{X}$ with model density $f(x; \alpha)$, where α (possibly a vector) is a fixed but unknown member of Λ, the parameter space of the model. Then the i.i.d. assumption entails that the joint distribution of the data, $f(x_1, x_2, ..., x_N; \alpha)$, can be written as

$$f(x_1, x_2, \ldots, x_N; \alpha) = \prod_{i=1}^{N} f(x_i; \alpha)$$

for some fixed $\alpha \in \Lambda$. This is exactly the perspective that was developed for MPT models described in the earlier section, "Brief Review of Multinomial Processing Tree Models."

A hierarchical version of the model just mentioned assumes that the observations are not identically distributed from the model with a fixed $\alpha \in \Lambda$ because of variation in the parameters over observations. For hierarchical models, the assumption is that each X_i has a marginal distribution $f(x; \alpha_i)$, for some fixed value of α_i in Λ. In addition, the N α_i are observations of a sequence of random variables, $\alpha_1, \alpha_2, ..., \alpha_N$, that are i.i.d. as a random variable α, with some distribution $g(\alpha; \tau)$, where τ is called the *hyperparameter* of the model and has its own parameter space, T. Because of the i.i.d. assumption, the joint distribution of the model's parameters (the α_i) is given by

$$g(\alpha_1, \alpha_2, ..., \alpha_N; \tau) = \prod_{i=1}^{N} g(\alpha_i; \tau) \qquad (1.16)$$

for some fixed but unknown hyperparameter τ. In addition, the data random variables are conditionally independent on the sampled parameters ($\alpha_1, \alpha_2, ..., \alpha_N$) in the sense that

$$f(x_1, x_2, ..., x_N | \alpha_1, \alpha_2, ..., \alpha_N) = \prod_{i=1}^{N} f(x_i | \alpha_i). \qquad (1.17)$$

Viewed in this way, the marginal distribution of X_i that depends on a fixed τ can be obtained by integrating over the parameter space of α,

$$h(x; \tau) = \int_{\Lambda} f(x|\alpha) g(\alpha; \tau) d\alpha, \qquad (1.18)$$

and, further, the X_i are i.i.d. with density $h(x; \tau)$ for some fixed $\tau \in T$. Thus, the hierarchical model in Equations 1.16, 1.17, and 1.18 involves two component models: (a) the basic model density, $f(x; \alpha)$, for some $\alpha \in \Lambda$; and (b) a distribution, $g(\alpha; \tau)$, for some $\tau \in T$, governing variability in the model's parameter(s).

Consider the case of an MPT model with S parameters, $(\varphi_1, \varphi_2, ... \varphi_s)$ $\in \Omega = (0,1)^S$, and suppose each participant-item observation X_{ij} is generated by the model with its own parameter vector $\theta_{ij} = (\theta_{ij,1}, \theta_{ij,2}, ... , \theta_{ij,S}) \in \Omega$. Without further model specification, this idea is completely unworkable, because there are $N \cdot M \cdot S$ parameters required to explain the $N \cdot M$ category observations (for one possible approach to this issue, see Batchelder, Kumbasar, & Boyd, 1997). One way to make a workable hierarchical model for participant differences is to retain the assumption of item homogeneity within a participant and postulate that participants' parameters θ_i are drawn i.i.d. from some joint distribution on Ω. One convenient joint distribution to use is characterized by independent beta distributions on each of the S parameters (cf. Batchelder, 1998). In fact, this is the assumption of parameter variability represented in the simulation option of Hu's software for analyzing MPT models discussed earlier.

Now we are in a position to formulate this parameter variability assumption into an explicit hierarchical MPT model rather than just a simulation option. Let θ_s be one of the parameters in an MPT model, and assume that it is drawn marginally over participants from the beta distribution in Equation 1.8. Now the assumption that each parameter in the MPT model has an independent beta distribution requires that the hierarchical model has a $2 \cdot S$ dimensional hyperparameter given by $\tau = \langle \tau_{1,s}, \tau_{2,s} \rangle_{s=1}^{S}$. Then the parameters of the participants are i.i.d. with density given by

$$g(\theta_1, \theta_2, \ldots, \theta_S; \tau = \langle \tau_{1,s}, \tau_{2,s} \rangle_{s=1}^{S}) = \prod_{s=1}^{S} g(\theta_s; \tau_{1,s}, \tau_{2,s}), \quad (1.19)$$

where $g(\theta_s; \tau_{1,s}, \tau_{2,s})$ is given by Equation 1.8. The hierarchical model in Equation 1.19 has $2 \cdot S$ parameters, and it was analyzed by Batchelder and Smith (2003).

The distribution in Equation 1.19 is somewhat restricted, because the independence assumption precludes the possibility of correlations between parameters. Positive correlations between parameters across participants are a definite possibility (especially for clinical populations), because a participant who is strong in one particular cognitive capacity may well be strong in other, related capacities. Klauer (2006) has introduced a family of hierarchical latent class MPT models that assume that the participants are drawn from several latent classes, where participants' responses in any class can be regarded as i.i.d. Klauer's approach is based on postulating that participants' data come from a finite mixture model (see Titterington, Smith, & Makov, 1985), where the base model for each class is a particular MPT model, and the parameters can vary across classes. This approach allows parameters to be correlated over participants.

When one considers a hierarchical version of an MPT model, it is natural to consider the conditions under which it will be identifiable. As Klauer (2006) showed, a necessary condition for identifiability is that the base model for each participant be identified. The good news is that in addition to this requirement, there is only the additional requirement that the number of parameters not exceed the number of possible data patterns that can be observed across participants. In general, there are a huge number of ways that a participant's M responses can be fit into K categories; for example, there are 84 ways that a participant could place just six responses into four categories. Thus, when an identified MPT model is posed as a hierarchical model, one can postulate distributions with many hyperparameters for the distribution of the parameters of the base model.

Even though it is easy to pose a variety of hierarchical models for any identified MPT model, there are substantial computational issues that have to be overcome to analyze the model. Batchelder and Smith (2003) developed the computational tools to handle the simple hierarchical model in Equation 1.19, and Klauer (2006) provided the details for latent class MPTs and developed the software for carrying out the computations, which is called HMMTree and can be downloaded for free at http://www.psychologie. uni-freiburg.de/Members/stahl/HMMTree. In general, the computational approach that most researchers favor in analyzing such models involves Markov Chain Monte Carlo methods (see Gelman et al., 2004; Gill, 2002). It is beyond the scope of this chapter to delve more deeply into the computational issues involved in hierarchical modeling. Suffice it to say that we expect that hierarchical modeling will be at the cutting edge of further applications of MPT models in the clinical area, and thus it is a goal of future work to develop software to enable routine formulation and analysis of hierarchical MPT models of the sort constructed in this subsection.

CONCLUSION

MPT models are a popular class of mathematical models that have been used to study a wide range of theoretical issues in a number of different experimental paradigms. Their application to clinical studies, however, is a relatively recent development. In most experimental applications, individual differences in participant populations are purposely minimized and ignored; in contrast, in clinical applications differences in the abilities of participants are usually the primary focus of inquiry. This raises a number of special issues and concerns when using MPT models to study clinical populations. We have attempted to address some of these issues in chapter 1 as well as to outline some specific options and recommendations to researchers with clinical interests.

Our first recommendation for clinical applications of MPT models is, whenever feasible, to use homogeneous items and to calculate parameter estimates for each individual participant. This will require collecting enough data observations for each individual, possibly over several sessions, to achieve stable estimates. To determine how many data observations to collect per individual, one may need to conduct simulation studies for the MPT model (for how these types of simulations can be conducted, see Riefer & Batchelder, 1991b). However, with stable individual estimates, it is then possible to compare groups using traditional statistics, compute measures of effect size, and determine whether parameter values are correlated with other relevant clinical variables. If it is not feasible to collect a sufficient number of data observations from each individual, then it is still possible to compare clinical groups with their controls by pooling the responses across the members of each group. In this case, we recommend that researchers examine the raw frequencies for the participants in each group and use the chi-square test based on Equation 1.12 to determine whether individual differences exist. If the hypothesis of no individual differences is rejected, then we recommend either of two approaches. The first, which is easier but less desirable, is to conduct hypothesis tests with the pooled data as if there were no individual differences. The D-M model in Equation 1.14 is then fit to the data to estimate the variances to be used in Hu's simulation option to see whether the scientific conclusions remain unchanged. The second approach, namely, to explicitly construct a hierarchical MPT model such as the one in Equation 1.19, is more desirable. Analysis of the data with such a model will enable researchers to estimate parameters and conduct hypothesis tests both within and between groups without a need to worry about the presence of individual differences.

Each of the options outlined above is relatively straightforward and computationally tractable. This highlights one of the major advantages of MPT models as data analysis tools: Their simple structure and design make it easy to use a wide variety of statistical techniques to explore issues of individual differences, hypothesis testing, sample size, and many others. Because of their statistical flexibility, MPT models have been used with great success to study cognitive processing in many areas of experimental psychology. Our goal in this chapter has been to demonstrate that they can also be powerful tools for assessing cognitive deficits in clinical populations.

REFERENCES

Adam, S., Van der Linden, M., Collette, F., Lemauvais, L., & Salmon, E. (2005). Further exploration of controlled and automatic memory processes in early Alzheimer's disease. *Neuropsychology, 19*, 420–427.

Agresti, A. (2002). *Categorical data analysis* (2nd ed.). New York: Wiley.

Aleman, A., Böcker, K. B. E., Hijman, R., de Haan, E. H. F., & Kahn, R. S. (2003). Cognitive basis of hallucinations in schizophrenia: Role of top-down information processing. *Schizophrenia Research, 64*, 175–185.

American Psychiatric Association. (2000). *Diagnostic and statistical manual of mental disorders* (4th ed., text revision). Washington, DC: Author.

Baldi, P., & Batchelder, W. H. (2003). Bounds on variances of estimators for multinomial processing tree models. *Journal of Mathematical Psychology, 47*, 467–470.

Bastin, C., Van der Linden, M., Charnallet, A., Denby, C., Montaldi, D., Roberts, N., & Mayes, A. R. (2004). Dissociation between recall and recognition memory performance in an amnesic patient with hippocampal damage following carbon monoxide poisoning. *Neurocase, 10*, 330–344.

Batchelder, W. H. (1998). Multinomial processing tree models and psychological assessment. *Psychological Assessment, 10*, 331–344.

Batchelder, W. H., Chosak-Reiter, J., Shankle, W. R., & Dick, M. B. (1997). A multinomial modeling analysis of memory deficits in Alzheimer's and vascular dementia. *Journal of Gerontology: Psychological Sciences, 52B*, 206–215.

Batchelder, W. H., Kumbasar, E., & Boyd, J. P. (1997). Consensus analysis of three-way social network data. *Journal of Mathematical Sociology, 22*, 29–58.

Batchelder, W. H., & Riefer, D. M. (1980). Separation of storage and retrieval factors in free recall of clusterable pairs. *Psychological Review, 87*, 375–397.

Batchelder, W. H., & Riefer, D. M. (1986). The statistical analysis of a model for storage and retrieval processes in human memory. *British Journal of Mathematical and Statistical Psychology, 39*, 120–149.

Batchelder, W. H., & Riefer, D. M. (1990). Multinomial processing models of source monitoring. *Psychological Review, 97*, 548–564.

Batchelder, W. H., & Riefer, D. M. (1999). Theoretical and empirical review of multinomial process tree modeling. *Psychonomic Bulletin & Review, 6*, 57–86.

Batchelder, W. H., & Smith, J. B. (2003, July). *Modeling cognition with hierarchical models.* Paper presented at the 36th Annual Meeting of the Society for Mathematical Psychology, Ogden, UT.

Bellezza, F. S. (2003). Evaluation of six multinomial models of conscious and unconscious processes with the recall-recognition paradigm. *Journal of Experimental Psychology: Learning, Memory, and Cognition, 29*, 779–796.

Bishop, Y. M. M., Fienberg, S. E., & Holland, P. W. (1975). *Discrete multivariate analysis: Theory and practice.* Cambridge, MA: MIT Press.

Buchner, A., Erdfelder, E., & Vaterrodt-Plunnecke, B. (1995). Toward unbiased measurement of conscious and unconscious memory processes within the process dissociation framework. *Journal of Experimental Psychology: General, 124*, 137–160.

Chechile, R. A. (2004). New multinomial models for the Chechile–Meyer task. *Journal of Mathematical Psychology, 48*, 364–384.

Chosak-Reiter, J. (2000). Measuring cognitive processes underlying picture naming in Alzheimer's and cerebrovascular dementia: A general processing tree approach. *Journal of Clinical and Experimental Neuropsychology, 22*, 351–369.

Curran, T., & Hintzman, D. L. (1995). Violations of the independence assumption in process dissociation. *Journal of Experimental Psychology: Learning, Memory, and Cognition, 24*, 531–547.

Del Vecchio, N., Nei, M., Sperling, M., & Tracy, J. (2004). A dissociation between implicit and explicit verbal memory in left temporal lobe epilepsy. *Epilepsia, 45*, 1124–1133.

Erdfelder, E., & Buchner, A. (1998). Process-dissociation measurement models: Threshold theory or detection theory? *Journal of Experimental Psychology: General, 127*, 83–97.

Evans, M., Hastings, N., & Peacock, B. (2000). *Statistical distributions.* New York: Wiley.

Folstein, M. F., Folstein, S. E., & McHugh, P. R. (1975). "Mini-mental state": A practical method for grading the cognitive states of patients for the clinician. *Journal of Psychiatric Research, 12*, 189–198.

Gelman, A., Carlin, J. B., Stern, H. S., & Rubin, D. B. (2004). *Bayesian data analysis* (2nd ed.). London: Chapman & Hall.

Gill, J. (2002). *Bayesian methods: A social and behavioral sciences approach.* New York: Chapman & Hall/CRC.

Greeno, J. G., & Bjork, R. A. (1973). Mathematical learning theory and the new "mental forestry." *Annual Review of Psychology, 24*, 81–116.

Harvey, P. D. (1985). Reality monitoring in mania and schizophrenia: The association between thought disorder and performance. *Journal of Nervous and Mental Disease, 173*, 67–73.

Hay, J. F., Moscovitch, M., & Levine, B. (2002). Dissociating habit and recollection: Evidence from Parkinson's disease, amnesia and focal lesion patients. *Neuropsychologia, 40*, 1324–1334.

Hays, W. L. (1981). *Statistics* (3rd ed.). New York: Holt, Rinehart & Winston.

Hu, X., & Batchelder, W. H. (1994). The statistical analysis of general processing tree models with the EM algorithm. *Psychometrika, 59*, 21–47.

Hu, X., & Phillips, G. A. (1999). GPT.EXE: A powerful tool for the visualization and analysis of general processing tree models. *Behavior Research Methods, Instruments, and Computers, 31*, 220–234.

Jacoby, L. L. (1991). A process dissociation framework: Separating automatic from intentional uses of memory. *Journal of Memory and Language, 30*, 513–541.

Jacoby, L. L. (1998). Invariance in automatic influences of memory: Toward a user's guide for the process-dissociation procedure. *Journal of Experimental Psychology: Learning, Memory, and Cognition, 24*, 3–26.

Jermann, F., Van der Linden, M., Adam, S., Ceschi, G., & Perroud, A. (2005). Controlled and automatic uses of memory in depressed patients: Effect of interval lengths. *Behaviour Research and Therapy, 43*, 681–690.

Johnson, M. K., Hashtroudi, S., & Lindsay, D. S. (1993). Source monitoring. *Psychological Bulletin, 114*, 3–28.

Johnson, N. L., & Kotz, S. (1969). *Discrete distributions.* New York: Wiley.

Kaplan, E., Goodglass, H., & Weintraub, S. (1983). *Boston Naming Test.* Philadelphia: Lea & Febiger.

Kazes, M., Berthet, L., Danion, J.-M., Amado, I., Willard, D., Robert, P., & Poirier, M.-F. (1999). Impairment of consciously controlled use of memory in schizophrenia. *Neuropsychology, 13*, 54–61.

Keefe, R. S. E., Arnold, M. C., Bayen, U. J., & Harvey, P. D. (1999). Source monitoring deficits in patients with schizophrenia; a multinomial modeling analysis. *Psychological Medicine, 29,* 903–914.

Keefe, R. S. E., Arnold, M. C., Bayen, U. J., McEvoy, J. P., & Wilson, W. H. (2002). Source-monitoring deficits for self-generated stimuli in schizophrenia: Multinomial modeling of data from three sources. *Schizophrenia Research, 57,* 51–67.

Kessels, R. P. C., Feijen, J., & Postma, A. (2005). Implicit and explicit memory for spatial information in Alzheimer's disease. *Dementia and Geriatric Cognitive Disorders, 20,* 184–191.

Klauer, K. C. (2006). Hierarchical multinomial processing tree models: A latent-class approach. *Psychometrika, 71,* 1–31.

Knapp, B. R., & Batchelder, W. H. (2004). Representing parametric order constraints in multi-trial applications of multinomial processing tree models. *Journal of Mathematical Psychology, 48,* 215–229.

Knight, R. G. (1998). Controlled and automatic memory process in Alzheimer's disease. *Cortex, 34,* 427–435.

Koivisto, M., Portin, R., Seinelä, A., & Rinne, J. (1998). Automatic influences of memory in Alzheimer's disease. *Cortex, 34,* 209–219.

Linscott, R. J., & Knight, R. G. (2001). Automatic hypermnesia and impaired recollection in schizophrenia. *Neuropsychology, 15,* 576–585.

Linscott, R. J., & Knight, R. G. (2004). Potentiated automatic memory in schizotypy. *Personality and Individual Differences, 37,* 1503–1517.

McDougall, P., Borowsky, R., MacKinnon, G. E., & Hymel, S. (2005). Process dissociation of sight vocabulary and phonetic decoding in reading: A new perspective on surface and phonological dyslexias. *Brain and Language, 92,* 185–203.

Moore, D. S., & McCabe, G. P. (1999). *Introduction to the practice of statistics* (3rd ed.). New York: Freeman.

Morris, J. C., Heyman, A., Mohs R. C., Hughes J. P., van Belle, G., Fillenbaum, G., et al. (1989). The Consortium to Establish a Registry for Alzheimer's Disease (CERAD): Part I. Clinical and neuropsychological assessment of Alzheimer's disease. *Neurology, 39,* 1159–1165.

Mosimann, J. E. (1962). On the compound multinomial distribution, the multivariate beta distribution, and correlations among proportions. *Biometrika, 49,* 65–82.

Moulds, M. L., & Bryant, R. A. (2004). Automatic versus effortful influences in the processing of traumatic material in acute stress disorder. *Cognitive Therapy and Research, 28,* 805–817.

Nieznanski, M. (2005). Reality monitoring failure in schizophrenia: Relation to clinical symptoms and impairment of self-concept. In J. E. Pletson (Ed.), *Progress in schizophrenia research* (pp. 45–76). Hauppauge, NY: Nova Science.

Read, T. R. C., & Cressie, N. A. C. (1988). *Goodness-of-fit statistics for discrete multivariate data*. New York: Springer-Verlag.

Riefer, D. M., & Batchelder, W. H. (1988). Multinomial modeling and the measurement of cognitive processes. *Psychological Review, 95,* 318–339.

Riefer, D. M., & Batchelder, W. H. (1991a). Age differences in storage and retrieval: A multinomial modeling analysis. *Bulletin of the Psychonomic Society, 29,* 415–418.

Riefer, D. M., & Batchelder, W. H. (1991b). Statistical inference for multinomial processing tree models. In J.-P. Doignon & G. Falmagne (Eds.), *Mathematical psychology: Current developments* (pp. 313–336). New York: Springer-Verlag.

Riefer, D. M., Hu, X., & Batchelder, W. H. (1994). Response strategies in source monitoring. *Journal of Experimental Psychology: Learning, Memory, and Cognition, 20,* 680–693.

Riefer, D. M., Knapp, B. R., Batchelder, W. H., Bamber, D., & Manifold, V. (2002). Cognitive psychometrics: Assessing storage and retrieval deficits in special populations with multinomial processing tree models. *Psychological Assessment, 14,* 184–201.

Rothkegel, R. (1999). AppleTree: A multinomial processing tree modeling program for Macintosh computers. *Behavior Research Methods, Instruments, & Computers, 31,* 696–700.

Rouder, J. N., & Lu, J. (2005). An introduction to Bayesian hierarchical models with an application in the theory of signal detection. *Psychonomic Bulletin & Review, 12,* 573–604.

Schmitter-Edgecombe, M. S., Marks, W., Wright, M. J., & Ventura, M. (2004). Retrieval inhibition in directed forgetting following severe closed-head injury. *Neuropsychology, 18,* 104–114.

Seinelä, A., Hämäläinen, P., Koivisto, M., & Ruutiainen, J. (2002). Conscious and unconscious uses of memory in multiple sclerosis. *Journal of the Neurological Sciences, 198,* 79–85.

Simons, J. S., Verfaellie, M., Galton, C. J., Miller, B. L., Hodges, J. R., & Graham, K. S. (2002). Recollection-based memory in frontotemporal dementia: Implications for theories of long-term memory. *Brain, 125,* 2523–2536.

Smith, J. A., & Knight, R. G. (2002). Memory processing in Alzheimer's disease. *Neuropsychologia, 40,* 666–682.

Smith, J. B., & Batchelder, W. H. (2003, November). *Assessing participant and item homogeneity in memory modeling.* Poster presented at the 44th Annual Meeting of the Psychonomic Society, Vancouver, British Columbia, Canada.

Titterington, D. M., Smith, A. F. M., & Makov, U. E. (1985). *Statistical analysis of finite mixture distributions.* New York: Wiley.

von Hecker, U., & Meiser, T. (2005). Defocused attention in depressed mood: Evidence from source monitoring. *Emotion, 5,* 456–463.

Yonelinas, A. P. (2002). The nature of recollection and familiarity: A review of 30 years of research. *Journal of Memory and Language, 46,* 441–517.

Yonelinas, A. P., Kroll, N. E. A., Dobbins, I., Lazzara, M., & Knight, R. T. (1998). Recollection and familiarity deficits in amnesia: Convergence of remember-know, process dissociation, and receiver operating characteristic data. *Neuropsychology, 12,* 323–339.

2

A MODEL-BASED STORAGE–RETRIEVAL ANALYSIS OF DEVELOPMENTAL DYSLEXIA

RICHARD A. CHECHILE

The field of psychological assessment has played a central role in clinical, educational, and industrial–organization psychology. Consequently, there has been a close linkage between those applied subfields of psychology and psychometrics. In contradistinction to psychometrics, mathematical psychology has emerged as a branch of quantitative psychology with a tight linkage with experimental psychology. To nonquantitative psychologists, psychometrics and mathematical psychology might appear to be similar areas. Both use stochastic models as well as other mathematical tools. However, to quantitative psychologists, these fields are distinctly different. In psychometrics, the data examined are frequently a multiple-item questionnaire or a psychological test. For such tests, a single question does not capture the psychological construct, but the test administrator hopes that the concept is represented by a configuration of responses to a number of questions. Also, the data in many psychometric applications do not originate from an experiment with multiple conditions. In mathematical psychology, the relevant data usually pertain to multiple-condition experiments. Moreover, the dependent variables in experiments, such as response time, percentage correct, or the trade-off of speed and accuracy, are examined for a set of homogeneous items. For example, a pool of nonsense syllables that are controlled for length and preexperimental meaningfulness might be used as the stimuli for a memory experiment. Instead of questions that are designed to be different, experimental psychologists use stimuli that are designed to be as similar as possible. Whereas the focus in psychometrics is with psychological measurement, in mathematical psychology, the focus is on the development of quantitative theories to account for the experimental results. The linkage between mathematical psychology and experimental psychology is thus analogous to the relationship between theoretical and experimental physics.

Despite the focus on theories for experimental data, some of the models developed in mathematical psychology can also function as a psychological assessment tool. For example, Batchelder (1998); Chechile and Roder (1998); and Riefer, Knapp, Batchelder, Bamber, and Manifold (2002) have used a class of mathematical models that are called *multinomial processing tree* (MPT) models as a vehicle to examine special participant populations.

In this chapter, I use MPT modeling to explore questions about the fundamental reasons for forgetting. More specifically, when there is a decline in the rate for retaining information, is the forgetting due to a failure to retrieve stored information, a degradation of the memory representation, or a combination of both storage and retrieval factors? Given a specially designed memory testing procedure, it is possible to estimate the proportion of events that are stored sufficiently well to support the recall of the target information. It is also possible to estimate the proportion of the stored memory traces retrieved at the time of testing. Consequently, when forgetting occurs, it is possible to ascertain how much of the memory loss is due to storage decrements and how much is due to retrieval failures. In this chapter, I use the memory measurement model to examine the memory processes of dyslexic children, and I provide evidence that there is a marked difference between the memory processes of dyslexic children and normal readers even for words correctly read initially. Before tackling the issue of storage and retrieval measurement, in the next section I make the argument that a general model-based measurement is essential for understanding underlying cognitive processes.

WHY IS PSYCHOLOGICAL MEASUREMENT VITAL FOR COGNITIVE PSYCHOLOGY?

Without a model for measuring underlying processes, it is difficult to make progress in cognitive psychology. The dependent variables recorded in psychological experiments do not reflect the influence of a single cognitive process. This point is clearly accepted for the problem of detecting a faint signal. The percentage correct on target-present trials and the percentage incorrect on target-absent trials do not directly measure the strength of the stimulus. The decision criterion influences both the hit and false-alarm rates. Signal detection (Green & Swets, 1966) is perhaps the most widely recognized and used model from mathematical psychology and was developed to disentangle decision and signal-strength measures. Although there is a consensus that the data from target-present/target-absent experiments require a mathematical model to unravel the mixture of cognitive processes that influence the recorded responses, many investigators have not generalized this approach to other dependent measures common in psychological research. However, a major point in this chapter is that the dependent variables in psychological experiments usually reflect an entanglement of psychological processes, and the best available solution for this measurement problem is to use mathematical models to recover measures of the underlying psychological processes.

To highlight the problem of process entanglement, consider some common dependent variables used in experimental psychology. One such dependent variable is the participant's response time. For example, a psycholinguist might be interested in using the response time on a lexical decision task to learn about the nature of lexical memory. In a lexical decision task, the respondent is presented with a string of visually presented letters, which may or may not be a word. Although the organization of lexical memory can affect the response time, other processes, such as the respondent's alertness, accuracy, confidence, decision criterion, and motor speed, also can influence the response time. If there are differences among groups of respondents on the mean lexical decision time, how can one be sure which processes are different among the groups? Dissatisfaction with response time as the key measure in lexical decision research has motivated some researchers to use neurological measures of brain activity as alternative dependent measures for studying underlying language processes. For example, Holcomb and Neville (1990) used event-related electrical brain potentials to study lexical access time, yet the event-related potentials are also susceptible to the influence of a number of other processes. It would be surprising and wonderful to find a direct neuropsychological signal that is present only when a basic psychological process is in operation and that otherwise is absent. Until clear evidence of this type emerges, researchers are left with the problem of gaining access to the processes of interest from dependent variables that are influenced by multiple processes. In contradistinction to a purely experimental approach, mathematical psychologists have developed models for response time and accuracy data that are applicable to a lexical decision task. For example, random-walk models, such as Link and Heath's

(1975) relative judgment random-walk model, can account for the experimental data in terms of latent processes that have parameters that can be estimated. Many such models of response time have been developed (see Van Zandt, 2002), and these models can potentially be used to examine differences among participant populations.

More central to the issues examined in this chapter is that memory measures, such as the correct recall rate or the correct recognition rate, are not directly associated with a single psychological process. For example, if there is a change in the correct recall rate, then that change might be caused by a change in the storage of the targets, a change in retrieval, or a combination of changes in both storage and retrieval. Some researchers (e.g., Belmont & Butterfield, 1969; Buschke, 1974) have attempted to use the approach of experimental dissociation to study storage and retrieval processes. The objective of the dissociation approach is to identify an independent variable that affects only one of the underlying processes. For example, an independent variable, such as the time allowed to recall, should not affect the probability of item storage, but it could affect the likelihood of retrieving a stored item. However, experimental dissociation by itself is not a measurement system. Relatively few independent variables are known to affect only a single psychological process. If one of the few independent variables that does affect only one memory process is used, then a subsequent change in memory retention produced by manipulating that variable is merely an exercise in confirming what is already known. Experimental dissociation research does not partition the probability of correct recall into storage and retrieval components. However, if a mathematical model is developed that does unravel storage and retrieval processes from a set of dependent measures, then experimental dissociation is a powerful means for assessing the validity of the measurement model. For example, suppose that a model-based measure of memory storage is affected by the above-mentioned recall time manipulation: That would be evidence against the measurement model. The ability of a measurement model to survive validation tests of this type helps to build confidence in the model itself. Later in this chapter, I discuss other methods of model assessment.

If one accepts the general notion that the dependent variables of cognitive psychology experiments tap more than a single process, then a measurement technique is required to extract measures of the latent processes of interest. Consequently, both mathematical psychology and psychometrics share a common interest in measurement despite historical differences and differences in focus. Once a valid measurement system has been developed, then that procedure can be used as an assessment tool to study various subpopulations. Conversely, if latent psychological processes are not measured, then differences between experimental conditions and differences between subpopulations of research participants will not be understood. In this chapter, a model-based measurement procedure is used to study storage and retrieval differences among subpopulations of children who vary widely in reading skill.

MODELING STORAGE AND RETRIEVAL PROCESSES

A number of models for storage and retrieval measurement have been developed. In psychology, when multiple theories are in current use, then there are usually some deep disputes among the theorists. However, that is not the case among modelers of storage and retrieval processes. One of the key reasons for the multiple models pertains to the fact that there are different experimental tasks. The common approach embraced by the various theorists who are interested in measuring storage and retrieval processes is to model the specific experimental task. If there is a different task, then the task model will be different. For example, Chechile and Meyer (1976) examined a task that involved three types of test trials: (a) recall, (b) old recognition, and (c) new (or foil) recognition. The experimental procedure also involves the random intermixing of the three trial types during testing so that participants do not know in advance how they will be tested. Moreover, the participants were required to give 3-point confidence judgments on their "yes" or "no" recognition decision. The storage and retrieval model emerged from the analysis of the multinomial data collected from this experimental paradigm. This is the approach that has come to be called *MPT modeling*. Chechile (1998) and Chechile and Soraci (1999) also have provided another task for collecting data to measure storage and retrieval. For this experimental procedure, there is an initial free-recall test that is followed by a series of forced-choice recognition tests, that is, an initial four-alternative forced-choice test that is followed up with additional forced-choice tests. Because the multinomial data are different for this experimental test procedure, there is a different MPT model for storage–retrieval measurement. Yet another testing procedure is one in which associative learning is assessed with a free-recall test along with a pair-clustering test. Batchelder and Riefer (1980) developed an MPT model for this task. Furthermore, Riefer and Rouder (1992) and Rouder and Batchelder (1998) have developed a storage–retrieval measurement model for a task that involves free and cued recall. Consequently, the multiplicity of storage–retrieval measurement models is due in part to the fact that the testing procedures are different. Despite the differences in models, there is general agreement on the basic concepts of storage and retrieval among the various models. Batchelder and Riefer (1999) provided an extensive review of many MPT models developed in psychological research; only some of those models are designed to tackle the problem of storage and retrieval measurement.

Another source of difference among the models pertains to simplifying assumptions about secondary processes. For example, for the procedure in which there is a random intermixing of recall and old–new recognition test trials with confidence ratings, Chechile and Meyer (1976) provided four MPT models for measuring storage and retrieval. These models make different assumptions about the latent processes. Recently, I (Chechile, 2004) critiqued the earlier Chechile and Meyer MPT models and developed three additional models for the task. Later in this chapter, I describe one of these new models in more detail and relate it to the other models for this task.

The recall test is central for understanding and defining the concepts of storage and retrieval. In a recall test, the respondent is given a noninformative cue to output the previously presented memory items. For example, a tone or a nondescript cue, such as the word *recall*, is presented. With a properly designed recall task, the probability of being correct by chance alone is virtually zero. Thus, correct recall of an item occurs when the item is both stored and retrieved. The proportion of test items that are sufficiently stored is denoted as θ_S. The insufficient-storage probability is the proportion of items that have degraded and cannot support the complete reconstruction of the memory target. The missing information can be either partial or total. Insufficient storage results in a failure to recall the target completely. However, sufficient storage does not necessarily result in correct recall. To recall a memory target, the individual must also gain access to that memory representation at the time of the test. That search process can fail to find the target under the time constraints imposed by the experiment. The probability of successfully retrieving a sufficiently stored target is denoted as θ_r. Consequently, the probability of correct recall is equal to the product $\theta_S\theta_r$. Conversely, either the retrieval failure of a stored item, with probability $\theta_S(1 - \theta_r)$, or the insufficient storage of the item, with probability $1 - \theta_S$, results in a recall error. A probability tree representation for the underlying psychological processes involved in the recall task is provided in Figure 2.1.

Note that the above analysis of the recall task underscores the earlier point that the dependent variable (the proportion of correct recall) is a result of an entanglement of two important psychological processes. If only recall tests are used, then it is impossible to know whether a change in the correct recall rate is due to changes in either storage, retrieval, or both storage and retrieval.

Chechile and Meyer's (1976) experimental task also includes old and new recognition test trials that are followed up with a 3-point confidence rating. The information extracted from these recognition test trials provides one with a means to disentangle storage and retrieval measures. There were four different models for these trials in the original Chechile and Meyer article. More recently, I (Chechile, 2004) critiqued all of those models and

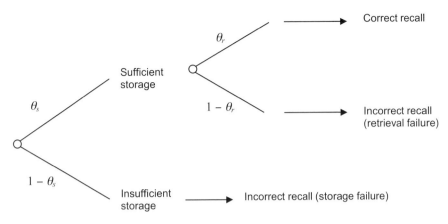

Figure 2.1. The process tree model for recall trials.

provided three new models for the recognition trials. The model that will be used in this article is the 6P model from Chechile (2004).

The process trees for recognition test trials for the 6P model are provided in Figure 2.2. Let us first examine the processes involved in old recognition. Note that the same storage parameter, θ_S, is shown for the first branch of the old recognition tree. In Chechile and Meyer's (1976) experimental task the random intermixing of the three test trials (recall, old recognition, and new recognition) results in a lack of predictability on the part of the respondent as to how a given memory target will be tested. It is reasonable and has been demonstrated that accurate participant knowledge about how they will be tested influences their initial encoding processes (see Balota & Neely, 1980; Hall, Grossman, & Elwood, 1976; and Neely & Balota, 1981). If participants know that the target will be examined by a recall test, then they can, and do, store the targets at the time of learning differently than when they know that the target will be examined by recognition methods. However, with the Chechile and Meyer task, the participants cannot accurately predict how they will be tested, so it is reasonable to assume that the same probability of sufficient storage defined for the recall test trials is applicable during old recognition test trials. If there is sufficient storage, then it is assumed that the old recognition probe triggers a data-driven, bottom-up reelicitation of the stored target. In essence, one assumes here that if the memory target is stored, then the participant recognizes the target through a direct reactivation of the initial encoding; that is, a conceptually driven, top-down search of memory is bypassed. It is also assumed that the participant has highest confidence when the target is stored. However, if the target is insufficiently stored (fractional storage or

Old Recognition Tree

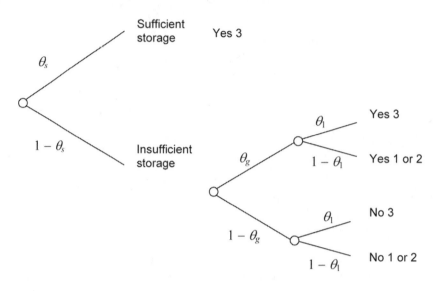

New Recognition Tree

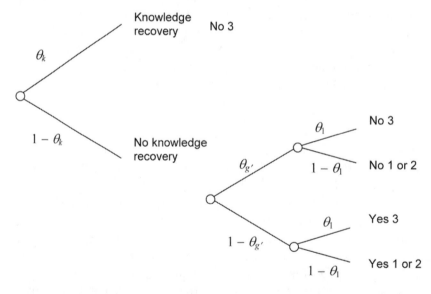

Figure 2.2. The process tree for old and new recognition trials for the 6P model.

no storage), then the participant still can be correct on a yes–no old recognition test. The parameter θ_g is the probability that the participant will give the correct "yes" response in old recognition in the case of insufficient storage. The θ_1 parameter is the probability that the participant will give a high confidence rating despite insufficient storage of the target. This model for old recognition is the same as Chechile and Meyer's Model 2 for old recognition trials.

For the 6P model, there is a fundamental difference in how new recognition is represented compared with the earlier Chechile and Meyer (1976) models. Those earlier models assumed that the same storage parameter, θ_S, was also involved on foil trials. However, I have critiqued that assumption (Chechile, 2004). A foil is different than the target, and it is not likely that a novel item will trigger a data-driven, bottom-up process activation of the target item. Nonetheless, the participant might still recollect some aspect of the target and on the basis of that information reject the foil with certainty. After all, there is some nonzero probability that the whole target can be recalled in the absence of any cue, so there should be some probability of recovering enough of the target to reject the foil. The probability for such a knowledge-based decision during foil recognition test trials is a new parameter, θ_k. The introduction of this parameter is the key difference between the 6P model and the earlier Chechile and Meyer models. If no target knowledge is recovered during foil testing, there is still a chance that the participant will correctly respond "no." The $\theta_{g'}$ parameter is the probability of a correct guess in foil recognition. Thus, the correct guessing rates are not assumed to be equal between the old and new recognition tests. Yet the same θ_1 parameter is used in the 6P model for the probability of giving a high-confident response when there is guessing.

The model is called the *6P model* because there are six parameters, that is, θ_S, θ_r, θ_k, θ_g, $\theta_{g'}$, and θ_1. I (Chechile, 2004) also provided two additional models (each with seven parameters). Those models differed in regard to the assumption of the equivalence of the θ_1 parameter in all cases where there is guessing. For the seven-parameter models, an additional parameter (θ_2) is introduced. This parameter is the rate for using a high-confidence rating in new recognition after an incorrect "yes" response. For Model 7A, θ_2 is also the rate of a high-confidence rating in new recognition after a correct "no" guess. For Model 7B, θ_2 is the rate of a high-confidence guess after a "yes," and θ_1 is the corresponding rate after a "no" response. On the basis of Monte Carlo simulations, I have recommended that the 6P model be used as a default model until there is a statistical departure from the 6P model in favor of one of the other two seven-parameter models (Chechile, 2004).

ESTIMATING MODEL PARAMETERS

When the parameters are estimated, one has measured some of the fundamental memory processes represented in the model. There are several ways that the parameters of the 6P model can be estimated; for more details, see Chechile (2004). General-purpose software for obtaining maximum likelihood estimates for MPT models can be used (see Hu & Phillips, 1999). Another method for parameter estimation is called *population-parameter mapping* (PPM). I (Chechile, 2004) have shown that the two methods converge for large sample sizes of 1,000 recall, 1,000 old, and 1,000 new recognition trials. However, for smaller sample sizes, Monte Carlo studies demonstrated that PPM estimation had less error in recovering known parameter values. Consequently, the PPM method is used for the research reported in this chapter.

PPM is a method of estimation that yields (a) point estimates for the model parameters, (b) a probability distribution for each parameter, and (c) an estimate of the coherence of the model itself. PPM is a variant of Bayesian estimation, but it bypasses some of the computational complex aspects of a Bayesian analysis. Bayesian statistics is an alternative system of statistical inference that is based on the assumption that the parameters can be represented by probability distributions; see Box and Tiao (1973), Congdon (2001), Hartigan (1983), Lad (1996), Lee (1989), and Press (1989). Classical statistical methods do not allow for population parameters to possess a probability description (see von Mises, 1957). However, De Finetti (1937/ 1964) introduced a subjective probability framework that enables parameters to be represented by probability distributions. Although Bayesian statistics is not prevalent in psychological research, it is a rigorous system of statistical inference that is firmly based on probability theory and has a strong following in contemporary statistics. However, Bayesian statistics often results in difficult computational problems. PPM originally emerged as a method for circumventing some of the computational problems with Bayesian inference for the case of estimating the latent model parameters associated with multinomial data, yet PPM has an advantage over a standard Bayesian analysis in that it is able to assess the quality of the model itself. I have discussed these issues (Chechile, 1998, 2004), and the details about how the PPM method is applied to the 6P model is provided in Appendix 2.1.

The 6P model has been used to examine experiments that explore (a) the effect of retention interval in short-term memory, (b) the effect of retrieval time, and (c) the effect of target–foil similarity (Chechile, 2004). These studies were conducted using the Brown–Peterson experimental paradigm, which involves a series of tests for individual target items. For a typical trial, a subspan memory target (e.g., a nonsense item, such as *BXT*) is briefly presented and is followed by materials designed to keep the respondent busy during the retention interval. For example, after the target is presented, the participants might be required to *shadow*, or repeat, an auditory string of digits presented in the retention interval. In the last stage of a Brown–Peterson trial, the participants are tested on their memory of the target item.

The results of several Brown–Peterson experiments have provided evidence for the validity of the 6P model (Chechile, 2004). For example, in one experiment with a fixed duration for the retention interval, the time allowed for recalling the target in the test phase of the Brown–Peterson paradigm was varied (either 1.5 seconds or 3.5 seconds). Increasing the time during testing cannot meaningfully increase the probability of sufficient storage; however, increased time should affect the retrieval of stored targets, because the participant is given slightly more time to search his or her memory. The only reliable change found for the increased recall time was an increase in the retrieval parameter (Chechile, 2004). Had the storage measure changed, then there would be evidence against the storage–retrieval MPT model. The finding that only retrieval is affected by recall time is thus powerful support for the 6P model. Furthermore, in another experiment the time allowed for recall was fixed, but the length of the retention interval was varied (either 4 seconds, 8 seconds, or 12 seconds). Memory declined for longer retention intervals, but only the storage parameter varied with retention interval (Chechile, 2004). Hence, there are independent variables that selectively influence either one or the other of the two components of recall, that is, either the storage or retrieval components of the correct recall rate. Moreover, the recall-time experiment underscores that the components successfully map onto one's conceptual understanding of storage and retrieval processes.

Additional validation evidence has been reported based on the study of the similarity between targets and foils (Chechile, 2004). When items used in foil recognition are highly similar to the target, there is a substantial increase in the false-alarm rate. However, a valid decomposition of recall into storage and retrieval components should not be affected by the degree of the similarity between the targets and the foils that were used in recognition testing. The only parameter that did change with the similarity of the foils to the targets was the θ_k parameter (Chechile, 2004). If the foils are dissimilar to a target, then it does not require very much information about the target to be recovered to reject the foil. However, if the foil is very similar to a target, then more of the target must be recovered in order to reject the foil on the basis of recollected information. Hence, it is reasonable that target–foil similarity results in different θ_k estimates. It is important, however, that the storage and retrieval measures did not change with the similarity between targets and foils.

Further support for the 6P model has been obtained from the PPM estimation method. With the PPM method, there is a probability associated with the coherence of the model itself, that is, $P(coh)$. A low value for $P(coh)$ will occur if the data are inconsistent with the MPT model. In each condition for the above three experiments, the probability of model coherence, $P(coh)$, exceeded .995. This finding and the aforementioned validation evidence provide a strong basis of support for the 6P model. In the balance of this chapter, the 6P model is used to study the effects of developmental dyslexia.

COGNITIVE PROCESSES UNDERLYING DEVELOPMENTAL DYSLEXIA

The term *dyslexia* is commonly used to denote a developmental problem in which a child's reading performance is substantially below the level expected given the child's age and IQ. The *Diagnostic and Statistical Manual of Mental Disorders* (American Psychiatric Association, 2000) used the phrase *reading disorder* instead of *dyslexia*, although the *International Classification of Diseases, Clinical Modification* (U.S. Department of Health and Human Services, Centers for Disease Control and Prevention, National Center for Health Statistics, n.d.), used by neurologists, does accept the term *dyslexia*. For school-age children, the prevalence of dyslexia is commonly reported to be about 4% to 5% (Galaburda, 1999).

To be successful in reading, a host of cognitive processes must operate smoothly. Eye tracking, visual encoding, lexical access, phonological access, semantic integration, and memory trace persistence are some of the cognitive processes that must function well for reading to be effective. Impairment with any of these processes can result in reading difficulties. Consequently, the classification of dyslexia might include a mixture of individuals who have a variety of cognitive deficits that interfere with reading.

Early research on dyslexia emphasized the idea of distortions in sensory processing (Bryan, 1974; Vellutino, 1977). Poor quality of the iconic or acoustic encoding of words was thought to underlie the reading impairment. However, there have been challenges to this notion. Research by Doering and Rabinovitch (1969); McGrady and Olson (1970); and Morrison, Giordani, and Nagy (1977) have provided evidence that neither the quality nor the quantity of information in the iconic store differs between good and poor readers. For example, Morrison et al. found that good and poor readers' recognition rates were comparable if the delay between presentation and test was less than 300 milliseconds. For longer delays, the poor readers' recognition rates were below that of normal readers; thus, the problem does not appear to be with the initial perceptual encoding. In fact, Stanley and Hall (1973) demonstrated that poor readers have an iconic image that persists beyond that of normal readers. Lovegrove, Martin, and Slaghuis (1986) and Lovegrove, Garzia, and Nicholson (1990) also have found evidence of a deficiency in the visual transient system, and this defect is responsible for longer visual persistence for many reading-disadvantaged children. These studies indicate that for many poor readers, the visual problem is not an inaccurate encoding but an iconic representation that persists for an unusually long time.

Reading also involves the development of phonological information. There is agreement among researchers that poor readers typically have problems with reading aloud. Many investigators (e.g., Liberman & Shankweiler, 1985; Stanovich, 1988; Vellutino & Scanlon, 1987) have identified the problem with phonological processing as the fundamental basis for dyslexia. However, other investigators (e.g., Farmer & Klein, 1995; Tallal, 1984; Tallal & Curtiss, 1990) have argued that the phonological problems are a symptom of a deficit with the processing of information in a rapid temporal sequence. Yet the hypothesis of a rapid temporal processing deficit has also been criticized. Martin (1995); Rayner, Pollatsek, and Bilsky (1995); and Studdert-Kennedy and Mody (1995) have argued against the idea that dyslexia is fundamentally caused by a deficit in rapid temporal processing.

Although the debate about the mechanism of the phonological deficit is currently not settled, there is evidence that the cognitive problems experienced by poor readers are partially due to short-term memory difficulties (Chechile & Roder, 1998). Even after poor readers correctly articulated a word, there were difficulties in short-term retention of the words. If a child cannot remember the words, then reading comprehension clearly will suffer. This finding by Chechile and Roder (1998) indicates that the phonological deficit in itself is not the only reason why dyslexic individuals have difficulties.

The above-mentioned Chechile and Roder (1998) study was designed to examine the differences between good and poor readers in terms of storage and retrieval processes. Chechile and Roder's experiment used the previously discussed Chechile and Meyer (1976) task of randomly intermixing recall, old recognition, and new recognition test trials. Chechile and Roder used Model 4 from Chechile and Meyer's study to obtain measures for storage and retrieval. However, I have critiqued the earlier Chechile and Meyer models and have developed improved models for this experimental task— for example, the previously discussed 6P model (Chechile, 2004). Consequently, it is important to reexamine Chechile and Roder's data with the more recent 6P model.

AN ANALYSIS OF CHECHILE AND RODER'S (1998) DATA WITH THE 6P MODEL

A detailed description of the participant populations, materials, experimental task, and data are provided in Chechile and Roder's (1998) chapter. I begin with a brief summary to set the stage for the subsequent analyses and discussion.

Summary of the Test Procedures

From a total of 219 fourth-grade children, 39 carefully screened children were selected to serve in the experiment. The screening was based on IQ, age, gender, and reading scores. Three groups were formed on the basis of reading performance. The groups corresponded to poor, average, and above average readers. Reading comprehension scores were obtained by school officials using the Metropolitan Achievement Tests. The reading performance for the children in the poor reader group was 1 or more years below grade level. For the average reader group, the reading level was at grade level (±6 months), and the above average group was 1 or more years beyond grade level. The age, gender, and IQ of the three groups were comparable by design.

The memory targets were words selected from Entwisle's (1966) word association norms of first-grade children. Words were selected to form four types of lists that varied in intralist similarity. The lists were composed to be either (a) dissimilar (e.g., *stars, fan, race, always*); (b) phonologically similar (e.g., *blue, to, shoe, zoo*); (c) semantically similar (e.g., *bad, awful, evil, mean*); or (d) orthographically similar (e.g., *pals, slap, spill, lips*).

The experimental task was a delayed serial probe task using Chechile and Meyer's (1976) procedure of randomly intermixing recall, old, and new recognition trials. Each child received 16 lists of six words. For any given list, the children saw a 6 × 2 array of face-down index cards. For each of the six cards in the first row, the children (a) turned over the card, (b) read the word on the card aloud three times within 2 seconds, and (c) turned the card over again. Misread words were noted so those items could be omitted later in the data analysis. After the presentation phase of the six words, there was a delay period during which the child verbally repeated a set of 15 digits. After this delay, the second row of six index cards was used to assess the children's memory of the target words. Two trials per list were recall tests, two were old recognition tests, and two were new recognition tests. For the recall tests, the experimenter turned over a blank card below one of the cards on the first row and asked the child to recall the word in that position. For the recognition tests, the experimenter turned over a card and asked, "Was this word here?" In the case of an old recognition test, the word on the card was a duplicate of the word in the position above. For the new recognition trials, the word on the card was a list item from a different position. After a recognition test, the child was required to give a 3-point confidence judgment (i.e., "sure," "maybe," or "just guessing"; we scored these as 3, 2, and 1, respectively, but the child just gave the verbal responses).

The 6P Model Analysis

Chechile and Roder (1998) used Model 4 from Chechile and Meyer (1976) to study the differences among the reading groups. The model was used separately for each participant, and the statistical analysis was based on an analysis of variance of the point estimates from Chechile and Meyer's Model 4. In the current reanalyses of Chechile and Roder's data, four key differences are made. First, the 6P model was used (Chechile, 2004); the rationale for this decision was discussed earlier. Second, the PPM method of parameter estimation was used as opposed to the standard Bayesian method of parameter estimation used by Chechile and Roder; Appendix 2.1 contains the details about this method, and I have described the advantages of the PPM method in previous work (Chechile, 1998, 2004). Third, the assessment of condition differences was based on the distributional information that was obtained from the PPM method. Fourth, the parameter estimation was done on the basis of the grouped data for each reading group as opposed to conducting the estimation on an individual basis and later averaging the parameter estimates. In general, grouping data can be problematic whenever there are extreme differences among the individuals within a condition; however, large within-group differences were reduced in this study because the participants were screened on the basis of IQ, age, gender, and reading scores. The goal of the study was to examine differences among the reading groups rather than differences among the individuals within a group, so grouping did not compromise the research objectives. Grouping also had a distinct advantage that warrants further discussion.

For small-sample studies, the factoring of the correct recall rate into storage and retrieval components is less resolved compared with studies that have larger sample sizes. From a Bayesian perspective, the probability distributions that describe the model parameters are broadly dispersed when the sample size is small. To illustrate this subtle point, consider the hypothetical case where $\theta_S = .8$, $\theta_r = .4$, $\theta_g = .6$, $\theta_{g'} = .7$, $\theta_k = .5$, and $\theta_1 = .2$. Let us further suppose that we observe a "perfect" sample with 10 recall trials, 10 old recognition trials, and 10 new recognition trials. By a "perfect" sample I mean that the multinomial cell frequencies are the expected frequencies according to the model within the rounding to the nearest integer. In this case, the estimated values for θ_S and θ_r are .59 and .58, respectively. These values are considerably discrepant from the correct values of .8 and .4 for the respective storage and retrieval parameters. This discrepancy is mainly due to the fact that the posterior distributions for the model parameters are too broad with this sample size. Moreover, the averaging of fuzzy individual point estimates does not guarantee that the mean converges to the correct value. Averaging data for a group of people with these inaccurate values for storage and retrieval will result in means that are also inaccurate, because the error caused by insufficient sample size is not necessarily random over the participants in the group. The solution to this problem is to use more data. For example, suppose that there are 100 recall, 100 old recognition, and 100 new recognition test trials. Given "perfect" data, the estimates for storage and retrieval are .76 and .43, respectively, which are close to the correct values. In general, the sharpness in factoring the storage and retrieval components of recall and the accuracy of the estimates is a function of both the sample size and the model. For the 6P model, I found good parameter recovery for the case in which there are 100 recall trials, 100 old recognition trials, and 100 new recognition trials (Chechile, 2004). Consequently, in the reanalysis of Chechile and Roder's (1998) data, I pooled all the information for a common list type and reading group, especially because I am interested in group differences rather than individual differences.

For PPM estimation, there is a posterior distribution for each parameter. In practice, there are 100 intervals of width .01, and for each interval there is a posterior probability for the parameter being in the interval. Let us denote $P_i(\theta_S \mid D)$ as the posterior probability that the storage parameter is in the ith interval given the data (D); for example, $P_{30}(\theta_S \mid D)$ is the probability that the storage parameter is within the (.29, .30] interval. If we are interested in assessing the difference in the storage parameter between two different conditions, then the probability of a difference can be directly computed. Let us denote the two conditions as (I) and (II). The posterior probability that the storage parameter is larger in the (I) condition is computed as $P[\theta_S(I) > \theta_S(II) \mid D] = \sum_{j=1}^{99} P_j(\theta_S(II) \mid D) \sum_{i=j+1}^{100} P_i[\theta_S(I) \mid D]$. If the probability for a difference equals or exceeds .95, then it is considered highly likely that there is a credible difference in the parameter between the two experimental conditions. However, if the probability of a difference is less than .95, then one should regard the result as being below the desired probability level for reporting a reliable effect. Consequently, with PPM estimation, hypotheses about condition differences can be directly assessed via probability theory without using the classical method of testing hypotheses by assuming a null hypothesis and evaluating whether there is a significant departure from the null hypothesis.

The data for each group were reported previously by Chechile and Roder (1998); consequently, the focus here is on the 6P model analyses.

In order to concentrate only on the participants' memory, the data have been excluded for any item that was not initially read correctly three times. The 6P model was used to examine the grouped data for each reading group and list type. The mean parameter estimates and standard deviations are provided in Table 2.1.

In comparing the poor readers with the other two groups in regard to the storage parameter, there is a statistically reliable deficit for the orthographically similar memory list. The probability of a storage deficit for the poor readers compared with the average readers is .9971, and the probability of storage deficit compared with the above average readers is .9986. For the other list types, the poor readers did not demonstrate a storage deficit relative to both of the other reading groups. Although the storage means for the phonologically similar and semantically similar lists are less for the poor readers compared with the average readers, the above average readers and poor readers have very close storage values for those list types. Even if the data are pooled for all the lists other than the orthographically similar list, there is not a reliable difference in the storage probability between the poor readers and the control participants. Consequently, there is a reliable storage deficit for the poor readers only when the list is orthographically similar. The same conclusion for storage was reached in the Chechile and Roder (1998) analysis that used Model 4 from Chechile and Meyer (1976). However, the storage means obtained in the current analysis with the 6P model are very different from those reported by Chechile and Roder. In all 12 conditions, the storage means in Chechile and Roder's study were larger than the values obtained with the 6P model. For example, the storage means in Chechile and Roder's analysis for poor readers were .32, .73, .67, and .62, for the orthographically similar, phonologically similar, semantically similar, and dissimilar conditions, respectively.

Unlike the storage measure, the retrieval process was not impaired for the poor readers. In fact, the poor readers had relatively high retrieval values. Because of the large standard deviations for the retrieval estimates, the retrieval parameter for poor readers demonstrates only two reliable between-groups differences. The poor readers had reliably better retrieval than the above average readers when the list was orthographically similar; the probability of a difference was .9727. Also, for dissimilar lists the poor readers had better retrieval than above average readers; the probability of a difference was .9846. Thus, poor readers were not demonstrating any difficulties with respect to memory retrieval.

In all 12 conditions, the retrieval estimates were higher in the current analysis than the values reported in Chechile and Roder's (1998) analysis. In addition, the 6P model was able to detect some highly probable group differences in the retrieval measure that were not detected in Chechile and Roder's analysis. There is also one noteworthy within-group retrieval

TABLE 2.1
Mean Parameter Estimates and Standard Deviations for 6P Model Parameters

Group and condition	θ_S		θ_r		θ_k		θ_g		θ_g		θ_1	
	M	SD	M	SD	M	SD	M	SD	M	SD	M	SD
Poor readers												
OS	.086	.045	.851	.248	.281	.133	.432	.061	.618	.092	.691	.049
PS	.286	.114	.773	.250	.412	.197	.691	.082	.705	.119	.806	.059
SS	.353	.087	.829	.184	.446	.129	.597	.084	.525	.118	.721	.060
DS	.399	.097	.557	.188	.272	.118	.496	.097	.554	.090	.651	.058
Average readers												
OS	.400	.097	.556	.188	.271	.117	.495	.097	.554	.089	.651	.058
PS	.516	.099	.630	.164	.511	.114	.546	.111	.609	.104	.651	.072
SS	.564	.090	.660	.073	.496	.101	.580	.106	.546	.106	.604	.073
DS	.407	.101	.405	.177	.531	.072	.502	.097	.314	.093	.611	.061
Above average readers												
OS	.380	.076	.365	.129	.436	.065	.649	.071	.451	.078	.338	.062
PS	.332	.101	.507	.216	.424	.103	.699	.073	.679	.081	.509	.075
SS	.442	.079	.834	.151	.224	.125	.657	.081	.641	.080	.633	.064
DS	.454	.075	.215	.080	.463	.074	.608	.079	.618	.076	.354	.069

Note. Means and standard deviations for the 6P model parameters for poor readers, average readers, and above average readers and for lists that are orthographically similar (OS), phonologically similar (PS), semantically similar (SS), and dissimilar (DS).

difference. One of the best list types from which to retrieve information is one in which the items are semantically similar, whereas one of the most difficult list types from which to retrieve information is a list of unrelated items. For each reading group, the retrieval estimate was larger in the semantically similar condition compared with the dissimilar condition. However, this difference was statistically reliable only for the above-average readers; that is, the probability of a difference was .9994.

The θ_k parameter is a novel feature of the 6P model compared with the original Chechile and Meyer (1976) models. Only one reliable group difference was identified by this parameter. The poor readers on dissimilar lists had a lower value for θ_k relative to the average readers; the probability of difference was .9728.

The other model parameters (i.e., θ_g, $\theta_{g'}$, and θ_1) are "nuisance" parameters that are valuable only for correcting the recognition data for factors such as the guessing rates and the rate of high confidence when storage is incomplete. Yet, one noteworthy observation about the θ_1 parameter warrants further examination. Note that in general, the values for θ_1 were higher for the poor readers than the average readers, who in turn had higher θ_1 values than the above average readers. This ordering suggests that there may have been differences among the groups in the conditional probabilities for using the highest confidence rating when incorrect. Those conditional probabilities were .755, .640, and .455, respectively, for the poor, average, and above average readers. These conditional probabilities did vary directly with the θ_1 values. Consequently, the model correctly adjusted the recognition data to account for differences in the use of the confidence scale.

It is also important to look at the conditional probabilities for correct recognition, given that the confidence was high versus low. For the poor readers, $P_r(\text{correct} \mid \text{high}) = .761$, and $P_r(\text{correct} \mid \text{low}) = .604$. For average readers, $P_r(\text{correct} \mid \text{high}) = .808$, and $P_r(\text{correct} \mid \text{low}) = .520$. For above average readers, $P_r(\text{correct} \mid \text{high}) = .859$ and $P_r(\text{correct} \mid \text{low}) = .631$. Thus, for each group, these conditional probabilities improved with confidence. The increase of these conditional probabilities with confidence level is an indication that the children were using the confidence scale in a meaningful fashion. The increase in accuracy with confidence is also consistent with the 6P model, because reduced confidence is reflective of either insufficient storage in the case of old recognition or the absence of any target knowledge for foil recognition. However, high confidence can occur with either sufficient or insufficient storage.

With the PPM method for estimating the 6P model parameter it is possible to assess the probability of the coherence of the model itself. The mean probability of coherence across the 12 conditions is .834. The following question arises: What is the expected coherence probability? I conducted an extensive set of Monte Carlo simulations in which the data were drawn from a "true" 6P model (Chechile, 2004). Moreover, these studies were conducted for various sample sizes. For a sample size of 100 recall trials, 100 old recognition trials, and 100 new recognition trials, the average coherence probability was found to be .838 (Chechile, 2004). In this chapter, the actual data had some variability in the sample size because trials on which the child could not articulate the memory target during learning were omitted in the analysis. Without any omitted trials, there were 104 recall, 104 old recognition, and 104 new recognition trials for each condition. Consequently, the mean coherence probability of .834 is very close to the expected coherence probability for the 6P model for the sample size used.

Finally, it is instructive to examine the difference in the correct recall rate between poor readers and above average readers for orthographically similar lists. These rates are .058 and .125 for the poor and above average groups, respectively. The difference in the correct recall rate is not significant, $\chi^2(1, N = 206) = 2.69$, $p > .1$, but there was a reliable deficit for storage for the poor readers, and these children also had better retrieval. In essence, the 6P model was able to detect differences between reading groups for both storage and retrieval even in a case where the product of the storage and retrieval measures (i.e., the correct recall rate) was not significantly different.

DISCUSSION

Model-based measurement is a powerful tool for examining underlying cognitive processes. Without a mathematical model to structure the interplay of cognitive processes, the dependent measures used in experimental studies cannot be directly tied to a particular process. Model-based measurement, however, disentangles these processes. Furthermore, model-based measurement can uncover effects that do not manifest themselves in terms of behavioral measures. For example, with orthographically similar lists the recall rate is not significantly different between poor readers and above average readers, yet for orthographically similar items the storage and retrieval model is able to detect two effects (in opposite directions). Relative to the above average readers, poor readers demonstrate a reliable storage deficit, but the poor readers also have better retrieval of the information that is stored. The opposite direction of the storage and retrieval changes between the two groups obscures the detection of a difference on the correct recall rate because the recall rate is the product of the storage and retrieval probabilities. The detection of these two effects illustrates a powerful advantage of model-based measurement.

The question arises as to why retrieval is superior for the poor readers when the memory list has high orthographic similarity. Although the poor readers did well retrieving stored items in the other list conditions, they were not reliably better than the control participants, so the superior retrieval for the poor readers was restricted to the condition with high orthographic similarity. However, in that condition the average poor reader stored only about 2.1 words out of a possible total of 24 words. For comparison purposes, the average poor reader stored about 8.4 words for each of the other list types. Hence, the poor readers encoded the words on the orthographically similar list in a fashion that resulted in few items being retained, but those items were highly retrievable.

In this experiment, the children were required to know both the identity of the words and the location of the words within the list. A storage difficulty could be either a problem with the loss of item information or the loss of position information. In either case, an increased rate of storage problems is an impediment to effective reading. The memory of a sequence of words is essential for language comprehension. Consequently, a partial explanation of the learning disability experienced by the poor readers is their lower rate of memory storage. Yet poor readers showed a storage decrement only for orthographically similar items. When the memory lists were phonologically similar, semantically similar, or dissimilar, then the dyslexic participants did not have any additional problems with storing the memory targets. Also, the retrieval of stored traces was excellent for the poor readers.

When trying to understand the differences among subpopulations, a number of difficulties must be addressed (see, e.g., Baumeister, 1967; Chapman & Chapman, 1974). One problem is the suitability of control or comparison groups. If one group is superior to another group on all measures, then one just might not have a suitable comparison group. One way to address this concern is to identify an interaction effect. In this study, the isolation of the storage deficit to only orthographically similar lists and the finding of better retrieval for poor readers are reflective of an interactive effect. It is clear that the average and above average groups were not performing better under all conditions and for all processes. This finding provides support for the suitability of comparison groups used to assess the memory processes of dyslexic children.

In this chapter, the more recent 6P model (Chechile, 2004) was used instead of the model used by Chechile and Roder (1998). The older storage-retrieval separation model made a questionable assumption about foil recognition. The θ_k parameter represents the success rate in foil recognition test trials for recovering enough target information to reject the foil with high confidence. It is not reasonable to assume the equality of θ_k and θ_S, as was done in Chechile and Roder's analysis.

For each of the 12 conditions in this study, the resulting estimates for θ_S are substantially different from the values previously reported by Chechile and Roder (1998). Despite these large differences, the between-conditions differences detected for storage are still similar to those discussed by Chechile and Roder. In both analyses, a storage deficit was detected for poor readers (compared with the other reading groups) only for orthographically similar lists. Consequently, Chechile and Roder's interpretation as to why this pattern occurs for poor readers is still reasonable.

Chechile and Roder's (1998) account for the pattern of storage changes stressed the overreliance of the poor readers on visual encodings. Chechile and Roder pointed out that poor readers can understand spoken language without difficulty. Comprehending spoken language requires the activation of semantic memory codes from phonetic input. In this experiment, the targets had to be articulated correctly three times over a 2-second interval or else the target was excluded in the later data analysis. Each target was presented in a visual form. Thus, it would seem reasonable to assume that for a word correctly read aloud, the children developed, at the time of reading, suitable visual, phonetic, and semantic codes for the word. Yet this multifaceted encoding needed to be linked to list position information. It seems reasonable to assume that the multifaceted information was concurrent with the positional information in a very short-term, immediate, perceptual trace. However, the three components of the item information (visual, phonological, and semantic) need not be equally "strong." Chechile and Roder argued that good readers are flexible in their encoding emphasis. In most cases, a good reader might stress the semantic code in linking the item information to the position information. However, these good readers might switch to a different encoding emphasis for the semantically similar list, that is, either a phonological or an orthographic emphasis. Such a switch would reduce intralist interference. Chechile and Roder suggested that poor readers tended to rely on an orthographic encoding. Orthographic encoding will work fine for all list types except for the orthographically similar lists. Chechile and Roder hypothesized that poor readers do not spontaneously switch to a different encoding emphasis under conditions of high orthographic similarity. This hypothesis is consistent with those of other investigators who have provided support for the idea that poor readers overuse visual encoding (e.g., Fay, Trupin, & Townes, 1981; Gordon, 1984; Rack, 1985; Snowling, 1991). Recall that Stanley and Hall (1973) found a more persistent iconic image for children with reading disabilities. Also, there is some physiological evidence of abnormalities in the brains of dyslexic individuals in the magnocellular layer of the lateral geniculate nucleus (i.e., Livingstone, Rosen, Drislane, & Galaburda, 1991). The magnocellular system is sensitive to low spatial frequency and visual persistence (see, e.g., Di Lollo, Hanson, & McIntyre, 1983; Lovegrove, Martin, & Slaghuis, 1986).

The hypothesis that poor readers place excessive emphasis on visual processing provides another perspective in the debate concerning the phonological deficit hypothesis (e.g., Farmer & Klein, 1995; Liberman &

Shankweiler, 1985; Stanovich, 1988; Vellutino & Scanlon, 1987). Is the demonstrated difficulty in the articulation of printed words due in part to the overreliance on visual information? It is important to note, however, that the problems in memory storage for orthographically similar lists cannot be attributed to articulation problems, because mispronounced items were excluded in the data analysis. Furthermore, the memory targets were presented slowly in this study, so it is difficult to argue that the reading disability is due to problems with processing a rapid temporal sequence (cf. Tallal, 1984; Tallal & Curtiss, 1990). Also, the hypothesis of a deficit in rapid temporal processing cannot explain why the poor readers in this study performed normally with all lists other than the orthographically similar lists.

Finally, many cognitive processes are involved in effective reading, and if any of these processes are inefficient, then reading difficulties can be expected. Understanding which processes are impaired requires measures that are validly linked to cognitive processes. Yet behavioral measures do not reflect the influence of only one cognitive process, and furthermore, physiological differences detected in the brains of dyslexic individuals (e.g., Livingstone, Rosen, Drislane, & Galaburda, 1991) do not result in an unambiguous interpretation in terms of information-processing mechanisms. The central thesis of this chapter is that model-based measurement is the best available approach for understanding differences in underlying cognitive processes. Both storage and retrieval mechanisms can and do fail, and the rate of these failures can vary with different participant populations. Model-based measurement should become a routine feature in the assessment of condition and population differences.

SUMMARY

A central concern in psychological assessment is the measurement of processes that are not directly tapped by a single behavioral response. In this chapter, a case is advanced for the general need to examine mathematical models of the latent processes as a means for measuring the set of entangled cognitive processes. This approach is illustrated for the problem of understanding the causes for forgetting in terms of storage and retrieval processes. The measurement model is also a vehicle for examining differences in clinical subgroups. In this chapter, a storage and retrieval measurement model was used to study the memory processes of dyslexic children. The measurement model uncovered a massive storage problem exhibited by the poor readers only when the memory items were orthographically similar.

APPENDIX 2.1

Population Parameter Mapping Method

A key concept in understanding the population parameter mapping (PPM) method is the distinction between two sets of population parameters. Chechile and Meyer's (1976) experimental task and the 6P model have six population parameters (θ_S, θ_r, θ_k, θ_g, $\theta_{g'}$, θ_1; see main text). The second set of population parameters is the set of population proportions corresponding to the observational categories. Although the psychological parameters are denoted by subscripts to a theta (θ) symbol, the population proportions for the mutually exclusive and exhaustive response categories are denoted by subscripts to a phi (φ) symbol. More specifically, the population proportions for correct and incorrect recall are φ_1 and $\varphi_2 = 1 - \varphi_1$, respectively. In old recognition, the population proportions for "no 3," "no 1 or 2," "yes 1 or 2," and "yes 3" responses are, respectively, φ_3, φ_4, φ_5, $\varphi_6 = 1 - \varphi_3 - \varphi_4 - \varphi_5$. The corresponding population proportions for the new recognition trials are, respectively, φ_7, φ_8, φ_9, $\varphi_{10} = 1 - \varphi_7 - \varphi_8 - \varphi_9$. When data are collected, there will be observed frequencies $n_1, \dots, n_{10}$ for the 10 response categories. For a Bayesian analysis in terms of the response category proportions, $\varphi_1, \dots, \varphi_{10}$, it is necessary to specify a prior probability for the parameters. I have recommended a multivariate uniform prior (see Chechile, 1998, 2004), which can be represented as

$$P_r(\{\varphi_1, \dots, \varphi_{10}\}) = K' \varphi_1{}^{n'1} \dots \varphi_{10}{}^{n'10},$$

where $n'_1 = n'_2 = \dots = n'_{10} = 0$, $\varphi_2 = 1 - \varphi_1$, $\varphi_6 = 1 - \varphi_3 - \varphi_4 - \varphi_5$, $\varphi_{10} = 1 - \varphi_7 - \varphi_8 - \varphi_9$, and $K' = 36$. The subsequent posterior distribution based on the observed data D, that is, frequencies $n_1, \dots, n_{10}$, is

$$P(\{\varphi_1, \dots, \varphi_{10}\} | D) = K \varphi_1{}^{n1} \dots \varphi_{10}{}^{n10},$$

where K is a known constant given the values for $n_1, \dots, n_{10}$. I have shown how a random vector $\{\varphi_1, \dots, \varphi_{10}\}$ can be sampled from the posterior distribution (see Chechile, 1998, 2004). If random sampling is repeated many times, then the multivariate posterior distribution is approximated by the distribution of the sampled vectors. However, we are not particularly interested in the distribution of response category proportions. Our goal is to obtain the corresponding distribution for the 6P model parameters. PPM is designed to achieve this goal.

PPM estimation involves a two-step procedure that is repeated many times. The first step is the drawing of a random vector $\{\varphi_1, \dots, \varphi_{10}\}$ from the posterior distribution. The second step is to map that random vector to a corresponding vector of parameters in the 6P model. I have developed the following set of equations for this mapping (see Chechile, 2004):

$$\theta_S = \text{maximum of either } (\varphi_6 - c_1 c_2)/(1 - c_1 c_2) \text{ or } \varphi_1;$$
$$\theta_r = \text{minimum of either } \varphi_1 (1 - c_1 c_2)/(\varphi_6 - c_1 c_2) \text{ or } 1;$$
$$\theta_k = \text{maximum of either } (\varphi_7 - c_1 c_3)/(1 - c_1 c_3) \text{ or } 0;$$
$$\theta_g = (\varphi_5 + \varphi_6 - \varphi_1)/\varphi_2, \text{ if } \theta_S = \varphi_1; \text{ otherwise, } c_2;$$
$$\theta_{g''} = \varphi_7 + \varphi_8, \text{ if } \theta_k = 0; \text{ otherwise, } c_3;$$
$$\theta_1 = c_1, \text{ where}$$
$$c_1 = (\varphi_3 + \varphi_{10})/(\varphi_3 + \varphi_4 + \varphi_9 + \varphi_{10});$$
$$c_2 = \varphi_5/(\varphi_4 + \varphi_5);$$
$$c_3 = c_8/(c_8 + c_9).$$

However, the resulting vector $\{\theta_S, \theta_r, \theta_k, \theta_g, \theta_{g'}, \theta_1\}$ might be discrepant from what is permitted according to the 6P model. To understand this point, let us consider the reverse mapping that is obtained by substituting the values for the $\{\theta_S, \theta_r, \theta_k, \theta_g, \theta_{g'}, \theta_1\}$ vector back into the process trees to obtain predicted values for the response category proportions. We denote the predicted vector as $\{\varphi^{(p)}_1, \varphi^{(p)}_2, ..., \varphi^{(p)}_{10}\}$. If the sampled vector $\{\varphi_1, \varphi_2, ..., \varphi_{10}\}$ is perfectly consistent with the 6P model, then it will be the same as the $\{\varphi^{(p)}_1, \varphi^{(p)}_2, ..., \varphi^{(p)}_{10}\}$ vector. However, it might not be exactly consistent with the 6P model. Because the number of dimensions of the 6P model parameter space (i.e., six) is less than the number of dimensions of the response category space (i.e., seven), there will be points in the response category space that are not exactly consistent with the model but are very close to a point in the response category space that is consistent with the model; that is, there might be small modeling error. I have defined the modeling error for the 6P model as $\delta = \max (|\varphi_i^{(p)} - \varphi_i|)$, $i = 1, ..., 10$. If δ is too large, then the mapped vector $\{\theta_S, \theta_r, \theta_k, \theta_g, \theta_{g'}, \theta_1\}$ is considered inconsistent with the model, and it is rejected (Chechile, 2004). In the research with the 6P model, the maximum tolerance for the modeling error is taken as .05. The two-step process of PPM is repeated N times ($N = 30,000$ for the work reported in this chapter). The number of consistent vectors divided by N approximates the probability of model coherence.

The set of acceptable $\{\theta_S, \theta_r, \theta_k, \theta_g, \theta_{g'}, \theta_1\}$ vectors is the basis for describing each of the model parameters. With the PPM procedure, an entire probability distribution can be approximated for each model parameter. The mean of the distribution for a parameter is taken as a unique point estimate of the latent processes. The distribution itself can also be used in assessing hypotheses about condition differences.

REFERENCES

American Psychiatric Association. (2000). *Diagnostic and statistical manual of mental disorders* (4th ed., text revision). Washington, DC: Author.

Balota, D. A., & Neely, J. H. (1980). Test-expectancy and word-frequency effects in recall and recognition. *Journal of Experimental Psychology: Learning, Memory, and Cognition, 6,* 576–597.

Batchelder, W. H. (1998). Multinomial processing tree models and psychological assessment. *Psychological Assessment, 10,* 331–344.

Batchelder, W. H., & Riefer, D. M. (1980). Separation of storage and retrieval factors in free recall of clusterable pairs. *Psychological Review, 87,* 375–397.

Batchelder, W. H., & Riefer, D. M. (1999). Theoretical and empirical review of multinomial process tree modeling. *Psychonomic Bulletin & Review, 6,* 57–86.

Baumeister, A. A. (1967). Problems in comparative studies of mental retardates and normals. *American Journal of Mental Deficiency, 71,* 869–875.

Belmont, J. M., & Butterfield, E. C. (1969). The relation of short-term memory to development and intelligence. In L. P. Lipsitt & H. W. Reese (Eds.), *Advances in child development and behavior* (Vol. 4, pp. 29–82). New York: Academic Press.

Box, G. E. P., & Tiao, G. C. (1973). *Bayesian inference in statistical analysis.* Reading, MA: Addison-Wesley.

Buschke, H. (1974). Components of verbal learning in children: Analysis by selective reminding. *Journal of Experimental Child Psychology, 18,* 488–496.

Bryan, T. H. (1974). Learning disabilities: A new stereotype. *Journal of Learning Disabilities, 7,* 304–309.

Chapman, L. J., & Chapman, J. P. (1974). Alternatives to the design of manipulating a variable to compare retarded and nonretarded subjects. *American Journal of Mental Deficiency, 79,* 404–411.

Chechile, R. A. (1998). A new method for estimating model parameters for multinomial data. *Journal of Mathematical Psychology, 42,* 432–471.

Chechile, R. A. (2004). New multinomial models for the Chechile–Meyer task. *Journal of Mathematical Psychology, 48,* 364–384.

Chechile, R., & Meyer, D. L. (1976). A Bayesian procedure for separately estimating storage and retrieval components of forgetting. *Journal of Mathematical Psychology, 13,* 269–295.

Chechile, R. A., & Roder, B. (1998). Model-based measurement of group differences: An application directed toward understanding the information-processing mechanisms of developmental dyslexia. In S. A. Soraci & W. J. McIlvane (Eds.), *Perspectives on fundamental processes in intellectual functioning: A survey of research approaches* (Vol. 1, pp. 91–112). Stamford, CT: Ablex.

Chechile, R. A., & Soraci, S. A. (1999). Evidence for a multiple-process account of the generation effect. *Memory, 7,* 483–508.

Congdon, P. (2001). *Bayesian statistical modelling.* West Sussex, England: Wiley.

De Finetti, B. (1964). Foresight: Its logical laws. In H. E. Kyburg & H. E. Smokler (Eds.), *Studies in subjective probability* (pp. 93–158). London: Wiley (Original work published 1937)

Di Lollo, V., Hanson, D., & McIntyre, J. S. (1983). Initial stages of information processing in dyslexia. *Journal of Experimental Psychology: Human Perception and Performance, 9,* 923–935.

Doering, D. G., & Rabinovitch, M. S. (1969). Auditory abilities of the children with learning problems. *Journal of Learning Disabilities, 2,* 467–474.

Entwisle, D. R. (1966). *Word associations of young children.* Baltimore: John Hopkins University Press.

Farmer, M. E., & Klein, R. M. (1995). The evidence for a temporal processing deficit linked to dyslexia: A review. *Psychonomic Bulletin & Review, 2,* 460–493.

Fay, G., Trupin, E., & Townes, B. D. (1981). The young disabled reader: Acquisition strategies and associated deficits. *Journal of Learning Disabilities, 14,* 32–35.

Galaburda, A. M. (1999). Dyslexia. In R. A. Wilson & F. C. Keil (Eds.), *The MIT encyclopedia of the cognitive sciences* (pp. 249–251). Cambridge, MA: MIT Press.

Gordon, H. W. (1984). Dyslexia. In R. E. Tarter & G. Goldstein (Eds.), *Advances in clinical neuropsychology* (Vol. 2, pp. 181–205). New York: Plenum Press.

Green, D. M., & Swets, J. A. (1966). *Signal detection theory and psychophysics.* New York: Wiley.

Hall, J. W., Grossman, L. R., & Elwood, K. D. (1976). Differences in encoding for free recall vs. recognition. *Memory & Cognition, 4,* 507–513.

Hartigan, J. A. (1983). *Bayes theory.* New York: Springer-Verlag

Holcomb, P. J., & Neville, H. J. (1990). Semantic priming in visual and auditory lexical decision: A between modality comparison. *Language and Cognitive Processes, 5,* 281–312.

Hu, X., & Phillips, G. A. (1999). GPT.EXE: A powerful tool for the visualization and analysis of general processing tree models. *Behavior, Research, Methods, Instruments, & Computers, 31,* 220–234.

Lad, F. (1996). *Operational statistical methods.* New York: Wiley.

Lee, P. M. (1989). *Bayesian statistics: An introduction.* New York: Wiley.

Liberman, I. Y., & Shankweiler, D. (1985). Phonology and the problems of learning to read and write. *Remedial and Special Education, 6,* 8–17.

Link, S. W., & Heath, R. A. (1975). A sequential theory of psychological discrimination. *Psychometrika, 40,* 77–105.

Livingstone, M., Rosen, G., Drislane, F., & Galaburda, A. (1991) Physiological and anatomical evidence for magnocellular defect in developmental dyslexia. *Proceedings of the National Academy of Sciences USA, 88,* 7943–7947.

Lovegrove, W., Garzia, R., & Nicholson, S. (1990). Experimental evidence for a transient system deficit in specific reading disability. *Journal of the Ophthalmology Society of America, 61,* 137–146.

Lovegrove, W., Martin, F., & Slaghuis, W. (1986). A theoretical and experimental case for a visual deficit in specific reading disability. *Cognitive Neuropsychology, 2,* 225–267.

Martin, R. C. (1995). Heterogeneity of deficits in developmental dyslexia and implications for methodology. *Psychonomic Bulletin & Review, 2,* 494–500.

McGrady, H. J., & Olson, D. A. (1970). Visual and auditory learning processes in normal children and children with specific learning disabilities. *Exceptional Children, 36,* 581–589.

Morrison, F. J., Giordani, B., & Nagy, J. (1977, April 1). Reading disability: An information-processing analysis. *Science, 196,* 77–79.

Neely, J. H., & Balota, D. A. (1981). Test-expectancy and semantic-organization effects in recall and recognition. *Memory & Cognition, 9,* 283–300.

Press, S. J. (1989). *Bayesian statistics: Principles, models, and applications.* New York: Oxford University Press.

Rack, J. (1985). Orthographic and phonetic coding in developmental dyslexia. *British Journal of Psychology, 76,* 325–340.

Rayner, K., Pollatsek, A., & Bilsky, A. B. (1995). Can a temporal processing deficit account for dyslexia? *Psychonomic Bulletin & Review, 2,* 501–507.

Riefer, D. M., Knapp, B. R., Batchelder, W. H., Bamber, D., & Manifold, V. (2002). Cognitive psychometrics: Assessing storage and retrieval deficits in special populations with multinomial processing tree model. *Psychological Assessment, 14,* 184–201.

Riefer, D. M., & Rouder, J. N. (1992). A multinomial modeling analysis of the mnemonic benefits of bizarre imagery. *Memory & Cognition, 20,* 601–611.

Rouder, J. N., & Batchelder, W. H. (1998). Multinomial models for measuring storage and retrieval processes in paired associate learning. In C. E. Dowling, F. S. Roberts, & P. Theuns (Eds.), *Recent progress in mathematical psychology: Psychophysics, knowledge representation, cognition, and measurement* (pp. 195–225). Mahwah, NJ: Erlbaum.

Snowling, M. J. (1991). Developmental reading disorders. *Journal of Child Psychology and Psychiatry, 32,* 49–77.

Stanley, G., & Hall, R. (1973). Short-term visual information processing in dyslexics. *Child Development, 44,* 841–844.

Stanovich, K. E. (1988). Explaining the differences between the dyslexic and the garden-variety poor reader: The phonological-core variable-difference model. *Journal of Learning Disabilities, 21,* 590–604.

Studdert-Kennedy, M., & Mody, M. (1995). Auditory temporal perception deficits in the reading-impaired: A critical review of the evidence. *Psychonomic Bulletin & Review, 2,* 508–514.

Tallal, P. (1984). Temporal or phonetic processing deficit in dyslexic? That is the question. *Applied Psycholinguistics, 5,* 167–169.

Tallal, P., & Curtiss, S. (1990). Neurological basis of developmental language disorders. In A. Rothenberger (Ed.), *Brain and behavior in child psychiatry* (pp. 205–216). New York: Springer-Verlag.

U.S. Department of Health and Human Services, Centers for Disease Control and Prevention, National Center for Health Statistics. (n.d.). *International classification of diseases, clinical modification*. Hyattsville, MD: Author. (Available from the National Center for Health Statistics Web site: http://www.cdc.gov/nchs/icd9.htm)

Van Zandt, T. (2002). Analysis of response time distributions. In H. Pashler & J. Wixted (Eds.), *Stevens' handbook of experimental psychology* (Vol. 4, pp. 461–561). New York: Wiley.

Vellutino, F. R. (1977). Alternative conceptualizations of dyslexia: Evidence in support of a verbal-deficit hypothesis. *Harvard Educational Review, 47,* 334–354.

Vellutino, F. R., & Scanlon, D. M. (1987). Phonological coding, phonological awareness, and reading ability: Evidence from a longitudinal and experimental study. *Merrill–Palmer Quarterly, 33,* 321–363.

von Mises, R. (1957). *Probability, statistics and truth.* New York: Dover.

3

COGNITIVE MODELS FOR EVALUATING BASIC DECISION PROCESSES IN CLINICAL POPULATIONS

ELDAD YECHIAM, ELIZABETH S. VEINOTT, JEROME R. BUSEMEYER, AND JULIE C. STOUT

Severe frontal lobe brain injury is often associated with impairment in decision-making ability (Damasio, 1996). After observing a patient with ventromedial frontal lobe damage whose cognitive abilities were intact but whose decision making was impaired, Bechara, Damasio, Damasio, and Anderson (1994) developed a task, now referred to as the *Iowa gambling task*, to identify and assess this neurological deficiency. Poor performance on this task has been observed in patients with ventromedial damage as characterized by a greater tendency to focus on immediate rewards and ignore future larger negative consequences. Since the publication of Bechara et al.'s study, in the tradition of true interdisciplinary work, researchers interested in clinical neuroscience, psychopathology, and drug abuse have been using this task to assess both behavioral and neurological characteristics in different populations. Although this approach has been successful in determining that schizophrenia (Wilder, Weinberger, & Goldberg, 1998), panic disorders (Cavedini et al., 2002), and acute mania (Clark, Iversen,

& Goodwin, 2001) do not seem to be associated with ignoring future consequences, many more neurologically and psychologically distinct populations have demonstrated similar decision deficits on this task (e.g., Bartzokis et al., 2000; Bechara et al., 2001; Mazas, Finn, & Steinmetz, 2000; Petry, Bickel, & Arnett, 1998; Schmitt, Brinkley, & Newman, 1999; Stout, Roda-walt, & Siemers, 2001).

In the Iowa gambling task, participants select between four alternatives that appear as decks of cards. Each alternative produces gains and also occasionally losses, and outcomes vary in the size of the gains to losses and in the frequency of the losses. It has been suggested that poor performance on the Iowa gambling task is due to a breakdown in the emotion-based learning system, because this task cannot be performed successfully on the basis of a purely cognitive system alone (Bechara et al., 1994; Damasio, Tranel, & Damasio, 1991), thereby implying that this task involves an interaction of motivational and cognitive processes. The interaction of these underlying processes in this complex task poses a theoretical problem in that it is difficult to independently evaluate the contribution of each component process. Overall poor performance may be a result of deficits in different component processes in different populations rather than a single deficit. As we demonstrate in this chapter, cognitive models, often used in cognitive psychology and cognitive science, provide a tool for identifying the relative contributions of distinct subcomponents of a behavior and may be particularly useful to the study of decision-making deficits in different clinical populations.

Cognitive models provide a theoretical basis for identifying implicit basic processes that underlie complex task performance. Thus, they offer an elegant solution that facilitates the use of relatively complex tasks within the framework of clinical assessment because they enable one to produce independent measures of the component processes involved in a task. Cognitive models explain intelligent (human or animal) behavior by building models that simulate that behavior (usually on a computer). Within the approach, cognitive mechanisms are mapped onto computational algorithms, and cognitive representations are mapped onto computational data structures. Cognitive models range in their complexity and the types of problems that they are modeling. Some solve highly specific problems; for example, processing-tree theory (Batchelder & Riefer, 1999) produces independent measures of memory storage and retrieval. Other cognitive models (e.g., the executive-process/interactive control [commonly known as "EPIC"] model [Meyer & Kieras, 1999], and the adaptive control of thought—rational [commonly known as "ACT-R"] model [Anderson, 1991]) are designed to address a large family of problems and to simulate many different basic processes. In this chapter, we review the use of a model that is similar to the former class of models and has been specifically designed to simulate performance on the Iowa gambling task.

Cognitive models are powerful in that they use a quantitative approach whereby different variants of the model can produce testable predictions about performance levels (response time, errors, choice made, etc.) at different time points and under different conditions. The present model allows one to independently assess the motivational, learning, and response component processes that lead to the overall deficient decision-making behavior. It uses a quantitative learning model that predicts how people learn from experience. The predictions of the model are tested against the learning curves of performance, and the similarity represents the descriptive power of the model.

In this chapter, we demonstrate the use of computational models for the understanding of underlying processes in complex clinical assessment tasks, such as the Iowa gambling task. First, we describe the Iowa gambling task as an example of a complex behavioral task that is used in clinical assessment. Next, we present the quantitative model used to identify basic processes that lead to poor task performance. Because different cognitive models rely on different assumptions about the basic components, we describe and compare three alternative models. After that, we review three methods for model comparison (prediction, simulation, and bootstrapping) and discuss the advantages and disadvantages of the methods. The chapter closes with a review of the applications of the present approach for analyzing the Iowa gambling task. In previous work on this topic, Busemeyer and Stout (2002) tested three very different models for this task and fit the models to the empirical data. This chapter complements Busemeyer and Stout's work by analyzing three different variants of the best-fitting model from their article, providing a more detailed description of the modeling procedures for those interested in learning how to use computational models to study underlying processes and by applying this approach to the study of two disparate populations that show similar overt behavior on the Iowa gambling task: (a) patients with Huntington's disease and (b) cocaine abusers.

THE BEHAVIORAL TASK

For demonstrating the use of a cognitive model for distilling the basic processes involved in a complex decision task, we reexamine a series of studies in which the Iowa gambling task was used (Bechara et al., 1994). This popular task has been used for neurological assessment of patients with ventromedial prefrontal cortex (VMPFC) damage by examining a person's tendency to make risky choices in response to different reward structures.

Tally: 2,000

You won 50, but lost 50

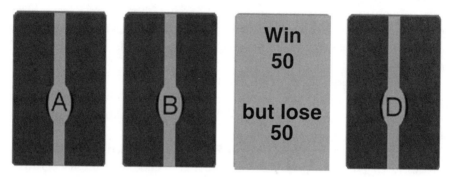

Figure 3.1. The layout of the Iowa gambling task (Bechara et al., 1994). There are four decks of cards, labeled A, B, C, and D. Each time a decision maker selects a deck, the outcome from that deck is shown. The feedback also includes the accumulated tally. Note that gains and losses can occur simultaneously on the same trial, as in this case (the decision maker chose Deck C and had a gain of $50 and a loss of $50).

In this task, participants start with $2,000 in play money and make a series of 100 choices from four decks of cards with the goal of maximizing their net payoff across trials. On each trial, the participant selects one card from any of the four decks and turns it over to learn the outcome of his or her choice. There is also an accumulating payoff counter, which is displayed constantly. In addition to the goal of maximizing their payoff, the participants are told that they can switch among the decks as often as they wish, but they are not told how many cards they will be choosing or anything about the decks. Information about the payoffs of the different decks is learned over time.

Each choice leads to a gain, and sometimes these gains are coupled with simultaneous losses (see Figure 3.1 and Table 3.1). Two of the four decks are disadvantageous because they lead to net losses across multiple selections. These decks are initially very attractive because they always pay $100, but they are also associated with larger, infrequent losses (up to $1,250). The average net loss per trial for these decks is $25. Good performance is achieved by avoiding these disadvantageous decks and instead choosing the two alternative decks, which lead to a net gain of $25 on

TABLE 3.1
The Payoff Scheme of the Four Alternatives in the Iowa Gambling Task

Deck	Wins	Losses	Description
A	$100 every card	.5 to lose $250	Disadvantageous: Risky
B	$100 every card	.1 to lose $1,250	Disadvantageous: Risky, rare loss
C	$50 every card	.5 to lose $50	Advantageous: Safe
D	$50 every card	.1 to lose $250	Advantageous: Safe, rare loss

Note. A = disadvantageous; losses in 50% of the selections; B = disadvantageous; losses in 10% of the selections; C = advantageous; losses in 50% of the selections; D = advantageous; losses in 10% of the selections.

average per trial. The two advantageous decks have smaller immediate payoffs of $50 but also losses of smaller magnitude. There are three main characteristics of this task: (a) It involves uncertainty regarding gains and losses associated with each deck of cards; (b) participants receive immediate feedback regarding their choices; and (c) the task is complex, because it requires both motivation (responses to gains and losses) and learning for participants to perform well.

Typical performance on this task involves initially favoring the disadvantageous decks because their immediate reward ($100) is twice as much as the advantageous decks. Over trials, healthy control participants learn that although the disadvantageous desks initially seem superior, they are not, because they are also associated with significantly larger losses, and thus these participants switch to preferring the advantageous decks. Examining the overall performance (percentage of disadvantageous decks chosen) on this task initially proved to be effective in differentiating individuals with bilateral damage to the VMPFCs from healthy control participants (Bechara et al., 1994). Individuals with VMPFC lesions possess normal mental capacities as measured by the Wisconsin Card Sorting Task (Milner, 1963) and working memory tasks. Moreover, these individuals do not show poor performance in simple choice tasks, such as decisions between safe and risky gambles (see, e.g., Leland & Grafman, 2005). Yet in real-world situations, these patients have been observed to have deficits in their decision-making behavior (Bechara et al., 1994; Eslinger & Damasio, 1985). Likewise, on the more complex Iowa gambling task, patients with VMPFC lesions also display poor performance (Bechara et al., 1994).[1]

---

[1]The use of relatively complex tasks, such as the Iowa gambling task, for clinical assessment thus has pluses and minuses. Complex tasks elicit cognitive processes that are different from those observed in simpler tasks, because they force individuals to deal with complex stimuli in environments that include nontrivial attention and memory demands (see Fabiani, Buckely, Gratton, Coles, & Donchin, 1989). On the positive side, complex task performance is assumed to be more similar to performance in real-world situations, which can be helpful for clinical assessment. On the negative side, however, when using complex tasks it is more difficult to interpret the findings and relate them to basic brain and cognitive mechanisms.

The Iowa gambling task has been used to test hypotheses regarding the underlying neuropsychology of different psychological disorders. To that end, no difference in performance on this task has been found between healthy control participants and patients with schizophrenia (Wilder et al., 1998), acute mania (Clark et al., 2001), or panic disorder (Cavedini et al., 2002). Together, these data suggest that the VMPFC is not affected in these particular psychological disorders. It is interesting that deficits similar to those in the VMPFC patients were also found in patients with many other neuropsychological disorders and clinical populations, such as Huntington's disease (Stout et al., 2001), obsessive–compulsive disorder (Cavedini et al., 2002), psychopathic individuals (Blair, Colledge, & Mitchell, 2001; Schmitt et al., 1999), persons with antisocial personality disorder (Mazas et al., 2000), and chronic drug abusers (Bartzokis et al., 2000; Bechara et al., 2001; Grant, Contoreggi, & London, 2000; Petry et al., 1998), making the theoretical interpretations of the behavior more difficult.

It is of course possible that a single deficit leads to choice of disadvantageous decks in these different populations, yet in this case one must conclude that the Iowa gambling task is not sensitive for differentiating among such distinct clinical populations. An alternative reason for this inability of the overt task performance measure to distinguish among the different populations is that there are different component processes that lead to the overt risk-taking behavior, and these may be different in distinct populations.

The behavioral outcomes of this task may appear on the surface to be relatively simple. However, on further evaluation, this task involves several different processes to accomplish it successfully. For example, there are motivational processes, such as evaluating feelings regarding immediate wins and infrequent larger losses; cognitive processes, such as learning long-term deck contingencies and remembering past wins and losses; and choice strategies, affected by individual strategies such as impulsiveness and need for consistency. Each of these processes could plausibly lead to the overt behavior observed.

For example, if a decision maker (DM) chooses from the disadvantageous decks, characterized by higher immediate gains coupled with higher infrequent losses, then maybe the DM is focusing more on gains than losses. This motivational explanation of the behavior is similar to the concept of promotion and prevention focus (Higgins, 1997). Whereas this first component that can lead to poor performance is motivational, an alternative component is related to learning and memory processes, denoting the degree of forgetting or discounting of past losses. Namely, if DMs discount (or forget) the past losses from the disadvantageous decks because they are infrequent, then they are likely to prefer these decks, because some of the time they supply a payoff that is relatively high. Accordingly, the second plausible explanation of poor performance in this task may be due to a memory component.

Finally, a third factor that may lead to poor performance is an erratic choice pattern due to such causes as loss of interest, boredom, impulsivity, or fatigue. This factor implies that although DMs may have high attention to losses initially, their attention wavers throughout the task, and the choice becomes more arbitrary as they continue in the task. This is another possible reason for not learning to choose the advantageous decks more often. These multiple interpretations provide a problem for theoretically understanding risk-tasking behavior observed in the Iowa gambling task.

In this chapter, we take the approach that to improve the sensitivity of the task to the underlying basic processes of different clinical populations, the overt behavior in the gambling task needs to be distilled so as to examine potential differences in underlying basic components. The change in these basic components (e.g., motivational, cognitive, choice consistency) may be different in distinct clinical populations and thus provide more insight into the psychological differences in these populations.

THE QUANTITATIVE LEARNING MODEL

For capturing the basic processes involved in the Iowa gambling task, we use a cognitive model called the *expectancy-valence model* that was initially developed by Busemeyer and Stout (2002). This cognitive model is a reinforcement learning model, because it simulates the behavior of a person who makes a series of choices, each based on the outcome from the previous choices, without any knowledge of the actual distribution of the payoff associated with each choice. Specifically, the model is a set of stochastic equations that mimic the psychological processes that are involved in the decision of which card to choose next in the trial. Each of the equations is a simple unit that performs a basic element of cognition. However, the emergent behavior of the ensemble becomes fairly complex, up to the level where the mathematical model can realistically mimic human behavior (see Busemeyer & Johnson, 2004)

Expectancy-Valence Model

According to this model, the DM integrates the gains and losses experienced on each trial into a single affective reaction called a *valence*. Expectancies about the valence produced by each deck are learned by an adaptive learning mechanism. Finally, these expectancies serve as the inputs into a probabilistic choice mechanism that selects the choice on each trial

(Busemeyer & Stout, 2002). The valences (or subjective reactions) and expectancies (which are the accumulated reactions for a deck) are updated after each selection on the basis of the outcome of the selection and the simulated attributes of the player.

As one might expect, when first faced with the four decks, people have no preference because they have no information about the decks, so they will randomly choose a card. Consequently, in the first trial, the response of the model is a random choice. In the next trial, the model's response depends on the outcome from the previous trial. The model receives this outcome as its input. Its output answers the question "What is the next choice ahead given the observed outcome?" The model assumes that there are three components of the Iowa gambling task and, consequently, the model: (a) attention to losses or wins, (b) memory for recent outcomes, and (c) consistency of the choice. Furthermore, recall that the power of this computational model is that each component can be individually assessed to provide a specific profile for each individual based on these three components, described next.

Attention to Losses and/or Wins: The Motivational Parameter

In the Iowa gambling task, the evaluation of the gains and losses is called a *valence* and is represented by a utility function that allows for different weights for gain and losses (Kahneman & Tversky, 1979). The utility is denoted $u(t)$ and is calculated as a weighted average of gains and losses for the chosen deck in trial t.

$$u(t) = W \cdot \text{win}(t) - (1 - W) \cdot \text{loss}(t), \qquad (3.1)$$

where $\text{win}(t)$ is the amount of money won on trial t, $\text{loss}(t)$ is the amount of money lost on trial t, and W is a parameter that indicates the weight given to gains versus losses. The attention weight is a motivational difference in attention distribution. The parameter is limited from 0, denoting attention only to losses, to 1, denoting attention only to gains. Values between 0 and 1 indicate the comparative weight of gains versus losses. This parameter captures and formally specifies the motivational component of poor performance in the Iowa gambling task. Specifically, poor performance in the Iowa task may be due to persistence in choosing from disadvantageous decks because of insensitivity to the large losses produced by these decks.

Imagine, for example, a DM who pays much more attention to gains than to losses (represented as a $W = .9$). This DM chooses a card from a disadvantageous deck and receives a gain of $100 and a loss of $250. According to the model, the utility is not a simple average of the two outcomes; instead, it is a weighted average in which for this DM, gains are more important than losses. In this case, $u(t)$ is equal to $.9 \times 100 - .1 \times 250$, or

$u(t) = 65$. Now let us say that the same person chooses from an advantageous deck and receives a $50 gain and a $50 loss. This leads to $u(t)$, which equals $.9 \times 50 - .1 \times 50$, or 40. Thus, for this DM the subjective outcome from this disadvantageous deck is higher; hence, according to the model, this deck is more likely to be chosen. This parameter is therefore useful for characterizing a motivational deficit (i.e., a strong preference for gains) that may lead to poor performance in the Iowa gambling task.

Influence of Memory for Recent Outcomes: The Recency Parameter

In the Iowa gambling task, the DM initially does not know anything about the payoff distributions for the different decks and must attempt to learn this information over choice trials. When DMs learn from experience, they need to decide whether to make their next choice on the basis of recent outcomes or on the basis of the outcomes observed over longer periods of time. Structural capacities may influence this choice, because some previous gains or losses are so distant that they are not recalled.

Formally, the term expectancy, E_j, is used to denote the accumulated expected utility for deck j or, in other words, the accumulated experience one has with a deck. High relative expectancy implies that the propensity to choose the corresponding deck would be high. The expectancy is updated by the affective response experienced when a card from a particular deck is chosen and is a function not only of the new valence or utility of the outcome for a given trial $u(t)$ but also of old valences from previous trials. A delta learning rule (see, e.g., Busemeyer & Myung, 1992; Sarin & Vahid, 1999) is used for updating the expectancy after each choice, as follows:

$$E_j(t) = E_j(t - 1) + \varphi \cdot [u(t) - E_j(t - 1)]\, \delta_j(t). \qquad (3.2)$$

On any trial t, the expectancy is equal to that endowed by the previous trials $E_j(t - 1)$. In addition, if deck j was selected in trial t, then the expectancy changes. The formula also includes $\delta_j(t)$, which is in essence a weight associated with the chosen deck. It equals 1 if deck j is chosen on trial t, and 0 otherwise. This means that for all the decks that were not chosen, the expectancy does not get updated because the second half of the equation is multiplied by zero. When the expectancy gets updated, $\delta_j(t) = 1$, then a change occurs in the direction of the prediction error given by $u(t) - E_j(t)$. That is, if the new outcome from deck j is higher than the stored outcome (i.e., the old expectancy), this improves the expectancy, and the propensity to select the deck increases. If the new outcome is lower, then the new expectancy of the deck becomes lower.

The recency parameter, φ, describes the degree to which expectancies of deck consequences reflect the influence of past experiences with particular decks or rather appear to be affected by the most recent outcome with a

TABLE 3.2
Simulated Expectancy Outcomes in Different Values of the
Memory Parameter (φ)

Trial	DM-A $\varphi = .9$		DM-B $\varphi = .1$	
	Expectancy	Outcome	Expectancy	Outcome
1	0	1	0	1
2	.9	1	.1	1
3	.99	1	.19	1
4	.999	1	.271	1
5	.9999	1	.3439	1
6	.99999	1	.40951	1
7	.999999	−12.5	.468559	−12.5
8	−11.15	1	−0.8283	1
9	−0.215	1	−0.64547	1
10	.8785	1	−0.48092	1
11	.98785	1	−0.33283	1
12	.998785	1	−0.19955	1
13	.999878	1	−0.07959	1
14	.999988	−12.5	.028368	−12.5
15	−11.15		−1.22447	

Note. DM-A = Decision Maker A; DM-B = Decision Maker B.

deck. This parameter is also limited from 0 to 1. Large values of φ indicate strong recency effects such that the most recent trials are more influential in determining the expectancy, whereas past outcomes are discounted. In other words, people's deck expectancies change quickly, are influenced strongly by recent outcomes, and are forgotten easily. In contrast, small values of φ indicate the persistence of influences of prior trial outcomes over longer spans of selections and are associated with slow forgetting and slower incorporating of new outcomes into expectancies. To demonstrate these processes in the model, we analyze a specific example.

Table 3.2 compares two DMs with different learning strategies (i.e., values of φ) who, for the purpose of comparing the effect of these learning strategies on chosen deck expectancies, are always choosing from a disadvantageous deck (Deck B). Decision Maker A (DM-A) has a φ of .9, implying high recency, whereas Decision Maker B (DM-B) has a φ of .1, implying low recency. The initial expectancy (in Trial 1) is assumed to be zero because there is no prior information about any of the decks. In Trial 1, DM-A chooses from a disadvantageous deck and receives a gain of 1. The gains (and losses) in the outcome column refer to the weighted average of gains and losses, $u(t)$. In the first trial, the expectancy for DM-A's chosen deck is accordingly updated as follows: $E(1) = 0 + .9 \times (1 - 0) \times 1 = .9$. Replacing the .9 with a .1 in this equation provides one with the updated expectancy for DM-B's chosen deck. The expectancy for all unchosen decks is still 0.

After selecting six more cards from the disadvantageous deck (DM-A or DM-B), leading to five more gains of 1, a loss of 12.5, and additional gains, an interesting difference between the two DMs' expectancies for the disadvantageous deck is observed. DM-A reacts more strongly to losses, which leads to a drastic decrease in the level of expectancy for the chosen deck in the trial following a large loss (see Trials 8 and 15 in Table 3.2). However, for DM-A, the expectancy for this disadvantageous deck recovers quickly and returns to an almost normal level after only two trials (see Trial 10). In contrast, for the low recency DM-B, the expectancy following the large loss does not return to its high preloss level as quickly. It is thus likely that DM-A would have a higher propensity to choose from the disadvantageous deck even after experiencing the losses associated with it. Therefore, the recency parameter enables the model to represent a second condition under which DMs might choose disadvantageous decks. This explains favoring disadvantageous decks because the DM does not remember infrequently occurring bad outcomes and consequently does not discount those decks appropriately.

Reliability of Choice Behavior: The Choice Consistency Parameter

The DM's choice on each trial is based not only on the expectancies produced by each deck but also on the reliability with which the DM applies those expectancies when making the selections. As we discussed above, people may be inconsistent in the application of expectancies if they are bored, impulsive, or tired. In terms of explaining risk-taking behavior, inconsistency may impair the DM's ability to learn to choose the advantageous decks. According to the expectancy-valence model, the probability of choosing a deck is a strength ratio of that deck relative to the sum of the strengths of all decks:

$$\Pr[G_j(t)] = \frac{e^{\theta(t) \cdot E_j(t)}}{\sum_k e^{\theta(t) \cdot E_k(t)}}. \tag{3.3}$$

The sum of strength formula is a commonly used decision rule in risky choices (see Luce, 1959). An alternative is chosen as a function of its relative expectancy compared with the sum of the expectancy of the other alternatives. The formula yields a probability for choosing each deck, and the probabilities sum to 1. These probabilities are later examined for their predictive value.

It is assumed that the consistency, denoted by $\theta(t)$, changes as a function of experience and can increase in magnitude, reflecting learning. It can also decrease, reflecting tiredness or a loss of interest. This is formalized by a power function for the consistency change over trials:

$$\theta(t) = (t/10)^c. \tag{3.4}$$

Reliability is represented by the choice consistency parameter, denoted as c. The parameter c controls the consistency of the choice probabilities and the expectancies. The parameter is bounded between -5 and $+5$. When the value of c is low, choices are inconsistent, random, impulsive, and independent of the expectancies. When the value of the consistency parameter is very high, then the deck with the maximum expectancy will almost certainly be chosen on each trial.

The choice consistency parameter represents a third facet of performance in the Iowa gambling task. Very low values of the parameter indicate an erratic choice pattern in which DMs do not update their choices on the basis of their expectancies, and this is a third reason that one might observe a DM choosing from disadvantageous decks. For example, patients with VMPFC damage may lose their ability to concentrate as the task proceeds and consequently become more inconsistent with their choices over time. To summarize, the expectancy-valence model has three independent parameters: (a) a motivational parameter, representing attention weight given to losses and gains; (b) a learning parameter, representing memory for past outcomes; and (c) a choice consistency parameter, representing the degree of coupling between choices and outcome expectancies. The power in using a cognitive model, such as the expectancy-valence model designed for the Iowa gambling task, is that it allows one to decompose overall individual performance on a task into the underlying component processes. Furthermore, it provides individual estimates of each parameter estimate for each component that can then be used to assess component differences at the group level.

Alternative Models

The next step in any type of cognitive modeling is to compare and test competing models for the task. The best-fitting model in this competition is selected and used to provide the basis for the underlying basic processes. In previous work, Busemeyer and Stout (2002) and Yechiam and Busemeyer (2005) have compared the expectancy-valence learning model, which is a reinforcement learning model, to two substantially different models: (a) a strategy-switching model (see, e.g., Payne, Bettman, & Johnson, 1988) and (b) a Bayesian model (see, e.g., Luce, 1959). Because the reinforcement-learning model was found to be superior to alternative models in these two previous works (i.e., Busemeyer & Stout, 2002; Yechiam & Busemeyer, 2005), it is particularly important to fine tune this model to find the variant of it that best describes a performer's behavior. In the next section, we provide a more stringent test of the expectancy-valence model by comparing it with two different reinforcement learning models: (a) a decay model and (b) a model with independent attention weights to gains and losses. As we discuss next, these models differ in terms of their psychological interpretation of the attention weight and learning parameters.

Interference Versus Decay

Two general classes of models have been proposed to account for the way new information is accumulated in a learning task. One is based on loss of information due to interference from new outcomes, and the other class is based on decay of information. Under one class of models, similar to the expectancy-valence model, the weight of an expectancy from an alternative changes only if the alternative is selected. Thus, the old expectancy from an alternative is discounted only if the alternative is selected again and new information, $u(t)$, is added about that alternative (in the form of new outcomes). This class of models has been labeled *interference models*, because the memory representation is modified only by relevant events and not simply as a function of time (e.g., Newell, 1992; Oberauer & Kliegl, 2001).

In an alternative class of models, the weight of the old expectancy of an alternative can decrease on each choice trial even if an alternative has not been selected and no new information about it is presented. Thus, expectations about a deck can change as a result of the selections of other decks. This class of models can be labeled *decay models*, because decay of memory occurs even without the occurrence of interfering events (e.g., Atkinson & Shiffrin, 1968; Broadbent, 1958). A popular decay model is the reinforcement-decay model used by Roth and Erev (1995). It has the following formula for updating the expectancy in each trial (this equation is used instead of Equation 3.2):

$$E_j(t) = \varphi \cdot E_j(t - 1) + \delta_j(t) \cdot u(t). \qquad (3.5)$$

Note that for this model the past expectancy is always discounted, regardless of whether any new payoff information is experienced. This is implemented by the fact that the past expectancy of all decks $E_j(t - 1)$ is multiplied in each trial by the recency parameter φ (whose value is ≤ 1). In other words, if an option is not chosen, then a payoff of zero is used to update the expectancy. The assumption of decay implies a difference in the psychological interpretation of the recency parameter. It is therefore important to discern the model that is most suited to describe performers' behavior. Of course, this does not rule out the possibility that the models provide complementary perspectives and that a third hybrid model would be needed to accurately simulate a DM's choices.

Independent Attention to Gains and Losses

In Equation 3.1, a single parameter is used to denote the relative attention to gains versus losses. In theory, though, the attention to gains and losses may not be necessarily dependent. For example, a DM may pay a lot of attention to both gains and losses very little attention to either. To more accurately describe the behavior of such DMs, a model should include the attention to gains and losses as separate components. This is implemented by providing independent parameters for the attention to gain and losses, as follows:

$$u(t) = W \cdot \text{win}(t) - L \cdot \text{loss}(t). \tag{3.6}$$

If one compares this equation with Equation 3.1, one can see that the term $1 - W$ has been replaced by the parameter L. This is an independent parameter that denotes the attention to losses. This would allow the modeling of a DM who has high or low values for both W and L. Accordingly, the values of L and W are not necessarily limited by 1 but can be limited by a higher value (e.g., in Yechiam & Busemeyer, 2005, a ceiling value of 3 was used). Furthermore, as opposed to the decay formula discussed in the preceding section, the implementation of the present formula increases the number of parameters in the model from three to four. The implication of this step, as we discuss in more detail in the "Model Evaluation" section, is that the model is less parsimonious.

Baseline Models

In addition to the two variants of the expectancy-valence model discussed above, a baseline model is examined as a standard for comparison with each cognitive model. There are different plausible baseline models. The most "naive" baseline model is an agent that makes choices arbitrarily, that is, randomly. A more sophisticated baseline model, which is at present used in the implementation of the expectancy-valence model, is a statistical model that generates choices with constant probabilities across trials. The probability of choosing a card from one of the four decks can be described in three free parameters (because the fourth deck choice proportion is equal to 1 minus the proportion of the other decks). Unlike the cognitive models, this baseline model does not assume any learning or other fluctuations in selections as a result of training experience. Instead, it assumes that the choices are identically distributed across trials. In the next section, we evaluate the two cognitive models and compare them with the baseline model. Accordingly, a cognitive model will be deemed to have performed better than the baseline model if it succeeds in explaining how choices are changed as a function of learning or other trial-to-trial dependencies.

MODEL EVALUATION

To evaluate the variants of the expectancy-valence models presented above, one needs to use multiple strategies. We review the use of a prediction, a simulation, and a bootstrapping approach, because they provide important and complementary evaluation metrics. For example, in the prediction method, we examine the accuracy of the one-step-ahead predictions generated by each model for each individual performer. In contrast, using the simulation method, predictions for the full learning path are generated and compared with the average performer's learning curve. Finally, bootstrapping is an evaluation strategy that does not use empirical data. Instead, the model is used to generate data, and then it is reused to fit its own data. We follow with an example that combines the use of different methods in assessing variants of the expectancy-valence model.

Prediction

The first method of model evaluation examines the accuracy of one-step-ahead predictions generated by each model for each individual. To be more specific, define $Y_i(t)$ as a $t \times 1$ vector, representing the sequence of choices made by individual i in t trials. Define $X_i(t)$ as the corresponding sequence of payoffs produced by these choices. Each model is given $X_i(t)$ and uses this information to generate the probability of choosing deck j next time, given the outcomes on that deck, $\Pr[G_j(t + 1) \mid X_i(t)]$. The accuracy of these predictions is measured using the log-likelihood criterion:

$$\ln(L \mid \text{model}) = \Sigma_t \, \Sigma_j \, \ln(\Pr[G_j(t + 1) \mid X_i(t)]) \cdot \delta_j(t), \qquad (3.7)$$

where $\delta_j(t) = 1$ if deck j was chosen on trial t, and zero otherwise.

In this process, a grid search of the parameter space is used to find the combination of parameters that has the best prediction for the next step ahead. One such method is the robust combination of grid-search and simplex-search methods (Nelder & Mead, 1965). In this method, each point on the grid serves as a starting position for the simplex search algorithm, which is then used to find the parameters that maximize the log likelihood for an individual. For example, the parameter W has a value that is constrained between 0 (denoting attention to losses only) and 1 (denoting attention to gains only). To use the grid search, several points along this space are selected as the starting positions of the search algorithm.

The final outcome is a set of solutions, one for each starting point on the grid. The best solution is the one that maximizes the log-likelihood criterion. Once this set of solutions is calculated for each model, one can compare the model fits, G^2. The difference in the fit of the predictions of a baseline model and a cognitive model is evaluated by comparing log-likelihood scores for two models. Equation 3.8 compares the fit of the baseline and the expectancy-valence model:

$$G^2 = 2 \cdot [\ln(L \,|\, \text{model}) - \ln(L \,|\, \text{baseline})]. \qquad (3.8)$$

Positive values of the G^2 statistic indicate that a learning model performs better than the baseline model, whereas negative values indicate the reverse. Note that the cognitive model that has two separate parameters representing attention to gains and losses includes an additional parameter, L. Because the baseline model has only three parameters, whereas this learning model has four parameters, we need to adjust the fit calculation (G^2) for this difference in number of parameters. This is accomplished by using the Bayesian information criterion (BIC) statistic (Schwartz, 1978) to compare models:

$$\text{BIC} = G^2 - k \cdot \ln(N). \qquad (3.9)$$

In Equation 3.9, k denotes the difference in the number of parameters, and N equals the number of observations. For our comparisons, we have $k = 1$ (a one-parameter difference). Assuming that the task has 150 trials, then $N = 150$ and $1 \cdot \ln(150) \approx 5$. This implies that for the four-parameters cognitive model, we subtract 5 from the G^2 value.

Notice that the advantage of the one-step-ahead prediction method is that parameter estimation uses each and every trial in the repeated-choice task as independent observations. The number of trials usually is quite high (in the Iowa gambling task, it is 100), and this is adequate for producing stable parameter estimates for individual performers (see chap. 1, this volume).[2]

In summary, the prediction method allows one to assess the degree of fit between the average predicted choices for trial $t + 1$ given outcomes for all previous trials. In the next section, we discuss an alternative method that predicts choice for k trials ahead without the advantage of the input of the actual outcomes of the player.

Simulation

With this approach, many simulations of the full learning paths are generated to produce a distribution of choice sequences from a given model. The simulation method does not use any information about the actual

---

[2]Comparative BIC, although not having a well-charted distribution, importantly penalizes according to parameter estimation. In addition, this criterion can be complemented by parameter recovery methods such as the one described in the "Bootstrapping" section.

choices made by any of the participants. Instead, the outcomes of the model's choices are entered for updating the valences and expectancies in each selection. The final results are averaged to produce the probability of choosing each deck on each trial. The predicted probability is then compared with the observed proportion of choices on each trial, averaged across participants.

This method might seem cruder than the prediction method because it does not test the model compared with individuals' performance but against the average learning curve. In theory, a simulation can be used to examine the fit of a model compared with a single individual. Yet the statistical power of the simulation is low, because it does not have information about payoffs. Accordingly, it is not feasible to use it at the individual DM level.

Complementing this disadvantage is the following advantage: Some models, such as the decay model described in the "Alternative Models" section, allow for faster updating based on new information. Thus, their predictions might be better, not because of their general ability to predict the next step but because of their ability to adapt well to performers who converge quickly into preferring a single alternative and select repeatedly from that alternative. For example, assume that a DM has to choose between 10 alternatives, labeled A_1 to A_{10}. Each alternative produces an equal payoff with an average of 1 and standard deviation of 1. For the purpose of the example, we assume a linear relationship between payoff and expectancy. Under an interference model, the weight of new information is .9 the weight of old information. Under a decay model, the weight of old information is reduced by .9 in each trial. Let us say that at some point the player chose Option A_1 six times. Under the interference model, the increase in the expectancy of A_1 is, on average, $(.9 \cdot 1) \cdot 6$, or 5.4. Under the decay model, the value of each of the nine options that were not chosen is reduced by $1 - .9^6$, or 47%. Thus, the decay model is expected to predict the next choice better but only because it was the sixth in a sequence of similar choices. This ability implies an inequality in the evaluation that favors the decay models in cases where individuals reach such a plateau.

Some researchers have indeed suggested that the value of different models is highly specific to the precise evaluation method (Erev & Haruvy, 2005; Feltovich, 2000). Specifically, they have argued that model evaluation based on the examination of group averages (e.g., the simulation method) can lead to different results than the examination of individuals' choices (e.g., the prediction method). Likewise, an evaluation based on the prediction of the next choice ahead may lead to different results than the simulation of many choices ahead. Because the two evaluation methods have complementary advantages and disadvantages, using both methods is usually recommended.

Bootstrapping

A markedly different strategy for model evaluation is the use of a simulated data set. In this method, called *bootstrapping* (Efron, 1979), the quantitative model itself is used to generate data. One might ask why this method should be used rather than testing the model's predictions with an actual data set generated by human performers. One reason that it is used is for estimating model fits errors when empirical approximations are not available or if they are unreliable (Golden, 1995). However, bootstrapping is often used to complement empirical data because it enables the comparison of numerous different agents that have exact specifications in their behavioral characteristics (i.e., a predetermined parameter value).

Here we give an example of a rudimentary form of a method of bootstrapping. This method is based on the data-informed parametric bootstrap cross-fitting method (Wagenmakers, Ratcliff, Gomez, & Iverson, 2004), in which the models used to generate the data have specific parametric values that have theoretical or empirical significance. The ability of the models to predict the next step ahead of selections in the generated data is then compared. This is done using the prediction or simulation method described in the preceding section. In the present implementation, a supplementary step is added: In addition to examining the fits of the models for the simulated data, we examine the accuracy of the estimated (or restored) parameters of the model compared with the original parameters used to generate the data.

An Example Using Simulated Data

To examine the capability of the different variants of the expectancy-valence model to capture major differences in the weighting of parameters, we considered data generated using markedly different parameter values. The values were empirically derived from data examined using the original model (Yechiam & Busemeyer, 2005) and reflect realistic differences in the possible values of these parameters in different individuals. First, we examined high attention to gains ($W = .67$, $L = .33$) versus low attention to gains ($W = .33$, $L = .67$). Second, we considered high recency ($\varphi = .99$) compared with low recency ($\varphi = .5$). For the value of c (consistency), we used a single value (.5) that represents relatively high consistency and is in the range of the median in our previous work. The final parameter values appear in Table 3.3.

We generated data using an experiment-like design of 2 (high vs. low recency) × 2 (attention to gain vs. losses) × 2 (interference vs. decay). The recency parameter (denoting the degree of recency) and the attention weight parameter were used as between-subjects conditions. In addition, we used two models to generate this data. One used an interference expectancy

TABLE 3.3
Parameter Values in the Simulated Data

Parameters	High recency		Low recency	
	High attention to gains	High attention to losses	High attention to gains	High attention to losses
φ	.99	.99	.5	.5
W	.67	.33	.67	.33
L	.33	.67	.33	.67
c	.5	.5	.5	.5

Note. φ = recency parameter; W = weight to wins parameter; L = weight to losses parameter; c = choice consistency parameter.

updating formula (Equation 3.2), and the other used a decay-based formula (Equation 3.5) for updating the expectancy. Eighty modeling agents were run in each of the conditions (a total of 720 agents). We then examined the capability of different variants of the expectancy-valence model to fit these data using the prediction method as well as to restore the original parameters following the process of optimization.

The results of this examination appear in Table 3.4. The table shows the BIC value as the fit index in each cell (in parentheses). Next to this score are the restored values of parameters W and L (for conciseness, the two other parameters are not included). The results show the following interesting differences between the models. First of all, an examination of the three-parameter interference model compared with the three-parameter decay model shows that the interference model has higher BICs (108.9 compared with 49.0 on average) and more accuracy in the restored parameters in data created by the interference model, whereas the same is true for the decay model in data created by the decay model (BICs of 125.3 vs. 63.2). On the basis of this analysis of fit, it is clear that neither model dominates the other. Consequently, an empirical test is necessary to determine which model is more accurate (see Yechiam & Busemeyer, 2005).

In contrast, a comparison of the models in which gains and losses are dependent (the three-parameter model) or independent (the four-parameter model) shows that the three-parameter model has on average better fit (in 12 of the 16 cells its BIC is higher; on average 86.3 compared with 84.9)[3] as well as better accuracy. Although the differences in the BIC are relatively small, the accuracy of the three-parameter model in restoring the original parameter values appears to be much better. In fact, severe distortions in the original values of parameters W and L appear in the four-parameter

---

[3]Note that even though the four-parameter model is more general, the addition of a parameter penalizes its BIC score.

TABLE 3.4

Model Fits and Restored Parameters for the Variants of the Expectancy Valence Model: Interference Versus Decay and Dependent Gains Versus Independent Gains and Losses

Interference and decay BIC score and parameters	Interference				Decay			
	High recency[a]		Low recency[b]		High recency[a]		Low recency[b]	
	$W=.67$, $L=.33$	$W=.33$, $L=.67$	$W=.67$, $L=.33$	$W=.33$, $L=.67$	$W=.67$, $L=.33$	$W=.33$, $L=.67$	$W=.67$, $L=.33$	$W=.33$, $L=.67$
Dependent gains and losses (three-parameter model)								
Interference								
BIC score	113.1	146.1	69.7	106.8	47.4	121.5	61.0	**22.7**
Restored parameters (gains)	.67	.32	.66	.29	.81	.37	.80	**.74**
Restored parameters (losses)	.33	.68	.34	.71	.19	.63	.20	**.26**
Decay								
BIC score	31.2	**102.4**	14.5	**43.6**	59.0	189.5	167.5	85.0
Restored parameters (gains)	.62	**.59**	.63	**.56**	.69	.32	.67	.31
Restored parameters (losses)	.38	**.41**	.37	**.44**	.31	.68	.33	.69
Independent gains and losses (four-parameter model)								
Interference								
BIC score	108.5	141.7	65.2	102.3	**50.9**	**137.8**	58.7	**19.3**
Restored parameters (gains)	.75	.46	.81	.41	**.29**	**.22**	.83	**.42**
Restored parameters (losses)	.37	.75	.41	.78	**.87**	**2.6**	.22	**.18**
Decay								
BIC score	**28.6**	101.9	**15.4**	44.5	54.8	185.1	163.3	81.0
Restored parameters (gains)	**.47**	.48	**.26**	.31	**.88**	.33	.67	.36
Restored parameters (losses)	**.28**	.33	**.15**	.26	**.47**	.69	.34	.81

Note. Each cell includes the Bayesian information criterion (BIC) score of the model in parentheses and the restored parameters of attention to gains and losses. The data were generated by the interference and decay models using high and low values of the recency, weight to win (W), and weight to losses (L) parameters. Data for which the parameters were not restored accurately (more than .2. difference) are in boldface type.
[a]Recency parameter: $\varphi = .99$. [b]Recency parameter: $\varphi = .5$.

model (see boldface type in Table 3.4). Note that this is not proof that the four-parameter model is dominated by the three-parameter model because we did not examine models generated by high or low values of both parameters using the four-parameter model. Yet the analysis shows that for typical values of these parameters, the three-parameter model outperforms the four-parameter model.

An analysis of the consistency parameter c shows that in those cases where the values of the parameters W and L are inflated in the four-parameter model, the value of c is also inflated. This suggests that the augmented values of W and L have different implications that interact with the choice component of the model. In particular, when both W and L are high, this improves the consistency of the choice. Thus, in essence a new parameter is created: a degree of consistency that is not dependent on time as in the case of the consistency parameter.[4] The downside is that this change distorts the value of the W and L parameters. In addition, the value of the c parameter becomes inflated to match the influence of the $W + L$ parameter. Finally, this "effort" does not result in an increased fit of the model compared with the original three-parameter model.

In this section, we used a bootstrapping method to examine different variants of the expectancy-valence model. The results reveal that whereas the currently used interference model does not appear to dominate the alternative decay model, there appears to be no advantage to the use of a four-parameter model in this parameter range. The addition of the parameter did not improve the model fit but led to strong and consistent distortions in the value of the parameters. This should serve as a warning for models that include many parameters and do not examine unpredicted interactions between different components.

In this section we also have shown that the original three-parameter expectancy-valence model is analytically shown to be more accurate than a more complex variant. In the next section, we describe applications of the expectancy-valence model to the evaluation of decision-making deficits on the Iowa gambling task in two different clinical populations: (a) patients with a neurological disorder, Huntington's disease, and (b) cocaine abusers.

APPLICATIONS OF THE EXPECTANCY-VALENCE MODEL

The expectancy-valence model creates three new measures in addition to the overt choice from disadvantageous decks: (a) an attention to gains–losses measure, (b) a learning or recency measure, and (c) a choice

---

[4]This is caused because the expectancy in both the numerator and denominator in the ratio of strength Equation 3.3 is multiplied by a value (>1) derived from $W + L$.

consistency measure. This allows one to compare the distribution of these three measures across groups in order to identify which are driving the observed group differences. As previously discussed, both Huntington's disease patients and cocaine abusers resemble VMPFC patients in terms of their overt behavior on the Iowa gambling task, but do they differ on the three component processes? In this section, we review studies that have examined the usefulness of these measures for increasing the sensitivity of the task to underlying differences between performers with distinct impairments in memory systems (patients with Huntington's disease) and motivational systems (cocaine abusers).

Huntington's and Parkinson's Disease

Huntington's disease is an extremely rare and fatal syndrome with a prevalence of approximately 2 to 5 cases per 100,000 people in the United States (Harper, 1996). Huntington's patients suffer from a gradual loss of neurons in the caudate nuclei and the putamen of the basal ganglia, cells that mediate the projections into the VMPFC. Similar to VMPFC patients, the behavior of Huntington's patients is described as impulsive, risky, and uncontrollable (see Stout et al., 2001). Therefore, it seems reasonable to hypothesize that Huntington's patients would show performance deficits that are similar to those of patients with VMPFC-lesions.[5]

To test this hypothesis, Stout et al. (2001) compared performance on the Iowa gambling task by Huntington's disease patients ($n = 14$); a healthy control group ($n = 33$); and a group with Parkinson's disease with no orbital frontal cortex damage ($n = 20$), which served as a clinical control group. The two clinical groups had no comorbid psychological diagnoses, and all three groups were matched for gender and education; the Huntington group and the healthy control participants were also matched for age. Each participant performed the Iowa gambling task, and a reanalysis of the overt performance level (see Figure 3.2) shows that as predicted, the Huntington's disease patients displayed poor performance in the task, whereas the Parkinson's disease patients performed similarly to the healthy control participants.

Busemeyer and Stout (2002) reexamined the data from Stout et al. (2001) using the expectancy-valence learning model to assess the contributing factors to the poor performance exhibited by Huntington's patients. Because of the neurological and behavioral similarities between patients with Huntington's disease and patients with VMPFC lesions, it was predicted that if the effect is indeed due to the role of somatic markers, a deficit in

---

[5]Note that early detection of cognitive impairments is crucial in Huntington's disease because it improves the assessment of the suitability of the medication to the phase of the illness (Stout et al., 2001).

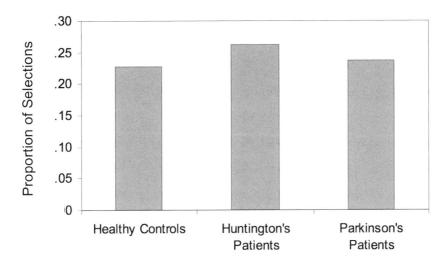

Figure 3.2. The reanalyzed results of Stout et al.'s (2001) study: proportion of selections from the disadvantageous decks in healthy control participants compared with individuals with Huntington's disease and Parkinson's disease.

one's ability to attach an emotional evaluation to cognitive stimuli (Damasio, 1996), then the most prominent role of the three parameters would be taken by the motivational attention weight factor. Table 3.5 presents a reanalysis of the results that uses the combination of grid-search and simplex-search methods (Nelder & Mead, 1965) discussed earlier, because the original analysis used a heuristic method for parameter optimization. The parameters of the models were optimized separately to fit the selections of each individual. The model fit was high, with 74% of the participants having a positive BIC score. Thus, the use of the expectancy-valence model improved the descriptive power of the performance data over an examination of the choice proportion of the different decks (similar to the description in Figure 3.2). The optimized parameters of the three populations are presented in Table 3.5.

TABLE 3.5
Parameter Estimates of the Expectancy-Valence Model:
Healthy Controls Compared With Individuals With Huntington's Disease
and Parkinson's Disease

Participants	Attention to recent outcome			Attention to gains/losses			Choice consistency		
	M	*Mdn*	*SD*	*M*	*Mdn*	*SD*	*M*	*Mdn*	*SD*
Healthy	0.28	0.12	0.37	0.65	0.69	0.28	0.91	1.31	2.10
Huntington's	0.41	0.20	0.46	0.77	0.88	0.34	1.40	0.77	3.25
Parkinson's	0.29	0.08	0.41	0.53	0.60	0.39	2.17	1.34	2.46

The results showed that indeed Huntington's patients had elevated attention to gains compared with losses. However, the difference along this dimension was not significant. The main difference between the Huntington's patients and healthy control participants was in the high recency displayed by Huntington's patients (see Table 3.5). For example, in the healthy control group, 18% of the participants had a recency parameter φ that was equal to 1 (denoting high recency). A similar proportion (20%) was observed in the group of Parkinson's patients. In contrast, the proportion of high-recency performers in the group of Huntington's patients was about 36% (an 89% increase; $Z = 1.34$, $p = .08$). This indicates that in contrast to the prediction based on the somatic marker hypothesis, memory is an important contributing factor to the performance impairments observed in Huntington's patients. This suggests that the Huntington's patients were not able to retain the outcomes from past choices as long as control participants were, and this led to their choosing more frequently from the disadvantageous decks. Indeed, Stout et al. (2001) found that for the Huntington's patient population, memory deficits on the Mattis Dementia Rating Scale (Mattis, 1988) were correlated with decision deficits in the gambling task. This is consistent with the theory that memory processes are partly responsible for the poor performance observed in this group.

Cocaine Abusers

Although Bechara et al. (2001) did not have specific predictions concerning Huntington's patients, they did contend that severe drug abusers display neuropsychological changes that are comparable to those of patients with lesions in their VMPFC. According to the National Institute on Drug Abuse (1999), in 1997 an estimated 1.5 million Americans age 12 and older were chronic cocaine users. An interesting and important topic of research has been to study the decision-making processes of chronic cocaine users. As part of this effort, several studies have demonstrated that cocaine abusers perform more poorly on the Iowa gambling task than do matched control participants, with drug abusers selecting more cards from the disadvantageous decks and fewer cards from the advantageous decks (e.g., Bechara, Dolan, & Hindes, 2002; Bechara et al., 2001; Grant et al., 2000).

To examine the underlying factors affecting the performance of drug abusers, Stout, Busemeyer, Lin, Grant, and Bonson (2005) examined the behavior of chronic cocaine abusers on the Iowa gambling task. They examined 12 cocaine-abusing individuals (average age 37, estimated IQ 93.7 ± 10.3) and 14 comparison, or nonabusing individuals (average age 30, estimated IQ 105.0 ± 7.62). Control participants were somewhat younger and had higher IQ levels than the drug abusers, but these differences were examined statistically and shown to have no effect on task performance.

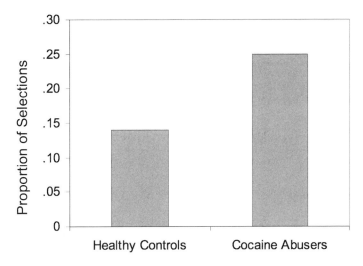

.30

.25

.20

.15

.10

.05

0

Proportion of Selections

Healthy Controls   Cocaine Abusers

Figure 3.3. The reanalyzed results of Stout et al.'s (in press) study: proportion of selections from the disadvantageous decks in healthy control participants compared with cocaine abusers.

The cocaine group reported current regular cocaine abuse, although all members of this group had past experience with other drugs of abuse (stimulants, depressants, marijuana, and opiates). Exclusion criteria included any history of significant medical illness or head trauma with loss of consciousness. The participants all performed 250 trials on the Iowa gambling task. The results appear in Figure 3.3.

These results demonstrate that cocaine abusers selected more cards from the disadvantageous decks. However, as demonstrated throughout this chapter, different reasons can account for failure to perform well on these tasks. The crucial question addressed in this study was whether the decision-making changes exhibited by drug abusers were caused by a memory component, as was found in the Huntington's patients, or by motivation or choice consistency. On the basis of an analysis of the data using the expectancy-valence learning model, it was found that the motivational processes were responsible for the decision-making deficit in drug abusers. Table 3.6 presents a reanalysis of the results from the first 100 trials that enables a comparison with the modeling results from Busemeyer and Stout's (2001) Huntington's study.

The model fit was high, with 70% of the participants having positive BIC scores, denoting an advantage of the expectancy-valence model over the baseline model. The attention weight parameter was significantly higher for the cocaine abuse group than the comparison group, $t(24) = 1.88$, $p < .05$, one-tailed, indicating that the card selections of the cocaine abuse group were more influenced by gains than were the comparison group. This

TABLE 3.6
Parameter Estimates of the Expectancy-Valence Model:
Healthy Controls Compared With Cocaine Abusers

Participants	Attention to recent outcome			Attention to gains–losses			Choice consistency		
	M	Mdn	SD	M	Mdn	SD	M	Mdn	SD
Healthy controls	0.35	0.19	0.39	0.34	0.24	0.35	0.64	−0.01	2.33
Cocaine abusers	0.58	0.60	0.39	0.61	0.79	0.40	−0.33	0.18	2.46

suggests that differences in motivational processes are a likely source of the differences in the decision-making styles of cocaine abusers, which is consistent with several major accounts in the drug abuse literature (e.g., Bechara et al., 2001, 2002; Grant et al., 2000; Kirby, Petry, & Bickel, 1999; London, Ernst, Grant, Bonson, & Weinstein, 2000).

Summary and Additional Studies

The reviewed studies of Huntington's patients and cocaine abusers show that in overt gambling task performance, there were no differences between these two populations. Both clinical populations displayed poor performance, with more choices from the disadvantageous decks compared with healthy control participants. However, the quantitative learning model was sensitive enough to detect different underlying processes that led to the choice of disadvantageous decks in the Iowa gambling task. In the case of the Huntington's patients, the overt disadvantageous choices were attributed to the memory component and possibly reflect the effect of memory impairments. In cocaine abusers, poor choices were attributed to the motivational component, with higher attention to gains on the part of the chronic drug abusers.

The present model is in its first phases of validation. So far, the effect of relevant manipulations (memory, explicit attention to gains and losses) has not been examined directly, yet several correlational examinations have demonstrated the construct validity of the model parameters. In one study, Johnson, Yechiam, Murphy, and Stout (in press) examined the association between the choice consistency parameter and a self-report measure of indecisiveness (Frost & Shows, 1993) in healthy adolescents. The results showed a strong negative correlation between choice consistency and indecisiveness ($rs = −.76$ on a child report and $−.68$ on a parent report). Another study, conducted by Yechiam, Hayden, Bodkins, O'Donnell, and Hetrick (2006), examined the association between the model parameters and measures of motivation, the Behavioral Inhibition System and Behavioral Activation System Scales (Carver & White, 1994). The results showed significant associations between attention to losses and high Behavioral Inhibition Scale scores, denoting increased behavioral inhibition (in a nonclinical group, $r = .39$, and in a bipolar patient group, $r = .46$). Finally, although there are no results linking the recency parameters directly with memory impairment, it should be noted that new findings show that recency was found to be elevated in chronic cannabis abusers (see Yechiam, Busemeyer, Stout, & Bechara, 2005), and an acute administration of cannabis increased the recency effect (Lane, Yechiam, & Busemeyer, 2006). This is consistent with the negative effect of cannabis on working memory capacity (Solowij, 1998).

CONCLUSION

In this chapter, we have presented a modeling approach that solves theoretical issues involved when poor performance on a task can be due to different component processes, such as in the case of the Iowa gambling task. We demonstrated that the use of a quantitative learning model can help in identifying the basic components that determine the performance characteristics. At the component level, changes in the motivation, learning, and consistency parameters distinguish among different clinical populations when the overall task performance failed to do so. Furthermore, the results of the analysis using our cognitive model are consistent with the behavioral and neurological characterizations of different clinical syndromes. The cognitive modeling approach is an important step in building a bridge between the study of neuroscience and behavior.

REFERENCES

Anderson, J. R. (1991). The place of cognitive architectures in a rational analysis. In K. Van Len (Ed.), *Architectures for intelligence* (pp. 1–24). Hillsdale, NJ: Erlbaum.

Atkinson, R. C., & Shiffrin, R. M. (1968). Human memory: A proposed system and its control processes. In K. W. Spence & J. T. Spence (Eds.), *The psychology of learning and motivation* (Vol. 2, pp. 89–195). New York: Academic Press.

Bartzokis, G., Lu, P. H., Beckson, M., Rapoport, R., Grant, S., Wiseman, E. J., & London, E. D. (2000). Abstinence from cocaine reduces high-risk responses on a gambling task. *Neuropsychopharmacology, 22,* 102–103.

Batchelder, W. H., & Riefer, D. M. (1999). Theoretical and empirical review of multi-nomial process tree modeling. *Psychonomic Bulletin and Review,* 6, 57–86.

Bechara, A., Damasio, A. R., Damasio, H., & Anderson, S. (1994). Insensitivity to future consequences following damage to human prefrontal cortex. *Cognition, 50,* 7–15.

Bechara, A., Dolan, S., Denburg, N., Hindes, A., Anderson, S. W., & Nathan, P. E. (2001). Decision-making deficits, linked to a dysfunctional ventromedial prefrontal cortex, revealed in alcohol and stimulant abusers. *Neuropsychologia, 39,* 376–389.

Bechara, A., Dolan, S., & Hindes, A. (2002). Decision-making and addiction (Part II): Myopia for the future or hypersensitivity to reward? *Neuropsychologia, 40,* 1690–1705.

Blair, R. J. R., Colledge, E., & Mitchell, D. G. V. (2001). Somatic markers and response reversal: Is there orbitofrontal cortex dysfunction in boys with psychopathic tendencies? *Journal of Abnormal Child Psychology, 29,* 499–511.

Broadbent, D. E. (1958). *Perception and communication.* London: Pergamon Press.

Busemeyer, J. R., & Johnson, J. G. (2004). Computational models of decision making. In D. Koehler & N. Harvey (Eds.), *Handbook of judgment and decision making* (pp. 133–154). New York: Blackwell.

Busemeyer, J. R., & Myung, I. J. (1992). An adaptive approach to human decision-making: Learning theory, decision theory, and human performance. *Journal of Experimental Psychology: General, 121,* 177–194.

Busemeyer, J. R., & Stout, J. C. (2002). A contribution of cognitive decision models to clinical assessment: Decomposing performance on the Bechara gambling task. *Psychological Assessment, 14,* 253–262.

Carver, C. S., & White, T. L. (1994). Behavioral inhibition, behavioral activation, and affective responses to impending reward and punishment: The BIS/BAS scales. *Journal of Personality and Social Psychology, 67,* 319–333.

Cavedini, P., Riboldi, G., D'Annucci, A., Belotti, P., Cisima, M., & Bellodi, L. (2002). Decision-making heterogeneity in obsessive–compulsive disorder: Ventromedial prefrontal cortex function predicts different treatment outcomes. *Neuropsychologia, 40,* 205–211.

Clark, L., Iversen, S. D., & Goodwin, G. M. (2001). A neuropsychological investigation of prefrontal cortex involvement in acute mania. *American Journal of Psychiatry, 158,* 1605–1611.

Damasio, A. R. (1996). The somatic marker hypothesis and the possible functions of the prefrontal cortex. *Philosophical Transactions of the Royal Society of London, B, Biological Sciences, 351,* 1413–1420.

Damasio, A. R., Tranel, D., & Damasio, H. C. (1991). Somatic markers and the guidance of behavior: Theory and preliminary testing. In H. S. Levin & H. M. Eisenberg (Eds.), *Frontal lobe function and dysfunction* (pp. 217–229). London: Oxford University Press.

Efron, B. (1979). Bootstrap methods: Another look at the jackknife. *Annals of Statistics, 7,* 1–26.

Erev, I., & Haruvy, E. (2005). Generality, repetition, and the role of descriptive learning models. *Journal of Mathematical Psychology, 49,* 357–371.

Eslinger, P. J., & Damasio, A. R. (1985). Severe disturbance of higher cognition after bilateral frontal lobe ablation: Patient EVR. *Neurology, 35,* 1731–1741.

Fabiani, M., Buckely, J., Gratton, G., Coles, M., & Donchin, E. (1989). The learning of complex task performance. *Acta Psychologica, 71,* 259–300.

Feltovich, N. (2000). Reinforcement-based vs. beliefs-based learning in experimental asymmetric-information games. *Econometrica, 68,* 605–641.

Frost, R. O., & Shows, D. L. (1993). The nature and measurement of compulsive indecisiveness. *Behavior Research Therapy, 31,* 683–692.

Golden, R. M. (1995). Making correct statistical inferences using a wrong probability model. *Journal of Mathematical Psychology, 39,* 3–20.

Grant, S., Contoreggi, C., & London, E. D. (2000). Drug abusers show impaired performance in a laboratory test of decision making. *Neuropsychologia, 38,* 1180–1187.

Harper, P. S. (1996). *Huntington's disease.* Philadelphia: Saunders.

Higgins, E. T. (1997). Beyond pleasure and pain. *American Psychologist, 52,* 1280–1300.

Johnson, S. A., Yechiam, E., Murphy, R. M., & Stout, J. C. (in press). Decision-making in Asperger's disorder. *Journal of the International Neuropsychological Society.*

Kahneman, D., & Tversky, A. (1979). Prospect theory: An analysis of decision under risk. *Econometrica, 47,* 263–291.

Kirby, K. N., Petry, N. M., & Bickel, W. K. (1999). Heroin addicts have higher discount rates for delayed rewards than non-drug-using controls. *Journal of Experimental Psychology: General, 128,* 78–87.

Lane, S., Yechiam, E., & Busemeyer, J. R. (2006). Application of a computational decision model to examine acute drug effects on human risk taking. *Experimental and Clinical Psychopharmacology, 14,* 254–264.

Leland, J. W., & Grafman, J. (2005). Experimental tests of the somatic marker hypothesis. *Games and Economic Behavior, 52,* 386–409.

London, E. D., Ernst, M., Grant, S., Bonson, K., & Weinstein, A. (2000). Orbito-frontal cortex and human drug abuse: Functional imaging. *Cerebral Cortex, 10,* 334–342.

Luce, R. D. (1959). *Individual choice behavior.* New York: Wiley.

Mattis, S. (1988). *Dementia Rating Scale: Professional manual.* Odessa, FL: Psychological Assessment Resources.

Mazas, C. A., Finn, P. R., & Steinmetz, J. E. (2000). Decision-making biases, antisocial personality, and early-onset alcoholism. *Alcoholism: Clinical and Experimental Research, 24,* 1036–1040.

Meyer, D. E., & Kieras, D. E. (1999). Précis to a practical unified theory of cognition and action: Some lessons from EPIC computational models of human multiple-task performance. In D. Gopher & A. Koriat (Eds.), *Attention and performance XVII: Cognitive regulation of performance: Interaction of theory and application* (pp. 17–88). Cambridge, MA: MIT Press.

Milner, B. (1965). Visually-guided maze learning in man: Effects of bilateral hippo-campal, bilateral frontal, and unilateral cerebral lesions. *Neuropsychologia, 3,* 317–338.

National Institute on Drug Abuse. (1999). *NIDA research report—Cocaine abuse and addiction* (NIH Publication No. 99-4342). Bethesda, MD: National Institutes of Health.

Nelder, J. A., & Mead, R. (1965). A simplex method for function minimization. *Computer Journal, 7,* 308–313.

Newell, A. (1992). Unified theories of cognition and the role of Soar. In J. A. Michon & A. Anureyk (Eds.), *Soar: A cognitive architecture in perspective* (pp. 25–75). Dordrecht, The Netherlands: Kluwer Academic.

Oberauer, K., & Kliegl, R. (2001). Beyond resources—Formal models for complexity effects and age differences in working memory. *European Journal of Cognitive Psychology, 13,* 187–215.

Payne, J. W., Bettman, J. R., & Johnson, E. J. (1988). Adaptive strategy selection in decision making. *Journal of Experimental Psychology: Learning, Memory, and Cognition, 14,* 534–552.

Petry, N. M., Bickel, W. K., & Arnett, M. (1998). Shortened time horizons and insensitivity to future consequences in heroin addicts. *Addiction, 93,* 729–738.

Roth, A., & Erev, I. (1995). Learning in extensive form games: Experimental data and simple dynamic models in the intermediate term. *Games and Economic Behavior, 8,* 164–212.

Sarin, R., & Vahid, F. (1999). Payoff assessments without probabilities: A simple dynamic model of choice. *Games and Economic Behavior, 28,* 294–309.

Schmitt, W. A., Brinkley, C. A., & Newman, J. P. (1999). Testing Damasio's somatic marker hypothesis with psychopathic individuals: Risk takers or risk averse? *Journal of Abnormal Psychology, 108,* 538–543.

Schwartz, G. (1978). Estimating the dimension of a model. *Annals of Statistics, 6,* 461–464.

Solowij, N. (1998). *Cannabis and cognitive functioning.* Cambridge, England: Cambridge University Press.

Stout, J. C., Busemeyer, J. R., Lin, A., Grant, S. R., & Bonson, K. R. (2005). Cognitive modeling analysis of the decision-making processes used by cocaine abusers. *Psychonomic Bulletin & Review, 11,* 742–747.

Stout, J. C., Rodawalt, W. C., & Siemers, E. R. (2001). Risky decision making in Huntington's disease. *Journal of the International Neuropsychological Society, 7,* 92–101.

Wagenmakers, E. J., Ratcliff, R., Gomez, P., & Iverson, J. (2004). Assessing model mimicry using the parametric bootstrap. *Journal of Mathematical Psychology, 48,* 28–50.

Wilder, K. E., Weinberger, D. R., & Goldberg, T. E. (1998). Operant conditioning and the orbitofrontal cortex in schizophrenic patients: Unexpected evidence for intact functioning. *Schizophrenia Research, 30,* 169–174.

Yechiam, E., & Busemeyer, J. R. (2005). Comparison of basic assumptions embedded in learning models for experience-based decision making. *Psychonomic Bulletin & Review, 12*, 387–402.

Yechiam, E., Busemeyer, J. R., Stout, J. C., & Bechara, A. (2005). Using cognitive models to map relations between neuropsychological disorders and human decision-making deficits. *Psychological Science, 16*, 973–978.

Yechiam, E., Hayden, E. P., Bodkins, M., O'Donnell, B. F., & Hetrick, W. P. (2006). *Decision making in bipolar disorder: A cognitive modeling approach.* Manuscript submitted for publication.

4

MODELING VISUAL ATTENTION AND CATEGORY LEARNING IN PATIENTS WITH AMNESIA, STRIATAL DAMAGE, AND NORMAL AGING

W. TODD MADDOX AND J. VINCENT FILOTEO

In this chapter, we review a body of work conducted in our laboratories that applies quantitative methods, developed from studies of healthy young adults, to better understand the perceptual and cognitive processes in certain clinical populations and healthy older adults. In keeping with the mission of this volume, we emphasize the details of the methodology but will supplement these with findings from specific clinical applications. Our aim is to provide a thorough enough presentation of the technical details (and relevant references) for readers to be able to apply these techniques in their own research.[1]

This research was supported in part by National Institutes of Health Grant R01 MH59196 to W. Todd Maddox, National Institute of Neurological Disorders and Stroke Grant R01 41372 to J. Vincent Filoteo, and a James McDonnell Foundation grant. We thank Jim Neufeld for several helpful comments on an earlier version of this chapter.
[1]Many terms introduced in this chapter are technical. Some are defined in the Glossary. More extensive definitions for many terms can be found at http://www.wikipedia.com.

All of our quantitative methods derive from general recognition theory (GRT; Ashby & Townsend, 1986), a multidimensional extension of signal detection theory (e.g., Green & Swets, 1966). GRT acknowledges the existence of noise in the perceptual system and assumes that repeated presentations of the same stimulus yield unique perceptual effects. Each stimulus presentation is represented by a point in a multidimensional psychological space, and the distribution of percepts over trials is described by a multivariate probability distribution. GRT also acknowledges the importance of separating perceptual processing assumptions from decisional processing assumptions. A detailed understanding of human behavior requires knowledge of the interplay between perceptual and decisional processes and thus requires a theory that acknowledges their separate and unique influences.

The focus of this chapter is on applications of GRT, and the toolbox of quantitative methods it holds, toward an understanding of perceptual and cognitive functioning in clinical populations and normal aging. Our review focuses on the study of attentional processes and category learning in patients with medial temporal lobe amnesia; patients with striatal damage, such as patients with Parkinson's disease (PD) or Huntington's disease (HD); and healthy older adults. Even though we have focused on these specific cognitive processes and populations in the past, the techniques described in this chapter are general enough to be applied to a number of other cognitive domains and participant populations.[2]

The chapter is organized as follows. In the first (next) section, we review briefly the assumptions of GRT. Although much previous research (not reviewed here) has provided empirical support for many of the theoretical assumptions of GRT, others have been questioned. Regardless of the validity of the theory as a whole, the quantitative methods underlying GRT provide an excellent descriptive tool for understanding perceptual and cognitive processing and were used as such in the work reviewed below. In the second section, we describe an experimental paradigm called the *general recognition randomization technique* (Ashby & Gott, 1988; hereafter referred to as the *perceptual categorization task*), which has been used in all of our research. The task is flexible enough that a number of important properties of attention and category learning can be examined but is rigid enough that powerful control can be maintained to alleviate the possibility of experimental confounds. The third section provides some background details regarding

---

[2]Our aim is to use quantitative modeling techniques to go beyond simple measures of accuracy in an attempt to draw substantive conclusions about perceptual and cognitive processing. Even so, it is important to acknowledge up front that experimental validation of the models and the construct validity of the parameters and their direct link to perceptual and cognitive processing is an ongoing process. A strong test of the validity of the models follows when experimental manipulations have predictable and separable effects on model parameters. As we discuss in the review below, in many cases experimental manipulations do lead to predictable and separable effects on model parameters.

the general modeling approach. In the fourth section, we outline some GRT-based techniques that we have applied to attentional processing in PD and normal aging and provide a brief summary of the most important findings. In the fifth section, we outline some GRT-based techniques that we have applied to category learning and memory in people with medial temporal lobe amnesia, PD, and HD and in normal elderly individuals, and we provide a brief summary of some of the more important findings from these studies. We conclude the chapter with some general comments.

GENERAL RECOGNITION THEORY

GRT provides an extension of signal detection theory to stimuli that vary along multiple dimensions. Within the framework of GRT, perceptual processes and decision processes are separate and distinct.

Perceptual Processes

GRT takes as its fundamental axiom that perceptual noise exists (i.e., repeated presentations of the same stimulus yield different perceptual effects because of such things as spontaneous neural activity, sensory adaptation, etc.) and assumes that a single multidimensional stimulus i can be represented perceptually by a multivariate probability distribution (Ashby & Lee, 1993). If stimulus i is a line of length l_i, and orientation o_i, then a bivariate normal distribution, $f_i(x,y)$, is assumed to describe the set of percepts where x denotes the perceptual dimension associated with line length and y denotes the perceptual dimension associated with line orientation. A bivariate normal distribution is described by a mean (μ_{ix}, μ_{iy}) and variance (σ^2_{ix}, σ^2_{iy}) along each dimension, as well as a covariance term, cov_{ixy}.

Decision Processes

In GRT, the experienced participant learns to divide the perceptual space into response regions and assigns a response to each region. The partition between response regions is called a *decision bound*. On each trial, the participant determines the location of the perceptual effect and gives the response associated with that region of the perceptual space. Several versions of the theory can be formulated depending on how the participant divides the perceptual space into response regions. We detail most of these in later sections devoted to the specific applications, but for now we introduce one that is of special importance, namely, the *optimal classifier*. The optimal classifier is a hypothetical device that uses the strategy that maximizes long-run accuracy. All other strategies lead to lower accuracy rates. Observers typically perform suboptimally because of the perceptual and decisional noise associated with human observation and thus tend to perform at levels lower than the optimal classifier.

Suppose there are two stimuli, 1 and 2, composed of two dimensions whose percepts are denoted by the bivariate normal distribution, $f_1(x,y)$ and $f_2(x,y)$. For any given percept (x,y), the optimal classifier computes the likelihood ratio, $l_o(x,y) = f_1(x,y)/f_2(x,y)$. Assuming no bias toward one response or the other, the optimal classifier uses the following decision rule:

If $l_o(x,y) > 1.0$, then respond "1"; otherwise, respond "2." (4.1)

With bivariate normally distributed percepts, the decision bound associated with the optimal classifier will always be linear or a quadratic curve. The shape of the optimal decision bound and the associated parameter values are determined by the set of percepts that satisfy $l_o(x,y) = 1.0$ (for details, see Ashby & Townsend, 1986). We turn now to a description of the perceptual categorization task.

PERCEPTUAL CATEGORIZATION TASK

The perceptual categorization task (Ashby & Gott, 1988) has been used extensively to study attention, learning, and memory processes in healthy young adults. In a typical perceptual categorization task the experimenter specifies two normally distributed categories of stimuli. In most cases, the stimuli are two dimensional (examples are provided in Figure 4.1), and thus each category is defined by a specific bivariate normal distribution. The experimenter generates a large number of random samples from each bivariate normal distribution (generally 50 to 100 random samples). Scatter plots of stimuli sampled from two bivariate normally distributed category structures are displayed in Panel A of Figure 4.2. Suppose that the stimulus on each trial is a single line of some fixed length and orientation. On each trial, one of the two predefined categories is chosen randomly with equal probability; a stimulus is sampled randomly from this category and is presented to the participant until he or she generates a response. Using Panel A of Figure 4.2 categories as an example, on the first trial, Category A might be selected, and the stimulus might be a short line of low angle. The participant will view this item and, when he or she is ready, press either the "A" or "B" button. Once the participant responds, corrective feedback is provided, a short intertrial interval consisting of a blank screen follows, and the next trial is initiated. Participants typically complete several hundred trials (400 to 600 in a 1-hour session). What constitutes category membership will depend on the specific task under study.

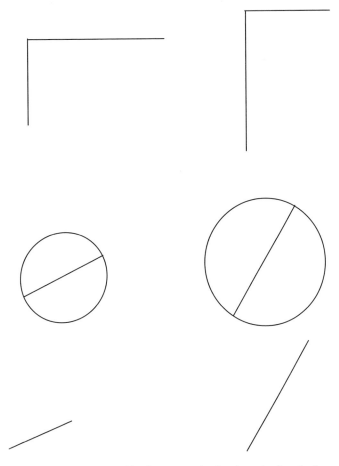

Figure 4.1. Example stimuli used in the perceptual categorization task.

In GRT, the perceptual distribution for each stimulus is assumed to be normally distributed, and the optimal classifier partitions the perceptual space into response regions associated with each stimulus (see Equation 4.1). Applications using the perceptual categorization task also assume normally distributed perceptual distributions, but they make more straightforward assumptions because the stimuli are perceptually discriminable (i.e., the stimuli within the experiment vary to a greater extent on the various dimensions) and exposure durations are longer (i.e., stimulus presentations are terminated after a participant makes a response). In the perceptual categorization task, variability is shifted from the perceptual distributions to the category distributions, and the collections of stimuli in each category are normally distributed. Because the categories are normally distributed, a single optimal decision bound can be derived in a fashion similar to that

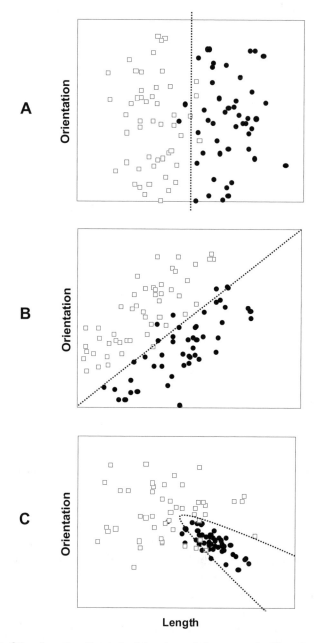

Figure 4.2. Stimuli and optimal decision bound from a selective-attention or uni-dimensional rule-based condition (A), a linear-integration condition (B), and a nonlinear integration categorization condition (C). Open squares denote Category A items, and filled circles denote Category B items.

outlined in Equation 4.1. The only difference is that the perceptual distributions are replaced with the category distributions. Suppose there are two bivariate normally distributed categories, A and B, defined by the probability density functions $f_A(x,y)$ and $f_B(x,y)$. For any given stimulus (or percept associated with the presentation of a stimulus), the optimal classifier computes the likelihood ratio, $l_o(x,y) = f_A(x,y)/f_B(x,y)$. Assuming no bias toward one category over the other, the optimal classifier uses the following decision rule:

$$\text{If } l_o(x,y) > 1.0, \text{ then respond ``A''; otherwise, respond ``B.''} \quad (4.2)$$

Note the similarity between this decision rule at the category level and the Equation 4.1 decision rule at the stimulus level. When one acknowledges the existence of perceptual noise, then the decision rule used to identify two stimuli, 1 and 2, is essentially equivalent to that used to categorize stimuli from two categories, A and B. As with Equation 4.1, the optimal decision bound will be either linear or a quadratic curve. The shape of the optimal decision bound and the associated parameter values are determined by the set of percepts that satisfy $l_o(x,y) = 1.0$ (see Ashby, 1992a; Maddox & Ashby, 1993). We outline a number of specific optimal decision rules below, but for now we show examples from three important classes of rules.

Because the stimuli are two dimensional, each stimulus can be denoted by a point in a two-dimensional space. Panel A of Figure 4.2 depicts the distribution of stimuli that might be used in an experiment that examines selective-attention processes using the single-line stimuli displayed in Figure 4.1. The x-axis represents the length of the line, and the y-axis represents the orientation of the line. The open squares in Figure 4.2 denote Category A stimuli, and the closed circles denote Category B stimuli. The broken vertical line in Panel A of Figure 4.2 denotes the experimenter-defined (optimal) categorization rule. Notice that this optimal rule requires the participant to place all of his or her attention on the length of the lines and to ignore the orientation of the lines. The participant is to set a criterion on line length and respond "A" to short lines and "B" to long lines. This is also referred to as a *unidimensional rule-based category structure*, because only one dimension is relevant, and the optimal decision strategy is able to be verbalized (we discuss rule-based categorization tasks in detail in the section "Applications of General Recognition Theory to Category Learning and Memory"). Panel B of Figure 4.2 depicts a case in which the optimal rule requires the participant to integrate information about line length and orientation and apply a linear integration rule. With these stimulus dimensions, the optimal decision strategy is not able to be verbalized in that optimal responding requires that the participant make comparisons between stimulus dimensions that are in different perceptual units (i.e., length and orientation). Finally, Panel C of Figure 4.2 depicts a case in which the optimal (not able to be verbalized) rule requires the participant to integrate information about line length and orientation and apply a nonlinear integration rule.

In the perceptual categorization task, the experimenter has a great deal of control over potentially important aspects of the categories, such as the maximum accuracy rate, the structural properties of the categories (e.g., the distributions), the number of categories, the number of stimuli sampled from each category, and the shape of the experimenter-defined categorization rule (e.g., selective attention/rule based, linear integration, nonlinear integration), to name a few. It is important to note that the experimental conditions for the three category structures described above are identical in a number of respects except for the exact form (i.e., shape and orientation) of the experimenter-defined categorization rule. Specifically, they use the same stimulus dimensions (i.e., a line length and line orientation; see Figure 4.1), number of unique stimuli (100), optimal accuracy rate (95%), and response requirements (select one of the two categories on each trial). Thus, any observed performance differences must be due to the nature of the experimenter-defined categorization rule.[3] This level of experimental control minimizes the possibility of extraneous confounding factors.

An additional advantage of the perceptual categorization task is that a number of quantitative models have been developed specifically for application to data collected in this task (Ashby, 1992a; Ashby & Maddox, 1993; Maddox & Ashby, 1993). The specifics of each model will be reserved for the two sections on applications ("Applications of General Recognition Theory to Attentional Processes" and "Applications of General Recognition Theory to Category Learning and Memory"), but some general comments regarding the modeling approach are in order.

GENERAL MODELING APPROACH

Generating Predicted Response Probabilities From a General Version of the Model

Humans rarely use the optimal decision rule but will often use the same strategy as the optimal classifier (e.g., Ashby & Maddox 1990, 1992).

---

[3] The conditions depicted in Panels A and B of Figure 4.2 include additional controls, because the stimuli in Panel B were derived from the stimuli in Panel A by applying a 45-degree rotation around the center of the length-orientation space. Under these conditions, the within-category scatter and category coherence are identical in both conditions.

Ashby and Maddox (1993) proposed *decision bound theory*, which assumes that the participant attempts to use the same strategy as the optimal classifier but with less success because of the effects of perceptual and criterial noise. *Perceptual noise* exists because there is trial-by-trial variability in the perceptual information associated with each stimulus. As outlined above, and using the same single-line stimulus example, we assume that the participant's percept of stimulus i on any trial is $x_{pi} = (x_i, y_i)'$, where $x_{pi} = l_i + e_p$, $y_{pi} = o_i + e_p$, l_i is the length of stimulus i, o_i is the orientation of stimulus i, and e_p is a univariate normal random variable with mean of zero and standard deviation, σ_p, that represents the effect of perceptual noise. *Criterial noise* exists because there is trial-by-trial variability in the memory for the decision bound. The simplest decision bound model is the *optimal decision bound model*. The optimal decision bound model is identical to the optimal classifier (Equation 4.2) except that perceptual and criterial noise are incorporated into the decision rule. Specifically,

$$\text{if } l_o(\mathbf{x}_{pi}) > 1 + e_c, \text{ then respond ``A''; otherwise, respond ``B,''} \quad (4.3)$$

where e_c is a univariate normally distributed random variable with zero mean and standard deviation σ_c that represents the effects of criterial noise. The most general version of the model abandons the likelihood ratio on the left side of Equation 4.3 for a general function $h(\mathbf{x}_{pi})$, although we generally assume that h will be linear or quadratic. Because $h(\mathbf{x}_{pi})$ is linear or quadratic, the optimal likelihood ratio value of 1.0 is absorbed into the intercept of the linear bound or the constant term in the quadratic bound, and we are left with

$$\text{if } h(\mathbf{x}_{pi}) > e_c, \text{ then respond ``A''; otherwise, respond ``B.''} \quad (4.4)$$

Assuming the Equation 4.4 decision rule, the probability of responding A, $P_r(R_A | \mathbf{x})$, is

$$P_r(R_A | \mathbf{x}) = P[h(\mathbf{x}_p) > e_c | \mathbf{x}] = \quad (4.5)$$
$$P_r[h(\mathbf{x}_p) - e_c > 0 | \mathbf{x}] = P_r[h(\mathbf{x}_p) + e_c > 0 | \mathbf{x}].$$

The latter equality holds because e_c is symmetrical with a mean of zero. Assuming that $h(\mathbf{x}_p)$ is normally distributed, which holds exactly if $h(\mathbf{x}_p)$ is linear and is approximate only when $h(\mathbf{x}_p)$ is quadratic, then Equation 4.5 can be evaluated from the cumulative normal distribution. The mean and variance depend on the form of the $h(\mathbf{x}_p)$ and were derived by detail in Ashby (1992a, pp. 459–467). A method for approximating the cumulative normal distribution was given by Ashby (1992b, p. 4, Equation 9).

Parameter Estimation and Model Testing

Any time a mathematical model is applied to a set of data, two issues need to be addressed. First, one needs to estimate the model parameters that provide the best fit to the data. Second, one needs to assess the model's ability to accurately describe the data. In our work, we use maximum likelihood procedures ($-\ln L$) to estimate the unknown parameters. The details of this procedure have outlined in several excellent texts (e.g., Ashby, 1992b; T. D. Wickens, 1982) and are not repeated here. Suffice it to say that, in most applications, maximum likelihood is superior to other procedures (e.g., sum of squared errors). In all of our work, we compare a number of models in their ability to account for a set of data. If the models are nested, in the sense that a simpler model can be derived from a more general model by setting some of the parameters of the more general model to constants, then we use likelihood ratio G^2 tests to determine whether the extra free parameters of the more general model might provide a statistically significant improvement in fit. As a concrete example, suppose that the optimal decision bound, $l_o(\mathbf{x}_{pi})$, was linear in Equation 4.3 and that the more general decision bound, $h(\mathbf{x}_{pi})$, in Equation 4.4 was also linear. Under these conditions, the optimal decision bound would be nested under the more general linear decision bound and would be equivalent when the slope and intercept of the more general linear bound were equal to the optimal slope and intercept. Again, the specifics of these procedures are available in numerous sources (e.g., Ashby, 1992b; T. D. Wickens, 1982). If the models are non-nested, then some other procedure is needed to compare the models. The Akaike information criterion (AIC; Akaike, 1974) can be applied with non-nested models, and this is the approach we have taken in most of our work. The AIC measure penalizes a model for each free parameter (i.e., parameters estimated from the empirical data) and is computed as follows: $AIC = 2(-\ln L) + 2n$, where n is the number of free parameters. The best-fitting model is the model with the smallest AIC value.

Depending on the research question of interest, we have used our modeling approach in one of two ways to facilitate our understanding of the attentional and category learning abilities of various clinical populations and older adults. The first approach focuses on a comparison of model fit values or model parameter values across experimental and control groups. For example, to determine how well an experimental group learns the optimal decision bound, we might compare the fit value for the optimal decision bound model across experimental and control groups. Similarly, to determine whether there is more (or less) variability across groups in the application of the participant's decision bound, we might compare the criterial noise (also referred to as the *rule application variability*) parameter across experimental and control groups. The second approach we have used focuses on model comparisons to determine whether groups differ in their approach to solving the task. For example, we might ask whether one group of participants is more likely to use an information-integration approach to solving an information-integration task than another group. Although these two approaches are clearly related, they address different research questions.

Individual-Participant Analyses

In all of our work, the models are applied at the level of the individual participant; data are never averaged across participants before model-based analyses are conducted. There is strong evidence that averaging can lead to incorrect conclusions regarding perceptual and cognitive processing in healthy young adults (e.g., Ashby, Maddox, & Lee, 1994; Estes, 1956; Maddox, 1999), and it is highly likely that these incorrect conclusions would be magnified in clinical populations. This approach allows us to identify subgroups of participants who show particular patterns of behavior and has been extremely fruitful with clinical populations. Of course, individual-participant analysis is not always viable with clinical populations. One solution is to ascertain the relative homogeneity of aggregated sets that are subjected to modeling. Data from participants providing a limited number of trials in principle can be combined and modeled (as a "homogeneous participant"). Individual-participant analysis is an ideal for which we should strive. However, when this approach is unrealistic other strategies for resolving potential interparticipant heterogeneity of model composition or parameters may be impelled by clinical constraints.

This concludes our general methodological review. We turn now to specific applications of our approach to attentional processing.

APPLICATIONS OF GENERAL RECOGNITION THEORY TO ATTENTIONAL PROCESSES

Several past studies have indicated that PD patients are impaired on tasks of attention (Filoteo et al., 1994, 1997), especially when participants are asked to attend selectively (Brown & Marsden, 1988; Maddox, Filoteo, Delis, & Salmon, 1996; Sharpe, 1990, 1992). Although these particular studies indicate that PD patients have impaired selective attention, not all studies have found such deficits (Brown & Marsden, 1988; Rafal, Posner, Walker, & Friedrich, 1984), and even those that have found impairment have not been able to specify the nature of such deficits. That is, selective-attention deficits in PD patients could be due to impairment in perceptual processes, decisional processes, or both, or to processing deficits in specific subcomponents of each domain. Another complication in characterizing attentional impairment in PD patients is that this disease is heterogeneous in that cognition is not affected equally in all patients (Dubois, Boller, Pillon, & Agid, 1991; Mayeux & Stern, 1983). Thus, we reasoned that studies of attentional processes in patients with PD could benefit from an approach whereby the specific processes involved in selective attention could be assessed and attentional processes could be evaluated at the level of the individual participant.

With these issues in mind, we attempted to characterize the selective-attention deficits in PD by applying the GRT-based modeling techniques outlined above to data collected in the perceptual categorization task (Filoteo & Maddox, 1999). Three experimental conditions were constructed. The (broken line) optimal decision bound along with the response region assignments (A and B) are summarized in the left-most column of Figure 4.3. The three conditions include (a) a *linear integration* condition, in which the participant had to place equal attention on both stimulus dimensions and use a linear integration rule; (b) a *selective attention* condition, in which the participant had to ignore one stimulus dimension and set a criterion along the other stimulus dimensions; and (c) a *baseline* condition that was identical to the selective-attention condition except that the irrelevant dimension was absent from the stimulus display. Optimal accuracy was 97% in all conditions. (The selective-attention and baseline conditions were run twice so that each dimension could serve as the relevant dimension and each could serve as the irrelevant dimension. For ease of exposition, our discussion focuses on data collapsed across these two conditions.) Each of the three conditions was run with the two-line stimuli and the circle stimuli.[4] Sample stimuli from each category in each condition are displayed in the right-most column of Figure 4.3 separately for each of the three experimental conditions. A group of PD patients and matched elderly control participants took part, and each participant completed 30 practice trials followed by 100 experimental trials in each condition. The PD patients were all in the early stages of the disease in terms of their level of motor impairment, were not experiencing any deficits in terms of global cognition, and were not having any problems performing their normal activities of daily living. Thus, the patients in the study were functioning at a rather high level. Nevertheless, on the basis of previous findings, we predicted that the PD patients would be impaired in the selective-attention condition relative to

---

[4] One focus of this study was to examine the effects of stimulus separability–integration on attentional processes. The two-line stimuli are thought to be integral, and the circle stimuli are thought to be separable (for a review, see Maddox, 1992). In this review, we collapse the results across the two types of stimuli.

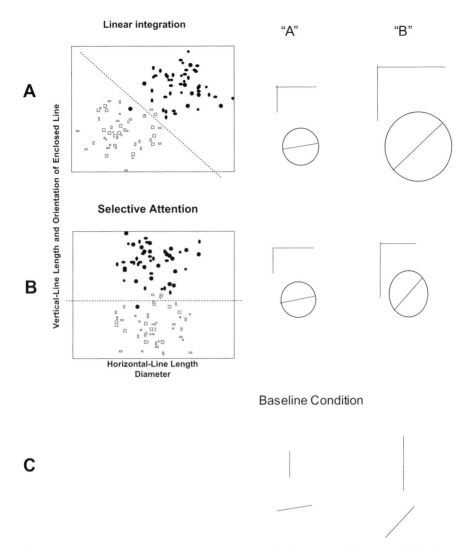

Figure 4.3. Category structures and sample stimuli used in Filoteo and Maddox (1999). Open squares denote Category A items, and filled circles denote Category B items. "A" = sample stimuli from Category A; "B" = sample stimuli from Category B.

the control participants but that the two groups would not differ in either the linear-integration condition or the baseline condition, in which selective attention is not required.

Because the focus of this study was on attentional processes and not category learning per se, the participants were given a verbal description of the optimal decision rule in each condition before the experiment started. For example, in the line orientation selective-attention condition, the participant was told to ignore the diameter of the circle and to respond "A" to shallow lines and "B" to steep lines. Thus, participants did not have to learn the basic aspects of the rule when performing the task but rather had to either attend selectively (as in the selective-attention condition) or integrate information across the two stimulus dimensions (as in the linear-integration condition).

Details of the Modeling Approach

Model-based analyses are useful for many reasons. One of the most important is that model-based analyses allow the researcher to tease apart the effects of different perceptual and cognitive processes that are usually nonidentifiable at the level of global accuracy. For example, with respect to selective-attention processes, a deficit in a participant's ability to learn the optimal decision criterion or a deficit in his or her ability to accurately apply the rule on each trial will both lead to an accuracy decrement. Model-based analyses are required to tease apart the effects of these different attentional processes and to uniquely identify the locus of the deficit.

Our modeling approach had two aims. The first aim was qualitative in the sense that we were interested in determining what type of decision bound participants used in each experimental condition. One possibility is that the participant used the optimal decision bound. The decision bound and response regions from hypothetical participants using the optimal decision bound in both the linear-integration and selective-attention conditions are depicted in Panels A of Figure 4.4. Another possibility is that the participant uses a suboptimal decision bound but one that is of the same form as the optimal decision bound. For example, in the linear-integration condition, the participant might use a linear bound with a suboptimal slope and/or intercept, or in the selective-attention condition, the participant might use a suboptimal decision criterion to separate small circles from large circles. Decision bounds and response regions from hypothetical participants using suboptimal linear integration and suboptimal selective attention strategies in the linear-integration and selective-attention conditions, respectively, are depicted in Panel B of Figure 4.4. A final possibility is that the participant uses a suboptimal decision bound but one of a different form from the optimal decision bound. For example, in the linear-integration condition the participant might use a selective-attention bound, or in the selective-attention condition the participant might use a suboptimal linear-integration strategy. Decision bounds and response regions from hypothetical participants using these two strategies are depicted in Panel C of Figure 4.4. Each model type was fit to each participant's linear-integration and selective-attention data. Only the optimal and suboptimal selective-attention models were fit to the baseline data. Because these models are nested, likelihood ratio tests were used to determine the model that provided the most parsimonious

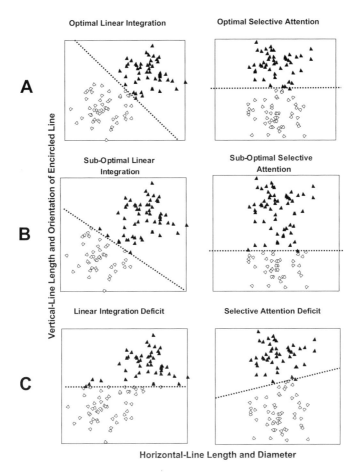

Optimal Linear Integration

Optimal Selective Attention

A

Sub-Optimal Linear Integration

Sub-Optimal Selective Attention

B

Linear Integration Deficit

Selective Attention Deficit

C

Vertical-Line Length and Orientation of Encircled Line

Horizontal-Line Length and Diameter

Figure 4.4. Hypothetic response regions from a participant using the optimal rule (A), a suboptimal rule (B), or a deficit rule (C). Open diamonds = Category A responses; filled triangles = Category B responses.

account of the data where the most parsimonious model was defined as the model with the fewest free parameters whose fit could not be significantly improved on by a more general model.

The second aim of the modeling was more quantitative in nature. The most parsimonious model provides information about the type of decision bound used by each participant, but the model parameters provide an esti-mate of the magnitude of any linear-integration or selective-attention deficit. For example, we can examine the slope of the selective-attention deficit model and compare it with the optimal slope of zero to determine the magnitude of a selective-attention deficit. A large selective-attention deficit would be associated with a slope of 1 or −1, because both imply equal attention to both dimensions, whereas a slope closer to zero implies only a small selective-attention deficit. Similarly, the best-fitting decision criterion from the suboptimal selective-attention model can be compared with the optimal selective-attention decision criterion. In addition to the parameters of the decision bound, each model includes a criterial noise parameter (see Equations 4.4 and 4.5). The criterial noise parameter provides information about the participant's ability to accurately apply his or her decision bound on each trial. We refer to the criterial noise estimate as a measure of *rule application variability*. The smaller the magnitude of the rule application variability, the less variable is the participant's trial-by-trial application of the rule. Although the decision bound parameters and rule application variability estimates both provide information about decision processes, each constitutes a unique subcomponent that should and can be examined separately using GRT. A selective-attention deficit at the level of the decision bound, or a large criterial noise variance, would each lead to reduced accuracy rates and thus are nonidentifiable at the level of accuracy. Fortunately, the GRT-based analyses make these two distinct forms of selective-attention deficit identifiable and hence observable.

Brief Summary of the Results

The accuracy rates for PD and normal control (NC) participants in the linear-integration, selective-attention, and baseline conditions are depicted in Panel A of Figure 4.5. Three comments are in order. First, PD patients showed significantly worse selective-attention performance relative to the NC participants. Second, PD and NC participants showed a statistically equivalent linear-integration performance, suggesting no deficit in PD participants' ability to integrate information across the two dimensions. Finally, PD patients were as good as NCs in the baseline condition, suggesting no difficulty setting a criterion along a single stimulus dimension when no other irrelevant dimension was present.

To determine the locus of the selective-attention deficit and to provide a better understanding of the types of strategies used by each participant, we fit the models depicted in Figure 4.4 (as outlined above). Panel B in Figure 4.5 displays the percentage of participants whose data were best fit by the optimal, suboptimal, or deficit-in-responding models for the PD and NC participants in the linear-integration and selective-attention conditions. Three comments are in order. First, approximately half of the PD and half of the NC participants used the optimal rule in the linear-integration condition, and the remaining half were distributed among the suboptimal and deficit models. Second, whereas approximately half of the PD participants used the optimal rule in the selective-attention condition, over 60% of the NC participants used the optimal rule. Finally, only a small number

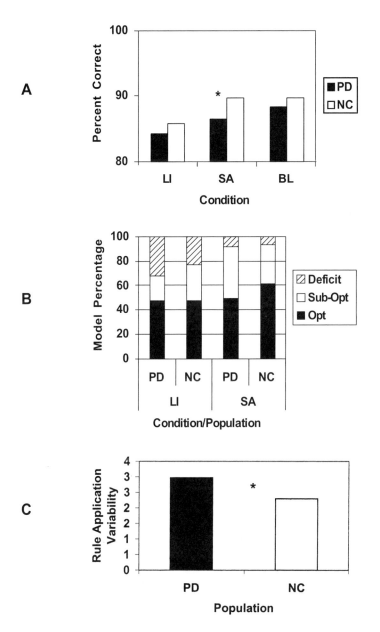

Figure 4.5. Data from Filoteo and Maddox (1999). Accuracy rates (A), best-fitting model distributions (B), and rule application variability (C). Asterisks denote a statistically significant performance difference ($p < .05$). PD = Parkinson's disease; NC = normal control participants; LI = linear integration; SA = selective attention; BL = baseline; Sub-Opt = suboptimal; Opt = optimal.

(<10%) of PD and NC participants showed a deficit in the selective attention condition.

Taken together, the model-based analyses suggest that accuracy rates were the same for the PD and NC participants in the linear-integration condition, because approximately equal numbers used the optimal decision rule. On the other hand, the PD selective-attention deficit was likely due to the fact that a larger proportion of PD participants used a suboptimal selective-attention rule. It is important to note that these findings indicate that PD patients' accuracy deficits in the selective-attention condition were not due to the patients' inability to attend selectively, because if this had been the case, the deficit-in-responding model would have accounted for a greater number of the patients' performances. Instead, PD patients were able to attend selectively, but they did so less optimally than NC participants.

To isolate the locus of PD patients' suboptimal selective-attention performance more fully, we examined the decision criterion estimates and the rule application variability estimates from the suboptimal selective-attention model. The decision criterion estimates did not differ across PD and NC participants, indicating that the PD patients did not develop a different criterion than NCs when attending selectively to the relevant stimulus dimension. That is, their deficit was not due to the use of a more suboptimal decision criterion. In contrast, however, the rule application variability estimates were larger for PD patients than NC participants, as shown in Panel C of Figure 4.5, suggesting that the patients' deficits were due to greater variability in the placement of the decision criterion. Such differences in the model parameters were not observed in either the linear-integration or the baseline conditions, only when an irrelevant stimulus dimension was present in the display (i.e., the selective-attention condition). Thus, the results of this study suggest that suboptimal selective attention in PD patients is secondary to greater response application variability in the presence of irrelevant visual information. If we had not applied the quantitative models to our data then we would have not been able to determine, first, that the PD patients were able to attend selectively but just did so at suboptimal levels and second, that the nature of this suboptimality was secondary to a deficit in applying a decision criterion consistently.

This example represents only one application of the GRT-based approach. Maddox et al. (1996) examined a different set of attention problems in patients with PD, and using the same experimental paradigm as that used by Filoteo and Maddox (1999), Maddox, Filoteo, and Huntington (1998) examined the impact of normal aging on various aspects of attention. In that study, Maddox et al. (1998) found no age-related difference in selective-attention performance but did find that older participants were more likely to be suboptimal when required to integrate information. We direct interested readers to these research reports for further details.

It is also worth mentioning that this approach, and the perceptual categorization task, can be used to tease apart perceptual forms of selective attention from decisional forms of selective attention. Perceptual forms of selective attention should affect the perceptual variance along the attended dimension, whereas decision forms of selective attention should affect the decision bound—that is, whether the decision bound is parallel to one of the coordinate axes. For applications of this sort, we again direct interested readers to several recent reports (Maddox, 2001, 2002; Maddox, Ashby, & Waldron, 2002).

In our GRT-based model applications to attentional processing, our aim was to take category learning out of the equation as much as possible. We achieved this goal by informing participants verbally of the relevant strategy before they took part in each experimental condition. By doing so, we learned a great deal about the nature of attentional deficits in patients with striatal damage and normal aging. We also have a strong interest in category learning and memory processes. In the next section, we review some GRT-based techniques that we have applied to category learning in clinical populations, including patients with medial temporal lobe amnesia, patients with PD or HD, and normally aging individuals.

APPLICATIONS OF GENERAL RECOGNITION THEORY TO CATEGORY LEARNING AND MEMORY

Categorization is an important skill that is critical to the survival of all organisms. Researchers recently have begun to investigate the possible neural substrates involved in this important cognitive process. One of the most successful multiple systems models of category learning, and the only one that specifies the underlying neurobiology, is the COmpetition between Verbal and Implicit Systems (COVIS; Ashby, Alfonso-Reese, Turken, & Waldron, 1998; Ashby, Noble, Filoteo, Ell, & Waldron, 2003; Ashby & Waldron, 1999) model. COVIS postulates two systems that compete throughout learning. COVIS assumes that the explicit system uses working memory and executive attention and is mediated primarily by the anterior cingulate, the prefrontal cortex, and the head of the caudate nucleus. This system appears to learn through a conscious process of hypothesis generation and testing. COVIS assumes that the implicit system is based on procedural learning and is mediated largely within the tail of the caudate nucleus (Ashby et al., 1998; Ashby & Ell, 2001; Willingham, 1998). It has been proposed that a dopamine-mediated reward signal is critical for learning in this system. The idea is that an unexpected reward causes dopamine to be released from the substantia nigra into the tail of the caudate nucleus and that the presence of this dopamine strengthens recently active synapses (e.g., Schultz, 1992; J. Wickens, 1993).

In COVIS, the explicit, hypothesis-testing system is assumed to dominate the learning of rule-based tasks, whereas the implicit, procedural learning system dominates the learning of information-integration tasks. *Rule-based category learning tasks* are those in which the category structures can be learned by means of some explicit reasoning process. In general, the rule that maximizes accuracy (i.e., the optimal rule) is easy to describe verbally (Ashby et al., 1998) and often involves setting a criterion along one dimension while placing no weight in the decision on the other, irrelevant dimension. An example of a rule-based task is provided in Panel A of Figure 4.2. In this case, the participant sets a criterion on line length and responds "A" to short lines and "B" to long lines, completely ignoring the line orientation. (Notice that the selective-attention tasks reviewed earlier are rule based; see Figure 4.3, Panel B.) *Information-integration category learning tasks*, on the other hand, are those in which accuracy is maximized only if information from two or more stimulus components is integrated at some predecisional stage that occurs outside of conscious awareness, such as when participants adopt a weighted linear combination of the dimensional values (Ashby & Gott, 1988). Panels B and C of Figure 4.2 display information-integration tasks. (Notice that the linear integration tasks reviewed earlier in the attentional processing section are information-integration tasks; see Figure 4.3, Panel A.) In most cases, the optimal rule in information-integration tasks is difficult or impossible to describe verbally, often because the two dimensions are measured in different physical units (Ashby et al., 1998). In contrast to information-integration rules, a conjunctive rule (e.g., respond "B" if the line is long and of shallow orientation; otherwise, respond "A") is one in which the participant applies separate decisions about each dimension (e.g., short or long and shallow or steep) and then combines the outcome of these decisions when making his or her categorization decision (integration is not predecisional). Such rules can be applied to information-integration conditions, but they generally lead to suboptimal levels of accuracy. Unlike information-integration rules, conjunctive rules are easy to verbalize. As we will see shortly, conjunctive rules are often used to solve information-integration category learning tasks.

Comparisons between rule-based and information-integration category learning that use the perceptual categorization task allow for strong experimental controls, with many aspects of the task (e.g., optimal accuracy, nature of the stimuli, number of categories, etc.) held constant while only the form of the optimal decision bound is manipulated. The additional advantage is that GRT-based modeling techniques are available to tease apart many subcomponents of perceptual and decisional processing in this task. We turn now to a description of these modeling techniques as applied to category learning. As we make clear in this section, the modeling techniques that we use to study category learning are very similar to those that we used to study attention.

Categorization Rule Learning and Rule Application Variability Analyses

Our modeling approach to category learning has evolved over the years. In our early work, we focused on a comparison of model fit values and model parameter values across experimental and control groups. In our more recent work, we have focused on model comparisons to determine whether groups differed in their approach to solving the task. In three early studies conducted in our laboratories, we tested patients with amnesia, PD, and HD and healthy control participants in their ability to learn a nonlinear information-integration rule with the two-line stimuli shown in Figure 4.1 (Filoteo, Maddox, & Davis, 2001a, 2001b; Maddox & Filoteo, 2001).[5] The stimuli and optimal decision bound are displayed in Figure 4.6. The optimal rule cannot be verbalized and instead is defined by a quadratic function of the horizontal and vertical line lengths. In both conditions, optimal accuracy was 95%. Each experimental condition consisted of six 100-trial blocks.

The aim of our modeling approach with these data was twofold. First, we were interested in determining how well a participant learned the optimal decision rule. To achieve this goal, we fit the optimal decision bound model (Equation 4.3) to each block of data separately for each participant. As a measure of categorization rule learning, we examined the goodness-of-fit value (i.e., the maximum likelihood value, $-\ln L$, negative log likelihood) from the optimal model. The smaller the fit, the better the optimal rule describes the data. Second, as we outlined in the section titled "Applications of General Recognition Theory to Attentional Processes," we also examined the magnitude of rule application variability. To achieve this goal, we fit a suboptimal model that assumed a quadratic decision bound but allowed the decision bound parameters to be estimated from the data. As a measure of rule application variability, we examined the criterial noise estimate from this suboptimal model. It is important to note that poor categorization rule learning and high rule application variability will lead to performance decrements at the level of accuracy. Thus, at the level of accuracy rates these very different processes are nonidentifiable. Only with the model-based approach can these two subprocesses be teased apart and made identifiable.

The asymptotic accuracy rates obtained during the final block of trials (i.e., Trials 501–600) for the amnesiac, PD, HD, and the relevant control

---

[5] The PD and HD studies also included a rule-based category learning condition that we do not review here.

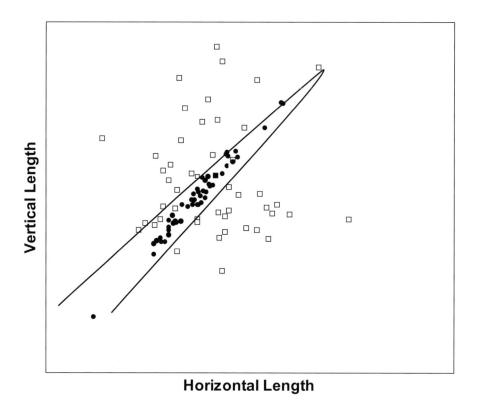

Horizontal Length

Figure 4.6. Nonlinear information-integration category structures used in three studies conducted in our laboratories. Open squares denote Category A stimuli, and filled circles denote Category B stimuli. The broken quadratic curve denotes the optimal decision bound.

participants are depicted in Panel A of Figure 4.7. Notice that asymptotic performance was equivalent between the amnesiac patients and the control participants,[6] whereas both the PD and HD participants showed clear category learning deficits. To determine the locus of the information-integration category learning deficit in PD and HD participants, we examined the

_____

[6] Some researchers have argued that amnesic patients learn categorization rules using working or short-term memory processes (Nosofsky & Zaki, 1999; Palmeri & Flanery, 1999). For example, it has been suggested that amnesic patients are able to take advantage of the repeating stimuli during some categorization tasks, and this information is then used to categorize (Nosofsky & Zaki, 1999). One amnesic patient and 1 control participant returned for a second session in the experiment. During the first block of trials in the second session, the amnesic patient and control participant again showed equivalent performance, and in fact performance during the first block of the second session was slightly better than that during the final block of trials from the first session, even though the amnesic patient had no memory of the task. These results indicate that the categorization rule was retained over the 1-day delay period and refute the possibility that working or short-term memory processes mediated category learning in amnesia.

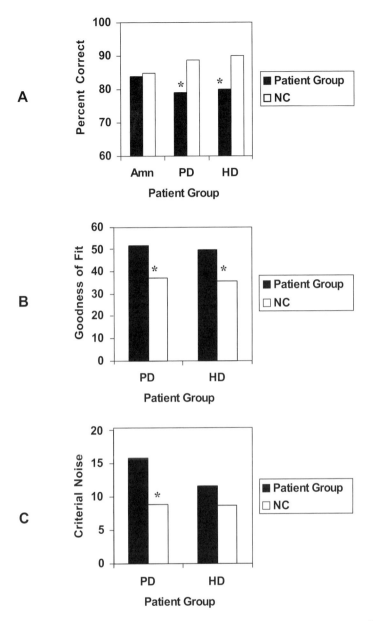

Figure 4.7. Accuracy rates (A), categorization rule learning (B), and rule application variability estimates (C) from three studies conducted in our laboratories. Asterisks denote a statistically significant performance difference (*p* < .05). NC = normal control participants; Amn = amnesiac; PD = Parkinson's disease; HD = Huntington's disease.

categorization rule learning and rule application variability estimates from the final block of trials. These values are displayed in Panels B and C of Figure 4.7. The HD patients showed categorization rule learning deficits, but not rule application variability deficits (although the trend is in that direction), suggesting that their performance deficit was due to an inability to learn the optimal rule but not due to more variability in the application of their rule. The PD patients evidenced categorization rule learning and rule application variability deficits, suggesting that their accuracy deficit was due to an inability to learn the optimal rule and to greater variability in the application of the rule that they had learned. A regression analysis indicated that PD patients' goodness-of-fit values and criterial noise values uniquely predicted their accuracy performance on the categorization task, suggesting that both categorization learning and rule application variability were each important factors in determining the degree to which the rule was learned.

Taken together, the results support the prediction that patients with striatal damage, such as those with PD or HD, should show deficits in information-integration category, whereas amnesiac patients with medial temporal lobe damage should not. This makes sense, because information-integration category learning is assumed to be mediated within the tail of the caudate, a region that is affected in patients with PD or HD. The results also suggest that the locus of the PD and HD participants' deficits was in their ability to learn the optimal decision bound, with the additional difficulty for PD patients in accurately applying the rule that they have learned. Our previous attentional studies with PD patients have indicated that their deficits in information-integration category learning such as those we just described were not due to an impairment in attending to the two relevant stimulus dimensions. Recall that PD patients performed normally relative to control participants when they were told they had to attend to both stimulus dimensions. Thus, the deficit in information-integration category learning observed in PD patients is likely due to striatal dysfunction impairing the processes specific to category learning.[7]

---

[7] As we elaborate in detail in the next section, these data provide support for a multiple-systems approach to category learning. Some single-system advocates, however, have argued that single-system models can account for many of the classic category learning data that have been offered in support of multiple systems (Nosofsky & Zaki, 1998). For example, Nosofsky and Zaki (1998) argued that a single-system exemplar-based model could account for the performance dissociations observed in amnesiac and PD patients by Knowlton and Squire (1993; Squire & Knowlton, 1995). Although page constraints preclude a detailed discussion, Nosofsky and Zaki suggested that a single-system exemplar model could account for Knowlton and Squire's amnesia data by assuming that amnesiacs have poorer memory sensitivity. We tested this model on our data and found that poorer memory sensitivity was unable to account for our results, mainly because we found no performance deficit at any stage of learning. Nosofsky and Zaki suggested also that Knowlton and Squire's PD data could be accounted for by a single-system exemplar model if it was assumed that PD patients were more likely to use a probabilistic response strategy than control participants. We tested this model on our

The data reviewed thus far represent only one application of the GRT-based approach to category learning. In a recent study, Maddox, Aparicio, Marchant, and Ivry (2005) examined rule-based category learning in PD patients and patients with cerebellar damage using a task similar to that displayed in Panel A of Figure 4.2. They found lower accuracy rates for PD patients relative to control participants but no performance deficit for patients with cerebellar damage. PD patients did not show rule-based deficits in the sense that they did not attempt to integrate information inappropriately; instead, they used highly suboptimal decision criterion values and showed large rule application variability deficits.

In our more recent work, we have begun to focus on the PD information-integration category learning deficit. We wish to determine the breadth of the information-integration category learning deficit in PD (i.e., can we identify conditions for which no deficit is observed?) and to examine in greater detail the types of strategies used by participants. We turn now to a brief review of the modeling approach taken in this work and to a brief review of the results from one study.

Quantitative Analyses of Response Strategies in Information-Integration Category Learning

The focus of our early work was twofold. First, we were interested in examining category learning by using the perceptual categorization task in patients with amnesia and patients with striatal damage. Our interest was to determine whether the striatal patients showed category learning deficits in the same categorization condition that amnesiac patients showed normal learning. We achieved this goal and found that PD patients (and HD patients) were impaired at learning a nonlinear, information-integration category task, whereas amnesiac patients performed normally. Second, we were interested in determining whether the accuracy deficit was due to a deficit in the participants' ability to learn the optimal decision rule, a deficit in their ability to accurately apply their rule on each trial, or both. We found that PD patients showed categorization rule learning and rule application variability deficits, whereas HD patients showed only categorization rule learning deficits.

Because PD patients showed clear deficits in information-integration category learning, our more recent work has focused on developing a clearer understanding of the nature of this deficit by examining category learning

---

data and found that it could account for some aspects of the data but not others. Although single-system models are often flexible enough to account for a single data set, it is more important for a model to account for a complete body of data. The multiple-systems approach seems to achieve this goal, whereas the single-system exemplar model does not.

across qualitatively different information-integration category structures. In a recent study, Filoteo, Maddox, Salmon, and Song (2005) tested a group of PD patients and healthy elderly control participants by using the linear information-integration and nonlinear information-integration conditions displayed in Panels B and C, respectively, of Figure 4.2 with the single-line stimuli. Each participant completed six 100-trial blocks in each condition. It is important to reiterate that because this work is couched within the framework of the perceptual categorization task, a number of important factors (e.g., optimal accuracy) are equated across conditions, and only the form of the optimal decision bound is manipulated.

Since we completed our early work (summarized earlier), the focus of our modeling approach has also changed slightly. Instead of focusing on estimates of categorization rule learning and rule application variability, we have begun to attempt to characterize the strategy that participants are actually using. One conclusion we have drawn from our parallel work with healthy young adults is that participants will often try to solve information-integration tasks using hypothesis-testing strategies when the experimental conditions are not conducive to learning with the procedural learning system (for a review, see Maddox & Ashby, 2004). This might also occur with PD patients. Because the neurobiological machinery necessary to solve information-integration tasks that use the tail of the caudate is damaged in PD, it might be that PD patients attempt to use hypothesis-testing (or rule-based) strategies. Another possibility is that PD patients use the same approach as control participants when learning information-integration categories but that they do so less well than control participants. To investigate these possibilities, we developed a large number of models that were applied to the data from each block of trials separately for each participant. Some of these models were hypothesis-testing models, and some were information-integration models.

Figure 4.8 displays hypothetical decision bounds and the resulting response regions from specific response strategies that might be applied in the linear information-integration condition. The four models in the left-most column are hypothesis-testing models, and the three models on the right are information-integration models. The top two hypothesis-testing models instantiate *unidimensional* rule strategies. One model assumes that the participant sets a criterion on length and ignores orientation, whereas the other assumes that the participant sets a criterion on orientation and ignores length. The bottom two hypothesis-testing models instantiate *two-dimensional, conjunctive* rule strategies. Each model assumes that the participant sets a criterion on the length dimension and a separate criterion on the orientation dimension. In the first case, the participant responds "A" if the length is short and the orientation is steep; otherwise, the participant responds "B." In the second case, the participant responds "B" if the length

Hypothesis-Testing Strategies   **Information-Integration Strategies**

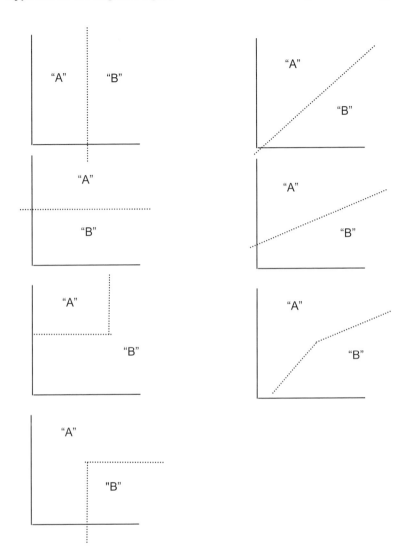

Figure 4.8. Hypothetical response regions from participants using hypothesis-testing (panels on the left) and information-integration (panels on the right) strategies to solve the linear information-integration task. "A" and "B" indicate participant responses (see text).

is long and the orientation is shallow; otherwise, the participant responds "A." The top-most information-integration strategy assumes that the participant uses the optimal decision bound. The middle model assumes that the participant uses a linear decision bound but allows the slope and intercept to be suboptimal. The bottom model assumes that the participant uses two linear decision bounds. This model is called the *striatal pattern classifier* (Ashby & Waldron, 1999), and it was developed as a computational model of the tail of the caudate. The model assumes that there are four units in the length orientation space, with two being assigned to Category A and two to Category B. On each trial, the participant determines which unit is closest to the perceptual effect and gives the associated response. The model results in two minimum-distance-based decision bounds. This model has been found to provide a good computational model of participants' response regions in previous information-integration category learning studies (e.g., Ashby & Waldron, 1999; Ashby, Waldron, Lee, & Berkman, 2001; Maddox, 2001, 2002; Maddox, Filoteo, Hejl, & Ing, 2004). Similar response strategies might be applied in the nonlinear information-integration condition. For example, the Figure 4.8 hypothesis testing models were applied in the nonlinear information-integration condition, and nonlinear variants of the information-integration models were applied. Each model was applied separately to the data from each block of trials for each individual participant.

We turn now to a brief summary of the results. The asymptotic accuracy rates obtained during the final block of trials (i.e., Trials 501–600) for the PD patients and control participants is depicted in the top panel of Figure 4.9. Notice that PD patients showed relatively normal linear information-integration learning but a deficit in nonlinear information-integration learning. The middle left panel shows the percentage of participants whose final block data were best fit by an information-integration model or a rule-based model. Notice that the model percentages are similar across PD and control participants for the linear and nonlinear information-integration conditions, but many fewer PD and control participants attempted to use hypothesis-testing strategies in the nonlinear condition. To gain additional insight into the locus of the PD nonlinear information-integration learning deficit, we focused only on participants whose data were best fit by an information-integration model. We computed the accuracy rate for these participants (displayed in the middle right panel of Figure 4.9) as well as the categorization rule learning and rule application variability indices (displayed in the bottom two panels of Figure 4.9). These analyses suggest that PD patients who used information-integration strategies to solve the linear information-integration task were as accurate as control participants, showed equivalent rule learning, and demonstrated equivalent variability in the application of their rule. For PD patients who used information-integration strategies to solve the nonlinear information-integration task, on the other hand, accuracy was lower, categorization rule learning was poorer, and variability in the application of their rule was higher than that of control participants.

Taken together, these results suggest that PD patients perform relatively normally on solving linear information-integration tasks but show clear and large deficits in their ability to solve more complex nonlinear information-

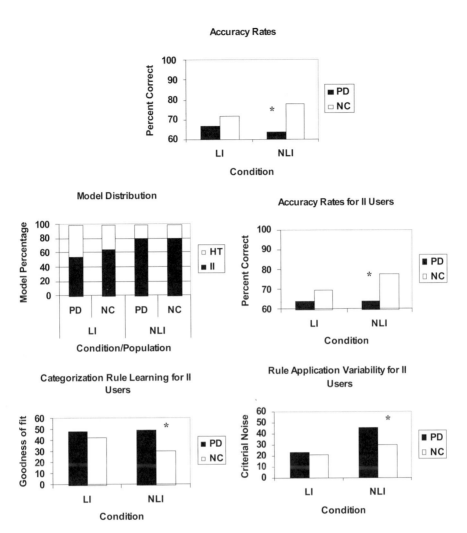

Figure 4.9. Data from Filoteo et al. (2005). Final block overall accuracy rates, model distributions, accuracy rates, categorization rule learning, and rule application variability estimates for participants whose data were best fit by an information-integration model. Asterisks denote a statistically significant performance difference (*p* < .05). PD = Parkinson's disease; NC = normal control participants; LI = linear information integration; NLI = nonlinear information integration; HT = hypothesis-testing model fit best; II = information-integration model fit best.

integration tasks. It seems reasonable to suppose (although this is speculative) that the resolution of the perceptual decision space in the tail of the caudate must be higher to solve more complex nonlinear information-integration tasks than to solve simpler linear information-integration tasks. Because the tail of the caudate is dysfunctional in PD, it perhaps can be expected that performance in tasks that require more striatal units might be impaired in

PD relative to performance in tasks that require fewer striatal units. This is one important line of work that we continue to actively pursue in our laboratories.

This example represents only one application of this sort. We recently published a study that examined information-integration category learning in healthy older adults using the categories depicted in Panels B and C of Figure 4.2 (Filoteo & Maddox, 2004). It is well known that subcortical dopamine levels are reduced as a result of the normal aging process (Carlsson & Winblad, 1976). In light of this fact, we predicted, and found, that normal elderly individuals display information-integration category learning deficits.

We are currently examining PD patients' ability to learn other information-integration tasks and a series of rule-based tasks. We have also begun to apply this modeling approach to data collected using functional magnetic resonance imaging (Filoteo, Maddox, Simmons, et al., 2005; Nomura et al., in press). It would also be straightforward to apply this approach with other clinical populations (e.g., participants with attention-deficit/hyperactivity disorder, Alzheimer's disease, etc.) as well.

CONCLUSION

The aim of this chapter was to review the details of a quantitative model-based approach that we have taken to the study of attentional and category-learning processes in clinical populations. Our theoretical approach is grounded in GRT, which is an extension of signal detection theory to multidimensional stimuli. The fundamental axiom of GRT is that perceptual processing is noisy and that perceptual and decisional processes are separate and should be uniquely identifiable. Taking a GRT-based approach, we were able to examine attentional processes in PD and, importantly, were able to identify and study subgroups of participants who showed qualitatively different attentional-processing strategies. These types of subgroup analyses are very important and useful in clinical settings, where within-group variability is so high. We found that PD patients were able to integrate information from two stimulus dimensions when required to, whereas a large subgroup of PD patients showed deficits in their ability to attend selectively to one stimulus dimension while ignoring the other. We also found that this deficit was restricted primarily to their inability to accurately apply their decision rule on each trial. Using a similar approach, we were able to examine category learning in persons with amnesia, PD, and HD. We found that individuals with amnesia showed normal information-integration category learning, whereas PD and HD patients showed large information-integration category learning deficits. The deficit for both PD and HD patients was due to poor learning of the categorization rule, and only for the PD patients was there an additional deficit in consistently applying the learned rule. Further examination of information-integration learning in PD patients suggested that these patients show normal learning when the categorization rule is linear, and their deficit is restricted to cases in which the categorization rule is highly nonlinear. When the decision rule is highly nonlinear, PD patients show poor categorization rule learning and highly variable application of the learned rule.

Many of the conclusions we have drawn from our past studies would have been missed if we had relied solely on traditional measures of performance (e.g., accuracy rates or reaction times). We hope that through our review readers have achieved a greater appreciation of our measurement techniques and how they can lead to a better understanding of the nature and degree of cognitive changes in various patient populations. We also hope that this will inspire others to incorporate similar approaches into their own research programs.

REFERENCES

Akaike, H. (1974). A new look at the statistical model identification. *IEEE Transactions on Automatic Control, 19*, 716–723.

Ashby, F. G. (1992a). Multidimensional models of categorization. In F. G. Ashby (Ed.), *Multidimensional models of perception and cognition* (pp. 449–484). Hillsdale, NJ: Erlbaum.

Ashby, F. G. (1992b). Multivariate probability distributions. In F. G. Ashby (Ed.), *Multidimensional models of perception and cognition* (pp. 1–34). Hillsdale, NJ: Erlbaum.

Ashby, F. G., Alfonso-Reese, L. A., Turken, A. U., & Waldron, E. M. (1998). A neuropsychological theory of multiple systems in category learning. *Psychological Review, 105*, 442–481.

Ashby, F. G., & Ell, S. W. (2001). The neurobiological basis of category learning. *Trends in Cognitive Sciences, 5*, 204–210.

Ashby, F. G., & Gott, R. E. (1988). Decision rules in the perception and categorization of multidimensional stimuli. *Journal of Experimental Psychology: Learning, Memory, and Cognition, 14*, 33–53.

Ashby, F. G., & Lee, W. W. (1993). Perceptual variability as a fundamental axiom of perceptual science. In S. C. Masin (Ed.), *Foundations of perceptual theory* (pp. 369–399). Amsterdam: Elsevier.

Ashby, F. G., & Maddox, W. T. (1990). Integrating information from separable psychological dimensions. *Journal of Experimental Psychology: Human Perception and Performance, 16*, 598–612.

Ashby, F. G., & Maddox, W. T. (1992). Complex decision rules in categorization: Contrasting novice and experienced performance. *Journal of Experimental Psychology: Human Perception and Performance, 18*, 50–71.

Ashby, F. G., & Maddox, W. T. (1993). Relations between prototype, exemplar, and decision bound models of categorization. *Journal of Mathematical Psychology, 37*, 372–400.

Ashby, F. G., Maddox, W. T., & Lee, W. W. (1994). On the dangers of averaging across subjects when using multidimensional scaling or the similarity-choice model. *Psychological Science, 5*, 144–151.

Ashby, F. G., Noble, S., Filoteo, J. V., Ell, S. W., & Waldron, E. M. (2003). Category learning deficits in Parkinson's disease. *Neuropsychology, 17*, 115–124.

Ashby, F. G., & Townsend, J. T. (1986). Varieties of perceptual independence. *Psychological Review, 93*, 154–179.

Ashby, F. G., & Waldron, E. M. (1999). The nature of implicit categorization. *Psychonomic Bulletin & Review, 6*, 363–378.

Ashby, F. G., Waldron, E. M., Lee, W. W., & Berkman, A. (2001). Suboptimality in human categorization and identification. *Journal of Experimental Psychology: General, 130*, 77–96.

Brown, R. G., & Marsden, C. D. (1988). Internal versus external cues and the control of attention in Parkinson's disease. *Brain, 111*, 323–345.

Carlsson, A., & Winblad, B. (1976). Influence of age and time interval between death and autopsy on dopamine and 3-methoxytyramine levels in human basal ganglia. *Journal of Neural Transmission, 38*, 271–276.

Dubois, B., Boller, F., Pillon, B., & Agid, Y. (1991). Cognitive deficits in Parkinson's disease. In F. Boller & J. Grafman (Eds.), *Handbook of neuropsychology* (Vol. 5, pp. 195–240). New York: Elsevier Science.

Estes, W. K. (1956). The problem of inference from curves based on group data. *Psychological Bulletin, 53*, 134–140.

Filoteo, J. V., Delis, D. C., Demadura, T., Salmon, D. P., Roman, M. J., & Shults, C. (1994). Abnormally rapid disengagement of covert attention to global and local stimulus levels may underlie the visual-perceptual impairment in patients with Parkinson's disease. *Neuropsychology, 8*, 218–226.

Filoteo, J. V., Delis, D. C., Salmon, D. P., Demadura, T. L., Roman, M. J., & Shults, C. W. (1997). An examination of the nature of attentional deficits in patients with Parkinson's disease: Evidence from a spatial orienting task. *Journal of the International Neuropsychological Society, 3*, 337–347.

Filoteo, J. V., & Maddox, W. T. (1999). Quantitative modeling of visual attention processes in patients with Parkinson's disease: Effects of stimulus integrality on selective attention and dimensional integration. *Neuropsychology, 13*, 206–222.

Filoteo, J. V., & Maddox, W. T. (2004). A quantitative model-based approach to examining aging effect on information-integration category learning. *Psychology and Aging, 19*, 171–182.

Filoteo, J. V., Maddox, W. T., & Davis, J. D. (2001a). A possible role of the striatum in linear and nonlinear category learning: Evidence from patients with Huntington's disease. *Behavioral Neuroscience, 115,* 786–798.

Filoteo, J. V., Maddox, W. T., & Davis, J. D. (2001b). Quantitative modeling of category learning in amnesic patients. *Journal of the International Neuropsychological Society, 7,* 1–19.

Filoteo, J. V., Maddox, W. T., Salmon, D. P., & Song, D. D. (2005). Information-integration category learning in patients with striatal dysfunction. *Neuropsychology, 19,* 212–222.

Filoteo, J. V., Maddox, W. T., Simmons, A. N., Ing, A. D., Cagigas, X. E., Matthews, S., & Paulus, M. P. (2005). Cortical and subcortical brain regions involved in rule-based category learning. *NeuroReport, 16,* 111–115.

Green, D. M., & Swets, J. A. (1966). *Signal detection theory and psychophysics.* New York: Wiley.

Knowlton, B. J., & Squire, L. R. (1993, December 10). The learning of categories: Parallel brain systems for item memory and category knowledge. *Science, 262,* 1747–1749.

Maddox, W. T. (1992). Perceptual and decisional separability. In F. G. Ashby (Ed.), *Multidimensional models of perception and cognition* (pp. 147–180). Hillsdale, NJ: Erlbaum.

Maddox, W. T. (1999). On the danger of averaging across observers when comparing decision bound and generalized context models of categorization. *Perception & Psychophysics, 61,* 354–374.

Maddox, W. T. (2001). Separating perceptual processes from decisional processes in identification and categorization. *Perception & Psychophysics, 63,* 1183–1200.

Maddox, W. T. (2002). Learning and attention in multidimensional identification and categorization: Separating low-level perceptual processes and high-level decisional processes. *Journal of Experimental Psychology: Learning, Memory, and Cognition, 28,* 99–115.

Maddox, W. T., Aparicio, P., Marchant, N., & Ivry, R. B. (2005). Rule-based category learning is impaired in patients with Parkinson's disease but not patients with cerebellar disorders. *Journal of Cognitive Neuroscience, 17,* 707–723.

Maddox, W. T., & Ashby, F. G. (1993). Comparing decision bound and exemplar models of categorization. *Perception & Psychophysics, 53,* 49–70.

Maddox, W. T. & Ashby, F. G. (2004). Dissociating explicit and procedural-learning based systems of perceptual category learning. *Behavioural Processes, 66,* 309–332.

Maddox, W. T., Ashby, F. G., & Waldron, E. (2002). Multiple attention systems in perceptual categorization. *Memory & Cognition, 30,* 325–339.

Maddox, W. T., & Filoteo, J. V. (2001). Striatal contributions to category learning: Quantitative modeling of simple linear and complex nonlinear rule learning in patients with Parkinson's disease. *Journal of the International Neuropsychological Society, 7,* 710–727.

Maddox, W. T., Filoteo, J. V., Delis, D. C., & Salmon, D. P. (1996). Visual selective attention deficits in patients with Parkinson's disease: A quantitative model-based approach. *Neuropsychology, 10,* 197–218.

Maddox, W. T., Filoteo, J. V., Hejl, K. D., & Ing, A. D. (2004). Category numerosity impacts rule-based but not information-integration category learning: Further evidence for dissociable category learning systems. *Journal of Experimental Psychology: Learning, Memory, and Cognition, 30,* 227–235.

Maddox, W. T., Filoteo, J. V., & Huntington, J. R. (1998). Effects of stimulus integrality on visual attention in older and younger adults: A quantitative model-based analysis. *Psychology and Aging, 13,* 472–485.

Mayeux, R., & Stern, Y. (1983). Intellectual dysfunction and dementia in Parkinson's disease. In R. Mayeux & W. G. Rosen (Eds.), *The dementias* (pp. 211–227). New York: Raven Press.

Nomura, E. M., Maddox, W. T., Filoteo, J. V., Ing, A. D., Gitelman, D. R., Parrish, T. B., et al. (in press). Neural correlates of rule-based and information-integration visual category learning. *Cerebral Cortex.*

Nosofsky, R. M., & Zaki, S. R. (1998). Dissociations between categorization and recognition in amnesic and normal individuals: An exemplar-based interpretation. *Psychological Science, 9,* 247–255.

Nosofsky, R. M., & Zaki, S. R. (1999). Math modeling, neuropsychology, and category learning: Response to B. Knowlton (1999). *Trends in Cognitive Sciences, 3,* 125–126.

Palmeri, T. J., & Flanery, M. A. (1999). Learning about categories in the absence of training: Profound amnesia and the relationship between perceptual categorization and recognition memory. *Psychological Science, 10,* 526–530.

Rafal, R. D., Posner, M. W., Walker, J. A., & Friedrich, F. J. (1984). Cognition and the basal ganglia: Separating mental and motor components of performance in Parkinson's disease. *Brain, 107,* 1083–1094.

Schultz, W. (1992). Activity of dopamine neurons in the behaving primate. *Seminars in Neuroscience, 4,* 129–138.

Sharpe, M. H. (1990). Distractibility in early Parkinson's disease. *Cortex, 26,* 239–246.

Sharpe, M. H. (1992). Auditory attention in early Parkinson's disease: An impairment in focused attention. *Neuropsychologia, 30,* 101–106.

Squire, L. R., & Knowlton, B. J. (1995). Learning about categories in the absence of memory. *Proceedings of the National Academy of Sciences, USA, 92,* 12470–12474.

Wickens, J. (1993). *A theory of the striatum.* New York: Pergamon Press.

Wickens, T. D. (1982). *Models for behavior: Stochastic processes in psychology.* San Francisco: Freeman.

Willingham, D. B. (1998). A neuropsychological theory of motor skill learning. *Psychological Review, 105,* 558–584.

5

A MATHEMATICAL PROCESS ACCOUNT OF GROUP AND INDIVIDUAL DIFFERENCES IN MEMORY-SEARCH FACILITATIVE STIMULUS ENCODING, WITH APPLICATION TO SCHIZOPHRENIA

RICHARD W. J. NEUFELD, DAVID VOLLICK, JEFFREY R. CARTER, KRISTINE BOKSMAN, LAWRENCE R. LEVY, LEONARD GEORGE, AND JENNIFER JETTÉ

Variations in cognitive performance across clinical or other populations may stem from one or a combination of sources. Such variation usually comprises systematic differences in duration, correctness of task performance across multiple trials, or both. Factors affecting these response properties may have to do with architecture of the cognitive system executing the

Sources of support for this research included an operating grant from the Social Sciences and Humanities Research Council of Canada, awarded to Richard W. J. Neufeld; a research operating grant from the Workplace Safety and Insurance Board, Canadian Institutes of Health Research (Richard W. J. Neufeld, coinvestigator); and a grant from the Canadian Institutes of Health Research New Emerging Teams Program (Richard W. J. Neufeld, coinvestigator). We also thank Julie Stout, who served as action editor for this chapter.

task, such as its design with respect to the handling of task components concurrently or successively. Another aspect of the system brought to bear is that of its capacity for dispatching constituent task components per unit of time, or the "amount of work" or rate of output over a given interval of which the system is capable. Still a third aspect of the processing system impinging on the above response properties entails termination criteria, notably whether processing ceases on completion of transactions sufficient for emitting a response or continues beyond the necessary complement (for elaboration from a clinical science perspective, see chap. 7, this volume, and Townsend, Fific, & Neufeld, in press).

Interest nevertheless may lie not only with accounts of cognitive performance characterizing groups and their differences but also with respect to performance when it comes to the individual. The issue of mediating group-level findings to the individual is a long-standing one (e.g., Davidson & Costello, 1969; Neufeld, 1977, chap. 2). Motivation to address individual differences may emanate from clinical exigencies, as in the case of client-specific clinical assessment and intervention. It may arise as well because certain quantitative accounts of cognitive performance, known as *mixture models*, provide for random variation in model properties. This variation potentially is identified with inequities in performance from one individual to the next, thus becoming tantamount to individual differences in model expression. So, because such a mixture model simultaneously provides for group and individual levels of performance, data from both levels impinge on its validity. Coherence of model predictions at both levels of analysis thereby qualify as part of the arsenal of methods for model evaluation and selection (cf. Myung, Forster, & Browne, 2000; Wagenmakers & Waldorp, 2006). In this way, mixture models not only assess cognitive performance at the individual level, without leaving group-level findings behind, but also prescribe tactics for empirically evaluating their own effectiveness in doing so.

Specifics as to how the above possibilities play out in the present context and how such potential might be realized are explained in this and the following paragraph. We use the method of illustration, incorporating a given set of data pertaining to memory search in schizophrenia (elaborated on below), but we hasten to note that the espoused strategy is general. Focus is on a specific form of processing capacity, whose composition is quantitatively defined (cf. Townsend & Ashby, 1983, chap. 4) and concomitantly takes account of both system architecture and termination criteria (Townsend & Wenger, 2004). We then examine the benefits and practical challenges of the presented computations. Substantive significance of the results are drawn out, including discernment of spared and disorder-affected cognitive functions and possible implications for cognition-intensive forms of coping with stress. Clinically significant extensions available from the present developments are described.

The presentation is organized to convey three things: (a) how research findings obtained from groups of participants, typifying clinical cognitive science, can be mediated to the individual participant; (b) how such individual-difference technology can evaluate efficacy of the proposed explanatory measurement model; and (c) to explicate a specific form of cognitive abnormality in schizophrenia that instantiates (a) and (b). First, we describe the paradigm activating the addressed cognitive performance and supplying the performance data. Doing so sets the stage for the subsequent modeling by illustrating the nature of the cognitive operations of interest and the pattern of deviations attending schizophrenia psychopathology. Methodological details necessary to appreciate the experimental particulars serving for the present illustration are provided along the way. Rounding out the description of the phenomenon being modeled is a description of the precise data summaries to which modeling is addressed. These necessary preliminaries usher in the proposed mixture model of performance. Specifics of evaluating the model predictions of both group and representative individual data sets are set forth. To enhance the context of this evaluation, we compare the efficacy of the proposed model with that of a principled, closely related competitor and with that of a nonmixture model.

EXPERIMENTAL PARADIGM, EMPIRICAL FINDINGS, AND MODEL DESCRIPTION AND TESTING

Paradigm

We begin this section with an overview of the procedural details, to follow. The present paradigm was designed initially for the study of functional asymmetry of brain hemispheres in schizophrenia (George & Neufeld, 1987). Specifically addressed were deviations in patterns of response to presentations of visual stimuli composed of words or pictures. When presented in the left hemifield (right visual field), verbal stimuli are processed more quickly and/ or accurately than when presented in the right hemifield, the opposite being the case for pictorial stimuli (Alwitt, 1981; Moscovitch & Klein, 1980; Sergent, 1982). The main experimental factors, then, were stimulus type (four-letter words or pictures of faces) and right or left visual field of presentation. Individuals were required to indicate as quickly and accurately as possible whether a presented word or picture matched the one presented immediately before. Other aspects of the stimulus complex and associated task requirements were incidental with respect to the present analysis. They were implemented to tax differentially processing demands on the hemisphere deemed to be specialized for processing of the given trial's stimulus type (left hemisphere for words and right hemisphere for faces). The rationale for their inclusion, and related manipulations, were enumerated by George and Neufeld (1987). These manipulations are briefly described below, because they are accommodated in the comprehensive task performance model.

Participants numbered 14 in each of five groups. Note that modeling is expedited by application to two of these five groups: (a) the paranoid schizophrenia participants and (b) the student control participants. Because results nevertheless generalize more broadly to other schizophrenia–control pairings among the groups at large, all five groups are enumerated. These were paranoid and nonparanoid schizophrenia patients, nonschizophrenia psychiatric control participants (13 of the 14 having an affective disorder), general control participants solicited from Employment Canada and local newspaper advertisements (similar in age and other demographics to the patient groups), and university undergraduates (to monitor effects of the constructed manipulations among the individuals who have provided most of the literature's data on behavioral lateralities involving brief visual displays). Provision for diagnostic aspects of group formation and demographic and clinical variables extraneous to the present purposes, including any sex differences in group composition and performance (absent throughout), are detailed in the original report.

Trials proceeded as follows. A target item, either a four-letter word or a black-and-white photograph of a face, appeared in the central visual field for 1.5 seconds and was immediately followed by a probe–stimulus display. This display consisted of three items. If the target was a word, two words were presented: one in the left visual field and one in the right field. The central field held an item prescribed by the concomitant hemisphere-load manipulations. These manipulations were directed to processes appurtenant to those of the current focus but nevertheless are accommodated in the performance model, as described above.

If the target was a face, items in the respective visual fields were faces. Probes were displayed for 20 milliseconds in the case of words and 200 milliseconds for faces (calibrated through extensive pilot testing). Participants were requested to press a "yes" key as quickly and accurately as possible if the probe, presented in either the left or right field, was the same as the target; if neither element matched the target, they were to press the "no" key as quickly and accurately as possible.

The central-field items of the probe display varied according to four levels of concomitant-task load directed toward the left or right hemisphere for the word and picture judgments, respectively. For words, the central field in the first load condition was blank; it contained a face, to be ignored in the second load condition. In the third condition, the central field contained a word to be ignored, and in the fourth, it contained a word to be spoken aloud after executing the yes–no probe–match response. Similar central-field manipulations attended the pictorial target, except that faces were used in the center rather than words, and words for faces. The fourth load for the picture stimuli required participants to dispatch the yes–no match response and then to indicate which of four faces displayed on a card was the one that had just appeared in the central visual field. Order of the eight task conditions (face vs. word-matching task × four central-field load levels) was randomized across participants; within conditions, positive and negative trial types were randomized, as were right- versus left-field placements of matching items, in the case of positive trials. Practice trials preceded test trials up to a criterion of four consecutive correct responses for each of the eight task conditions.

Each condition was assigned 32 trials, 16 positive and 16 negative. Of the positive trials, 8 probe-to-target matches appeared in the right visual field, and 8 appeared in the left field. There were therefore a total of 32 trials of the right visual field (left-hemifield compatible) target-matching words and 32 trials of left visual field target-matching words. Pictorial items had corresponding trial numbers of right- and left-hemifield compatible presentations. Only positive trials, generating differential task load according to side of matching-item presentation, were addressed in the present analysis.

Results

The principal dependent variable is latency of correct responses. Error rates (presented below) differed significantly across groups but not so as to compromise interpretation of the latency data (viz., apropos of speed–accuracy trade-off, e.g., Pachella, 1974; moreover, analyses of variance [ANOVAs] including and excluding incorrect responses differed trivially).

The principal result of the ANOVA on the correct response time data, as far as the present developments are concerned, was that of a significant Visual Field × Stimulus Type interaction, $F(1, 60) = 10.41$, $p \approx .002$. There was a significant main effect of groups ($p < .00005$), but despite the latter's heterogeneity, the Visual Field × Stimulus Type interaction remained stable, $F(4, 60)$, for its further interaction with groups: 1.085, $p = .37215$.

The present modeling approach is expedited, without expense to generality of chief inferences, by expressing the essential configuration of results in the form of a 2×2 factorial layout, with one of the two-level factors comprising diagnostic group status and the other comprising task load (more vs. less hemifield-compatible probe item presentation; e.g., Neufeld, Carter, Boksman, Jetté, & Vollick, 2002; Neufeld & Williamson, 1996). Representative groups evincing the Stimulus Type × Visual Field interaction were the paranoid schizophrenia patients and the student control participants. The second two-level factor entailed right versus left field of target-matching probe item presentation, specifically for the verbal stimuli. Word item data were selected because word-related simple main effects of the Stimulus Type × Visual Field interaction (i.e., faster responding to words presented in the left hemifield than to those presented in the right hemifield and to words presented in the left hemifield than to pictures presented in the left hemifield) were slightly more pronounced than were corresponding simple main effects for pictures.

Overall Interpretation

In this section, we enumerate cognitive transactions to which modeling is addressed, specifically those considered to underlie identification of a target–probe item match. They include the following: encoding the left- or right-field presented probe word into a task-facilitative (item comparison) format; the target–probe item comparison itself; and response processes, including selection of the yes–no response, prescribed by results of the memorial comparison as well as response execution. Reaction time data subjected to modeling may be affected as well by processing of the probe display's central-field item associated with the concomitant task, above. The model layout to be presented accommodates this contribution as a residual component of latency.

Delayed encoding of the presenting target–match item into a comparison-facilitative format was identified as the agent of group differences in task performance latency. Detailed accounts of data patterns supporting this and the following related deductions have been presented by Neufeld, Vollick, and Highgate (1993); Neufeld and Williamson (1996); and sources cited in these reviews. Memory scanning and response processes were deemed to be unimpaired among the schizophrenia participants. Similarly, times for central-field item concomitant-task operations were held to be common across the groups.

Moreover, as further detailed in Neufeld et al. (1993, 2002) and Neufeld and Williamson (1996), schizophrenia participants' protracted encoding has been identified with a specific aspect of the encoding process. Probe item encoding is considered to entail extracting physical features, accessing semantic properties, and related preparatory operations providing for ascertainment of probe–target item identity. Mathematical models of performance data have been constrained to maintaining a constant rate of dispatching the component encoding operations while allowing the number of constituent operations themselves to increase among schizophrenia participants (Neufeld et al., 1993, 2002; Neufeld & Williamson, 1996). This composition of elongated encoding—additional subprocesses of the encoding process (cf. Townsend, 1984)—again is a primary feature of model design, as applied to the representative data described above. Possible cognitive–behavioral agents of the added subprocesses are considered in the Discussion section, after description and evaluation of the implementing model.

Model-Predicted Performance Data

Data for the 2 × 2 factorial layout were amalgamated as follows. Performance was summarized in terms of the first two moments of the empirical latency distributions, comprising their means and variances, computed within participants, across trials. The first two moments were selected in the interests of moment stability and accuracy of parameter estimation (e.g., Townsend & Ashby, 1983). Each cell, in turn, was represented in the form of a "homogeneous participant" (cf. Townsend, 1984).

For each participant, then, mean latencies were computed for correct posttrial responses, separately for each visual field of target–matching probe item presentation and within each of the four concomitant-task loads. Likewise, participants' variances in correct-trial latencies were computed within each of these combinations. The means and variances then were averaged within participants, across the concomitant-task loads, separately for each visual field of the target-matching word. These mean and variance averages, in turn, were collapsed across the 14 individuals within the respective diagnostic groups. Maximum likelihood estimates of variances (Evans, Hastings, & Peacock, 2000) were used throughout, which can be shown to positively bias slightly the tests of fit appropriated here—if anything, disfavoring model acceptance. The resulting values, along with mean error rates, are presented in Table 5.1.

Data-Predicting Model

The constructed mixture model comprises two categories of distributions: (a) base distributions and (b) mixing distributions. A *base distribution* is used to characterize the dispersion of encoding latencies across trials for an individual participant. *Mixing distributions* convey individual differences in these base distributions. They do so by treating parameters of base distributions as random variables in their own right. This hierarchical relation of distributions thus provides for added sources of variability in performance data overall. Moreover, its Bayesian format, casting mixing distributions as Bayesian priors, affords potentially important computational options (which we expand on below).

Mixing distributions can remain constant across experimental factors, or they can vary, depending on how the base-distribution parameters they embrace are implicated in the configuration of summary performance data. In the present instance, one of the mixing distributions embodies variation

TABLE 5.1

Observed Mean Latencies in Seconds, (Average Latency Variances)$^{1/2}$, Error Rates, and Predictions of Proposed and Competing Models for Diagnostic Groups and Encoding Load (Hemifield Compatibility of Probe Item Presentation)

Diagnostic group	Encoding load	Mean			(Average variance)$^{1/2}$		
		Observed (error rate)	Model prediction	Competing model prediction	Observed	Model prediction	Competing model prediction
Control	Lower	0.830 (.04)	0.844	0.833	0.22	0.217	0.217
	Higher	0.880 (.09)	0.874	0.874	0.243	0.242	0.253
Paranoid schizophrenia	Lower	1.468 (.16)	1.465	1.449	0.508	0.534	0.553
	Higher	1.483 (.23)	1.496	1.49	0.603	0.545	0.568

in the number of subprocesses composing the encoding process, and the other embodies the rate, or capacity, of transacting these subprocesses. Considering data patterns in conjunction with model composition (e.g., Neufeld et al., 2002; Neufeld & Williamson, 1996), the former distribution tenably is elevated with heightened encoding load (less compatible hemifield of probe-item presentation), equally for controls and paranoid-schizophrenia patients. Likewise, paranoid-schizophrenia status elevates this distribution by a constant amount, under lower and higher encoding conditions.

In contrast, the distribution of parameter values corresponding to rates of subprocess completion (seconds per subprocess) defensibly is held constant across all four factorial combinations. These selective changes in mixing distributions across experimental factors can be shown to cohere parsimoniously with the absence of nonadditivity of factor effects regarding mean latencies (above) but also regarding within-participant variances (Vollick, 1994; Vollick & Neufeld, 2006). The required additivity is apparent in model predictions (see Table 5.1, and developments that follow). The present model architecture, then, in the first instance fits with qualitative properties of the data pattern. Additional tests of fit to group and, further, to individual participant data, are taken up in the section titled Tests of Model Fit and Competing Model Fit.

We now turn to details of the appropriated base distribution. Individual intertrial encoding latencies defensibly were considered to be Erlang distributed (e.g., Evans et al., 2000), a distribution that has two parameters: (a) k' (the shape parameter), in this instance expressing the number of encoding subprocesses, and (b) v (the intensity parameter), expressing their rate of dispatch (seconds per subprocess). With $k' = 1$, the Erlang distribution reduces to the exponential distribution but becomes increasingly similar to the normal distribution as k' increases. The mean latency for a given base distribution becomes k'/v, and the variance becomes k'/v^2. This distribution's probability density function $f(t)$, proportional to the relative frequency of process completions over time t, is $(vt)^{k'-1}/(k'-1)! \, ve^{-vt}$. Figure 5.1 depicts four latency distributions, hypothetically identified with 4 participants, each having an unique pair of values for k' and v. The mean of each one is k'/v, with variance k'/v^2.

The distribution of v is designated to be gamma, with parameters k (shape) and r (intensity). The parameter k is identified with task-related performer competence, and r is identified with susceptibility to stress effects on performer efficiency (Neufeld, in press). The mean and variance of v, according to this distribution, are k/r and k/r^2, respectively. The probability density function of v is $(rv)^{k-1}/\Gamma(k) \, re^{-rv}$. The symbol Γ stands for the gamma function, a continuous analog of the factorial; where k is an integer, $\Gamma(k) = (k-1)!$ (e.g., Beyer, 1984). A gamma distribution of v, with $k = 30$, and

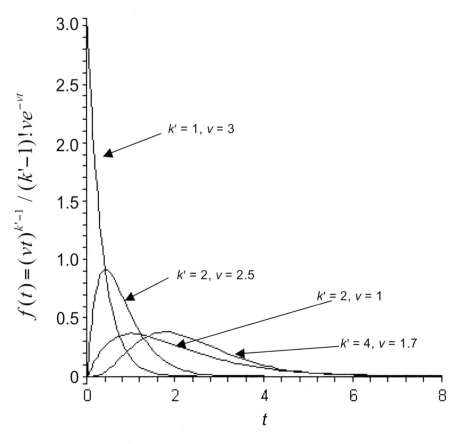

Figure 5.1. Erlang distributions, expressing hypothetical individual differences in values of *k'* and *v*.

$r = 10.743$, is presented in Figure 5.2. Interpretation of this distribution's parameters r and k was dealt with at some length by Neufeld (in press).

As for the base distribution's parameter k', its distribution in turn is designated as Poisson, the latter having parameter m (see, e.g., Kenny & Keeping, 1963). Both the mean and variance of this distribution are m, and its probability function for k', $\Pr(k')$, is $m^{k}/k'!\ e^{-m}$. The value of m for controls under the low encoding load conditions is m'; m' is incremented by h and/or g, with heightened encoding load and/or paranoid schizophrenia diagnostic status. This deployment of parameters again is based on consideration of empirical latencies conjoint with model composition (Neufeld et al., 2002). Figure 5.3 portrays Poisson distributions of k', for m ranging from 0.0971 to 1.858. A schematic of the mixture model's overall design is presented in Figure 5.4.

Selection of the parametric distributions used in this mixture model was defended by Neufeld et al. (2002). Note that such distributions have

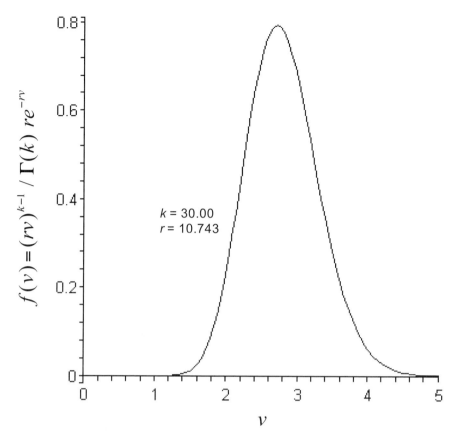

Figure 5.2. Mixing distribution of *v*, common to all combinations of encoding load and diagnostic status.

well-charted properties and can be members of larger families of prominently used distributions (Evans et al., 2000) and that their mixture-model implementation expedites individualized model appropriation through Bayesian methodology.

The model's prediction of mean latency for a cell of the 2 × 2 layout was structured as follows:

$$E(T; k,r,m)_{encoding} + Y + .160, \qquad (5.1)$$

where $E(T; k,r,m)_{encoding}$ is the mixture model's prediction of mean encoding latency, and Y is the time for processes auxiliary to probe item encoding, including a comparison of the encoded properties of the probe item to those of the memory-held target and any concomitant-task processing associated with the probe display's central-field item that precedes registration of the target–probe match response (as averaged across the four concomitant-

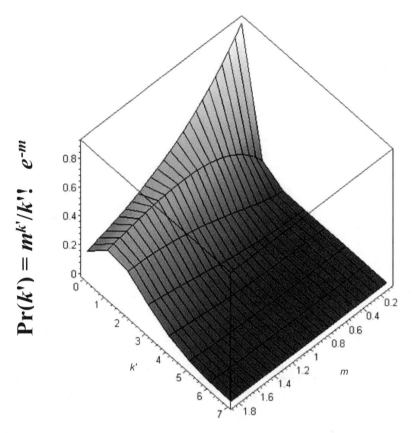

$$\text{Pr}(k') = m^{k'}/k'! \; e^{-m}$$

Figure 5.3. Tentative mixing distributions of *k'* for various values of *m*, which varies from 0.0971 to 1.858. As *m* increases, the mixing distribution's spread of *k'* increases toward higher values.

task conditions). Finally, the value of 0.160 seconds represents response movement time, as estimated by Woodworth and Schlosberg (1954). This value has served effectively in similar contexts (e.g., Townsend, 1984), and replacing it with a free, estimated parameter has rendered similarly small values with no improvement in model fit (Carter & Neufeld, 1999).

The mixture-model prediction of the average, or expected encoding latency $E(T; k,r,m)_{encoding}$ is

$$mr/(k - 1), \tag{5.2}$$

the parameter *m* being *m'* for control participants under the lower encoding load, with the addition to *m'* of *h*, *g*, or both, accompanying the higher encoding load, paranoid schizophrenia diagnostic status, or both.

The prediction of the variance in latency, averaged across participants in a cell of the 2 × 2 layout, in turn is

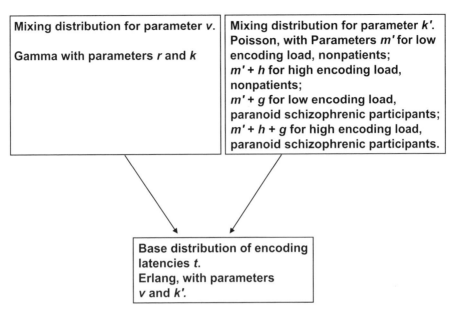

| Mixing distribution for parameter *v*.

Gamma with parameters *r* and *k* | Mixing distribution for parameter *k'*.
Poisson, with Parameters *m'* for low encoding load, nonpatients;
m' + *h* for high encoding load, nonpatients;
m' + *g* for low encoding load, paranoid schizophrenic participants;
m' + *h* + *g* for high encoding load, paranoid schizophrenic participants. |

Base distribution of encoding latencies *t*.
Erlang, with parameters *v* and *k'*.

Figure 5.4. Design of parameter-mixture model.

$$E[Var(T;\ k,r,m)]_{encoding} + Z + .001296, \qquad (5.3)$$

where $E[Var(T;\ k,r,m)]_{encoding}$ is the mixture model's prediction of average (i.e., expected) across-trial variance in encoding latency; Z is the estimated value of the variance in latency contributed by the same sources assigned to the parameter Y, above, again averaged across the four concomitant-task conditions; and 0.001296 is the across-trial variance in response-movement time (after Woodworth & Schlosberg, 1954). The model-predicted expected variance in encoding latency, $E[Var(T;\ k,r,m])_{encoding}$ is

$$mr^2/[(k-1)(k-2)]. \qquad (5.4)$$

Computations underlying the above model-predicted values were presented by Neufeld and Williamson (1996; see also Neufeld, in press).

Altogether, the estimated parameters (below) totaled six. There were eight observations and a mean and standard deviation for each of the four factorial combinations, leaving 2 degrees of freedom for testing of empirical model fit. Parameter values were estimated by means of a moment-fitting cost function (detailed by Townsend, 1984; see also Neufeld & McCarty, 1994), which was minimized using the classic and versatile search algorithm STEPIT 7.4 (Chandler, 1975, whose application was cross-checked against that of a search algorithm from Waterloo Maple, Waterloo, Ontario, Canada: MAPLE 9.0). The format of this cost function resembles that of chi-square but is not necessarily distributed as chi-square. It nevertheless serves well for parameter estimation. In the present case, the function settled at a value of 0.00793, indicating a successful search in terms of closeness of final predictions to observed values. Significance tests, however, required additional developments, as we describe in the next section.

As for the parameters themselves, k was fixed at the outset at 30, a tenable value considering the simplicity of the current encoding requirements, along with the substantive role of this parameter (Neufeld, in press). The remaining six parameters, and their estimated values, were $r = 10.7339$, $m' = .0971$, $h = .08175$, $g = 1.6793$, $Y = .64794$, and $Z = .031842$. The resulting model predictions are presented in Table 5.1.

Tests of Model Fit and Competing Model Fit

In this section, we consider empirical consequences of mixture-model composition and associated model tests. First, we consider the distributions of latency means and variances subjected to aggregation across participants. Next, we test fit of model predictions to group-level performance summaries. Comparison of empirical fit is made with that of a principled competing model. The predictions of both the proposed and competing models then are tested with respect to performance latencies of individual participants, using Bayesian analyses that synthesize individual performance samples with mixture models' parameter-mixing distributions—thus exploiting the latter's status as Bayesian priors. To round out, we compare predictive efficacy with that of classical methodology, which restricts individualized parameter estimation and model predictions to the performance sample itself.

Distribution of Aggregate Data

We begin by considering the distributions of data that have been aggregated across individuals, within factorial combinations of the present research design. If a mixture model stipulating parameter variation over individuals within a diagnostic-group–encoding-load combination is operative, then the data summaries for the participants tenably should arise from a single population. Moreover, considering the central limit theorem, the distribution arguably should be normal.

Note that a similar scenario holds for model testing with a homogeneous-participant strategy, where individual differences surrounding groupwise data aggregates are categorized as model-exogenous noise (Carter & Neufeld, 1999; Townsend, 1984; see also Shavelson & Webb, 1991). Regarding disorder-affected and spared cognitive functions, theoretical deductions drawn from model tests likely are the same whether individual differences are cast as theory-extraneous noise or mixture-model dispersions of base-distribution parameters (cf. Neufeld & Williamson, 1996). Viewing interparticipant variation in response protocols in terms of random dispersion of parameter values across individuals, however, potentially increases model comprehensiveness by incorporating stochastic data properties that otherwise would be regarded as error variance. The structure of the mixture models moreover opens up important computational options, because the parameter-mixing distributions de facto become Bayesian priors.

To evaluate the single-population assumption described above, each sample of individual mean latencies within each of the design's factorial combinations was subjected to a Kolgomorov–Smirnov test for departure from an hypothesized single normal distribution. The viability of regarding dispersions of performance latency as emanating from a single population was similarly tested. Standard deviations, averaged across concomitant-task conditions for each participant, again were subjected to a Kolgomorov–Smirnov test for departure from a single normal distribution.

Probability values for tests applied to the mean latencies, progressing from control participants under the lower encoding load through paranoid schizophrenia patients under the higher encoding load, were .905, .959, .433, and .997. Corresponding values for the measures of dispersion were .913, .990, .373, and .703. Test statistics therefore were well within the distributional envelope specified by the model-compatible null hypothesis.

Predictions of Group Performance Data

Model predictions of observed latencies and variances, enumerated in Table 5.1, were tested using the following ANOVA-based chi-square format (Carter & Neufeld, 1999; Snodgrass & Townsend, 1980):

$$(x_{observed} - \mu_{model\ predicted})^2 / \sigma^2_{model\ predicted}. \tag{5.5}$$

Here, $x_{observed}$ is the empirical sample statistic (e.g., mean or intertrial variance) drawn from the model-prescribed population, $\mu_{model\ predicted}$ is the population value of the statistic, and $\sigma^2_{model\ predicted}$ is the population variance of the statistic. The sample values are assumed to be normally distributed, by and large a reasonable assumption in the present case because of the summary statistics' aggregate format and operation of the central limit theorem.

For mean latency, the numerator of the chi-square statistic is $n(M_{observed} - \mu_{model})^2$, where n is taken to be the number of participants serving in each of the four cells of the design (14 in this case), and $\mu_{model} = mr/(k - 1) + Y + .160$.

Providing now for the composition of the denominator of the chi-square statistic $\sigma^2_{model\ predicted}$, the total mixture model variance can be partitioned into the required between- and within-participant terms. These terms are analogous to those used in the F statistic error term, for testing group effects in a split-plot factorial ANOVA (e.g., Kirk, 1995). The within-participant term is

$$(mr^2/[(k - 1)(k - 2)] + Z + .036^2)/q, \tag{5.6}$$

where q is designated to be the average number of correct trials among participants in the cell (unweighted approximation). The between-participant term, in turn, is

$$mr^2[(k - 1) + m]/[(k - 1)^2(k - 2)]. \tag{5.7}$$

Turning to variances, the numerator of the chi-square statistic is $n(V_{observed} - \Theta_{model})^2$, where Θ_{model} is the model's expected, or average within-participant variance in latencies across trials, which is

$$mr^2/[(k - 1)(k - 2)] + Z + .036^2. \tag{5.8}$$

As for the denominator $\sigma^2_{model\ predicted}$, between- and within-variance terms again are assembled. The model-defined between-participant variance, specifically with respect to the variance in latencies across trials, now is

$$\{m(m + 1)r^4/[(k - 1)(k - 2)(k - 3)(k - 4)]\} \tag{5.9}$$
$$- \{m^2r^4/[(k - 1)^2(k - 2)^2]\}.$$

Analogous to the expected within-participant variance in across-trial latencies, described earlier, within-participant variance in across-trial latency variances takes account of the population variance in encoding-latency variance for an individual with parameter combination k' and v, to which is added z and $.036^2$. The variance in across-trial sample variances, with q trials per sample, then becomes

$$2(k'/v^2 + Z + .036^2)^2/q. \tag{5.10}$$

To obtain the expected within-participant variance in such trial-wise variance, the above expression first is weighted by the probability density of the given combination of k' and v, which is then taken over all the current combinations of these two parameters.

The first term in braces of Equation 5.9 plus the expected within-participant term (temporarily ignoring Z and $.036^2$), constitute $E[Var(T | k',v)^2; k,r,m]$. The second term in braces of Equation 5.9 constitutes $[E(Var(T | k',v)); k,r,m]^2$, which is subtracted from $E[Var(T | k',v)^2; k,r,m]$ to give the modeled total variance in the within-participant intertrial variance $Var[Var(T | k',v); k,r,m]$. This operation altogether is a matter of computing the variance of any variate X, according to $Var(X) = E[X - E(X)]^2 =$

$E(X^2) - [E(X)]^2$, and is an instance of implementing relations between conditional and unconditional expectancies (Parzen, 1962, p. 55)

The resulting chi-square (df = 2) value was found to be 1.3356 (p = .51288). Note that the above within-participant term, Equation 5.10, assumes that the latency distribution for individual trials is normal, which would be dubious for the present values of m. The fit, however, was deemed to be close, because for each cell the value of the within-participant variance component was in essence dwarfed by that of the between-participant component, and the computed chi-square was at the median of the model-prescribed null hypothesis distribution. The specific probabilities stated here and below nevertheless should be taken *cum grano salis*.

Turning to the competing model, a structure similar to the proposed model's structure was put forth. The only difference was that for the competing model, k' was considered to vary over trials within participants as opposed to comprising an individual-difference parameter and thus remaining constant across trials. Rather than an Erlang distribution, therefore, the competing model's base distribution was one known as *Compound Poisson* (e.g., Ross, 1996). Now, m was fixed for each participant within a cell, the base value again being m' (newly estimated). To m' was added (newly estimated) h and/or g, as before, accompanying higher encoding load and/or paranoid schizophrenia diagnostic status.

Once more, additivity of expected latencies and expected variances was accommodated (see, e.g., Neufeld & Williamson, 1996). The minimized cost function was .006855, again indicating an excellent solution. Parameter values were k = 30 (defined as before), r = 5.88125, m' = .534, h = .202, g = 3.037, Y = .565, and Z = .000188.

In this case, the value of chi-square (df = 2), whose structuring (above) was adapted to the current model, was found to be 2.73989 (p = .2548). Thus, a reasonable fit to the group summary data emerged once more. The proposed and competing models therefore performed similarly well at the group-data level. Because of their Bayesian format, it was possible to carry the competition of these models to the individual-participant domain of analysis.

Before embarking on this evaluation, however, we note that selected observations on the present data representation of group performance, as set against the corresponding model predictions, provide a certain slant on these computations. According to the nature of the empirical data aggregates according to the proposed model, the mean latency is tantamount to that of a participant whose value of k' is m and whose value of v is $(k - 1)/r$. The latter is the modal value of a gamma-distributed$_{(r,k)}v$. Likewise, the expected variance is tantamount to that of a participant whose value of k' is m and whose value for v is $[(k - 1)(k - 2)]^{\frac{1}{2}}/r$. The competing model would stipulate the same requirements for v, with a fixed value of m governing variation in k' across trials, as described earlier.

Predictions of Individual-Performance Data

Inferences about task performance obtained from group data now are tailored to individuals as follows. The probability density of combinations of k' and v, prescribed by the prior distributions of the group with which an individual is identified, is combined with a sample of the individual's encoding-latency data. This synthesis is accomplished using Bayes's theorem:

$$\Pr(A|B) = \Pr(A \cap B)/\Pr(B) = \Pr(A)\Pr(B|A)/\Pr(B). \qquad (5.11)$$

In the present application, $\Pr(A)$ corresponds to the prior probability (currently, probability density) of the parameter combination k',v. Recall that the prior distribution of k' is Poisson, with its parameter m based on the participant's group membership and encoding load condition, whereas the prior distribution of v is gamma, with parameters r and k throughout (see Figures 5.2 and 5.3). The term $\Pr(B|A)$ is the Bayes's likelihood function, or conditional joint probability density of the sample of performance latencies, given k' and v. $\Pr(B)$ is the unconditional joint probability density of the performance sample, all combinations of k' and v considered.

In the present instance, a performance sample was taken as of four encoding-latency values, each one being an average of four correct-response encoding latencies obtained from the four concomitant-task loads. The sample is denoted $\{t_1, t_2, \ldots, t_N\}$, where in this case $N = 4$ and is written $\{*\}$ for short. This average-value format is in keeping with attenuation of model-exogenous noise and the nature of Y and Z as defined in the overall mixture model. One such sample was obtained for a control participant at each level of encoding load, and the same was done for a paranoid schizophrenia participant. With these four latency samples, and the prior distributions of k' and v in hand, we are poised to compute the individuals' Bayesian posterior means and variances under the respective encoding loads.

The desired quantities are calculated as follows (computational specifics and model-stipulated prepping of performance data are exposited in Neufeld et al., 2002, p. 285 and Appendix A; for a general exposition on Bayesian computations, see O'Hagan & Forster, 2004, chap. 6). First, the posterior probability density function of t given $\{*\}$ is obtained. To do so, the posterior probability density of k' and v, given $\{*\}$, is multiplied against the probability density of t, given k' and v, after which the product is integrated, and then summed, across all combinations of v and k'. Denoting the posterior density of t as $f(t\,|\,\{*\})_{k,r,m}$, the expected value of t^n given $\{*\}$, or $E(T^n\,|\,\{*\})_{k,r,m}$ is available by integrating $f(t\,|\,\{*\})_{k,r,m}\,t^n$ from $t = 0$ to $t = $ infinity. The posterior mean is $E(T^{n\,=\,1}\,|\,\{*\})_{k,r,m})$, and the posterior variance is $E(T^{n\,=\,2}\,|\,\{*\})_{k,r,m} - [E(T^{n\,=\,1}\,|\,\{*\})_{k,r,m}]^2$. These values, then, are the Bayesian individualized predictions, which present themselves for testing against corresponding moments of the individual's full set of correct-response data.[1] Analogous computations accompany the competing model, above, against whose predictive efficacy, that of the proposed model can be compared.

Predictions were tested using two versions of chi-square, each again fashioned according to Equation 5.5. The first, with the degrees of freedom equaling the total number of correct trials for the individual under the encoding-load condition, was formed as follows:

$$q(M_{latency,\ observed} - E(T|\{*\})_{k,r,m})^2/Var(T|\{*\})_{k,r,m} \qquad (5.12)$$
$$+ \sum_{i=1}^{q} (x_{latency\ i} - M_{latency,\ observed})^2/Var(T|\{*\})_{k,r,m}.$$

The other, with $df = 2$, was

$$q(M_{latency,\ observed} - E(T\,|\,\{*\})_{k,r,m})^2/Var(T\,|\,\{*\})_{k,r,m} \qquad (5.13)$$
$$+ (V_{latency,\ observed} - Var(T\,|\,\{*\})_{k,r,m})^2/[2\ (Var(T\,|\,\{*\})_{k,r,m})^2/q].$$

In these cases, q is the number of correct responses out of 32 for the current individual (values are 29, 28, 32, and 30 for the control participant under the lower encoding load through the paranoid schizophrenia participant under the higher encoding load). Note that the lack of any between-participants term reflects that both predictions and data now were participant specific.

The maximum-likelihood calculation of variance (i.e., using division by q, rather than $q - 1$; see Evans et al., 2000), stands to generate a slight positive bias disfavoring model acceptance all things considered. Also, assumption of normality undoubtedly is violated when it comes the individual observations in the 1-to-q summation of Equation 5.12 and the second denominator of Equation 5.13. The proposed and competing models, however, did vie head to head on the same (albeit inexact) testing platform.

Moreover, results (presented below) either were markedly inside or outside the proffered distribution. Other options, such as assumption-accommodating transformations, are decidedly contraindicated, in part because of the compromised interpretation of model-predicted latency.

Finally, by way of qualification, in each instance degrees of freedom are not attenuated from those corresponding to the full set of predicted observations; that is, degrees of freedom were not adjusted for incomplete separation of model predictions and observed data. The degrees of freedom nevertheless were left intact to facilitate computational exposition and illustration of Bayesian-enhanced predictive accuracy. Predicted individual

---

[1] Not surprisingly, these values are found to be close to those obtained from an Erlang-based distribution whose parameters k' and v are set according to $E(k'\,|\,\{*\})_{k,r,m}$ and $E(v\,|\,\{*\})_{k,r,m}$ (see Neufeld et al., 2002, Appendix A).

data were subsets of the data from the individual's group that provided parameter estimates of the Bayesian priors (albeit subsets comprising trivial proportions of the group data) and from which the person's performance sample was extracted. Note that the ideal prediction setup comprising independence among these data sets would be realized, for example, in the following alternate and realistic scenario: First, a client providing a sample of empirical latencies is not a member of an earlier prior-supplying group; second, allowing that model performance at the individual level is being predicted, the individual's predicted data could be arranged to exclude his or her performance specimen itself.

This said, the above chi-square tests on the Bayesian predictions are considered. Table 5.2 presents the latency samples for the control participants and paranoid schizophrenia participants, performing under the lower and higher encoding-load conditions; the empirical observations from individuals' larger data sets; predictions of the latter by proposed and competing models; and the respective chi-square tests of fit. For the proposed model, values of the test statistic stated in Equation 5.12 invariably were less than the expected value for a chi-square distribution, or its degrees of freedom, which in this case is q. In addition, two of the four tests associated with Equation 5.13 were nonsignificant. For the competing model, one test was significant using Equation 5.12, and two were very highly significant by Equation 5.13.

Recall that independent chi-squares can be added together and tested using the sum of their respective degrees of freedom. Each sum of the chi-square values for a pair of control and paranoid schizophrenia participants, obtained separately for each encoding load, therefore was tested with the pair's total degrees of freedom. Tested were both the proposed and competing models, using both Equations 5.12 and 5.13. Thus, for each model four chi-square summations were available.

Using Equation 5.12, resulting chi-squares for the proposed model under the lower and higher encoding loads, with 61 and 58 degrees of freedom, respectively, were 37.122, $p = .999$, and 42.45, $p = .937$. Corresponding values using Equation 5.13, with 4 degrees of freedom in each instance, were 27.84, $p \rightarrow 0$, and 7.031 ($p = .134$).

In the case of the competing model, $\chi^2(df = 61)$ using Equation 5.12 for the lower encoding load was 56.52, $p = .639$, and for the higher encoding load, $\chi^2(df = 58)$ was 96.616, $p = .001$. Using Equation 5.13 and 4 degrees of freedom, corresponding values were 20.21, $p = .0004$, and 39.311, $p \rightarrow 0$. Thus, one of these four tests on the proposed model was significant, but three of the four on the competing model were significant.

On balance, the proposed model performed discernably better at the individual-participant level than the competing model. Such competition of course could be extended to the remaining participants, and indeed new

TABLE 5.2

Performance Samples, Observed Means and Variances, Bayesian-Predicted Means and Variances, and Tests of Fit

Observations and predictions	Source of performance data			
	Control participants		Paranoid schizophrenia participants	
	Lower encoding load	Higher encoding load	Lower encoding load	Higher encoding load
Individual-participant latency samples	{0.965, 0.828, 0.885, 1.098}	{1.238, 0.938, 0.920, 1.028}	{1.350, 0.995, 1.025, 1.043}	{1.085, 1.235, 1.460, 1.200}
Observed mean, across q trials	0.905	1.022	1.0825	1.3775
Predicted mean (proposed model)	1.150	1.163	1.247	1.403
Predicted mean (competing model)	0.829	0.868	1.360	1.400
Observed variance	0.0415	0.135	0.095	0.1525
Predicted variance (proposed model)	0.15724	0.1666	0.2118	0.2798
Predicted variance (competing model)	0.042	0.057	0.227	0.240
Trials (q)	29	28	32	30
$\chi^2(df = q)$; Equation 5.12 (proposed model)	18.702 (<q; ns)	26.033 (<q; ns)	18.42 (<q; ns)	16.42 (<q; ns)
$\chi^2(df = q)$; Equation 5.12 (competing model)	32.65, $p = .292$	77.486, $p \to 0$	23.87 (< q; ns)	19.130 (<q; ns)
$\chi^2(df = 2)$; Equation 5.13 (proposed model)	18.900, $p \to 0$	3.855, $p = .146$	8.944, $p = .011$	3.176, $p = .204$
$\chi^2(df = 2)$; Equation 5.13 (competing model)	3.99, $p = .136$	37.288, $p \to 0$	16.22, $p \to 0$	2.023, $p = .364$

participants for whom the present priors are tenable (Neufeld et al., 2002, p. 294; see also description of desirable data sources and partitioning, above).

A chief point to be made is that individualized Bayesian-posterior predictions not only mediate group-level findings to individual participants but also harbor a potentially useful contribution to the methodology of model selection. As instantiated here, the proposed model tendering a combination of v and k' per participant is tenable and competitive.

Note that prior distributions in principle inform predictions about individual performance augmenting that of the performance sample itself. Referring a performance sample to the pertinent priors is analogous to the medical laboratory practice of bringing the larger body of hematological diagnostic knowledge to bear on a modest blood serum specimen. If prior-parameter distributions enlighten predictions about the individual's functioning then, compared with predictions that ignore the priors, those embracing them should be more accurate about the broader picture of the person's performance.

Accordingly, the same observations subjected to Bayesian posterior predictions, enumerated in Table 5.2, were subjected to predictions based on classical parameter estimates. Such estimates are derived from the respective performance samples and make no reference to the prior parameter distributions of the group to which the individual belongs. We used the method of *moment matching* (see Evans et al., 2000) to estimate k' and v for individual data in each of the 2×2 factorial combinations (adjusted for movement time and estimates of Y and Z of the proposed model). Predictions were submitted to tests corresponding to Equations 5.12 and 5.13. Now each of the eight calculations indicated the predictions were well wide of the mark; ps ranged from .035 to $.428(10^{-12})$, with the average being .007.

To be sure, sample sizes were very small, but no more so than those entered into the Bayesian posterior predictions. In the latter case, the prior distributions evidently exercised their correcting influence on the predictions of individual task transaction, through their involvement in Bayes's theorem.

A phenomenon at work in the above influence is known as *shrinkage* (e.g., O'Hagan & Forster, 2004). Specifically, classical parameter estimates gravitate toward the mean of their prior distribution (see Neufeld et al., 2002, Equation A6). Its operation is exemplified with respect to parameter v. The four classical estimates averaged 16.294, with a variance of 18.193. If error of estimation was assuaged via incorporation of the priors (as attested by the pattern of empirical fit tests), then the posterior estimates of v, $E(v \mid \{*\})_{k,r,m}$ should be "attracted" to their prior's mean $k/r = 2.796$. Such obviously was the case, as in each of the four instances the posterior estimate of v was 3.0. The current instance therefore supplies a rather stark example of the grounding effects conveyed by prior-lodged information.

On balance, because they bring to bear information about person-specific performance additional to that lodged in the obtained performance specimen (see, e.g., Neufeld et al., 2002, Equations A6 and A7 and the final mathematical Appendix equation), Bayesian posterior predictions fare considerably better than do classical method predictions. In their present application, the former nevertheless leave room for improvement. Such improvement may be attained through the use of larger performance samples (for more on the interplay of distributional properties and sample size in determining the posterior dispersion of base distribution parameter values, see chap. 2, this volume).

DISCUSSION

Overview

The foregoing developments comprise a formal dissection of spared and affected functions in targeted portions of a memory/visual search task. Presentation of the task's probe item was lateralized according to hemifield specialization for probe item processing. Focus was on a specific process, and form of deficit in that process. The targeted process comprised encoding of the presented probe into a cognitive format, facilitating collateral processes, including memory scanning and comparison. The specific parametric source of encoding elongation characterizing schizophrenia participants consisted of additional constituent operations, or subprocesses.

The tenability of this theoretical agent of performance deficit has cut across analytical (stochastic–mathematical, as illustrated here in the analysis of groupwise performance differences) and connectionist (simulational, computational; Carter & Neufeld, 2006) levels of modeling and has found support from diverse cognitive–behavioral and cognitive neurophysiological studies (Boksman et al., 2005; Carter & Neufeld, 1999; Neufeld & Williamson, 1996). The present developments extend the tenability of this source of deficit to the individual level of analysis. Symptom significance, with respect to thought-content disorder, and significance with respect to stress-negotiation deficit, in turn, have been drawn out elsewhere (Neufeld, 2005; Neufeld et al., 1993; Neufeld & Williamson, 1996).

Competing versions of this form of deficit were similarly viable when evaluated at the group level of analysis. However, when tested on a selection of individual-performance data, the model positing individual differences in the pair of parameters tenably governing individual performance-latency distributions was at least marginally superior to one restricting individual differences to only one of the parameters. Thus, support for the favored model went beyond the "aesthetic appeal" of each participant having his or her own set of parameter values.

Finally, the computations surrounding the present source of schizophrenia deviation illustrate an additional test for model selection. This option involves coherence of model performance at group and individual levels of prediction. It adds to the existing arsenal of Bayesian model selection and testing (cf. Karabatsos, 2006; Rubin, 1984; Wagenmakers, Ratcliff, Gomez, & Iverson, 2004) while taking account of clinical constraints on magnitude of cognitive performance specimens.

Elongated Encoding and Cognitive Capacity

The present modeled account of schizophrenia deviation points to a particular version of compromised cognitive performance capacity as follows. Axiomatically principled quantification of processing capacity, a very prominent construct in clinical science, is detailed in chap. 7, this volume. The capacity index (CI), described there, taps the amount of work done over an interval t. If sheer amount of work were identified with dispatching of encoding subprocesses, then schizophrenia and control participants would be comparable. Specifically, CI is affected by sources labeled *statistical advantage* and *capacity limitation* (specified in chap. 7, this volume). Scrutiny of the present account of protracted encoding contraindicates the involvement of either of these sources. The value of CI nevertheless is diminished.

The value of CI is computed as $-\ln[S(t)]$, or minus one times the natural logarithm of the survivor function of the process under consideration. The survivor function $S(t)$ is the integral of the probability density function of process completion, taken from t to infinity. For the mixture model adopted here, the survivor function of the encoding process, all combinations of v and k' considered is

$$\sum_{k'=0}^{\infty} [m^{k'}/k'!\exp(-m)] \; [\sum_{j=0}^{k-1} (\Gamma(j+k)t^j \cdot r^k)/(j!\Gamma(k)(r+t)^{j+k})]. \quad (5.14)$$

Inspection reveals that, other things being equal (notably, r and k), values will increase with the current model's schizophrenia-related increase in m, as follows. Considering the first square-bracketed term, the probability of higher amounts of k' go up with m; considering the second square-bracketed term, the summation obviously increases with k'. With higher probabilities and higher summations, the sum of the cross-products of the square-bracketed terms obviously increases. Because $S(t)$ increases, $\ln[S(t)]$ will increase, and $-\ln[S(t)] = CI$ will decrease, as m goes up.

The current decrease in CI, then, is attributable not to a reduction in cognitive work capable of being done but the amount necessary to be carried out to complete the encoding process. By this account, statistical advantage does not come into play (cf. chap. 7, this volume); neither are schizophrenia participants afflicted with diminished channel capacity, meaning a reduced rate of dispatching encoding subprocesses. Instead, presentation of the probe item is met with an endogenous increase in processing load, entailing the unleashing of additional constituent encoding operations (cf. Neufeld et al., 2002, footnote 4).

These observations point up the advantage of operationalizing cognitive capacity in quantitatively rigorous terms. Doing so indicates the need to pin down what is meant by capacity decline in psychopathology, as there potentially are several sources, any one or combination of which can issue in a diminution of CI.

Cognitive–Behavioral Correlates of Additional Encoding Subprocesses g

The precise cognitive–behavioral mechanisms behind an elevation in encoding subprocesses $g > 0$ remain to be determined. This state of knowledge is not an indictment of the present quantitative formulation. There is, after all, much in the way of accepted scientific precedent for mathematical necessity to precede identification of associated mechanisms (see, e.g., Braithwaite, 1968; Gleick, 2003; Kline, 1985; Penrose, 2004; Thorne, 1994). Moreover, as described at the outset of the Discussion section, the present quantitative formulation comes through whether attacks on the problem are sprung from analytical–mathematical or algorithmic–mathematical foundations. Selected cognitive–behavioral correlates of encoding elongation nevertheless present themselves as instantiating candidates of $g > 0$.

One such candidate consists of enhanced priming or "ramping up" of the processing system, which may involve orienting or other activities preliminary to engagement of encoding proper (Russell & Knight, 1977). Another is a reduced cognizance of previous informational transactions. This tendency can be termed *novelty excess*. It comprises failure to tag as "completed" previously transacted encoding subprocesses (cf. Hemsley, 1993, 1994), or a failure to store or recognize redundancy properties of component encoding operations (Steffy & Galbraith, 1980; Steffy & Waldman, 1993). In each case, the penalty is inefficient repetition of previous processing, potentially issuing in $g > 0$.

A further possibility relates to apparent negative-priming deficit (e.g., MacQueen, Tipper, Galway, & Goldberg, 2003).[2] It is made up of a reduction

---

[2] Thanks are extended to J. M. G. Williams for drawing Richard W. J. Neufeld's attention to this possibility.

in the usual tendency to inhibit distractors in the service of selective attention to target stimuli. This deficit could fit into the present context, not in terms of a failure to detect previousness but as a failure to edit it out.[3]

Again, the present quantitative formulation tenably antedates pinpointing the responsible cognitive–behavioral mechanism(s) and their associated neurocircuitry. It does nevertheless recruit the above and, possibly, other qualifying candidates.

Exigencies of Application

Advantages of appropriating the information conveyed by prior distributions to individual cognitive assessment are contingent on requisite stability of the specific prior-distribution parameters that are brought to bear. Acceptable stability requires a correspondingly sufficient corpus of data, which, as often as not, involves aggregation across similarly performing participants. The resulting prior distributions that are formed then may be integrated with a performance sample from a subsequent individual tenably belonging to the class of those to whom the prior distributions apply.

Aggregation of data submitted to prior-distribution mixture modeling brings into play the issue of acceptable homogeneity of that which is aggregated (see the Distribution of Aggregate Data section). Note that an oft-used technique in cognitive psychology for inducing data stability involves the running of participants through multiple multitrial sessions. This strategy of course has its limitations when participants are distressed and/or perform under stressing conditions. It also encounters its own potential problems of intersession heterogeneity of aggregated data. Apropos of the present exigencies, various tacks to addressing the issue of participantwise aggregation are available and have been reviewed and discussed by Carter, Neufeld, and Benn (1998; see also Neufeld & Gardner, 1990). They are taken up further in the Introduction to this volume.

The establishment of Bayesian priors can be challenging; they require stability-endowing data ensembles and the surmounting of barriers to valid assembly. Payoff, however, can be substantial. It can take the form of requiring only modest performance samples from subsequently assessed individuals. Such advantage is seen in the exemplary comparison between Bayesian posterior, and classical predictions, above—results that by dint of mathematical necessity are generally emblematic of improved accuracy conveyed by valid Bayesian priors.

---

[3] It currently is indeterminate whether extra subprocesses, $g > 0$, may be consequential to, or at the root of, these proffered cognitive–behavioral mechanisms. Mathematical exploration of negative-priming deficits reveals that the associated pattern of control–schizophrenia differences in principle can be explained by a Poisson mechanism incorporating schizophrenia-specific additional encoding subprocesses.

Bayesian posterior depictions of individual performance, as computed in this presentation, moreover can be embellished with plots of individualized posterior probability density and distribution functions (see detailed illustrations in Neufeld et al., 2002). Such stochastic dynamical trajectories, in turn, stand to be useful in assessing the time course of targeted functions for neurophysiological studies, such as those involving functional magnetic resonance imaging (Neufeld, in press; Neufeld et al., 2002).

Extensions

Selected extensions of the present developments unveil additional potentially important avenues of formally grounded cognitive assessment. Included are methods for monitoring an individual's treatment response over a course of intervention. Also provided are similarly dynamic strategies for evaluating the efficacy of a treatment regimen across participants at large. The computational techniques use formulations similar to those used here, conjoint with an extension to finite probability mixtures of priors (Neufeld, 2006; for background on such hierarchical mixtures, see, e.g., O'Hagan & Forster, 2004). Architectural and computational specifics of these models exceed the mandate and length of the present treatment; however, readers may access the requisite details in Neufeld (in press).

A different sort of extension pertains to substantive inferences of the current representation of encoding debility. It bears on stress-negotiation deficit in psychopathology. The emphasis is placed on cognition-intensive coping (Kukde & Neufeld, 1994; Morrison, Neufeld, & Lefebvre, 1988; Neufeld, 1999). Such forms of coping, and the efficiency in cognitive functions they implicate, can be set into terms of a nonlinear dynamical system (in the popular vernacular, a *chaos-theoretic system*), incorporating stress, coping, and related variables (specifics are available in Neufeld, 1999; see also Levy, Neufeld, & Yao, 2003; Yao, Yu, Essex, & Davison, 2006). This extension makes for a formal systems platform to explore the nature of cognition-related stress vulnerability in psychopathology.

CONCLUSION

In this chapter, we have applied a stochastic mixture model to a specific form of stimulus encoding in schizophrenia, thereby providing for individual differences in expression of the same basic dysfunction. The application ushers in Bayesian-based techniques of individual assessment as well as a method of competing model selection based on consistency of model performance at group and individual levels of testing.

Establishment of the quantitative infrastructure, notably Bayesian priors, may be methodologically demanding. However, once in place, returns can be substantial. In principle, and as demonstrated in the developments presented here, precision of assessment of incoming participants can be sharpened with much less taxation in the way of sampled cognitive performance than that of classical methodology.

In general, quantitative constraints tend to make plain prevailing limitations and uncertainties in a problem area but also provide clues as to directions for redress. Quantitative formulations, moreover, expedite progress by making previous efforts self-evident because of the explicitness such formulations enforce. Thus, blind alleys are exposed, countering wasteful recapitulation. These assets of quantification have been harnessed here by interlacing a delineated form of cognitive psychopathology with adaptations and extensions of contemporary formal cognitive science.

REFERENCES

Alwitt, L. F. (1981). Two neural mechanisms related to modes of selective attention. *Journal of Experimental Psychology: Human Perception and Performance, 7,* 324–332.

Beyer, W. H. (1984). *Standard mathematical tables.* Boca Raton, FL: CRC Press.

Boksman, K., Théberge, J., Williamson, P., Drost, D., Malla, A., Densmore, M., et al. (2005). A 4.0 Tesla fMRI study of brain connectivity during word fluency in first episode schizophrenia. *Schizophrenia Research, 75,* 247–263.

Braithwaite, R. B. (1968). *Scientific explanation.* Cambridge, England: Cambridge University Press.

Carter, J. R., & Neufeld, R. W. J. (1999). Cognitive processing of multidimensional stimuli in schizophrenia: Formal modeling of judgment speed and content. *Journal of Abnormal Psychology, 108,* 633–654.

Carter, J. R., & Neufeld, R. W. J. (2006). *Cognitive processing of facial affect: Neuro-connectionist modeling of deviations in schizophrenia.* Manuscript submitted for publication.

Carter, J. R., Neufeld, R. W. J., & Benn, K. D. (1998). Application of process models in assessment psychology: Potential assets and challenges. *Psychological Assessment, 10,* 379–395.

Chandler, J. P. (1975). STEPIT 7.4 [Computer software]. Stillwater: Oklahoma State University, Computer Science Department.

Davidson, P. O., & Costello, G. G. (1969). *N = 1: Experimental studies of single cases.* New York: Van Nostrand Reinhold.

Evans, M., Hastings, N., & Peacock, B. (2000). *Statistical distributions* (3rd ed.). New York: Wiley.

George, L., & Neufeld, R. W. J. (1987). Attentional resources and hemispheric functional asymmetry in schizophrenia. *British Journal of Clinical Psychology, 26,* 35–45.

Gleick, J. (2003). *Isaac Newton.* New York: Pantheon.

Hemsley, D. R. (1993). Perception and cognition in schizophrenia. In R. L. Cromwell & C. R. Snyder (Eds.), *Schizophrenia: Origins, processes, treatment and outcome* (pp. 135–150). New York: Oxford University Press.

Hemsley, D. R. (1994). Perceptual and cognitive normality as the basis for schizophrenic symptoms. In A. S. David & J. Cutting (Eds.), *The neuropsychology of schizophrenia* (pp. 97–116). Hillsdale, NJ: Erlbaum.

Karabatsos, G. (2006). Bayesian nonparametric model selection and model testing. *Journal of Mathematical Psychology, 50,* 123–148.

Kenny, J. F., & Keeping, E. S. (1963). *Mathematics of statistics* (3rd ed.). New York: Van Nostrand.

Kirk, R. E. (1995). *Experimental design: Procedures for the behavioral sciences* (3rd ed.). Monterey, CA: Brooks/Cole.

Kline, M. (1985). *Mathematics and the search for knowledge.* Oxford, England: Oxford University Press.

Kukde, M. P., & Neufeld, R. W. J. (1994). Facial electromyographic measures distinguish covert coping from stress response to stimulus threat. *Personality and Individual Differences, 16,* 211–228.

Levy, L., Neufeld, R. W. J., & Yao, W. (2003). Methodological challenges to capturing dynamical aspects of health-care acquisition. In L. Dube & D. Moscowitz (Eds.), *Emotional and interpersonal dimensions of health services: Enriching the art of care with the science of care* (pp. 138–150). Montreal, Quebec, Canada: McGill–Queens University Press.

MacQueen, G. M., Tipper, S. P., Galway, T. M., & Goldberg J. O. (2003). Impaired distractor inhibition in patients with schizophrenia on a negative priming task. *Psychological Medicine, 33,* 121–129.

Morrison, M. S., Neufeld, R. W. J., & Lefebvre, L. A. (1988). The economy of probabilistic stress: Interplay of controlling activity and threat reduction. *British Journal of Mathematical and Statistical Psychology, 41,* 155–177.

Moscovitch, M., & Klein, D. (1980). Material-specific perceptual interference for visual words and faces: Implications for models of capacity limitation, attention, and laterality. *Journal of Experimental Psychology: Human Perception and Performance, 6,* 590–604.

Myung, I. J., Forster, M. R., & Browne, M. W. (Eds.). (2000). Model selection [Special issue]. *Journal of Mathematical Psychology, 44*(1–2).

Neufeld, R. W. J. (1977). *Clinical quantitative methods.* New York: Grune & Stratton.

Neufeld, R. W. J. (1999). Dynamic differentials of stress and coping. *Psychological Review, 106,* 385–397.

Neufeld, R. W. J. (in press). Composition and uses of formal clinical cognitive science In B. Shuart, W. Spaulding, & J. Poland (Eds.), *Nebraska Symposium* on *Motivation: Vol. 52. Modeling complex systems.* Lincoln: University of Nebraska Press.

Neufeld, R. W. J., Carter, J. R., Boksman, K., Jetté, J., & Vollick, D. (2002). Application of stochastic modelling to group and individual differences in cognitive functioning. *Psychological Assessment, 14,* 279–298.

Neufeld, R. W. J., & Gardner, R. C. (1990). Data aggregation in evaluating psychological constructs: Multivariate and logical-deductive considerations. *Journal of Mathematical Psychology, 34,* 276–296.

Neufeld, R. W. J., & McCarty, T. (1994). A formal analysis of stressor and stress-proneness effects on basic information processing. *British Journal of Mathematical and Statistical Psychology, 47,* 193–226.

Neufeld, R. W. J., Vollick, D., & Highgate, S. (1993). Stochastic modelling of stimulus encoding and memory search in paranoid schizophrenia: Clinical and theoretical implications. In R. L. Cromwell & R. C. Snyder (Eds.), *Schizophrenia: Origins, processes, treatment, and outcome: The Second Kansas Series in Clinical Psychology* (pp. 176–196). Oxford, England: Oxford University Press.

Neufeld, R. W. J., & Williamson, P. (1996). Neuropsychological correlates of positive symptoms: Delusions and hallucinations. In C. Pantelis, H. E. Nelson, & T. R. E. Barnes (Eds.), *Schizophrenia: A neuropsychological perspective* (pp. 205–235). London: Wiley.

O'Hagan, A., & Forster, J. (2004). *Kendall's advanced theory of statistics: Vol. 2B. Bayesian influences* (2nd ed.). New York: Oxford University Press.

Pachella, R. (1974). The interpretation of reaction time in information processing research. In B. H. Kantowitz (Ed.), *Human information processing: Tutorials in performance and cognition* (pp. 41–82). Hillsdale, NJ: Erlbaum.

Parzen, E. (1962). *Stochastic processes.* San Francisco: Holden-Day.

Penrose, R. (2004). *The road to reality: A complete guide to the laws of the universe.* London: Jonathan Cape.

Ross, S. M. (1996). *Stochastic processes* (2nd ed.). New York: Wiley.

Rubin, D. B. (1984). Bayesianly justifiable and relevant frequency calculations for the applied statisticians. *Annals of Statistics, 12,* 1151–1172.

Russell, P. N., & Knight, R. G. (1977). Performance of process schizophrenics on tasks involving visual search. *Journal of Abnormal Psychology, 86,* 16–26.

Sergent, J. (1982). The cerebral balance of power: Confrontation or cooperation? *Journal of Experimental Psychology: Human Perception and Performance, 8,* 253–272.

Shavelson, R. J., & Webb, N. M. (1991). *Generalizability theory: A primer.* Newbury Park, CA: Sage.

Snodgrass, J. G., & Townsend, J. T. (1980). Comparing parallel and serial models: Theory and implementation. *Journal of Experimental Psychology: Human Perception and Performance, 6,* 330–354.

Steffy, R. A., & Galbraith, K. (1980). Relation between latency and redundancy-associated deficit in schizophrenic reaction time performance. *Journal of Abnormal Psychology, 89*, 419–427.

Steffy, R. A., & Waldman, I. (1993). Schizophrenics' reaction time: North star or shooting star? In R. L. Cromwell & C. R. Snyder (Eds.), *Schizophrenia: Origins, processes, treatment, and outcome* (pp. 111–134). New York: Oxford University Press.

Symbolic Computation Group. (2003). MAPLE 9.0 [Computer software]. Waterloo, Ontario, Canada: Waterloo Maple, Inc.

Thorne, K. S. (1994). *Black holes and time warps: Einstein's outrageous legacy.* New York: Norton.

Townsend, J. T. (1984). Uncovering mental processes with factorial experiments. *Journal of Mathematical Psychology, 28*, 363–400.

Townsend, J. T., & Ashby, F. G. (1983). *Stochastic modelling of elementary psychological processes.* Cambridge, England: Cambridge University Press.

Townsend, J. T., Fific, M., & Neufeld, R. W. J. (in press). Assessment of mental architecture in clinical/cognitive research. In T. A. Treat, A. Kraut, & T. Baker (Eds.), *Psychological clinical science: Recent advances in theory and practice.* Mahwah, NJ: Erlbaum.

Townsend, J. T., & Wenger, M. J. (2004). The serial–parallel dilemma: A case study in a linkage of theory and method. *Psychonomic Bulletin & Review, 11*, 391–418.

Vollick, D. (1994). *Models of encoding-latencies in paranoid schizophrenia.* Unpublished doctoral dissertation. University of Western Ontario, Waterloo, Ontario, Canada.

Vollick, D., & Neufeld, R. W. J. (2006). *Stochastic modelling of encoding-latency means and variances in paranoid schizophrenia.* Manuscript in preparation.

Wagenmakers, E.-J., Ratcliff, R., Gomez, P., & Iverson, G. J. (2004). Assessing model mimicry using the parametric bootstrap. *Journal of Mathematical Psychology, 48*, 28–50.

Wagenmakers, E., & Waldorp, L. (Eds.). (2006). Model selection [Special issue]. *Journal of Mathematical Psychology, 50*(2).

Woodworth, R. S., & Schlosberg, H. (1954). *Experimental psychology.* New York: Holt, Rinehart & Winston.

Yao, W., Yu, P., Essex, C., & Davison, M. (2006). Generalized competitive mode and its applications. *International Journal of Bifurcations and Chaos, 16*, 497–522.

6

CLINICAL COGNITIVE SCIENCE: APPLYING QUANTITATIVE MODELS OF COGNITIVE PROCESSING TO EXAMINE COGNITIVE ASPECTS OF PSYCHOPATHOLOGY

TERESA A. TREAT, RICHARD M. McFALL, RICHARD J. VIKEN,
JOHN K. KRUSCHKE, ROBERT M. NOSOFSKY, AND SHIRLEY S. WANG

Numerous theoretical approaches implicate a role for altered cognitive processing in the development, maintenance, and treatment of a wide range of clinically relevant behaviors. Clinical scientists have been slow, however, to capitalize on the wealth of contemporary theoretical, measurement, and analytical models of cognitive processing when constructing, evaluating, and extending these theoretical approaches to psychopathology (MacLeod, 1993; McFall & Townsend, 1998; McFall, Treat, & Viken, 1998). To date, the translation of cognitive science models to clinical science has occurred primarily at the measurement or task level, leading to an impoverished understanding and utilization of the multifaceted complexity of the relevant theoretical constructs, such as attention, classification, memory, and learning. As a result, clinical scientists have tended to collapse, or ignore the distinctions between, theoretical and measurement models of cognitive processes and to reify cognitive tasks as the theoretical constructs themselves (e.g., the emotional Stroop and dot-probe paradigms often are assumed to "be" attention and are pulled off the shelf whenever researchers need a measure of attention). Clinical scientists' failure to translate many of cognitive scientists' theoretically grounded analytical models also slows the advancement of clinical cognitive science. Fitting formal analytical models, or process models, not only forces clinical researchers to quantify and evaluate rigorously their theoretical assumptions about the operation of the cognitive processes of interest but also enhances their understanding of the mechanisms hypothesized to underlie variation in observed performance on cognitive-processing tasks.

The overarching aims of this chapter are to introduce a unified class of theoretical, measurement, and analytical models that can be used to examine research questions about clinically relevant cognitive processing and to illustrate the generalizability and applicability of these cognitive science models to more real-world research questions. This well-established class of models treats participants' perceptual organizations of stimuli as a primitive on which other processes—such as classification, memory, and learning—operate (for evidence of the validity of these models, see Kruschke, 1992; Kruschke & Johansen, 1999; Nosofsky, 1991, 1992a, 1992b). Formal process models specify mathematically the theorized links among these interrelated processes and afford rigorous examination of the mechanisms underlying task performance. Thus, this approach not only accounts simultaneously for the operation of multiple cognitive processes but also specifies well-integrated theoretical, measurement, and analytical models of these processes.

To examine the feasibility and utility of using this clinical cognitive approach, we deliberately have examined it in parallel across multiple areas of psychopathology, with a primary focus on problematic eating patterns and sexually aggressive behaviors. Theoretical approaches within both domains increasingly have focused on the role of information-processing patterns in the etiology and maintenance of these behaviors and in the development of prevention and intervention strategies (e.g., McFall, 1990; Schewe & O'Donohue, 1993; Vitousek, 1996; Ward, Hudson, Johnston, & Marshall, 1997; Wilson, 1999). In this chapter, we focus on the use of cognitive science methods to characterize individual differences in men's processing of women's facial affect and physical appearance, with implications for our understanding of sexual aggression, and individual differences in women's processing of other women's facial affect and body size, with implications for our understanding of eating disorders. We open this chapter with a section on stimulus-construction issues, given their centrality to the utility and validity of the approach.

STIMULUS SET DEVELOPMENT

Cognitive scientists commonly rely on simple, artificial stimulus sets that vary along a finite number of readily identifiable dimensions that are perceived in a relatively uniform fashion across participants (e.g., rectangles that vary in height and width, or color patches that vary in hue and saturation). These well-controlled and decontextualized stimulus sets facilitate investigation of cognitive scientists' research questions about process models of normative information processing. Clinical scientists, in contrast, more commonly are interested in characterizing individual differences in the processing of much more complex, socially relevant stimuli that vary along numerous dimensions. As a result, the development of an appropriate stimulus set is a critical and time-consuming process for clinical researchers.

Stimulus development begins by specifying explicitly a small number of dimensions of theoretical interest. In our experience, the incorporation of more than three or four systematically manipulated dimensions in a stimulus set becomes unwieldy, given the need to include multiple stimuli per dimension. Within the domain of eating disorders, for example, we have sought to evaluate questions about individual differences in women's processing of information about other women's body size and facial affect (Viken, Treat, Nosofky, McFall, & Palmeri, 2002). The stimulus set ideally should include both dimensions that are predicted to draw more attention from the clinical population of interest and dimensions that are predicted to draw equal or less attention from the clinical population. This strategy facilitates the examination of alternative explanations that are plausible but less theoretically interesting. For example, demonstrating that high-symptom women, relative to low-symptom women, attend both significantly more to body size and significantly less to facial affect is inconsistent with group differences in intelligence, motivation, level of perfectionism, and so on. Our use of formal process models to evaluate our hypotheses also facilitates the rigorous evaluation of competing models (cf. Knight & Silverstein, 2001; Neufeld, Vollick, Carter, Boksman, & Jetté, 2002).

The second step in stimulus development entails selection of an appropriate presentation medium. To date, we have relied primarily on photo stimulus sets, but alternatives include words or phrases describing objects or people, situations described in brief vignettes, audio or video clips of interpersonal interactions, and combinations of these possibilities (e.g., presenting photos with accompanying short text). The potential media vary in terms of the extent to which they provide ecologically valid representation of relevant stimulus features and the extent to which they afford control of irrelevant stimulus features. Ideally, the selected medium allows researchers to maximize variability along the dimensions of primary theoretical interest in an ecologically valid fashion and to minimize or eliminate variability along theoretically irrelevant dimensions.

Next, researchers develop a large potential stimulus pool that incorporates sufficient and representative variability along the dimensions of primary theoretical interest and minimizes or eliminates variability along unimportant dimensions. Thus, when developing the photo stimulus set for our eating-disorders research program, we photographed numerous college-age volunteers as they displayed happy, neutral, and sad facial expressions. The naturally occurring variability in body size among models was less pronounced than we had hoped, so we digitally altered the photographs to increase variability along this dimension. Variability in other aspects of appearance was of less interest theoretically but likely to draw attention, so we asked all volunteers to wear similar outfits, to remove makeup, and to pull their hair back from their faces. Photographs also were taken in front of a fixed background and under standard lighting conditions, in an effort to eliminate variability along these theoretically uninteresting dimensions.

The fourth step in stimulus development involves the collection of normative data along dimensions of potential relevance to participants' processing of the stimulus set and the selection of a preliminary stimulus set. Thus, we asked a sample of undergraduate women to make explicit ratings of the models' body size, facial affect, attractiveness, friendliness, and self-esteem along 10-point scales. The average ratings on these dimensions provided normative values for the stimuli along the body-size and affect dimensions. When selecting a subset of the stimuli for use in cognitive-processing studies, we retained only one photo per model and endeavored to include sufficient and representative variability both along and across the two theoretical dimensions of greatest interest to us (i.e., we included women in each of the four quadrants of the desired two-dimensional stimulus space). We also selected stimuli that minimized the correlation between the normative ratings of the two dimensions, because we were interested in characterizing the processing of the two dimensions as independently as possible.

The final step necessitates conducting a multidimensional scaling (MDS) study to evaluate four things: (a) whether the population of interest attends to the dimensions of theoretical interest when processing the stimuli (i.e., whether the psychological dimensions correspond to the physical dimensions); (b) whether participants attend too much to irrelevant dimensions, necessitating a retooling of the stimulus set; (c) whether the two dimensions are perceived relatively independently; and (d) whether individual differences in attention to the dimensions emerge. In the next section, we describe this process.

Overall, the stimulus development process aims to construct a set of stimuli that both represents the real-world variability along the dimensions of greatest theoretical interest and controls or constrains the real-world variability along the dimensions of least theoretical interest. This frequently necessitates construction of a stimulus set from scratch, because preexisting stimuli often fail to meet these criteria. In our experience, this process is time consuming but invaluable, because the validity and precision of all inferences about attention to, classification of, memory for, and learning about the theoretical dimensions of interest depend to a significant extent on the adequacy of the stimulus set.

PERCEPTUAL ORGANIZATION

Perceptual organization (PO) refers to the representation and organization of incoming stimuli in terms of their perceived similarity and dissimilarity. Numerous theoretical perspectives in clinical psychology are consistent with the perspective that psychopathology is determined or maintained partly by features of participants' POs, such as attention to stimulus dimensions, the perceived association between stimulus dimensions, and the organization of stimulus dimensions as discrete versus continuous (e.g., Beck, 1976; Kelly, 1955). The class of cognitive models of interest in this chapter treats participants' POs as representational bases for the operation of other higher order cognitive processes, such as classification, memory, and learning (Kruschke, 1992; Kruschke & Johansen, 1999; Nosofsky, 1991, 1992a, 1992b). For example, the process models outlined in subsequent sections predict that participants (a) should classify a presented stimulus into a category containing the most similar members, (b) should recognize a presented stimulus as previously viewed when it is highly similar to previously stored stimuli, and (c) should learn a category structure based on a particular stimulus feature more quickly when stimuli in different categories are perceived to be very dissimilar and stimuli in the same category are perceived to be very similar.

PO frequently is assessed using a similarity-rating paradigm, in which participants judge the similarity of pairs of stimuli on a scale anchored by *very different* and *very similar*. Participants are told that there are no right or wrong answers and usually are encouraged to respond quickly with their first impression rather than to deliberate extensively about their decisions. This task provides a relatively implicit assessment of participants' POs, because it neither specifies the stimulus attributes of interest nor directs participants to attend to particular stimulus attributes. In an alternative paradigm, participants judge as quickly as possible whether presented pairs of stimuli are the same or different; in this case, either participants' judgments or their reaction times can be submitted for subsequent analysis (Nosofsky, 1992b). Given the distinctiveness and complexity of the stimuli of interest to clinical researchers, this latter paradigm may prove to be less useful in applied contexts.

MDS analyses of participants' similarity ratings provide a spatial representation of participants' PO or *psychological space*, in which the perceived similarity between two stimuli, δ_{ij}, is modeled as a decreasing function of the distance, d_{ij}, between the perceived values of two stimuli, x_i and x_j (Davison, 1992; Treat et al., 2002). Thus, two stimuli that are judged to be very similar are scaled much closer in the psychological space than two stimuli that are judged to be very dissimilar (see Figure 6.1). The upper left-hand panel of Figure 6.1 presents the group psychological space of 24 photo stimuli that portray women who vary along facial-affect and body-size dimensions. Stimuli A and B, which were judged to be very similar, are scaled close together. In contrast, both stimuli are judged to be very dissimilar to stimulus C, which is scaled far away from stimuli A and B.

Metric scaling approaches assume that the function relating similarity and distance decreases linearly, whereas less restrictive nonmetric approaches assume only that this function decreases monotonically. Distances typically are computed using a Euclidean metric (i.e., $r = 2$ in Equation 6.1) when the M stimulus dimensions are processed more holistically, or integrally. In contrast, a city-block metric (i.e., $r = 1$) is assumed when the M stimulus dimensions are perceived more distinctively or separably (Nosofsky & Palmeri, 1996; Shepard, 1964). In our experience, the correct metric for the more complex, ecologically valid stimulus sets of interest to clinical researchers often lies between these two extremes. Thus, it may prove useful for researchers to estimate this parameter rather than fixing it at either 1.0 or 2.0:

$$d_{ij} = \left[\sum_{m=1}^{M} (x_{im} - x_{jm})^r \right]^{1/r}. \tag{6.1}$$

In the weighted MDS (WMDS) model, which also is known as the *individual differences scaling* (INDSCAL) model, individual differences in the k participants' similarity ratings, δ_{ijk}, are modeled as a decreasing function of interstimulus distances, d_{ijk} (Carroll & Chang, 1970). These distances vary as a function of individual differences in the participant-specific weighting of the M stimulus dimensions, w_{mk}, as specified in Equation 6.2:

$$d_{ijk} = \left[\sum_{m=1}^{M} w_{mk}(x_{im} - x_{jm})^r \right]^{1/r}. \tag{6.2}$$

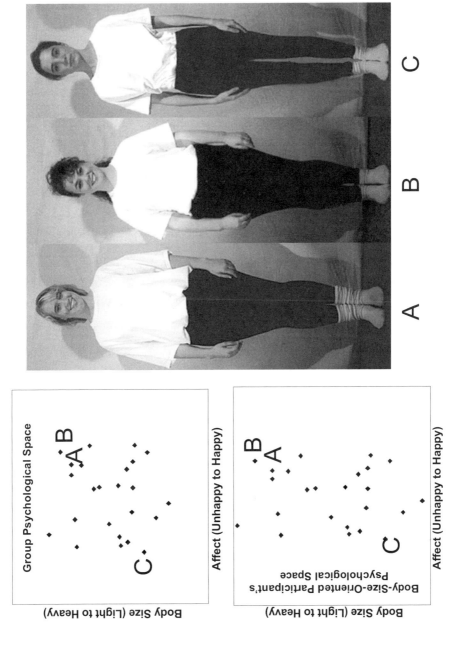

Figure 6.1. Multidimensional scaling representation of perceptual organizations of group and body-size-oriented participant.

Conceptually, these attention weights stretch and shrink the M dimensions of the group psychological space. The psychological space of a participant who attends much more to body size than to facial affect is presented in the lower left-hand panel of Figure 6.1. The large attention weight for body size increases the distance between the heavier and lighter photo stimuli, which reflects this participant's perception that heavier and lighter stimuli are very dissimilar to one another. In contrast, the small attention weight for affect shrinks the distance between the happier and sadder stimuli, consistent with the participant's judgment that happier and sadder stimuli are not particularly dissimilar. A particularly nice feature of the WMDS model is its simultaneous representation of both group- and participant-specific aspects of PO: Both the dimensions spanning the psychological space and the organization of the stimuli within each dimension are assumed to be shared by participants, whereas the relative attention to or importance of each dimension is allowed to vary across participants.

We have used the WMDS model to test hypotheses about clinically relevant individual differences in dimensional attention (Treat, McFall, Viken, & Kruschke, 2001, 2006; Viken et al., 2002; for an alternative approach to the evaluation of dimensional attention, cf. chap. 4, this volume). Within the realm of eating disorders, we have demonstrated that undergraduate women who report clinically significant symptoms of bulimia nervosa, compared with undergraduate women who report no bulimic symptoms, exhibit relatively greater attention to other women's body size than to their facial affect. Within the realm of sexual aggression, we have found that undergraduate men who display relatively greater attention to women's physical exposure (i.e., the extent to which the woman's clothing is revealing) than to women's facial affect (i.e., sad vs. happy) also construe the continuation of sexual advances toward an uninterested woman as more justifiable than men who attend relatively more to women's affect than exposure.

The WMDS model of participants' POs assumes that all participants organize the information within the dimensions to which they attend in the same way. Alternative MDS models of participants' POs, however, could be used to evaluate hypotheses about clinically relevant individual differences in the organization of stimuli within a dimension. For example, women who report eating-disorder symptoms might represent body-size information in a more discrete fashion as heavy or light, whereas control participants might perceive body size as varying more continuously. Evaluating this kind of research question typically would entail comparing the estimates of stimulus coordinates across individual-specific MDS solutions. Individual-specific MDS models estimate far more parameters than the WMDS model from the same amount of data, however. The resulting parameter estimates, therefore, likely will be very imprecise at the individual-participant level unless each participant provides more than one set of similarity ratings. Fortunately, Lee and Pope (2003) recently proposed a promising Bayesian model-fitting strategy that addresses these difficulties when analyzing all participants' data simultaneously by identifying subgroups of participants who share similar spatial representations of the stimuli and then estimating a separate MDS solution for each subgroup.

The WMDS model also assumes that participants perceive the stimulus dimensions to be uncorrelated (e.g., perception of body size is unrelated to perception of facial affect). A generalization of the WMDS model relaxes this constraint and allows investigators to characterize simultaneously both individual differences in dimensional attention and individual differences in the perceived correlation between dimensions (Tucker, 1972). It might be of interest, for example, to evaluate whether women with eating disorders, relative to control participants, perceive a stronger negative correlation between body size and affect, such that heavier women are perceived to be less happy and lighter women are perceived to be more happy. The same model could be used to evaluate whether sexually aggressive men perceive a stronger positive correlation between women's sexual interest and the provocativeness of women's dress than do control participants, whereby more provocatively dressed women are perceived to be more sexually interested and less provocatively dressed women are perceived to be less sexually interested.

All of the MDS models discussed to this point can be characterized as deterministic, because they model the location of stimuli in participants' psychological space as a single fixed point (i.e., stimulus values are assumed to be the same across trials). In contrast, probabilistic scaling approaches assume that the perceived value of the stimuli in psychological space fluctuates from trial to trial and represent stimulus locations as a multivariate normal distribution of values. MacKay and colleagues (MacKay & Zinnes, 1986; Zinnes & MacKay, 1992) have demonstrated that deterministic methods recover systematically biased estimates of stimulus coordinates whenever stimulus values are perceived variably, either across or within persons, and whenever stimuli are highly confusable. Under these circumstances, deterministic models tend to provide more extreme estimates of stimulus coordinates, such that high-variability stimuli are scaled toward the exterior of the psychological space (Zinnes & MacKay, 1992). Treat et al. (2002) demonstrated the potential incremental utility of probabilistic methods under more clinically relevant conditions by juxtaposing deterministic and probabilistic solutions for men's perceptual organizations of women after the men had consumed and absorbed either an alcoholic or a placebo beverage. Deterministic and probabilistic solutions differed markedly for men in the alcohol condition, in particular, as would be expected given the greater perceptual variability presumably induced by alcohol consumption. In particular, dimensions were more difficult to interpret in the deterministic solutions, and the estimated configurations were characterized by a large empty space in the interior of the scaling solutions. Additionally, perceptual variability was significantly greater in the alcohol condition than in the placebo condition, and estimates of perceptual variability for each stimulus along the dimensions of "appeal" and "provocativeness" varied in a predictable fashion (e.g., seminude women were perceived homogeneously along the provocativeness dimension but heterogeneously along the appeal dimension).

Probabilistic MDS methods show clear incremental utility for mapping participants' psychological spaces whenever marked inter- or intraindividual perceptual variability either is assumed to be present or is of particular theoretical interest. These methods not only provide increased confidence in the accuracy of the estimated stimulus configuration but also estimate the magnitude of inter- or intraindividual perceptual variability, which also may interest clinical researchers. Additionally, probabilistic approaches allow much more statistically rigorous hypothesis testing about the ideal dimensionality for scaling solutions and the equivalence of stimulus coordinates or variances than typically is possible when using deterministic methods (Zinnes & MacKay, 1992). The greater complexity of probabilistic models, however, places greater demands on the similarity-ratings data. As a result, currently available versions of probabilistic scaling methods do not estimate individual differences parameters, such as dimensional attention weights or interdimensional correlations. Additionally, replicated ratings are necessary for precise parameter estimation in individual-specific analyses.

In the subsequent sections of this chapter, we introduce a class of theoretical, measurement, and analytical models developed by cognitive scientists to account for classification, memory, and learning processes. These models account simultaneously for the operation of very different processes partly by positing a shared spatial representation of participants' perceptual organizations (Nosofsky, 1992b). Thus, using similarity-scaling models to map participants' psychological spaces not only allows clinical researchers to evaluate clinically relevant questions about participants' POs but also sets the stage for theoretically coherent and analytically rigorous investigations of research questions about other higher order cognitive processes.

IMPLICIT CLASSIFICATION

Implicit classification refers to the placement of stimuli into categories without experimenter instruction as to the stimulus characteristics on which to base classifications or feedback about the accuracy of classifications. Whereas identification entails the assignment of a different category label to each stimulus, classification involves the assignment of the same category label to multiple stimuli. Thus, classification involves treating different stimuli within the psychological space as functionally equivalent. When women are classified as "heavy" or "light," for example, the variation in body size that occurs within each category is ignored.

Individual differences in the basis for implicit classifications should be of interest to clinical researchers, because different behavioral responses to stimuli may be secondary to variation in partitioning of the psychological space. In a current ongoing study, for example, college-age men have classified undergraduate women depicted in photos as "likely to be responsive to sexual advances" or "not likely to be responsive to sexual advances." The women in the photos have varied orthogonally along two dimensions that may be relevant to men's classifications: (a) the provocativeness of the woman's clothing and (b) the woman's affect (i.e., the extent to which she is communicating strong sexual interest or strong sexual disinterest by means of her facial expression or body posture). In an alternative paradigm, the prototype-classification task, participants might classify stimuli as an example of one of two types of stimuli that vary along two orthogonal stimulus dimensions (Cohen & Massaro, 1992). In the current study, one type of woman might be represented by a sexually interested and provocatively dressed woman, whereas the other type of woman might be represented by an angry woman who is not dressed provocatively. Either paradigm could be used to assess individual differences in college men's sensitivity or attention to these two dimensions when judging a woman's responsiveness, which may contribute to individual differences in the extent to which college men exhibit sexually aggressive behavior.

To date, we have relied primarily on the prototype-classification task to assess individual differences in participants' sensitivity or attention to underlying dimensions. In a recent study that examined the role of classification processes in eating disorders, participants first viewed a "Type A woman," who was normatively sad and heavy, and a "Type B woman," who was happy and light (Viken et al., 2002). See Figure 6.2 for an example of similar prototypes. Participants then classified each of the remaining stimuli as more similar to a Type A or a Type B woman. As when completing the similarity-ratings paradigm, participants were urged to respond quickly, because their first impressions were of primary interest to the experimenter.

According to Nosofsky's (1987) weighted prototype model, individual differences in participants' classification patterns partially reflect individual differences in participants' sensitivity or attention to the underlying dimensions. Suppose, for example, that a participant must classify a normatively sad and light woman, labeled stimulus i in Figure 6.2. Classification of

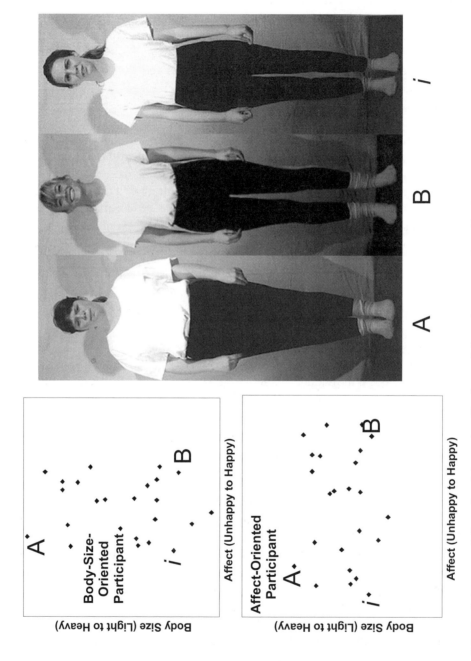

Figure 6.2. Spatial representation of prototype-classification task from the perspective of body-size-oriented and affect-oriented participants. Photos A and B are two prototypes, and stimulus *i* is to be presented.

stimulus i as a Type A woman suggests greater attention to affect, whereas classification as a Type B woman suggests greater attention to body size. Put more formally, the probability of classifying stimulus i as a member of Category A, or $P(A|i)$ in Equation 6.3, is modeled as a function of the bias-weighted relative perceived similarity of stimulus i to Prototypes A and B, or η_{iA} and η_{iB}:

$$P(A|i) = \frac{\beta_A \eta_{iA}}{\beta_A \eta_{iA} + (1-\beta_A)\eta_{iB}}, \; \eta_{iA} = e^{-cd_{iA}}, \; d_{iA} = \left(\sum_{m=1}^{M} w_m(x_{im} - x_{jm})^r \right)^{1/r}.$$

$$(6.3)$$

Perceived similarity is assumed to be an exponentially decreasing function of the weighted distance between stimulus i and the relevant prototype, or $-cd_{iA}$, where c indicates the overall level of stimulus discriminability. As in the previous distance formula, x_i and x_j specify the stimulus coordinates, M refers to the stimulus dimension, and w_m indicates dimensional attention. Biases in the use of the category responses, β_A and β_B, quantify participants' relative use of the two response categories. Thus, as illustrated in Figure 6.2, the probability of classifying stimulus i as a member of Category A will be large when stimulus i is perceived to be very similar to Prototype A and very dissimilar to Prototype B, because the distance between stimulus i and Prototype A will be much shorter than the distance between stimulus i and Prototype B. If a participant also uses the two category responses at a similar rate (i.e., β_A and β_B have similar values), then $P(A|i)$ will approach 1.0.

Viken et al. (2002) recently used Nosofsky's (1987) weighted prototype classification model to evaluate rigorously the hypothesis that a group of college women who reported clinically significant bulimic symptoms, relative to a group of control participants, would base their implicit classifications of other women relatively more on their body size than on their facial affect. In other words, we anticipated that a model specifying group-specific estimates of dimensional attention, or w_m, would fit bulimics' and control participants' classification patterns significantly better than a model that specified a shared estimate of dimensional attention across groups. The former model generalized the latter model (i.e., it adds a parameter to an otherwise identical set of parameters), so we were able to evaluate this hypothesis using nested model-comparison techniques (Wickens, 1989). As expected, the fit of the model to the data improved significantly when dimensional attention was assumed to be group specific but not when the remaining parameters were assumed to be group specific. Inspection of parameter estimates indicated that bulimic participants, compared with control participants, attended relatively more to body size than to facial affect.

The theoretical, measurement, and process models of implicit classification presented in this section could be used widely to examine clinically relevant questions about the role of classification processes in psychopathology. Group differences in dimensional attention estimates were of primary interest to Viken et al. (2002), because the implicit nature of the prototype-classification task tended to elicit highly homogeneous use of the response categories across participants (i.e., response bias estimates were nearly identical for the two categories). Response bias estimates should exhibit much greater variability in an explicit prototype-classification task, however. Suppose, for example, that participants were instructed to base their classifications on the women's body size. In this case, group differences in dimensional attention should decrease sharply, because both groups would direct their attention to body size, but group differences in response bias estimates should reflect bulimic participants' less frequent use of the category exemplified by the thinner woman. Alternatively, we might examine individual differences in the extent to which men's explicit classifications of women's affect are influenced by the provocativeness of women's dress. The extent to which men attend to women's provocativeness, even when directed to attend to their affect, should increase the likelihood of their exhibiting sexually aggressive behavior. Overall, the models presented in this section provide a flexible approach to examination of a variety of questions about the role of implicit and explicit classification processes in psychopathology.

RECOGNITION MEMORY

Recognition memory refers to the observer's classification of stimuli as previously viewed or not. Cognitive scientists typically refer to this memory process as *explicit*, because participants are instructed to indicate whether they remember viewing the stimuli previously. Individual differences in explicit memory for stimulus features interest clinical researchers because such differences presumably contribute to clinically relevant variability in behavioral responses to stimuli. For example, college men who exhibit excellent memory for the provocativeness of women's dress but poor memory for women's affect should be at higher risk of exhibiting behavior that is judged to be sexually inappropriate or aggressive, because they are acting on the basis of incomplete or distorted information. Similarly, college women who struggle with problematic eating patterns may experience interpersonal difficulties or construe thinness as a royal road to happiness partially because they retain impoverished or erroneous information about the affect and happiness of other women.

Individual differences in explicit memory for stimulus attributes commonly are assessed in a recognition-memory task, in which participants first view, study, or are exposed to a subset of stimuli. Participants typically are not forewarned about the upcoming memory test or the relevant stimulus dimensions, but manipulations of these task features may be of theoretical interest to some researchers. At test, participants view both old stimuli and new stimuli that were not viewed previously. Participants classify each stimulus as old or new. Participants also may judge how confident they feel about these classifications. In a recently completed study (Treat, McFall, et al., 2006), college women first studied 28 photos of women who varied along body-size and facial-affect dimensions for 3 seconds apiece. Next, participants completed the prototype-classification task described above with the same 28 stimuli. Finally, participants viewed 56 photos of women and indicated whether they had seen the exact photo previously and how confident they were about their judgment by responding "definitely yes," "probably yes," "maybe yes," "maybe no," "probably no," or "definitely no." Half of the 56 photos were identical to those viewed previously; the remaining 28 photos showed the same woman, but either her affect or body size differed from the original (see Figure 6.3). Participants were told at the time of test that either "the look on her face" or "the shape of her body" might have been altered in each photo.

Signal-detection theory (SDT) methods (Macmillan & Creelman, 1991) commonly are used to quantify individual differences in participant memory—that is, individual differences in participants' abilities to detect the old signal in the presence of either new-affect or new-body-size noise (for an alternative approach to modeling recall and recognition-memory data, see chap. 2, this volume). In the present case, we fit an SDT model to the observed frequencies of each participant's confidence ratings for old, new-affect, and new-body-size stimuli. Table 6.1 provides the observed data for a participant who displayed excellent memory for affect, as indicated by her correct classification of most of the old stimuli (n = 28) as definitely or probably seen previously, as well as her classification of most of the new-affect stimuli (n = 14) as definitely or probably not seen previously. In contrast, her memory for body size was quite poor, as indicated by her inability to discriminate well between old and new body-size stimuli. The SDT model for recognition memory in this case, as illustrated in Figure 6.4, assumes that the stimuli are arrayed along a dimension of perceived familiarity. The stimuli are members of either the old, the new-affect, or the new-body-size distributions, which are assumed to be normal in form. Exemplars from the old distribution presumably provoke a greater sense of familiarity on average, so this distribution is placed to the right of the other distributions in the figure. The new-affect distribution is placed to the left of the new-body-size distribution to reflect our expectation that memory will be greater for affect than for body-size information. Five boundaries, which are represented by dashed lines in the figure, partition the familiarity dimension into the six confidence rating categories. On a given trial, a stimulus is assumed to evoke a particular value along the familiarity

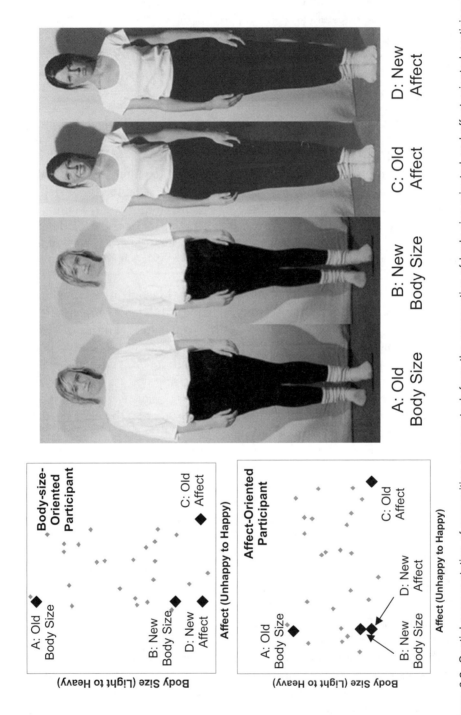

Figure 6.3. Spatial representation of recognition-memory task from the perspective of body-size-oriented and affect-oriented participants. "Old" photos were viewed by participants prior to the memory task; "new" photos presented during the memory task display the same women with opposite values along either the body-size or facial-affect dimensions.

TABLE 6.1

Data Structure and Sample Frequency Data for Recognition-Memory Task

Photo classification	Participant response to "Have you seen this EXACT PHOTO before?"					
	Definitely yes	Probably yes	Maybe yes	Maybe no	Probably no	Definitely no
Old	6	8	8	4	2	0
New affect	0	1	2	2	4	5
New body size	3	3	2	3	2	1

dimension and then is classified into the category associated with that value of familiarity. For example, presentation of a previously viewed woman with a startlingly different facial expression might provoke an extremely low feeling of familiarity that does not clear even the lowest boundary between "definitely no" and "probably no." Hence, the participant would respond "definitely no."

Fitting the SDT model to each participant's frequency data entails using maximum-likelihood methods to estimate the means and standard deviations of the two new distributions, because the mean and standard

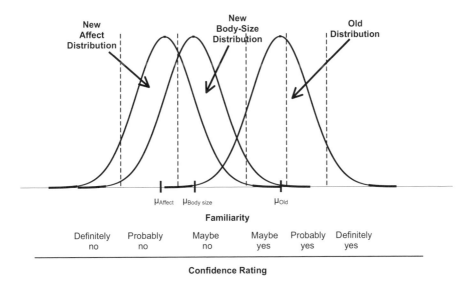

Figure 6.4. Signal-detection theory model for recognition-memory task, in which participants judge how confident they are that they have seen the exact photo previously. Stimuli from the "old" distribution were viewed by participants prior to the memory task; stimuli from the "new" distributions portray the same women with opposing values along either the body-size or facial-affect dimensions and are assumed to evoke a weaker feeling of familiarity. See text for further details.

APPLYING QUANTITATIVE MODELS OF COGNITIVE PROCESSING   195

deviation of the old distribution can be fixed at 0.0 and 1.0, respectively. The locations of the five boundaries separating the confidence regions also are estimated. Given these parameter estimates, the standardized distance between the mean of the old distribution and the mean of one of the new distributions indicates the strength of a participant's memory for either affect or body-size information. In spite of the sparseness of individual participants' data and the relatively large number of estimated parameters, individual differences in memory for body size and affect correlated reliably with women's self-reported symptoms of eating disorders. Relative to control participants, college women who reported clinically significant symptoms of eating disorders showed significantly and substantially impaired memory for affect information, consistent with their markedly decreased attention to affect in the prototype-classification task. In contrast, control participants and high-symptom participants showed similar levels of memory for body-size information, even though high-symptom participants showed significantly greater attention to body-size information than did control participants in the prototype-classification task. This finding suggests that future research should explore whether high-symptom participants, relative to low-symptom participants, store or retrieve body-size information differently or show decreased attention to body-size information during the recognition-memory task.

The SDT model is a commonly used process model of recognition memory in clinical research, as it specifies the decision-making processes that operate on the feeling of familiarity evoked by each stimulus to produce participant responses. The SDT model does not specify the representational and memory processes that give rise to the feeling of familiarity, however. In contrast, Nosofsky's (1991, 1992a, 1992b) process model of recognition memory emphasizes the central role of stimulus representation and memory processes in producing participant perceptions of stimulus familiarity, or F_i in Equation 6.4. Nosofsky's model operates on the stimulus similarities implied by the participant's psychological space and formalizes the notion that a stimulus presented at test, i, will tend to be recognized as old when its summed similarity to all J stimuli previously stored in memory, F_i, clears an estimated threshold. In the memory model in Equation 6.4, S_j refers to the strength with which stimulus j is stored in memory. As in the classification model described above, the similarity of the presented stimulus to each stored stimulus, η_{ij}, is modeled as an exponentially decreasing function of the dimensionally weighted distance between the two stimuli, d_{ij}:

$$F_i = \sum_{j=1}^{J} S_j \eta_{ij}, \ \eta_{ij} = e^{-cd_{ij}}, \ d_{ij} = \left(\sum_{m=1}^{M} w_m (x_{im} - x_{jm})^r \right)^{1/r}. \qquad (6.4)$$

Figure 6.3 illustrates the psychological space of the previously stored stimuli as well as the location of two new stimuli for both body-size and affect-oriented participants. Note that the Euclidean distance between the relevant old and the new stimulus—or the perceived dissimilarity of the relevant old and the new stimulus—varies markedly for these 2 participants. In particular, the distance between these stimuli is much greater when the altered dimension is the focus of attention for the participants (e.g., the distance between old- and new-affect stimuli is much greater for affect-oriented participants than for body-size-oriented participants). According to Equation 6.4, this increased distance translates into decreased similarity, which leads to a feeling of decreased familiarity, other things being equal. Thus, a body-size-oriented participant should perceive new affect stimuli to be more familiar than an affect-oriented participant. We anticipate that when we fit this model to our recently collected memory data, we should be able to account for the marked group differences in memory for affect by allowing w_{affect} to be significantly smaller and different for the women who report clinically significant symptoms of eating disorders. In a similar study examining individual differences in men's perceptions of women, we anticipate that men who exhibit sexually aggressive behavior will show deficient memory for women's affect that can be attributed to their significantly reduced attention to women's affect.

Clinical scientists could use the process model of recognition memory described above to address a wide variety of research questions about the role of explicit memory processes in psychopathology. To date, we have focused on the role of dimensional attention in accounting for group differences in recognition memory. Research questions also might focus on clinically relevant variability in other parameters, however, such as the estimated cutoffs for old–new or confidence-rating judgments, which capture individual differences in how conservatively or liberally participants use the response categories, and the memory strengths for individual stimuli or for stimuli in particular regions of the psychological space, which represent individual differences in the strength with which stimuli are stored in memory. Additionally, clinical researchers may be interested in the impact of various instructional manipulations on memory processes, as they move researchers in the direction of considering how to ameliorate problematic memory deficits. In the described study, participants were not told anything about the relevant stimulus attributes or the upcoming memory task. Future research should determine which (if any) of the following three manipulations improve high-symptom women's memory for affect substantially: (a) noting that the stimuli vary along affect and body-size dimensions before having participants study the stimuli; (b) alerting participants before they study the stimuli about the existence of an upcoming memory task for unnamed stimulus features; or (c) directing participants' attention, before they familiarize themselves with the stimuli, to the two relevant stimulus attributes for which memory will be assessed later. Thus, the theoretical, measurement, and analytical models presented in this section can be used to evaluate a plethora of research questions about the role of recognition memory processes in psychopathology.

CATEGORY LEARNING

In contrast to implicit classification, *category learning* refers to the placement of stimuli into categories with feedback about the accuracy of classification, although experimenter instruction about the stimulus characteristics on which to base classifications typically remains absent. Evaluating individual differences in category learning about clinically relevant information should prove to be of particular interest to clinical researchers, for several reasons. First, this approach facilitates investigations of individual differences in more dynamic aspects of cognitive processing, which may afford incremental prediction of clinical difficulties above and beyond more static characterizations of processing. For example, Viken et al. (2002) demonstrated previously that body-size-oriented women, who exhibit relatively greater attention to other women's body size than to facial affect, are more likely to report clinically significant symptoms of eating disorders. Body-size-oriented women presumably would exhibit variability in how rapidly they learn a simple affect category structure, however, in which happy women are in one category and sad women are in another. In this case, individual differences in how rapidly participants could learn an affect category structure might be more diagnostic of eating difficulties than individual differences in their pre-existing perceptual organizations.

Second, fitting formal process models of category learning to participants' observed data (e.g., their trial-by-trial responses) affords examination of the relative importance of various mechanisms that are hypothesized to underlie learning. Investigation of the processes underlying learning ultimately should facilitate the development of more targeted and efficient treatment approaches. Finally, category-learning paradigms may provide an alternative approach to cognitive therapy that draws on experimental cognitive psychology to retrain or modify deficient cognitive processing. Current cognitively oriented treatments rely on verbally mediated techniques that emphasize the identification and modification of specific maladaptive thoughts and beliefs. Using the tools of contemporary cognitive science, we may be able to develop performance-based interventions that target specific deficits in cognitive processing. For example, a new form of cognitive therapy might entail using learning paradigms to retrain attentional patterns, speed the gradual acquisition of relevant category structures, or facilitate attention shifting to relevant stimulus features under high-risk conditions.

Treat et al. (2001) illustrated the use of a category-learning task to assess individual differences in men's cognitive processing of the physical appearance and perceived affect of women. A stimulus set containing 26 photos of women from newsstand magazines varied along two dimensions of primary theoretical interest: women's physical exposure and women's facial affect. College men viewed one photo at a time, classified it as a member of one of two categories with arbitrary labels (e.g., "Category F" and "Category J"), and received feedback on the accuracy of their classifications (e.g., "Correct! She is a member of Category J"). Participants were told that initially they would be guessing, and they were not told the basis for the feedback. Participants also were told that the basis for the feedback might change during the course of the task and that they should attempt to learn the new category labels for the stimuli if this occurred. Participants first completed four blocks of either an exposure or affect category structure. In the affect category structure, for example, women exhibiting positive affect were in Category F, and women exhibiting negative affect were in Category J. After an unannounced shift to the other category structure, participants completed an additional four blocks of training. Before the category-learning task, participants had completed a similarity-ratings task with a subset of the stimuli, which allowed the experimenters to classify participants' perceptual organizations as either exposure oriented or affect oriented. As expected, exposure-oriented participants performed better at learning the exposure category structure than did affect-oriented participants, whereas affect-oriented participants performed better at learning the affect category structure. In other words, participants learned a category structure much more rapidly when it was congruent with their underlying perceptual organization.

Fitting formal process models of category learning to participants' observed data (e.g., their trial-by-trial responses) affords examination of the relative importance of various mechanisms that are hypothesized to underlie participants' observed responses. To date, we have relied on process models developed by Kruschke and colleagues (Kruschke, 1992; Kruschke & Johansen, 1999), because they also treat a spatial representation of participants' psychological space as the primitive, as do Nosofsky's (1987, 1991, 1992a, 1992b) prototype-classification and memory models. We fit Kruschke and Johansen's (1999) "rapid attention shifts 'n' learning" (RASHNL) model to the learning data described above, so that we could evaluate the importance of three potential influences on participants' learning and group differences in participants' learning (for explication of another formal quantitative approach to examination of category-learning processes, see chap. 4, this volume).

The first mechanism of interest, initial differences in relative attention to the psychological dimensions of physical exposure and facial affect, may facilitate or inhibit learning a particular category structure, depending on their congruence with the structure to be learned. For example, affect-oriented participants should be at a relative advantage over exposure-oriented participants when learning the affect category structure, because they perceive stimuli in the same category to be relatively more similar than stimuli in different categories. The second mechanism, shifting attention toward relevant dimensions and away from irrelevant dimensions, suggests that participants learn category structures by modifying their perceptual organization to be more consistent with the demands of the category structure. In other words, exposure-oriented participants could learn the affect category structure by increasing their attention to affect and decreasing their attention to exposure, thus modifying their perceptual organization to make it similar to that of the affect-oriented participant. This shift in dimensional attention would enhance the relatively greater perceived similarity of stimuli in the same category to stimuli in different categories. The third mechanism attributes participant learning to strengthened associations between regions of the psychological space and correct category responses. Participants could learn the affect category structure, for example, by gradually mapping the region of the psychological space that contains women displaying positive affect to the "F" response and the region of the psychological space that contains women exhibiting negative affect to the "J" response.

We fit the RASHNL model (Kruschke & Johansen, 1999) to the proportion-correct values of the exposure- and affect-oriented groups on each of the eight blocks in the learning task to evaluate the relative importance of these three mechanisms to participants' learning. Preliminary model fits indicated that participants perceived the stimulus dimensions in a holistic rather than a separable fashion, so the Euclidean metric was used to define interstimulus distances in the remaining analyses. As expected, the best-fitting RASHNL model necessitated retention of a group-specific estimate of initial differences in relative attention, with exposure-oriented participants showing significantly greater relative attention to exposure than to affect compared with the affect-oriented participants. This finding is consistent with the results of the initial statistical analyses of the observed data that we described above; however, fitting a process model to the data also provided group-specific estimates of relative attention to the psychological dimensions of interest.

Although extensive evidence supports a role for attention shifting in category learning within cognitive science, the best-fitting RASHNL model suggested that shifting attention toward relevant dimensions and away from irrelevant dimensions did not play a role in participants' learning. The "stickiness" of participants' perceptual organizations may be attributable in part to participants' more holistic processing of the stimulus dimensions, which increases the difficulty of shifting attention toward or away from specific dimensions (Nosofsky & Palmeri, 1996). Finally, the RASHNL modeling indicated that learning to map regions of the psychological space to the correct category label played a central but not group-specific role in participants' acquisition of the category structures. This association-learning mechanism produces more gradual, incremental improvement in performance than the attention-shifting mechanism.

The ability to shift attention to newly relevant stimulus information is highly adaptive under some conditions, such as when a person needs to shift attention away from a potential sexual partner's physical exposure or sexual characteristics and toward the partner's expressions of sexual interest. Thus, it may prove fruitful to develop novel treatment strategies that use category-learning paradigms therapeutically to modify problematic attention patterns. The present findings are somewhat discouraging in this regard, because the RASHNL model fits suggested that participants did not learn by optimizing their dimensional attention patterns. Participants' more integral processing of the stimulus dimensions presumably rendered attention shifting more difficult, but this will be a commonly occurring feature of the more complex stimulus sets of interest to clinical researchers. Thus, future research should investigate the learning conditions under which participants' perceptual organizations exhibit greater flexibility and malleability, even when the stimulus dimensions are perceived more holistically.

This extended presentation of Treat et al.'s (2001) category-learning study was intended to illustrate the potential utility of investigating clinically relevant category-learning processes as well as using formal process models to characterize the operation of mechanisms hypothesized to underlie both normal and abnormal learning patterns. This study relied on a relatively simple category-learning task, in which each category structure was based on a single dimension and a single unannounced shift to a new category structure occurred, but more complex associative-learning paradigms (e.g., forward- and backward-blocking paradigms, learned-inhibition paradigms) also should prove useful to clinical researchers. In a recently completed study using a more complex paradigm, for example, Treat, Kruschke, and McFall (2006) demonstrated that learning a category structure based on an initially irrelevant dimension is strikingly more difficult after learning a category structure based on an initially relevant dimension. In this study, a significant subgroup of body-size-oriented women were unable to learn an affect category structure (happy vs. sad) after learning a body-size category structure (heavy vs. light), although all body-size-oriented women were able to learn an affect category structure when it was presented first. Future research will examine whether women who struggle with eating-disorder symptoms are overrepresented in this subgroup, because deficient processing of affective information may help to account for the marked interpersonal and emotion-regulation difficulties that frequently characterize this population.

Additionally, Treat et al.'s (2001) study provided deterministic feedback to participants (i.e., each stimulus always received the same feedback within a particular category structure). The administration of probabilistic feedback (e.g., each stimulus might receive the same feedback 80% of the time) provides a much more externally valid approximation of real-world feedback, such as women's responses to sexual advances or women's feelings about themselves, which rarely are perfectly consistent across occasions. Thus, it should prove useful to characterize individual differences in participants' learning about clinically relevant information under more challenging probabilistic conditions.

CONCLUSION

In this chapter, we have provided an overview of an integrated class of cognitive science models that can be used to conceptualize, measure, and model clinically relevant individual differences in cognitive processing. The process models of classification, memory, and learning account simultaneously for performance on very different tasks by positing a shared representational substrate, which can be assessed using MDS methods (Nosofsky, 1992b). Thus, these models display a high degree of coherence and consistency across their theoretical, measurement, and analytical layers. Additionally, they afford examination of the mechanisms hypothesized to underlie observed task performance, which provides researchers with a much richer understanding of individual differences in the operation of the cognitive-processing system.

Several studies now have demonstrated the feasibility and utility of adopting this quantitative approach to clinical cognitive science, in which clinical scientists represent clinically relevant individual differences in cognitive processing within cognitive scientists' formal computational models by modifying parameter values or architectures (e.g., Busemeyer & Stout, 2002; Filoteo & Maddox, 1999; Neufeld et al., 2002; Treat et al., 2001, 2002; Viken et al., 2002). These studies highlight the generalizability of cognitive science theories, methods, and process models to more real-world circumstances, in which individual differences in the processing of socially complex information are the phenomenon of interest. These quantitative modeling efforts should advance clinical scientists' theories about cognitive influences on psychopathology, suggest novel intervention targets, and foster the development of novel forms of performance-based cognitive therapy.

REFERENCES

Beck, A. T. (1976). *Cognitive theory and the emotional disorders*. New York: International Universities Press.

Busemeyer, J. R., & Stout, J. D. (2002). A contribution of cognitive decision models to clinical assessment: Decomposing performance on the Bechara gambling task. *Psychological Assessment, 14*, 253–262.

Carroll, J. D., & Chang, J. J. (1970). Analysis of individual differences in multidimensional scaling via an N-way generalization of "Eckart–Young" decomposition. *Psychometrika, 35*, 283–320.

Cohen, M. M., & Massaro, D. W. (1992). On the similarity of categorization models. In F. G. Ashby (Ed.), *Multidimensional models of perception and cognition* (pp. 395–447). Hillsdale, NJ: Erlbaum.

Davison, M. L. (1992). *Multidimensional scaling*. Malabar, FL: Krieger.

Filoteo, J. V., & Maddox, W. T. (1999). Quantitative modeling of visual attention processes in patients with Parkinson's disease: Effects of stimulus integrality on selective attention and dimensional integration. *Neuropsychology, 13*, 206–222.

Kelly, G. A. (1955). *The psychology of personal constructs*. New York: Norton.

Knight, R. A., & Silverstein, S. M. (2001). A process-oriented approach for averting confounds resulting from general performance deficiencies in schizophrenia. *Journal of Abnormal Psychology, 110*, 15–30.

Kruschke, J. K. (1992). ALCOVE: An exemplar-based connectionist model of category learning. *Psychological Review, 99*, 22–44.

Kruschke, J. K., & Johansen, M. K. (1999). A model of probabilistic category learning. *Journal of Experimental Psychology: Learning, Memory, and Cognition, 25*, 1083–1119.

Lee, M. D., & Pope, K. J. (2003). Avoiding the dangers of averaging across subjects when using multidimensional scaling. *Journal of Mathematical Psychology, 47*, 32–46.

MacKay, D. B., & Zinnes, J. L. (1986). A probabilistic model for the multidimensional scaling of proximity and preference data. *Marketing Science, 5*, 325–344.

MacLeod, C. (1993). Cognition in clinical psychology: Measures, methods or models? *Behaviour Change, 10*, 169–195.

Macmillan, N. A., & Creelman, C. D. (1991). *Detection theory: A user's guide*. Cambridge, England: Cambridge University Press.

McFall, R. M. (1990). The enhancement of social skills: An information-processing analysis. In W. L. Marshall & D. R. Laws (Eds.), *Handbook of sexual assault: Issues, theories, and treatment of the offender* (pp. 311–330). New York: Plenum Press.

McFall, R. M., & Townsend, J. T. (1998). Foundations of psychological assessment: Implications for cognitive assessment in clinical science. *Psychological Assessment, 10,* 316–330.

McFall, R. M., Treat, T. A., & Viken, R. J. (1998). Contemporary cognitive approaches to studying clinical problems. In D. K. Routh & R. J. DeRubeis (Eds.), *The science of clinical psychology: Accomplishments and future directions* (pp. 163–197). Washington, DC: American Psychological Association.

Neufeld, R. W. J., Vollick, D., Carter, J. R., Boksman, K., & Jetté, J. (2002). Application of stochastic modeling to the assessment of group and individual differences in cognitive functioning. *Psychological Assessment, 14,* 279–298.

Nosofsky, R. M. (1987). Attention and learning processes in the identification and categorization of integral stimuli. *Journal of Experimental Psychology: Learning, Memory, and Cognition, 13,* 87–108.

Nosofsky, R. M. (1991). Tests of an exemplar model for relating perceptual classification and recognition memory. *Journal of Experimental Psychology: Human Perception and Performance, 17,* 3–27.

Nosofsky, R. M. (1992a). Exemplar-based approach to relating categorization, identification, and recognition. In F. G. Ashby (Ed.), *Multidimensional models of perception and cognition* (pp. 363–393). Hillsdale, NJ: Erlbaum.

Nosofsky, R. M. (1992b). Similarity scaling and cognitive process models. *Annual Review of Psychology, 43,* 25–53.

Nosofsky, R. M., & Palmeri, T. J. (1996). Learning to classify integral-dimension stimuli. *Psychonomic Bulletin & Review, 3,* 222–226.

Schewe, P., & O'Donohue, W. (1993). Rape prevention: Methodological problems and new directions. *Clinical Psychology Review, 13,* 667–682.

Shepard, R. N. (1964). Attention and the metric structure of the stimulus space. *Journal of Mathematical Psychology, 1,* 54–87.

Treat, T. A., Kruschke, J. K., & McFall, R. M. (2006). *Individual differences in blocking of socially relevant information.* Manuscript in preparation.

Treat, T. A., McFall, R. M., Viken, R. J., & Kruschke, J. K. (2001). Using cognitive science methods to assess the role of social information processing in sexually coercive behavior. *Psychological Assessment, 13,* 549–565.

Treat, T. A., McFall, R. M., Viken, R. J., & Kruschke, J. K. (2006). *The role of attention, memory, and correlation-detection processes in eating disorders.* Manuscript in preparation.

Treat, T. A., McFall, R. M., Viken, R. J., Nosofsky, R. M., MacKay, D. B., & Kruschke, J. K. (2002). Assessing clinically relevant perceptual organization with multidimensional scaling techniques. *Psychological Assessment, 14,* 239–252.

Tucker, L. R. (1972). Relations between multidimensional scaling and three-mode factor analysis. *Psychometrika, 37,* 3–27.

Viken, R. J., Treat, T. A., Nosofsky, R. M., McFall, R. M., & Palmeri, T. (2002). Bulimics and controls' differential attention to and classification of body-size and affect stimulus information. *Journal of Abnormal Psychology, 111*, 598–609.

Vitousek, K. B. (1996). The current status of cognitive–behavioral models of anorexia nervosa and bulimia nervosa. In P. M. Salkovskis (Ed.), *Frontiers of cognitive therapy* (pp. 383–418). New York: Guilford Press.

Ward, T., Hudson, S. M., Johnston, L., & Marshall, W. L. (1997). Cognitive distortions in sex offenders: An integrative review. *Clinical Psychology Review, 17*, 479–507.

Wickens, T. D. (1989). *Multiway contingency tables analysis for the social sciences.* Hillsdale, NJ: Erlbaum.

Wilson, G. T. (1999). Cognitive behavior therapy for eating disorders: Progress and problems. *Behaviour Research and Therapy, 37*, S79–S95.

Zinnes, J. L., & MacKay, D. B. (1992). A probabilistic multidimensional scaling approach: Properties and procedures. In F. G. Ashby (Ed.), *Multidimensional models of perception and cognition* (pp. 35–60). Hillsdale, NJ: Erlbaum.

7

QUANTITATIVE RESPONSE TIME TECHNOLOGY FOR MEASURING COGNITIVE-PROCESSING CAPACITY IN CLINICAL STUDIES

RICHARD W. J. NEUFELD, JAMES T. TOWNSEND, AND JENNIFER JETTÉ

The dichotomy of automatic versus controlled processing has been of great importance in cognitive psychology (Hasher & Zacks, 1979; Schneider & Shiffrin, 1977; Shiffrin & Schneider, 1977; Treisman & Gormican, 1988). These concepts have often been defined more or less operationally rather than strictly in terms of theoretical constructs. Performance maintaining its efficiency as opposed to deteriorating as workload increases has been the norm. For instance, Schneider and Shiffrin (1977), in a massive study of these phenomena in the context of visual search, saw automatic processing as being associated with flat or almost-flat response time functions as the

Sources of support for this research included an operating grant from the Social Sciences and Humanities Research Council of Canada awarded to Richard W. J. Neufeld, operating grants from the Workplace Safety and Insurance Board and the Canadian Institutes of Health Research (Richard W. J. Neufeld, coinvestigator), a grant from the Canadian Institutes of Health Research New Emerging Teams Program (Richard W. J. Neufeld, coinvestigator), and Grant NIMH-R01 MH57717-04A1 from the National Institute of Mental Health awarded to James T. Townsend. We thank Teresa A. Treat, who served as action editor for this chapter.

visual display set size increased. Increasing response time functions indicated ordinary controlled, or *effortful*, processing.

Nonetheless, theoretically oriented processing concepts have been associated, sometimes relatively loosely, sometimes quite tightly, with the dichotomy at least since the publication of Schneider and Shiffrin's (1977) seminal work, which suggested multifaceted change in information processing over the course of repetition. From this viewpoint, automatic processing entails the processing of task elements in parallel (or synchronously) rather than in serial (or successively) and does not tax processing capacity, whereby an increase in task load does not incur deterioration in performance efficiency (speed and/or accuracy).

Controlled processing, furthermore, has been thought to be *self-terminating*, meaning that search can cease as soon as sufficient information for a correct response is acquired. Nonetheless, the incorporation of unnecessary elements can be allowed in the case of automatic processing, at least for selected paradigms (Schneider & Shiffrin, 1977; see also Kahneman & Chajczyk, 1983; Shiffrin, 1988). Processing of all items in a trial is referred to as *exhaustive processing*; thus, it can be seen that automatic processing demands the satisfaction of several criteria on processing dimensions (see, e.g., Townsend, 1974; Townsend & Ashby, 1983).

To be sure, domains of clinical investigation invoking all or part of this multidimensional construct have included cognition in schizophrenia (C. S. Carter, Robertson, Chaderjian, Celaya, & Nordahl, 1992; Gold, Wilk, McMahon, Buchanan, & Luck, 2003; Granholm, Asarnow, & Marder, 1996a, 1996b; Magaro, 1983; Narr, Green, Capetillo-Cunliffe, Toga, & Zaidel, 2003; Nuechterlein & Dawson, 1984), affective disorders (Hartlage, Alloy, Vázquez, & Dykman, 1993; MacLeod & Rutherford, 1998; Sheppard & Teasdale, 2000), addictions (Baxter & Hinson, 2001), and anxiety disorders (Brewin, 1989; Brewin, Dalgleish, & Joseph, 1996; Brewin & Holmes, 2003; Teachman & Woody, 2003), among others. Even the search for possible leads for improvements in psychotherapy has not been exempt (Kirsh & Lynn, 1999).

As stated previously, the primary constituents of the automatic and controlled–effortful characterization of cognitive performance entail architecture of the processing system, notably whether task elements are transacted in parallel or serial fashion, capacity, and termination criteria. These components nevertheless are intrinsically bound up with one another in the ways they affect performance, and as will be apparent in the following discourse, measurement of any one must take account of the others (Townsend & Ashby, 1983; Townsend & Wenger, 2004a).[1] Despite being

---

[1] Analyses addressing conflation of these constituents occurring to their informal treatment in clinical science were presented by Neufeld (1996).

closely interlaced, these components are separable in empirically tractable ways but not without a methodology rigorously grounded in quantitative theorizing.

In this chapter, we spotlight what arguably is the most prominent member of the above trio from the standpoint of clinical science and assessment-processing capacity. Applications in the clinical arena of methods for deciphering architecture have been taken up in a separate venue (Townsend, Fific, & Neufeld, in press).

Over the course of presentation, mathematically entrenched measures and their empirical estimates will be described: the capacity index, $H(t)$; the Capacity Ratio (CR); and the Capacity OR Coefficient, $C_o(t)$. $H(t)$ is a general measure of cognitive work done over a given time interval. It is launched from an axiomatic definition of the capacity concept and is linked to work and energy in physics. CR compares values of $H(t)$ between two conditions of processing, or between groups under study. It is very versatile and is useful for bringing to bear the assets of $H(t)$ on the ubiquitous assessment of capacity of clinical compared with control groups. $C_o(t)$ is used to characterize a processing system of interest with reference to a benchmark system—one whose efficiency in processing a given cognitive load is unchanged with an increase in load. The studied system's response to increased cognitive load is classified as expressing *limited capacity*, whereby efficiency decreases with increased load; *unlimited capacity*, whereby, like the benchmark system, efficiency remains unchanged; or *super capacity*, whereby efficiency actually increases with increased load. $C_o(t)$ can be especially useful in assessing the system of interest as it operates under normal circumstances and then to evaluate whether and how it is perturbed with psychopathology. Each of the above quantities is developed with respect to specific clinical data.

Specific definitions and estimation of $H(t)$ and CR now lead off. They are developed and then illustratively applied to a study of cognitive functioning of anxiety-prone individuals. The remaining index, $C_o(t)$, similarly is developed and then illustrated, this time with respect to memory search in schizophrenia. Along the way, we examine challenges of implementation in clinical science and avenues to potential resolution.

QUANTIFYING PROCESSING CAPACITY

A measure of cognitive-processing capacity is presented here. It is prescribed by formal theoretical developments addressed to task performance response times. The measure has the desirable features of being robust, in terms of transcending individual and task differences in latency distributions, and empirically tractable, in terms of being readily computable from obtained data. As part and parcel of derivations emanating from fundamental mathematical concepts (axioms and rigorous definitions and assumptions), such measures qualify as being mandated specifically by theory, resembling measurement practices of longer established sciences (Meehl, 1978; cf. McFall & Townsend, 1998). An added bonus turns out to be the construct validity with which formal theoretical measures are endowed, owing to the substantive properties derived from their analytical infrastructure (Braithwaite, 1968; cf. the "construct representation" of Embretson, 1983).[2]

We begin by describing summary depictions of probability distributions (i.e., frequency functions) of events—in this case, cognitive process completions. That is, some type of cognitive task is performed, typically on a set of entities that can be perceptual or more cognitive, as in memory search. These distributions represent the quantitative building blocks of the present capacity index, $H(t)$. They also capture the essence of latency in its roles as dependent variable and performance index in studies of cognition generally. In this treatment, performance inaccuracy is deemed to be inconsequential, that is, relatively low, and not aligned with latency in ways that compromise inferences drawn from the latter (see, e.g., Townsend & Wenger, 2004a). Note that the distributions being characterized are both stochastic and dynamical, features of theory again earmarking longer established sciences (e.g., Penrose, 2004).

DISTRIBUTION PROPERTIES AND THEIR ROLES IN DEFINING THE CAPACITY INDEX: $H(t)$

Consider the completion of a cognitive task or task segment (process). The task, for example, may be one of memory search. The participant must detect the presence of a visually presented alphanumeric item (*probe item*) among a set of memorized items (*memory set*). Of course, the probe itself must somehow be transformed and prepared for the comparison process (*probe-item encoding*). Unless the interval between memory set presentation and presentation of the probe is very short, placement of the memory set in short-term memory should not influence the response times. The critical cognitive events, particularly the search through memory, obviously are not completed at the same point in time on every trial. Instead, completion times vary, and their relative frequencies produce a corresponding probability distribution. In the case of a continuous distribution, as a function of continuous time t, the frequency function is known as a *probability density function*,

---

[2] Such *ab initio* analytical construct validity contrasts that where the claimed substantive significance of a model parameter is supported from ensuing mathematical explorations of its properties (Neufeld, in press).

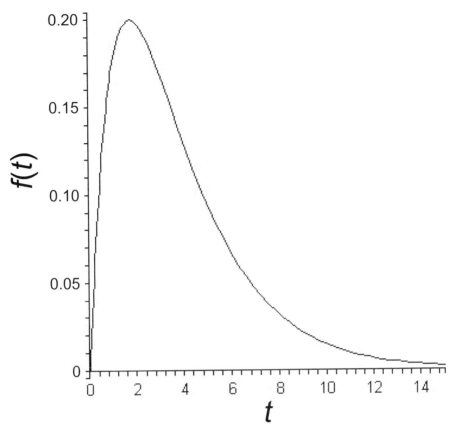

Figure 7.1. Density function *f(t)* for a theoretical distribution of processing latencies.

or simply *density function*, $f(t)$ (not to be confused with the ordinary concept of density in the field of physics). Hence, $f(t)$ is proportional to completion frequency (see Figure 7.1). The density function of time t is analogous to the height of the familiar normal distribution as a function of z.

The probability of event occurrence at or before a specific value of t (i.e., completion of processing before time t) comprises the cumulative probability distribution function $F(t)$. Replacing t with t' in $f(t)$, $F(t)$ is the integral (if time were discrete instead of continuous, it would be a sum) of $f(t')$ from 0 to t. The survivor function $S(t)$ is the complement of $F(t)$, or the probability of event occurrence after t, and is therefore just $S(t) = 1 - F(t)$. Accordingly, $S(t)$ is the integral of $f(t')$ from t to infinity. Finally, the hazard function, $h(t)$, expresses the instantaneous rate of event completion, given that it has not yet occurred, or $f(t)/S(t)$. That is, given that the event has not occurred by time t, $h(t)$ gives the likelihood that it will occur in the next instant. Its curious name derives from its use in actuarial science

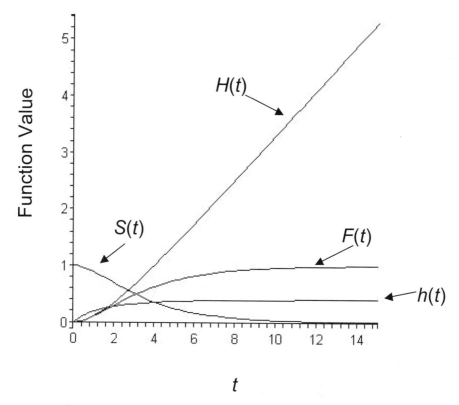

Figure 7.2. Distribution function F(t), survivor function S(t), hazard function h(t), and integrated hazard function H(t) corresponding with the density function f(t) of Figure 7.1.

to estimate likelihood of failure (e.g., of a refrigerator or a person [i.e., likelihood of death]) within the next small interval, assuming that failure has not occurred up until that time. These functions, as derived from $f(t)$ in Figure 7.1, are presented in Figure 7.2.[3]

The capacity index specifically exploits $h(t)$ and its denominator, $S(t)$. Note first that $h(t)$ is affiliated with the concept of power in physics (Wenger & Townsend, 2000). It tells us the momentary intensity of a system's work potential and stipulates the immediate pressure toward the state transition of a process, from that of incompletion to completion. It is nevertheless a transitory function of time and therefore difficult to estimate empirically. An index summarizing the collective momentary intensities over the continuous time interval t, however, is $H(t)$. Mathematically, this index is the definite

---

[3] Additional explication of these functions, from the standpoint of clinical science, were presented by Neufeld (1998).

integral of $h(t')$ between 0 and t, $\int_0^t h(t')dt'$ (see Figure 7.2). Just as work and energy in physics are associated with a summing or integration of power over a time interval, we can think of $H(t)$ as "energy expenditure" in cognitive operations (Townsend & Ashby, 1978, 1983). As an aggregate, its empirical estimation necessarily is more reliable than are approximations of its infinitesimal constituents $h(t')$. It will turn out that the relation of this integral to the empirically accessible $S(t)$ further increases the appeal of this measure.

The desired $H(t)$ is derived from $S(t)$ as follows. Because $S(t)$, by well-established probability theory, is equivalent to $e^{-H(t)}$, $H(t)$ is simply $-\ln[S(t)]$, where $\ln(x)$ stands for the so-called *Naperian* or *natural* logarithm of x. It can also be written as $\log_e(x)$. Consequently, an estimate of $H(t)$, denoted $\hat{H}(t)$, is supplied by $-\ln[\hat{S}(t)]$, where $\hat{S}(t)$ is a sample estimate of $S(t)$.[4] Owing to this composition, then, $\hat{H}(t)$ represents a mathematically principled confluence of two things: (a) the computational tractability and stability of statistical estimation bestowed by data aggregation and (b) the full salvaging of inferences originating with the preaggregate data format (Neufeld & Gardner, 1990).

Observe in passing that $H(t)$ can serve as a characterization of decline in task performance efficiency, historically of considerable interest to clinical scientists (see Maher, 1966, chap. 1). Wishner (1955), for example, conjectured that an earmark of psychopathology is a reduction in the expenditure of energy consummating a task at hand, relative to the total energy laid out during the task's transaction (see also George & Neufeld, 1985; Neufeld, 1990; Nuechterlein & Dawson, 1984). Reduced efficiency, in this view, is tantamount to a lower ratio of work accomplished to total resource investment. The value of $\hat{H}(t)$ obviously would make for a rigorous estimate of the numerator of this ratio, at least in the case of cognitive performance.

The capacity index in turn enters into two composite indexes of comparative capacity, CR and $C_o(t)$. CR provides a general estimate of inequalities in capacity across conditions of performance and/or groups. Whereas CR is a versatile measure that expresses capacity differences generally, $C_o(t)$ does so in liaison with specific increments in task load (detailed later). Coupled with an experimental paradigm for which it was expressly developed, this coefficient measures the change, if any, of capacity as workload is varied. Both of these composite indexes, moreover, can monitor comparative capacity repeatedly over time t.

---

[4]Further appreciation of this relation is available from the following explication of $H(t)$ (Townsend & Ashby, 1983, pp. 26, 27). $H(t) = \int_0^t H'(t')dt'$, where $H'(t') = d[-\ln(S[t'])]/dt' = d[-\ln(1 - F(t'))]dt'$, which by the chain rule is $f(t')/[1 - F(t')] = h(t')$.

These composite indexes, as will be seen, apply in somewhat different circumstances, depending on the paradigm and research questions involved. The CR is simply the ratio of $\hat{H}(t)$ obtained for one performance condition or designated group to that of a counterpart. We now explicate its application to the analysis of processing among stress-susceptible, anxiety-prone individuals.

PARADIGM, DATA, AND APPLICATION OF $H(t)$ AND THE CAPACITY RATIO TO HYPOTHESIZED STRESS-SUSCEPTIBILITY EFFECTS ON COGNITIVE PROCESSING

Vulnerability to stress activation has predictable effects on capacity to process visual stimuli and to strategically organize available capacity resources. We develop these points through use of CR, and so we begin by laying out the essential experimental paradigm used to illustrate such application. The resultant data and their organization for accommodating CR are then described. Following these descriptions are specific hypotheses about stress-susceptibility effects as translated in terms of CR. Complementing the subsequent implementation of CR is a section on selected analyses that entail a specific theoretical distribution for processing latencies. This extension elucidates further the nature of CR against this distributional backdrop and indicates additional nuances of formally defined processing capacity.

Note that $H(t)$, and hence CR and $C_o(t)$, are "distribution general" in that they require only that $f(t)$ be a continuous function of t. That is, their meaning is not predicated on a specific shape of the operative distribution, as defined by a particular composition of $f(t)$. Nevertheless, if a specific version of $f(t)$ makes for a parametric distribution that reasonably conforms to empirical observations, then other glimpses into processing operations may be forthcoming. Included are certain angles on the workings of $H(t)$. In addition, parameters of a tenable version of $f(t)$ can naturally align with clinically significant constructs, affording substantively meaningful analyses and associated predictions. In the present case, the tenable distribution happens to be a simple but useful one, the exponential (e.g., Evans, Hastings, & Peacock, 2000).

Paradigm

The following paradigm was used by Jetté (1997) in formally modeling effects of white noise stress and stress susceptibility (physical danger–discomfort trait anxiety) on visual information processing. It was closely fashioned after those of prominent studies of auditory noise effects on light-flash detection (Hockey, 1970a, 1970b). These studies produce data amenable to stochastic mathematical modeling of capacity deployment (Neufeld, 1996), implicating substantive issues of visual attention in the company of (noise) stress (Broadbent, 1971).

The participants observed an array of six lamps. Two lamps were positioned beside each other toward the center of the visual array, and four were positioned peripherally, two on the left and two on the right of the central region; a light signal emanated from one of the lamps on each trial. Instructions were to press with the left index finger the button on a six-button response panel corresponding to the location of the light, as soon as it appeared. The light signal remained on pending the correct button press.[5]

During the performance of light detection, participants engaged in a pursuit-rotor task with the right hand. This task entailed keeping an L-shaped stylus on the bright spot of a rotating disk. Although presented as the main task, pursuit-rotor activity was incidental to actual theoretical and empirical purposes; in essence, it provided for a common direction of gaze. As in previous work (Forster & Grierson, 1978; Hockey, 1970a, 1970b), rotor speed was calibrated to ensure performance of approximately 65% on target.

The performance measure of principal interest was latency of response to register light appearance. Half of the participants in each anxiety group (i.e., 23 in each condition out of a total of 46 in each group), described below, experienced an even distribution of light signals across the six lamp positions, specifically, 48 in each (unbiased distribution condition). For these participants, the central region produced one third of the total number of signals (96 central and 192 peripheral). For the other half of the participants, each central position produced 96 signals, and each peripheral position produced 24 signals, with two thirds of the signals in the central location (biased distribution condition).

The tasks were performed amidst intermittent 1-second bursts of white noise, delivered through headphones on average every 8 seconds, and always outside the light-signal intervals (Poulton, 1977). There were three levels of intensity: (a) 35 dbA, (b) 88 dbA, and (c) 100 dbA sound pressure level at the ear. Noise levels were evenly dispersed with respect to light signals in the respective spatial locations, and the order of prevailing levels was balanced across participants within each group–condition combination. Participants were 92 right-handed male undergraduates—right handed to reduce individual differences in manual dexterity aspects of performance and male because of documented sex differences in stress response (Neufeld, 1978).

Stress susceptibility was psychometrically identified using the physical danger portion of the Endler Multidimensional Anxiety Scale (Endler,

---

[5]Methodological details, otiose with respect to the present exposition, are available in Jetté (1997; see also Hockey, 1970a, 1970b).

Edwards, & Vitelli, 1991). The scale taps respondent apprehensiveness and perceived sympathetic reactions to physical danger, discomfort, or pain. Psychometric properties were enumerated by Endler et al. (1991), and suitability to the present investigative context has been well established (Lefave & Neufeld, 1980; Neufeld & McCarty, 1994). Participants were separated by whether their scores were in the upper (more stress susceptible) versus lower (less susceptible) half of the distribution. Within each division, half of the 46 participants were randomly assigned to the biased signal distribution, and the remainder were administered the unbiased distribution.

Before arranging data to facilitate calculation of $\hat{H}(t)$ and CR, each value was adjusted to throw into relief signal-processing aspects of latency. Note that collateral operations contributing to observed latencies, necessary for task transaction but not deemed to be part and parcel of the focus of modeling, are labeled *base processes*. For example, if memory search were of primary concern (see the section entitled Distribution Properties and Their Roles in Defining the Capacity Index: $H(t)$, above), probe item encoding would be considered a base process. Other base processes would include those involved in translating the results of memory search (probe item present–absent) into the corresponding response (yes–no) and registering it. Apropos of the present paradigm, base processes arguably involve mainly those of converting the result of signal processing into the corresponding location on the response panel and pressing the button (for an elaboration of methods for dealing with base processes, see Townsend & Nozawa, 1995; Townsend & Wenger, 2004a). Thus, estimated duration of response processes was subtracted from each measured response time. The estimate was 552 milliseconds, based on Townsend (1984), a value that turns out to be close to 514 milliseconds, as estimated independently by Bricolo, Gianesini, Fanini, Bundesen, and Chelazzi (2002).

The adjusted latency for correct responses (>95% throughout and not aligned with latency in any way that would undermine inferences from the latter) was aggregated across the group of 23 participants within each stress-proneness/signal-distribution combination. In turn, the data were separated according to central–peripheral regions of signal presentation and prevailing noise level. Latencies were partitioned into bins corresponding to times of 0–600 milliseconds, 600–800 milliseconds, 800–1,000 milliseconds, 1,000–1,200 milliseconds, and >1,200 milliseconds. (The boundary of 600 milliseconds was based on an arbitrary precedent of Hockey [1970a]). Thus, of the total number of trials per group, 736 were available per noise level for the central region under the unbiased distribution, and likewise for the peripheral region under the biased distribution; 1,472 trials per noise level in turn were available for the central and peripheral regions under the biased and unbiased distributions, respectively. Bin entries comprised the proportions of total adjusted latencies falling into the successive intervals, computed separately for each region and noise level, within each stress-proneness/signal-distribution group.

Aggregation of data across participants within these groups was undertaken in the interests of stability of modeled data and attenuation of model-exogenous noise (e.g., J. R. Carter & Neufeld, 1999; Neufeld & McCarty, 1994). To ensure that resulting data profiles of bin proportions did not conflate systematically differing individual profiles, we used coefficient alpha to estimate profile homogeneity. Accordingly, the computation $1 - (MS_{participants \times bins})/(MS_{participants})$ (Hakstian & Whalen, 1976) was replaced with $1 - (MS_{participants \times bins})/(MS_{bins})$, affording both statistical and interpretative validity (Neufeld & McCarty, 1994; cf. Schmitt, 1996). Data collectives submitted to modeling were verified as representative of their constituents, because alpha estimates ranged from .97 to .99. (Tactics to avoiding artifacts arising from data aggregation are discussed in more detail in this volume's Introduction; see also chaps. 1 and 4, this volume.)

Hypotheses

Hypothesized patterns of CR, as applied to the present data, stemmed from previous formal analyses of stress and stress-susceptibility effects on cognitive performance (Neufeld, 1996; Neufeld & McCarty, 1994). The set of hypothesized patterns now briefly is summarized, followed by the representative application of CR to their investigation.

First, visual-search processing capacity[6] is expected to increase with noise levels, albeit more so with respect to central signal location. Second, stress susceptibility is expected to be identified with diminished visual-search processing capacity. Remaining with stress susceptibility, the third expected pattern entails strategy in deploying available capacity. Stress susceptibility is deemed to impair the advantageous appropriation of resources to display regions, as dictated by target occurrence and task requirements. Investigation of the third hypothesized pattern is described in detail, because of the three, it involves the most comprehensive set of CR procedures.

---

[6] Inferences are restricted to visual-search performance, in light of the concurrent pursuit-rotor task. Stress-susceptibility differences in processing capacity applied to this task, making for an equal or possibly greater overall capacity resource pool among the more stress-susceptible individuals, cannot be ruled out. Such a possibility nevertheless is unlikely, considering the characteristics of the pursuit-rotor task, as described above. Moreover, the visual-search results from which the present hypothesis arose (Neufeld & McCarty, 1994) did not entail a concurrent psychomotor task. Postulated mechanisms of diminished processing capacity among more anxiety-prone individuals have been enumerated by Neufeld (1996) and by Neufeld and McCarty (1994).

Application of Capacity Ratio

Computed values of CR essentially endorsed expectations in each case. Specifically, noise elevation generated higher values of $H(t)$ for both stress-prone groups, especially when increasing from low to medium levels, this effect being most apparent for the central region and among participants experiencing the centrally biased signal distribution. Corresponding values of CR comprising $\hat{H}(t)_{lower\,noise\,level} / \hat{H}(t)_{higher\,noise\,level}$ were generally less than 1.0 and were homogeneously so under the above conditions. The disproportionate increase associated with the central region under biased conditions, notably for the low versus medium noise levels, corresponded to lower values of the above CR when computed for the central versus peripheral region. That is, $CR_{central} / CR_{peripheral}$, the "second-order CR," was less than 1.0. Computational details were, to all intents and purposes, identical to those addressing stress-susceptibility and strategies of capacity allocation, below.

The pattern of noise-related capacity changes was accordant with a noise-induced increased tendency to focus resources toward more important task features. Such a pattern has been proposed as a mechanism of selectively improved performance under noise conditions (Broadbent, 1971; Hockey, 1970a, 1970b). Other theoretical accounts of noise-associated capacity increase are available from a stochastic-modeling platform (Neufeld, 1994, 1996).

Note that the present set of inferences stemming from the application of CR were compatible with those from generic analyses of the adjusted latencies (e.g., significant analysis of variance higher order interaction among noise levels, signal distribution, and central–peripheral region, $p < .05$; cf. chap. 2, this volume, regarding instances of opposing inferences from formal modeling and generic analyses). A certain overlap notwithstanding, formal modeling stands to furnish the informational added value emanating from a disciplined mathematical abstraction of the process tenably responsible for the data summaries to which the generic analyses are applied. Added value includes interpretative insights, data-analytic extensions, and paradigmatic innovations, illustrated in this chapter and throughout the volume at large.

Table 7.1 presents proportions of adjusted observed latencies in the respective interval bins. Also listed are the estimated values of $H(t)$, obtained as $-\ln[\hat{S}(t)]$, where $\hat{S}(t)$ is equal to 1 minus the cumulative bin proportions; for example, $1.890 = -\ln(0.151) = -\ln[1 - (0.736 + 0.113)]$.

Lower values of $\hat{H}(t)$ accompanied higher stress susceptibility throughout. This result is exemplified in Table 7.1 for performance under medium noise and centrally biased signal frequency. (The full set of results is available in Jetté, 1997). On top of diminished capacity overall was evidence of its less advantageous deployment with respect to task conditions (in line with the third prediction, see Hypothesis section). In particular, adjusting avail-

TABLE 7.1
Observed Bin Proportions, Estimated Survivor Functions $\hat{S}(t)$,
and Capacity-Index $\hat{H}(t)$ Values for Each Group Under Medium
Noise Level and Centrally Biased Signal Distribution

Location estimates	Bin interval (milliseconds)			
	0–600	600–800	800–1,000	1,000–1,200
Low stress susceptable				
Peripheral				
Observed proportion	0.736	0.113	0.055	0.035
Estimated survivor function	0.264	0.151	0.096	0.061
Capacity index	1.332	1.890	2.343	2.797
Central				
Observed proportion	0.832	0.090	0.038	0.018
Estimated survivor function	0.168	0.078	0.04	0.022
Capacity index	1.784	2.551	3.219	3.817
High stress susceptible				
Peripheral				
Observed proportion	0.72	0.113	0.053	0.045
Estimated survivor function	0.28	0.167	0.114	0.069
Capacity index	1.273	1.790	2.172	2.674
Central				
Observed proportion	0.737	0.131	0.048	0.029
Estimated survivor function	0.263	0.132	0.084	0.055
Capacity index	1.336	2.025	2.477	2.900

able processing resources according to signal frequencies in the visual array stands to improve performance. The centrally biased distribution should draw more processing capacity to that region, and the opposite should be true for the unbiased distribution. Frequency-based strategy of allocation was more pronounced for the participants with lower stress proneness, as educed by $\hat{H}(t)$ and CR. The results for the biased distribution under the medium noise level provide a representative example of this pattern (see Table 7.1). Apropos of analysis of variance on the latency distributions, this representative selection is analogous to using a simple first-order interaction to dissect an obtained significant second-order Stress Proneness × Distribution Bias × Display Region interaction ($p < .05$ in the present case). Values of $\hat{H}(t)$ were greater for central than peripheral regions for both lower and higher stress-susceptibility groups, leading to $CR = \hat{H}(t)_{peripheral}/ \hat{H}(t)_{central} < 1.0$. Disproportionately greater deployment of processing capacity to the central region by the participants with lower susceptibility corresponded to values less than 1.0 for the second-order CR, $CR_{lower\ stress\ susceptibility}/ CR_{higher\ stress\ susceptibility}$; that is, more capacity was devoted to the central versus peripheral region for both groups, resulting in $CR < 1.0$ for each; the effect, however, was more pronounced for the low-susceptibility group, leading to their greater deflation of *CR*. Actual values of this second-order *CR*, corresponding to the respective bins in Table 7.1 (proceeding from left to right), are .78, .84, .83, and .80. The question of which group evinced a division of taskwise capacity closer to the optimum is examined in the following section.

Parametric Extension

Previous analysis of secondary data from experiments using paradigms similar to the present one (Hockey, 1970a, 1970b) encouraged consideration of the exponential distribution as a theoretical account of processing latencies (Neufeld, 1996, adapting Compound Parallel Model 1 of Townsend & Ashby, 1983, chap. 5). This distribution's density function is ve^{-vt}, where v is the rate of completion of a processed element (e.g., region of a visual array) and t is the elapsed time since processing commencement. The distribution function $F(t)$ is $\int_0^t ve^{-vt'}\, dt' = 1 - e^{-vt}$ and the survivor function $S(t) = e^{-vt}$, implying $-\ln[S(t)] = vt$. Dividing the density function by the survivor function, the hazard function $h(t)$ is seen to be equal to the rate parameter v and constant across all t. Finally, the mean of the distribution is $1/v$, and its variance is $1/v^2$.

The capacity index can be examined against the backdrop of this distribution. Note that the validity of this application is supported by multiple tests on empirical fit, applied both to the current binned proportions and to overall latencies. Probabilities for chi-square tests of goodness of fit ranged from .30 to .99, with an average of .71. Thus, results were solidly within the envelope prescribed by the hypothesized distribution.

The maximum likelihood estimate (MLE) of the exponential distribution's parameter v, MLE(v), based on a set of adjusted latencies of size N is $N/\sum_{i=1}^{N} t_{adj,i}$, or simply the reciprocal of the mean. This estimate entered into the above goodness-of-fit tests. Alternatively, $S(t)$ spawns its own version of MLE(v), specifically, $-\ln[\hat{S}(t)]/t$, or $\hat{H}(t)/t$, which shows $\hat{H}(t)$ to be a scaled maximum-likelihood estimator of capacity in the case of this distribution. Moreover, where the respective elements (regions) are processed in parallel, with each region's latencies independent of the other's, the estimated collective taskwise capacity is simply the sum of the individual estimates, in this case, $1/t[\hat{H}(t)_{central} + \hat{H}(t)_{peripheral}] = v_{central} + v_{peripheral}$ (Townsend & Ashby, 1983, p. 249).

Normative and Descriptive Models

The present parametric distribution affords the aforementioned observations not only on the capacity index but also on selected extensions. The slant on capacity endowed by this distribution bears on certain issues of potential import in clinical cognitive science, in this case involving the optimal allocation of taskwise capacity to central and peripheral regions of a visual display. Optimal division of processing capacity can be viewed as the most efficient division of attention in the present type of task, where vigilance for the occurrence of an environmental event is called for. The strategy that maximizes performance can be indicated by linking up the performance model and prevailing task characteristics.

Such a computed optimum is considered to be defined by a *normative model*, as identified with statistically prescribed idealized performance. A *descriptive model* depicts how individuals actually perform the task (Edwards, 1998). The descriptive model's capacity allocation for each of the low and high stress-susceptible participants can be compared for its proximity to optimal capacity allocation as computed from the normative model.

In the present context, optimal capacity deployment may be viewed as that resulting in the minimum latency for registering the appearance of a signal. A complementary angle deals with allocation that maximizes detection, given a specific time interval of signal duration t. The latter orientation coincides with the present overall tack to capacity measurement, because detection failure can be modeled in terms of the survivor function $S(t)$. This direction of analysis is developed using a signal interval of 600 milliseconds.

The current proportions of adjusted latencies equal to or less than 600 milliseconds now stand as a surrogate for the rates of detecting signals lasting only 600 milliseconds (the signal duration used in Hockey, 1970a), even though they actually remained on pending a response (as in Hockey, 1970b). Estimates of v for this analysis are obtained as $-\ln[\hat{S}(t)]/t$, where $t = 600$, and $\hat{S}(t)$ is $1 -$ (proportion of adjusted latencies equal to or less than 600 milliseconds). Results from this analysis are depicted graphically in Figure 7.3; reference to the figure may aid in following the steps described below.

We let the probability of a signal occurrence in the region with the higher frequencies be denoted w_H, and that in the lower frequency region be $w_L = 1 - w_H$. Processing capacity deployed to the w_H region is denoted v_H, and that to the w_L region is denoted v_L. Taskwise capacity is estimated as $v_H + v_L = c$. The probability of detection failure is

$$w_H S_H(t) + w_L S_L(t), \tag{7.1}$$

where, in the present instantiation, $S_H(t) = e^{-v_H t}$ and $S_L(t) = e^{-(c - v_H)t}$. After substituting these expressions in Equation 7.1, and applying the usual operations of differential calculus to find a minimum, Equation 7.1 is shown to be minimized with respect to v_H when the latter is equal to

$$1/(2t)[\ln(w_H) - \ln(w_L)] + c/2. \tag{7.2}$$

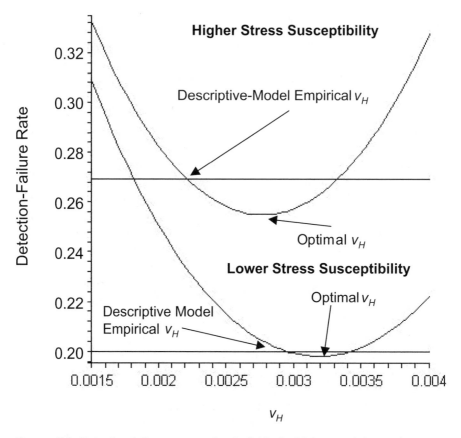

Figure 7.3. Detection-failure curves for individuals higher and lower in stress susceptibility. Higher elevation of the "higher stress susceptibility" curve reflects diminished taskwise capacity. Optimal values of v_H, as prescribed by the normative model, are those minimizing detection failures. Empirical estimates of v_H, for the descriptive model addressed to actual performance, correspond to the left-hand intersections of the curves with the horizontal lines, the latter in turn depicting resulting levels of empirical detection-failure rates.

A representative example of the computations for the normative and descriptive models is supplied by the combination of performance conditions made up of the centrally biased signal distribution delivered amidst a medium noise level. With $t = 600$, and $w_H = .67$ (corresponding to the central region light signal frequency), c for the lower susceptibility participants is estimated to be .00519, and optimal $v_H = .00318$. Corresponding values for the more highly susceptible individuals are .00435 and .00276.

As for the descriptive model, the value of v_H estimated for the lower susceptible participants is .00297, lower than the optimum by .00021, and that for the more highly susceptible counterparts is .00222, a departure from the optimum of .00054. By the normative model, optimal allocation for the lower susceptible individuals would result in a detection-failure rate of .198, close to the observed value of .200. If their capacity were equally divided between regions, the detection-failure rate would be .211. Optimal allocation for the more highly susceptible individuals would produce a detection-failure rate of .255, the observed value being .269. The amount corresponding to hypothetical equal allocation is .271. The increase in optimal allocation detection failure from .198 to .255, when going from the lower to more highly susceptible individuals, results from the lower value of c for the more highly susceptible group.

The optimal proportion of c to be dispatched to the central region is .6127 for the lower susceptible group. The estimated actual proportion is .5722, a difference of .04. For the more highly susceptible group, the calculated optimal proportion is .6348, compared with the empirical estimate of .5106, for a difference of .1242. Detection times for the central region, obtained as $1/v_H$, are 337 milliseconds for the lower susceptibility group, compared with 450 milliseconds for the more highly susceptible group; corresponding values for the peripheral region are 450 milliseconds and 469 milliseconds. Finally, note that a similar set of computations are available with respect to optimal division of capacity and performance maximization in terms of minimized processing latencies, rather than maximized light detection at time t (Neufeld, 1996).

To summarize, the present extension throws light on $H(t)$ according to its operation within a tenable parametric distribution. The parametric implementation of $H(t)$ offers up a quantitative gold standard against which measured performance can be assessed. It does so explicitly in terms of efficiency in adapting processing resources to the presenting task structure. Stress proneness associated with trait anxiety not only diminishes capacity to transact a given cognitive task (cf. Mogg, Bradley, Williams, & Mathews, 1993) but also compromises the interplay of remaining resources with task exigencies. Quantification of relations between task properties and processing capacity evidently yields pellucid mathematical expressions of selected cognitive vulnerabilities. Potential consequences, in the form of compromised negotiation of cognition-intensive coping, in turn have been drawn out from a nonlinear dynamical-systems ("chaos-theoretic") perspective in Neufeld (1999).

ANALYSIS OF MEMORY SEARCH IN SCHIZOPHRENIA

We turn now to the illustrative application of $C_o(t)$ to clinical data. A cognitive function that appears to have been spared among individuals with schizophrenia is that comprising the examination of material held in memory, a function known as *memory scanning*. In a typical memory-search task (Sternberg, 1975), for example, this function entails the search through memory for the presence of a visually presented probe item (see description in the Distribution Properties and Their Roles in Defining the Capacity Index section). Speed and accuracy of memory scanning evidently escape unscathed.[7] The collateral process of probe item encoding, however, decidedly is affected, an observation that is taken up further in chapter 5 of this volume.

Identifying and deciphering the nature of spared as well as affected aspects of cognition are important to producing a balanced profile of cognitive functioning characterizing a disorder. The discerned set of strengths and weaknesses arguably contributes to a fuller understanding of the symptom picture (George & Neufeld, 1985; Neufeld, Vollick, & Highgate-Maynard, 1993).

Also afforded is the possibility of exploiting apparent strengths in the service of intervention (cf. Penn & Spaulding, 1997). The capacity coefficient $C_o(t)$ can be used to penetrate capacity properties of cognitive processing in general and is applied here to memory-search operations deemed to be held in common by patients with schizophrenia and control participants. We again emphasize the much greater power and dynamic processing detail available with the current methods.

Paradigm

A study by Highgate-Maynard and Neufeld (1986) extended typical memory-search methodology by incorporating methods emanating from Paivio's (1986) dual-coding theory. Individuals with schizophrenia and control participants indicated "as quickly and accurately as possible" whether the real-life size—"overall volume"—of a presented item (a probe item comprising either an object or animal) was similar to that of a member of a previously memorized set of items (memory set). The number of items in the memory set (*memory-set size*) ranged from one to four. Each memory set of a given size was composed of its own set of items (e.g., breadcrumb, coffeepot, and bed for a set size of three; dot, teapot, dresser, and airplane for a set size of four), which in turn stayed the same for that set size throughout the experiment (known as a *fixed set procedure*). Correspondence versus absence of the probe's size properties to those of one of the members of the memory set (positive vs. negative trials) was balanced with respect to memory set size. The 4 × 2, Set Size × Positive Versus Negative trial, combinations were presented in random order. For reasons tangential to

---

[7] As with tenability of a parametric distribution according to goodness-of-fit testing, above, this inference currently is based on repeatedly negative statistical findings and stands to be supplemented with other recommended methods for "accepting the null hypothesis" (Cohen, 1988, pp. 16, 17).

memory scanning per se (Neufeld et al., 1993), half the participants in each group were presented with similar-sized drawings of probe items, whereas the other half were presented with their names.

Scanning memory-held items for the presence of the probe's size properties was considered to be comparatively taxing. It required comparison between the probe and memory-held items' overall volume, as set against subjective criteria of similarity in this property (Hockley & Murdock, 1987; Wright, 1977). Size attributes of items in the memory set were spaced such that the means of their normative-size ratings (Paivio, 1975) were at least 2 standard deviations of their Thurstonian discriminal-difference size dispersions apart (practically, at least 2 standard deviations of the distribution of difference scores between their normative size ratings; Highgate-Maynard & Neufeld, 1986). Responses were designated as correct or incorrect on the basis of whether they conformed to the following criteria for positive and negative trials. Negative trials, the correct response to which was a "no" button press, meant that the probe item's size did not resemble that of a memory-set item. Here, the probe item's mean real-life size rating was at least 1 standard deviation of the Thurstonian discriminal-difference dispersion from the normative mean rating of each item in the memory set. Positive trials, the correct response to which was a "yes" button press, were those where the mean of the probe item, and that of a memory-set member were, to all intents and purposes, identical. Practice trials, ensuring familiarity with task requirements and the nature of correct responding, were similar in number for each group.

Further specifics, including those surrounding provision for potentially confounding clinical and demographic variables and ascertainment of the viability of the paradigm for each diagnostic group of participants (e.g., applicability of normed item properties to each one), were detailed by Highgate-Maynard and Neufeld (1986) and were summarized by Neufeld, Carter, Boksman, Jetté, and Vollick (2002). Considering the current emphasis on latencies, we should emphasize that error rates were comparable across groups and did not contribute to latencies in any confounding way.

$C_o(t)$ in Light of the Memory-Search Paradigm

In explicating $H(t)$ and CR (see p. 210) we followed distribution-general developments with their instantiation in the exponential distribution. Conversely, it will be advantageous to launch developments of $C_o(t)$ from a parametric-distribution platform applicable to the results from this study. Doing so illustrates how the specific capacity properties embodied in the parametric distributions are expressed in terms of $C_o(t)$. Operations of these coefficients, illustrated in the given parametric case, nevertheless are distribution general.

The model applicable to memory search for this task, known as an *independent parallel model with moderately limited capacity* (IPMLC), was presented in Townsend and Ashby (1983). The rationale for its claimed viability here was detailed by Neufeld et al. (1993). Note that a stochastic model of parallel processing specifies that items are commenced simultaneously but that individual item completions are staggered stochastically across time. In the present model, memory-set items are processed in parallel, each completion is exponentially distributed with rate parameter v_n (see the description of the exponential distribution, above), and each is independent of any other completion. The capacity available to each item v_n nevertheless is partly degraded as the set size n increases.[8]

If capacity were unlimited rather than moderately limited, then the rate at which an individual item is processed, v_n, would be unaltered as n increases. The rate applicable to a single item being processed in isolation, $n = 1$, would remain in effect even as items are added to the memory set, $n = 2,3,4, \ldots$ (in the present case, n's maximum value being 4). Thus, $v_1 = v_2 = v_3 \ldots$. It is interesting that with parallel processing of a set size of n and unlimited capacity, times for the first item completion remain exponentially distributed, but with the rate parameter applicable to the first completion of the n-item set being $\sum_{i=1}^{n} v_n = nv_n$ (see Townsend & Ashby, 1983, pp. 90, 249, and the Parametric Extension section). This *independent-parallel unlimited capacity* (IPUC) model furnishes a benchmark for synthesizing IPMLCs' capacity attributes in terms of $C_o(t)$. Transdistribution properties of the IPUC processing architecture also provide a benchmark in the use of $C_o(t)$ to assess capacity aspects of examined systems in the distribution-general case, below.

For the IPMLC model, then, the decline in v_n as n increases is expressed as $v_n = v_1 / n \sum_{i=1}^{n} 1/i$, where v_1 is the rate for a single item processed by itself. As n increases from 2 through 4, for example, v_1 is scaled by .75, .61, and .52 to produce v_2, v_3, and v_4, respectively. This system's capacity is moderately limited because the decline in v_n with increasing n is less drastic than for a fixed-capacity system, where $v_n = v_1/n$. As with the IPUC model, the first completion again is exponentially distributed with rate parameter nv_n; however, v_n now is that prescribed by the IPMLC model.

The IPMLC model exemplifies certain properties of processing systems that elucidate the functioning of $C_o(t)$. One such property is *channel capacity*. It can be helpful to envision each of the set of n items as having a dedicated processing channel—analogous to a neural circuit but agnostic as to the

---

[8]Regarding the representativeness of individuals' memory-scanning performance by aggregated data subjected to modeling, pertinent alpha coefficients ranged from .92 to .94 (see "Paradigm" section).

circuitry involved. Among other variations, channel capacity can be unlimited, very limited, or moderately limited; consider the IPUC, the independent parallel fixed-capacity, and IPMLC models, respectively, described above.

Another concept brought to bear is that of *statistical advantage*. In an independent parallel system, the hazard function $h(t)$ for the next completion of a set of items in progress is the sum of their individual hazard functions. Thus, the instantaneous rate of an upcoming completion, given the continuation of all members of a set, increases with the size of the set. Formally, for n items,

$$h(t)_{min} = \sum_{i=1}^{n} h(t)_i, \qquad (7.3)$$

where $h(t)_{min}$ is the hazard function corresponding to the minimum of the n completion latencies, and $h(t)_i$ is the hazard function for item i, considered in isolation (befitting the independence provision); $i = 1, 2, ..., n$. Replacing t with t' in Equation 7.3 and integrating from $t' = 0$ to $t' = t$, we have $H(t)_{min} = \sum_{i=1}^{n} H(t)_i$. Furthermore, because the survivor function of the first completion $S(t)_{min}$ is equal to $e^{-H(t)_{min}}$, $-\ln[S(t)]_{min}$ is equal to $H(t)_{min}$.

These relations are instantiated in the case where the latencies for each item are exponentially distributed. Recall that with n items being processed independently and concurrently, each with rate parameter v_n, the rate parameter for the first completion is $\sum_{i=1}^{n} v_n = nv_n$, or n times $h(t)$ for the individual item.

A potentially useful, albeit rough analogy to the interplay of statistical advantage and channel capacity entails a set of randomly kinetic billiard balls, as follows. The speed with which the first ball drops into a pocket increases with the number of balls set in motion, roughly expressing statistical advantage. As for capacity limitation, with an increase in the number of balls rambling about on the playing surface, mutual interference, or momentary adverse effects on the playing surface (to stretch the analogy), may impair the balls' movement, prolonging the pocketing time.

We now examine how $C_o(t)$ captures the properties of statistical advantage and channel capacity. Results from applying this coefficient to assess targeted systems must be set against those from a system embodying a referent set of known properties. The IPUC model comes to the fore as the needed benchmark.

Paradigmatic requirements for the application of $C_o(t)$ entail redundant targets, as follows. In the case of visual search, more than 1 item of a visual array—say, 2—would match a previously presented target item. In the present case of memory search, the real life-size properties of more than one member of the memory set would match that of the probe item, according to the statistical criteria described above. With memory-set sizes n ranging between 1 and 2, on positive trials, there is a match between the probe and a single item, or a pair of memory-set items, respectively. Needless to say, such trials are balanced with randomly interspersed presentations of negative (no-match) trials. Participants are instructed to give a positive response ("yes" button press) if the probe's size properties are matched by those of the single member ($n = 1$), or either member ($n = 2$) of the memory set and to give a negative response otherwise. It is therefore assumed that responding is self-terminating, meaning that on positive trials where $n = 2$, processing ceases and responding occurs on detecting a match to the probe on the part of either member of the memory set. On these grounds, $H(t)_{min}$ is thrown into relief, with respect to $C_o(t)$. Note that for purposes of exposition, the present developments are based on an extrapolation of the actual procedures used by Highgate-Maynard and Neufeld (1986) combined with the IPMLC model inferred from those results.

Now, $C_o(t)$ simply comprises a certain ratio involving capacity indexes $H(t)$. Its numerator comprises $H(t)$ for the redundant-target trials, where both of the pair of memory-set items match the probe, denoted $H(t)_b$. The denominator consists of the sum of $H(t)$ for the single-target trials, or $2H(t)_s$, assuming as in the present case that the single-target distributions are identical. Consequently, $C_o(t)$ becomes $H(t)_b/2H(t)_s$. For the theoretical IPUC system, the survivor function for the first completion, allowing $n = 2$ (corresponding to $S[t]_b$) is $S(t)_s^2$, which in turn equals $[e^{-H(t)_s}]^2 = e^{-2H(t)_s}$. This expression makes $-\ln[S(t)_b] = 2H(t)_s$. The IPUC system thereby furnishes the denominator of $C_o(t)$, which anchors evaluation of the assessed system. The numerator of $C_o(t)$, in turn, is the value for that system of $H(t)_b = -\ln[S(t)_b]$ for the $n = 2$ trials.

If $C_o(t) = 1.0$, the most economical interpretation is that the examined system is one of independent processing and unlimited capacity (although note that some serial systems can mimic—are empirically equivalent to—IPUC systems; see, e.g., Townsend, 1990). If $C_o(t)$ is less than 1, then the examined system's task completion capacity is less than that of an IPUC system, or is one of limited capacity. If, on the other hand, $C_o(t)$ is greater than 1.0, then task-completion capacity exceeds that of the IPUC system, and supercapacity is said to be operative. Note that in practice each term of $C_o(t)$ is replaced by its empirically observed estimate.

Observe that $C_o(t)$ is distribution general. Its computation and interpretation presuppose no specific theoretical distributions, except that they are continuous across t. Second, we have specified that $C_o(t)$ addresses task-completion capacity. Values of $C_o(t)$ departing from 1.0 may indicate any or some combination of properties dislodging the system's capacity from that of the IPUC benchmark. Values less than 1.0 may signal, for example, a less efficient architecture (e.g., certain types of serial processing), deviation from a self-terminating stopping rule (notably, processing both items when one will suffice; recall that completions are stochastically distributed and therefore not synchronous), or limited channel capacity (reduction in each channel's speed, on concurrent processing). For that matter, one such property may have an elevating effect on $C_o(t)$ (e.g., mutual channel facilitation, as opposed to impedance), only to be overridden by another (e.g., exhaustive item processing).

Conversely, a value of $C_o(t)$ greater than 1.0, a signature of system supercapacity, may bespeak an architecture conducive to faster completions. One such architecture has a coactive, channel-summation parallel structure, whereby the products of channels processing concurrently are funneled into a repository channel, which is responsive to the cumulative output from its tributaries (Townsend & Nozawa, 1995; Townsend & Wenger, 2004a). Another possibility comprises the above mutual channel facilitation within a regular parallel architecture (Townsend & Wenger, 2004b). Clinical examples of supercapacity, and postulated mechanisms of its occurrence, include multidimensional stimulus encoding in schizophrenia (J. R. Carter & Neufeld, 1999) and the enhancing effects of stress on cognitive performance (Neufeld, 1996).

On balance, then, $C_o(t)$ is a mathematically moored, distribution-general coefficient that parsimoniously embodies the key ingredients of system capacity. It incorporates a principled benchmark system and suggests sources of departure of an assessed system in either direction. Moreover, $C_o(t)$ subsumes prominent system-capacity earmarks, known as the *Grice* inequality and the *Miller* inequality (see Townsend & Nozawa, 1995; Townsend & Wenger, 2004b). A comprehensive paradigm simultaneously monitoring $C_o(t)$, and its sources of departure from 1.0, is prescribed in Townsend and Wenger (2004a; this is known as "double factorial technology"; see also Townsend & Nozawa, 1995).

Application of $C_o(t)$ to Results From the Memory-Search Paradigm

Application of $C_o(t)$ to the current IPMLC system unveils the underlying interplay of statistical advantage and channel capacity. Simultaneous monitoring of $C_o(t)$ and the agents of its variation in the case at hand affords appreciation of candidate reasons for its precise value here and elsewhere.

Under the IPMLC model, statistical advantage remains in play, but individual channel capacity is diminished. The estimated value of v_1 in the present case was 1.23 (defensibly common to the clinical and nonclinical groups; Neufeld et al., 1993), the units of measurement now being seconds. As each item's completion latency is deemed exponentially distributed, the denominator of $C_o(t)$, specified by the IPUC model with $v_1 = 1.23$, is $2H(t)_s = 2[-\ln(S(t)_s)] = 2[-\ln(e^{-v_1 t})] = 2.46t$. Whereas the value of $v_{n=2}$ for the IPUC model remains 1.23, that defined by the IPMLC model is 0.9225. So, the numerator of $C_o(t)$ now is $-\ln[S(t)_b] = -\ln(e^{-2H(t)}) = -\ln[e^{-2(.9225)t}] = 1.8450t$. The resultant value of $C_o(t)$ is thus 0.75.

If the operative system were one of independent processing, and unlimited capacity, the numerator of $C_o(t)$ would be $-\ln[S(t)_b] = -\ln[e^{-2(1.23)t}] = 2.46t$, and $C_o(t)$ would be 1.0. Statistical advantage would be fully realized rather than being somewhat offset through moderately limited channel capacity.

The detraction from statistical advantage of the current moderately limited capacity, however, is less severe than that accompanying fixed capacity. There, the value of $v_1 = 1.23$ would be spread across the two items, resulting in $v_{n=2} = 0.615$, and $C_o(t) = 0.50$. In this case, statistical advantage would be completely offset by channel-capacity limitation.

A value of 0.50 for $C_o(t)$ also would occur if a regular serial architecture were in place (Townsend & Ashby, 1983, pp. 80, 88). Rather than parallel processing, with capacity being split between the two items, processing would begin with one of the items, its rate being 1.23. Statistical advantage no longer is fully offset by channel-capacity limitation. Instead, being intrinsic to parallel processing, it now is absent at the outset.

Values of $H(t) = -\ln[S(t)]$ entering into $C_o(t)$ are plotted in Figure 7.4. That for the IPUC benchmark composes the upper line. An assessed system with like architecture and capacity attributes generates identical values of $H(t)$ for the numerator of $C_o(t)$ (apart from sampling and measurement error), yielding $C_o(t) = 1.0$ throughout the range of t. Note that the constancy of $C_o(t)$ across time t in each of the present cases arises from latencies being exponentially distributed. Values of this coefficient of course can vary across t for other distributions (see, e.g., Wenger & Townsend, 2000).

Values for the IPMLC structure constitute the middle line, and those for independent parallel processing with fixed capacity (IPFC) constitute the lower line. To more closely resemble noise-infiltrated empirical data, each of the latter depictions is perturbed slightly with the addition of random values ranging from −0.05 to +0.05. Values of $C_o(t)$ for the IPUC system should approximate $[2(.9225)]/[2(1.23)] = 0.75$, and those for an IPFC system should approximate $[2(.615)]/[2(1.23)] = 0.50$.

In summary, the coordination of $H(t)$ with the redundant-target paradigm issues in a quantitatively principled measure of capacity of an assessed system, the capacity OR index, $C_o(t)$. The denominator of this index can be assembled from single-target trials so as to express the value that would occur with redundant-target trials, as seen in its numerator, if the system were of an independent parallel architecture with unlimited channel capac-

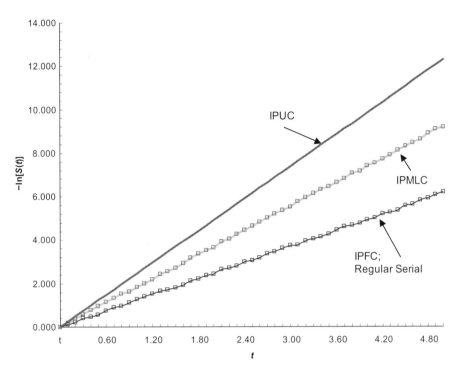

Figure 7.4. Values of the capacity coefficient $H(t) = -\ln[S(t)]$ portrayed for the independent-parallel unlimited capacity model (IPUC) benchmark, and independent parallel model with moderately limited capacity (IPMLC) and independent parallel model with fixed capacity (IPFC; empirically equivalent to standard serial for first-completion time), from $t = 0$ through $t = 5$, with $S(t)$ putatively sampled every 0.1 second. The value for v_1 for each structure is 1.23. Values specified by the IPMLC and IPFC models are randomly perturbed to convey some infiltration of empirical estimates by noise.

ity. Sources of departure from this reference system—channel-capacity limitation in the context of parallel-processing statistical advantage—provide a parametric glimpse into the overall workings of $C_o(t)$. In other words, selected mechanisms of cognitive-performance capacity captured by $C_o(t)$ are delineated as they take shape in the particular parametric case.

Some Clinical Inferences

Features of processing architecture affecting $C_o(t)$ stand to be shared by patients and control participants, because processing architecture in and of itself tends to remain intact with disorder (Neufeld & Broga, 1981; Neufeld et al., 2002; cf. Townsend et al., in press). Certain properties endowed by a given architecture therefore are no less present if its bearer is experiencing schizophrenia than otherwise. In the case at hand, such properties include statistical advantage accruing to an independent parallel structure.

Channel capacity conceivably could suffer with disorder. In the present instance, however, moderately limited capacity defensibly is shared by both groups. The absence of disproportionate channel-capacity limitation is reminiscent of findings for schizophrenia more generally, when capacity has been delineated within a formal theoretical framework (J. R. Carter & Neufeld, 2006; Neufeld et al., 1993; cf. chap. 5, this volume).

Although not that of unlimited capacity or supercapacity, the speed of ascertaining the status of an encountered stimulus over that of a fixed-capacity system stands to convey potentially important adaptive advantage in self-maintenance and meeting of environmental demands. Moreover, such comparative advantage potentially is compounded as memory-scanning requirements mount up in scanning-intensive tasks. It also arguably is ramified according to the constellation of other transactions contingent on the product of memory scanning (e.g., organizing a response appropriate to the memory-conveyed properties of a person, object, or event; cf. Schweikert, 1989; Wenger & Townsend, 2000). Again, to the degree that the present formulation can be brought forth, the temporal advantage imbued by an IPMLC structure over that of others, such as an IPFC or regular serial structure, is not lost with schizophrenia. This observation is in accord with other findings of intact memory search accompanying this disturbance (reviewed in Neufeld & Broga, 1981; see also Neufeld, 1991).

CONCLUSION

Cognitive processing capacity is a complex construct. Its meaning and measurement in a given application are intractable without the qualifications and constraints imposed by formal theory. Overall capacity to perform a cognitive task is available as the capacity index $H(t)$. Comparative taskwise capacity across performance conditions and/or groups can be evaluated using CR. Values are readily computed and have wide application.

The Capacity OR Coefficient $C_o(t)$ likewise is readily computable. It operates in lockstep with a collateral paradigm and assesses a submitted system against a standard of known architecture and channel-capacity characteristics. A system's unlimited capacity, limited capacity, or supercapacity depends on the absence, or the direction, of departure from the pivotal value of 1.0. Because $C_o(t)$ invokes a system with defined properties, candidate sources of $C_o(t)$'s value for the examined system are forthcoming.

A more recent capacity coefficient, complementing $C_o(t)$, is the Capacity AND Coefficient, $C_a(t)$ (Townsend & Wenger, 2004b). This coefficient resembles $C_o(t)$ in its computation and, like $C_o(t)$, prescribes an associated paradigm as well as the IPUC system as a benchmark. Its focus, however, is on exhaustive processing (as with completion of both items of a two-item memory set or visual array). Experimental trials of principal interest therefore are negative trials, whereby a target is not present in the memorized or visually inspected item set. Coupled with $C_o(t)$, this coefficient increasingly should make for a comprehensive picture of the operative system and act as a consistency test (Meehl, 1983) for inferences drawn from $C_o(t)$.

The capacity measures presented here inform the interpretation of generic data summaries, such as moments and other summary statistics. For example, allowing that reaction time reflects a continuous underlying latency distribution, mean reaction time is the integral from zero to infinity of the distribution's survivor function. The survivor function at time t is simply e exponentiated by -1 times the integral of the hazard function, taken between 0 and t. The hazard function, in turn, is explicitly tied to the concept of processing capacity. In this way, the mean reaction time has its own roots in an integrand that is elemental to formal capacity measures. Even the interpretation of a mean reaction time therefore is embellished by unveiling its dynamic stochastic composition.

The measures presented here clearly spring from decidedly formal theory. Experimental paradigms and forms of data partitioning are prescribed by the theoretical developments. Such results are in the spirit of theory-determined rather than off-the-shelf measurement (McFall & Townsend, 1998; Meehl, 1978), and they are in accord with the Einsteinian edict that "useful theory indicates where to look and provides a means of interpreting what is seen." The realization of dynamic stochastic properties in theory and measurement should advance assessment methodology for prominent concepts in clinical science as it has in other areas of psychology and older disciplines.

REFERENCES

Baxter, B. W., & Hinson, R. E. (2001). Is smoking automatic? Demands of smoking behavior on attentional resources. *Journal of Abnormal Psychology, 110*, 59–66.

Braithwaite, R. B. (1968). *Scientific explanation.* Cambridge, England: Cambridge University Press.

Brewin, C. R. (1989). Cognitive change processes in psychotherapy. *Psychological Review, 96*, 379–394.

Brewin, C. R., Dalgleish, T., & Joseph, S. (1996). A dual representation theory of posttraumatic stress disorder. *Psychological Review, 103*, 670–686.

Brewin, C. R., & Holmes, E. A. (2003). Psychological theories of posttraumatic stress disorder. *Clinical Psychology Review, 23*, 339–376.

Bricolo, E., Gianesini, T., Fanini, A., Bundesen, C., & Chelazzi, L. (2002). Serial attention mechanisms in visual search: A direct behavioral demonstration. *Journal of Cognitive Neuroscience, 14,* 980–993.

Broadbent, D. E. (1971). *Decision and stress.* New York: Academic Press.

Carter, C. S., Robertson, L. C., Chaderjian, M. R., Celaya, L. J., & Nordahl, T. E. (1992). Attentional asymmetry in schizophrenia: Controlled and automatic processes. *Biological Psychiatry, 31,* 909–918.

Carter, J. R., & Neufeld, R. W. J. (1999). Cognitive processing of multidimensional stimuli in schizophrenia: Formal modeling of judgment speed and content. *Journal of Abnormal Psychology, 108,* 633–654.

Carter, J. R., & Neufeld, R. W. J. (2006). *Cognitive processing of facial affect: Neuro-connectionist modeling of deviations in schizophrenia.* Manuscript submitted for publication.

Cohen, J. (1988). *Statistical power analysis for the behavioral sciences.* Hillsdale, NJ: Erlbaum.

Edwards, W. (1998). Tools for and experiences with Bayesian normative modeling. *American Psychologist, 53,* 416–428.

Embretson, W. S. (1983). Construct validity: Construct representation versus nomothetic span. *Psychological Bulletin, 93,* 179–197.

Endler, N. S., Edwards, J. M., & Vitelli, R. (1991). *Endler Multidimensional Anxiety Scales (EMAS): Manual.* Los Angeles: Western Psychological Services.

Evans, M., Hastings, N., & Peacock, B. (2000). *Statistical distributions* (3rd ed.). New York: Wiley.

Forster, P. M., & Grierson, A. T. (1978). Noise and attentional selectivity: A reproducible phenomenon? *British Journal of Psychology, 69,* 489–498.

George, L., & Neufeld, R. W. J. (1985). Cognition and symptomatology in schizophrenia. *Schizophrenia Bulletin, 11,* 264–285.

Gold, J. M., Wilk, C. M., McMahon, R. P., Buchanan, R. W., & Luck, S. J. (2003). Working memory for visual features and conjunctions in schizophrenia. *Journal of Abnormal Psychology, 112,* 61–71.

Granholm, E., Asarnow, R. F., & Marder, S. R. (1996a). Display visual angle and attentional scanpaths on the span of apprehension task in schizophrenia. *Journal of Abnormal Psychology, 105,* 17–24.

Granholm, E., Asarnow, R. F., & Marder, S. R. (1996b). Dual-task performance operating characteristics, resource limitations, and automatic processing in schizophrenia. *Neuropsychology, 10,* 11–21.

Hakstian, A. R., & Whalen, T. E. (1976). A *k*-sample significance test for independent alpha coefficients. *Psychometrika, 41,* 219–231.

Hartlage, S., Alloy, L. B., Vázquez, C., & Dykman, B. (1993). Automatic and effortful processing in depression. *Psychological Bulletin, 113,* 247–278.

Hasher, L., & Zacks, R. T. (1979). Automatic and effortful processes in memory. *Journal of Experimental Psychology: General, 108,* 356–388.

Highgate-Maynard, S., & Neufeld, R. W. J. (1986). Schizophrenic memory-search performance involving nonverbal stimulus properties. *Journal of Abnormal Psychology, 95*, 67–73.

Hockey, G. R. J. (1970a). Effect of loud noise on attention selectivity. *Quarterly Journal of Experimental Psychology, 22*, 28–36.

Hockey, G. R. J. (1970b). Signal probability and spatial location as possible bases for increased selectivity in noise. *Quarterly Journal of Experimental Psychology, 22*, 37–42.

Hockley, W. E., & Murdock, B. B., Jr. (1987). A decision model for accuracy and response latency in recognition memory. *Psychological Review, 94*, 341–358.

Jetté, J. (1997). *Formal models of the effects of exogenous stressors on information processing.* Unpublished master's thesis, University of Western Ontario, London, Ontario, Canada.

Kahneman, D., & Chajczyk, D. (1983). Tests of the automaticity of reading: Dilution of Stroop effects by color-irrelevant stimuli. *Journal of Experimental Psychology: Human Perception and Performance, 9*, 497–509.

Kirsh, I., & Lynn, S. (1999). Automaticity in clinical psychology. *American Psychologist, 54*, 504–515.

Lefave, M. K., & Neufeld, R. W. J. (1980). Anticipatory threat and physical-danger trait anxiety: A signal-detection analysis of effects on autonomic responding. *Journal of Research in Personality, 14*, 283–306.

MacLeod, C., & Rutherford, E. M. (1998). Automatic and strategic cognitive biases in anxiety and depression. In K. Kirsner, C. Speelman, M. Maybery, A. O'Brien-Malone, M. Anderson, & C. MacLeod (Eds.), *Implicit and explicit mental processes* (pp. 233–254). Mahwah, NJ: Erlbaum.

Magaro, P. A. (1983). Psychosis and schizophrenia. In W. D. Spaulding & J. K. Cole (Eds.), *Nebraska Symposium on Motivation: Vol. 31. Theories of schizophrenia and psychosis* (pp. 157–229). Lincoln: University of Nebraska Press.

Maher, B. (1966). *Principles of psychopathology: An experimental approach.* New York: McGraw-Hill.

McFall, R. M., & Townsend, J. T. (1998). Foundations of psychological assessment: Implications for cognitive assessment in clinical science. *Psychological Assessment, 10*, 316–330.

Meehl, P. E. (1978). Theoretical risks and tabular asterisks: Sir Karl, Sir Ronald, and the slow progress of soft psychology. *Journal of Consulting and Clinical Psychology, 46*, 806–843.

Meehl, P. E. (1983). Consistency tests in estimating the completeness of the fossil record: A neo-Popperian approach to statistical paleontology. In J. Earman (Ed.), *Minnesota studies in the philosophy of science: Vol. X. Testing scientific theories* (pp. 413–473). Minneapolis: University of Minnesota Press.

Mogg, K., Bradley, B. P., Williams, R., & Mathews, A. (1993). Subliminal processing of emotional information in anxiety and depression. *Journal of Abnormal Psychology, 102*, 304–311.

Narr, K. L., Green, M. F., Capetillo-Cunliffe, L., Toga, A. W., & Zaidel, E. (2003). Lateralized lexical decision in schizophrenia: Hemispheric specialization and interhemispheric lexicality priming. *Journal of Abnormal Psychology, 112,* 623–632.

Neufeld, R. W. J. (1978). Paranoid and nonparanoid schizophrenics' deficit in the interpretation of sentences: An information-processing approach. *Journal of Clinical Psychology, 34,* 333–339.

Neufeld, R. W. J. (1990). Coping with stress, coping without stress, and stress with coping: On inter-construct redundancies. *Stress Medicine, 6,* 117–125.

Neufeld, R. W. J. (1991). Memory in paranoid schizophrenia. In P. Magaro (Ed.), *The cognitive bases of mental disorders: Annual review of psychopathology* (Vol. 1, pp. 231–261). Newbury Park, CA: Sage.

Neufeld, R. W. J. (1994). *Theoretical stress and stress-proneness effects on information processing in light of mathematical models of stochastic processes* (Research Bulletin No. 720). London, Ontario, Canada: University of Western Ontario, Department of Psychology.

Neufeld, R. W. J. (1996). *Stochastic models of information processing under stress* (Research Bulletin No. 734). London, Ontario, Canada: University of Western Ontario, Department of Psychology.

Neufeld, R. W. J. (1998). Introduction to special section on process models in psychological assessment. *Psychological Assessment, 10,* 307–315.

Neufeld, R. W. J. (1999). Dynamic differentials of stress and coping. *Psychological Review, 106,* 385–397.

Neufeld, R. W. J. (in press). Composition and uses of formal clinical cognitive science In B. Shuart, W. Spaulding, & J. Poland (Eds.), *Nebraska Symposium on Motivation: Vol. 52. Modeling complex systems.* Lincoln: University of Nebraska Press.

Neufeld, R. W. J., & Broga, M. I. (1981). Evaluation of information-sequential aspects of schizophrenic performance: II. Methodological considerations. *Journal of Nervous and Mental Disease, 169,* 569–579.

Neufeld, R. W. J., Carter, J. R., Boksman, K., Jetté, J., & Vollick, D. (2002). Application of stochastic modelling to group and individual differences in cognitive functioning. *Psychological Assessment, 14,* 279–298.

Neufeld, R. W. J., & Gardner, R. C. (1990). Data aggregation in evaluating psychological constructs: Multivariate and logical deductive considerations. *Journal of Mathematical Psychology, 24,* 276–296.

Neufeld, R. W. J., & McCarty, T. (1994). A formal analysis of stressor and stress-proneness effects on basic information processing. *British Journal of Mathematical and Statistical Psychology, 47,* 193–226.

Neufeld, R. W. J., Vollick, D., & Highgate-Maynard, S. (1993). Stochastic modelling of stimulus encoding and memory search in paranoid schizophrenia: Clinical and theoretical implications. In R. L. Cromwell & R. C. Snyder (Eds.), *Schizophrenia: Origins, processes, treatment, and outcome: The second Kansas series in clinical psychology* (pp. 176–196). Oxford, England: Oxford University Press.

Nuechterlein, K. H., & Dawson, M. E. (1984). Information processing and attentional functioning in the developmental course of schizophrenic disorders. *Schizophrenia Bulletin, 2,* 160–203.

Paivio, A. (1975). Perceptual comparisons through the mind's eye. *Memory & Cognition, 3,* 635–647.

Paivio, A. (1986). *Imagery and verbal processes.* Hillsdale, NJ: Erlbaum.

Penn, D. L., & Spaulding, P. W. (1997). Introduction: Factors underlying social functioning in schizophrenia: Information processing and social perception. *Psychiatry, 60,* 279–280.

Penrose, A. (2004). *The road to reality.* New York: Knopf.

Poulton, E. C. (1977). Continuous intense noise masks auditory feedback and inner speech. *Psychological Bulletin, 84,* 977–1001.

Schmitt, N. (1996). Uses and abuses of coefficient alpha. *Psychological Assessment, 8,* 350–353.

Schneider, W., & Shiffrin, R. M. (1977). Controlled and automatic human information processing: I. Detection, search, and attention. *Psychological Review, 84,* 1–66.

Schweikert, R. (1989). Separable effects of factors on activation functions in discrete and continuous models: d' and evoked potentials. *Psychological Bulletin, 106,* 318–328.

Sheppard, L. C., & Teasdale, J. D. (2000). Dysfunctional thinking in major depressive disorder: A deficit in metacognitive monitoring? *Journal of Abnormal Psychology, 109,* 768–776.

Shiffrin, R. M. (1988). Attention. In R. C. Atkinson, R. J. Herrnstein, G. Lindzey, & R. D. Luce (Eds.), *Stevens' handbook of experimental psychology* (2nd ed., pp. 739–811). New York: Wiley.

Shiffrin, R. M., & Schneider, W. (1977). Controlled and automatic human information processing: II. Perceptual learning, automatic attending, and a general theory. *Psychological Review, 84,* 127–190.

Sternberg, S. (1975). Memory scanning: New findings and current controversies. *Quarterly Journal of Experimental Psychology, 27,* 1–32.

Teachman, B., & Woody, S. (2003). Automatic processing among individuals with spider phobia: Change in implicit fear associations following treatment. *Journal of Abnormal Psychology, 112,* 100–109.

Townsend, J. T. (1974). Issues and models concerning the processing of a finite number of inputs. In B. H. Kantowitz (Ed.), *Human information processing: Tutorials in performance and cognition* (pp. 133–168). Hillsdale, NJ: Erlbaum.

Townsend, J. T. (1984). Uncovering mental processes with factorial experiments. *Journal of Mathematical Psychology, 28,* 363–400.

Townsend, J. T. (1990). Serial and parallel processing: Sometimes they look like Tweedledum and Tweedledee but they can (and should) be distinguished. *Psychological Science, 1,* 46–54.

Townsend, J. T., & Ashby, F. G. (1978). Methods of modeling capacity in simple processing systems. In J. Castellan & F. Restle (Eds.), *Cognitive theory* (Vol. III, pp. 199–239). Hillsdale, NJ: Erlbaum.

Townsend, J. T., & Ashby, F. G. (1983). *Stochastic modelling of elementary psychological processes.* Cambridge, England: Cambridge University Press.

Townsend, J. T., Fific, M., & Neufeld, R. W. J. (in press). Assessment of mental architecture in clinical/cognitive research. In T. A. Treat, A. Kraut, & T. Baker (Eds.), *Psychological clinical science: Recent advances in theory and practice.* Mahwah, NJ: Erlbaum.

Townsend, J. T., & Nozawa, G. (1995). Spatio-temporal properties of elementary perception: An investigation of parallel, serial, and coactive theories. *Journal of Mathematical Psychology, 39,* 321–359.

Townsend, J. T., & Wenger, M. J. (2004a). The serial–parallel dilemma: A case study in a linkage of theory and method. *Psychonomic Bulletin & Review, 11,* 391–418.

Townsend, J. T., & Wenger, M. J. (2004b). A theory of interactive parallel processing: New capacity measures and predictions for a response time inequality series. *Psychological Review, 111,* 1003–1035.

Treisman, A., & Gormican, S. (1988). Feature analysis in early vision: Evidence from search asymmetries. *Psychological Review, 95,* 15–48.

Wenger, M., & Townsend, J. T. (2000). Basic response time tools for studying general processing capacity in attention, perception, and cognition. *Journal of General Psychology, 127,* 67–99.

Wishner, J. (1955). The concept of efficiency in psychological health and psychopathology. *Psychological Review, 62,* 69–80.

Wright, B. D. (1977). Solving measurement problems with the Rasch model. *Journal of Educational Measurement, 14,* 97–116.

8

USING A SPEECH PERCEPTION NEURAL NETWORK SIMULATION TO STUDY NORMAL NEURODEVELOPMENT AND AUDITORY HALLUCINATIONS IN SCHIZOPHRENIA

RALPH E. HOFFMAN AND THOMAS H. McGLASHAN

Schizophrenia has a lifetime prevalence of 0.8% to 1.0% that varies little across countries, cultures, and socioeconomic strata. This illness has devastating consequences arising from symptoms such as delusions and hallucinations as well as from cognitive impairments and behavioral difficulties. Important advances in understanding pathophysiology have unfolded over the past 25 years. These efforts have led to drug therapies that reduce some symptoms. However, a comprehensive understanding of the neurobiological basis of schizophrenia, as well as definitive treatments, still elude us, and

Support for this research was provided by National Institute of Mental Health Grants RO1-MH50557 (to Ralph E. Hoffman) and KO5-MH01654 (to Thomas H. McGlashan).

long-term negative outcomes in terms of disability and suffering remain all too common.

In this chapter, we describe how computer simulations of complex neural networks may provide new insights into the pathophysiology of schizophrenia. The focus of this investigation was on auditory hallucinations, a disruptive and often-disabling manifestation of this illness. Insofar as these hallucinations are typically experienced as spoken speech, they can be approached using computer modeling methods that capture normal aspects of speech perception. Our point of departure is to consider studies of normal neurodevelopment during adolescence. These studies emphasize a loss of neural connections during this time period. Schizophrenia is an illness that emerges during late adolescence and early adulthood. Many studies appear to demonstrate loss of neural connectivity in schizophrenia as well, suggesting that this disorder reflects an extension of normal adolescent neurodevelopment. When reductions in connectivity were imposed on a simulated speech perception neural network, percepts were generated by the network spontaneously—in the absence of any input—thereby emulating hallucinations. These results therefore provide a conceptual linkage between the actual clinical manifestations of schizophrenia and a potential pathophysiology that has its origins in neurodevelopmental processes.

SCHIZOPHRENIA VIEWED AS A
NEURODEVELOPMENTAL DISTURBANCE

Researchers have long hypothesized that schizophrenia is a neurodevelopmental disorder (Feinberg, 1982–1983; Margolis, Chuang, & Post, 1995; Weinberger, 1987). This view arises from the fact that this illness generally emerges within a relatively restricted age range—late adolescence or young adulthood for men (roughly between the ages of 18 and 25), with a somewhat later onset for women (roughly between ages 20 and 30). The relative constraints on age of onset suggest that maturational or developmental processes in the brain referable to that time period may play a role in illness expression.

A characteristic feature of human brain development during adolescence is the large-scale elimination of cortical synapses in the association cortex. This process was first highlighted in humans by a now-classic study reported by Huttenlocher (1979). Examining postmortem tissue obtained from the middle frontal cortex from normal subjects, synaptic density was found to peak during childhood with a subsequent decline of 30% to 40% at adulthood. A more recent postmortem study by Huttenlocher and Dabholkar (1997) compared synaptic density in the auditory cortex with that of the prefrontal cortex and found that synaptic elimination was much more prolonged in the latter, extending well into adolescence. Different time frames of pruning for different cortical regions appear to be a human-specific neurodevelopmental feature. In primates, by comparison, synaptic density appears to be rise and fall in parallel across different cortical regions.

Feinberg (1982–1983) first speculated that there may be a specific relationship between normal adolescent synaptic elimination and the characteristic age of onset of schizophrenia and postulated either excessive, retarded, or abnormal pruning as the primary cause of the disorder. Insofar as the prefrontal cortex exhibits especially extended synaptic pruning ordinarily, this view suggests that the prefrontal cortex may be central to neural dysfunction in schizophrenia.

Early studies of cerebral blood flow and metabolic brain activation appeared to support the view that the prefrontal cortex played a key role in the pathophysiology of schizophrenia (for a review, see Weinberger, Aloia, Goldberg, & Berman, 1994). Studies generally found that the prefrontal cortex in schizophrenic patients activates less robustly during performance of cognitive tasks. In addition, magnetic resonance imaging studies have detected subtle reductions in prefrontal gray matter in this patient group (Buchanan, Vladar, Barta, & Pearlson, 1998; Gur, Cowell, et al., 2000). Consistent with these functional and volumetric findings are postmortem studies examining neural density (for a review, see Selemon & Goldman-Rakic, 1999). For instance, neuronal density in prefrontal area 9 was 17% higher than normal in schizophrenic brains relative to normal brains (Selemon, Rajkowski, & Goldman-Rakic, 1995). A parallel study of prefrontal area 46 found a 21% elevation in neuronal density of schizophrenic brains relative to normal brains (Selemon, Rajkowski, & Goldman-Rakic, 1998). Given that the actual number of neurons the cortex of schizophrenic brains is not increased (Pakkenberg, 1993), the most likely basis for these findings is that *neuropil volume*, that is, the entanglement of axons and dendrites between neurons, is diminished in schizophrenia, at least in prefrontal areas. Consistent with this view is a postmortem study by Glantz and Lewis (2000) that used a Golgi stain method to quantify dendritic spines. They found a 23% reduction of spines in deep layer 3 pyramidal neurons in prefrontal area 46 of postmortem schizophrenic brains relative to normal control brains. Another study by Garey et al. (1998) found even more dramatic reductions of spine density in schizophrenic brains for this cell type and brain area. Also suggestive of loss of synaptic terminal are immunolabeling studies demonstrating that *synaptophysin*, a phosphoprotein marker of synaptic terminals, is reduced in frontal brain regions of schizophrenic patients relative to normal control participants (Glantz & Lewis, 1997; Honer et al., 1999; Karson et al., 1999).

Other studies of schizophrenia, however, also suggest functional, volumetric, and/or molecular alterations in other brain regions, such as the hippocampus (Blennow, Bogdanovic, Gottfries, & Davidsson, 1999; Gur, Turetsky, et al., 2000; Heckers et al., 1998; Velakoulis et al., 1999; Weinberger, Berman, Suddath, & Torrey, 1992), the entorhinal cortex (Akil, Edgar, Pierri, Casali, & Lewis, 2000; Arnold, 2000), and the cingulate gyrus (Blennow et al., 1999; Tamminga, Vogel, Gao, Lahti, & Holcomb, 2000). Reduced synaptophysin and SNAP-25, another synapse-associated protein, have been reported in the medial temporal cortex of schizophrenic patients (Eastwood & Harrison, 1995; Young et al., 1998). Therefore, a focus on the prefrontal cortex alone probably will miss important aspects of the pathophysiology of this disorder.

As data have emerged suggesting that brain disturbances in schizophrenia are more widespread, studies have begun to focus on nonfocal abnormalities in cortical connectivity that may involve the prefrontal cortex as well as other cortical or subcortical regions. *Diffusion tensor imaging* quantifies directional coherence and, possibly, connectivity of white matter fibers linking cortical areas. Using this method, Lim et al. (1999) demonstrated that white matter directional coherence in patients with schizophrenia was reduced. Abnormal findings were detected in both hemispheres and were widespread, extending from the frontal to occipital brain regions. Friston and Frith (1995) used a time series analysis of regional brain activation assessed with positron emission tomography. Schizophrenic patients demonstrated differences in the level and direction of correlations across prefrontal and temporal brain regions compared with normal control participants. These data were interpreted as indicating a disruption of prefrontal–temporal interactions. Another study used positron emission tomography to delineate cortical activation during performance of a verbal fluency task (Spence et al., 2000). The most prominent feature distinguishing patients with schizophrenia from normal control participants was not level of activation in a particular brain area but reduced correlation of prefrontal and cingulate activation, which again suggests a breakdown in functional connectivity linking these brain regions. Finally, metachromatic leukodystrophy provides a neurological condition that can mimic schizophrenia (Hyde, Ziegler, & Weinberger, 1992). A variant of this disorder that emerges during adolescence and young adulthood can produce hallucinations, delusions, and disorganized thinking that is initially indistinguishable from that of schizophrenia and only later evolves into a degenerative picture characteristic of diffuse neurological impairment. This variant of the disorder attacks white matter mediating corticocortical connections, especially in frontal regions, while sparing gray matter. The selectivity of the neuropathology in its early stages again supports the hypothesis that schizophrenia arises from disrupted corticocortical connectivity.

SIMULATING AUDITORY HALLUCINATIONS OF SPEECH

Computer models are central to scientific disciplines ranging from meteorology to physical chemistry. Their usefulness lies in simulating complex, interactive systems. A good model does not attempt to re-create "reality" in its entirety—if that were the case, the best model would be the real-life system itself. Instead, model construction proceeds by incorporating a limited number of properties or observations. The model will have informative value if, when simulated, critical phenomena that have been previously unexplained are exhibited or if phenomena previously appearing unrelated are shown to emerge from a single process. Along these lines, we review in this chapter a neural network computer simulation of certain aspects of speech perception (Hoffman & McGlashan, 1997; McGlashan & Hoffman, 2000). Although this simulation represents a vast simplification of actual cortical networks, some interesting properties were exhibited by the network that included context-dependent information processing and efficient learning that suggest plausibility of the model's "perceptual" capacities. The central purpose of the model was to explore a possible pathophysiology of auditory hallucinations, a core symptom of schizophrenia. In the process of exploring the model's properties, an unanticipated finding emerged that was not deliberately engineered into the simulation. This new finding may provide insights into normal brain development and suggests a linkage between the pathophysiology of schizophrenia and neurodevelopmental processes. With some cleverness, one can often get models to do rather complicated things that appear to provide support for a wide range of hypotheses. Thus, it is unanticipated and unsought simulation findings that may have the most value in advancing knowledge.

Our strategy was not to simulate the entirety of schizophrenia—clearly an impossible task—but to explore a single exemplar symptom, auditory hallucinations. This symptom is reported by approximately 50% to 80% of patients with schizophrenia (Andreasen & Flaum 1991; Sartorius, Shapiro, & Jablonsky, 1974). If patients manifest auditory hallucinations during one episode, there is a high likelihood they will recur on subsequent episodes (Chaturvedi & Sinha, 1990), often with very similar phenomenological characteristics. Auditory hallucinations therefore appear to delineate a relatively stable vulnerability that warrants additional study.

One clue as to the neurobiological basis of these hallucinations is that they typically consist of spoken speech or "voices." This phenomenological feature suggests that hallucinated speech involves neural systems dedicated to auditory speech perception. This view is reinforced by neuroimaging evidence of auditory–linguistic association cortex activation when "voices" occur. Functional magnetic resonance imaging studies have highlighted activation of primary auditory and language association cortex during hallucination periods (Dierks et al., 1999; Shergill, Brammer, Williams, Murray, & McGuire, 2000). Along these lines, an evoked-potential study elicited by sound stimuli in hallucinating schizophrenic patients suggested endogenous activation (Tiihonen et al., 1992). Finally, a study of speech perception capacity under noisy conditions compared schizophrenic patients with and without auditory hallucinations (Hoffman et al., 1995; Hoffman, Rapaport, Mazure, & Quinlan, 1999). Selective impairments in discerning conversational spoken speech contaminated with background noise were detected in the former group. In general, these patients were not hallucinating during the task performance itself. Therefore, perceptual impairments were likely not due to distraction or interruption by the hallucinations themselves. These findings suggest that speech perception systems themselves are functionally altered in patients with these hallucinations.

Nonlinguistic mechanisms of hallucinated speech, such as sensory gating abnormalities, have been proposed. In support of this perspective are studies indicating that patients with schizophrenia are less able to filter out irrelevant information when responding to certain types of sensory inputs (Braff, Swerdlow, & Geyer, 1999; Judd, McAdams, Budnick, & Braff, 1992). There are, however, no studies directly testing this hypothesis by determining whether such filtering impairments distinguish schizophrenic patients who are vulnerable to auditory hallucinations and those who are not. Another popular view is that voices actually are ordinary inner thoughts or auditory imagery that have been misidentified as deriving from an external, nonself source (Frith & Done, 1989). In support of this hypothesis, McGuire et al. (1995) reported reduced activation in patients with auditory hallucinations compared with nonhallucinators when participants imagined hearing speech spoken by others. The authors argued that these brain activation failures, which emerged in the left middle temporal gyrus and the supplementary motor areas, reflect a defective capacity to remain aware that these images are self-generated. However, it remains possible that reduced activation elicited during task performance by hallucinating patients could be due to higher levels of baseline engagement of these brain areas. A parallel cognitive study has found impairments in distinguishing self versus nonself vocalizations heard on headphones in hallucinating versus nonhallucinating patients (Johns & McGuire, 1999). In this study, biases in attributing phonetically distorted reproductions of one's own voice as being spoken by another speaker were studied. Schizophrenic patients were found to have a greater attributional bias of this sort compared with nonhallucinating patients; however, this bias could be due to behavioral effects of hallucinations themselves—that is, hallucinators may be conditioned to expect a higher frequency of putatively nonself speech percepts compared with nonhallucinators. Finally, if one asks patients to generate inner speech or verbal thought, they do not report the subsequent experience as a voice or hallucination (Hoffman, 1986). If the primary difficulty were misattribution of verbal thought, then these simple exercises should result in hallucinated voices.

Our strategy for modeling auditory hallucinations therefore was to simulate certain aspects of the speech perception system based on neuro-imaging findings suggesting modality-specific involvement of the association cortex in various types of hallucinations (Shergill et al., 2001) as well as on our own psycholinguistic studies suggesting direct involvement of this neural system (Hoffman et al., 1995, 1999). A previous study by Hoffman and Dobscha (1989) examined effects of reduced synaptic density and network connectivity in associative memory simulations. Excessively pruned simulations revealed certain neural subassemblies within the larger network that failed to respond to inputs from elsewhere in the network, thereby producing "autonomous" outputs suggesting aspects of schizophrenia such as thought disorder and thought control. These neural assemblies demonstrated dynamical behaviors akin to "attractors" characterized by nonlinear systems theory. Attractor dynamics cause a nonlinear system to reorganize into a stable state. For overpruned networks, certain subassemblies would be relentlessly pulled into a particular attractor regardless of what was going on in the rest of the network.

On the basis of these earlier findings, our objective was to determine if pruning connections and eliminating synapses could also simulate hallucinated voices in a computer neural network simulation of aspects of speech perception. Hallucinations, by definition, are percepts that emerge in the absence of corresponding external sensory information. Our hope therefore was to explore conditions whereby these simulations produced speech percepts autonomously, that is, in the absence of any phonetic inputs.

NETWORK ARCHITECTURE

We developed a network architecture that detected words based on simplified "phonetic inputs" that are presented in sequence, expressing grammatical sentences. We targeted the working memory component of our neural network to explore effects of reduced corticocortical connectivity. Ordinary speech, when produced at normal rates, has significant acoustic ambiguity due to blurring of phonetic information and background sounds (Kalikow & Stevens, 1977; Warren & Warren, 1970). Consequently, perception of a word embedded in a stream of spoken speech depends not only on acoustic input corresponding to the word itself but also on previously perceived words and intrinsic knowledge of how words are sequenced grammatically and semantically into larger message units, a process reflecting a specialized working memory. Working memory impairments have been demonstrated in schizophrenia (Gold, Carpenter, Randolph, Goldberg, &

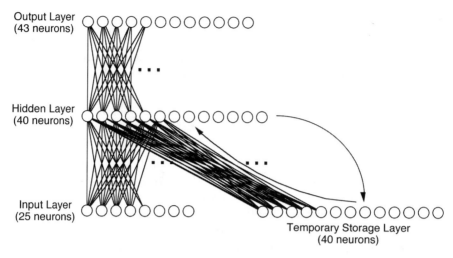

Output Layer
(43 neurons)

Hidden Layer
(40 neurons)

Input Layer
(25 neurons)

Temporary Storage Layer
(40 neurons)

Figure 8.1. A schematic diagram of the architecture of the network used in this study, which is based on Elman (1990). From "Synaptic Elimination, Neurodevelopment, and the Mechanism of Hallucinated 'Voices' in Schizophrenia," by R. E. Hoffman and T. H. McGlashan, 1997, *American Journal of Psychiatry, 154,* p. 1685. Copyright 1997 by the American Psychiatric Association; http://ajp.psychiatryonline.org. Reprinted by permission.

Weinberger, 1997; Park & Holzman, 1992) as well as disturbed interactions between frontal and medial temporal areas (Weinberger et al., 1992), two brain areas known to underlie this cognitive function (Goldman-Rakic & Friedman, 1991). A key functional component of our simulation, therefore, was the working memory component of a neural network that acquired knowledge regarding plausible, grammatical sequences of words in its vocabulary and used this knowledge to generate a sequential expectation that guided translation of the stream of "phonetic inputs" into sequences of word "percepts." We postulated first that verbal working memory in speech processing neurocircuitry of patients with auditory hallucinations was not only impaired but also produced spurious outputs and second, that these disturbances arose from reductions in working memory network connectivity.

Our simulation of sequential word processing was based on models developed by Elman (1990) and was a modification of an earlier simulation (Hoffman et al., 1995) that forced greater reliance on the working memory capacity of the system during training and reduced the number of neurons involved in working memory. The network, which consisted of 148 neuronal elements divided into a four-layered system (see Figure 8.1), was designed to translate phonetic inputs into perceptual outputs corresponding to strings of lexical elements. Actual acoustic data were not used. Instead, our simplifying assumption was that the phonetic representation of each word corresponded to a pattern of activation where roughly 25% of the neurons in the initial or *input layer* were turned "on" (see Table 8.1). Each of forty *hidden layer* neurons received a weighted sum of inputs from each of the 25 input neurons:

$$I(x) = \Sigma\, w_{yx}a_i(y), \qquad (8.1)$$

where $I(x)$ is information communicated from the input layer to neuron x in the hidden layer, w_{yx} is the weight (which can be positive or negative) of the projection from neuron y in the input layer to neuron x in the hidden layer, and $a_i(y)$ is the level of activation of neuron y in the input layer. Each hidden layer neuron also received input from every neuron in the *temporary storage* layer (also 40 neurons in size), which stored a replica of the pattern of activation of the hidden layer emerging from the preceding phonetic input.

The activation of each neuron in the hidden layer, $a_h(x)$, ranged from 0 to 1 and was computed as follows:

$$a_h(x) = 1/\{1 + \exp[-g * I(x) + \beta]\}, \qquad (8.2)$$

where g (gain) and β (bias) together determine response profiles of simulated neurons. When the combined input to a neuron was very negative, its activation approached zero. When the summed input was very positive, neural activation approached a maximum level of 1. Intermediate levels of firing were expressed as fractions. The *output layer* consisted of 43 neurons. Output layer neurons received inputs exclusively from the hidden layer (see Figure 8.1) and had the same activation function as hidden layer neurons.

Besides assignment of a phonetic code, each of the words in Table 8.1 was also assigned an activation pattern for the output layer where between three and six of these neurons were turned on for a given word. These neurons coded for semantic and syntactic features. For instance, the word *cop* was represented by activation of output neurons that individually coded for NOUN, ANIMATE, and HUMAN, as well as a particular neuron that referred to *cop* itself. A sample of output codes for individual words is provided in Table 8.2.

When the network produced an output layer activation pattern, an algorithm decided which word was the best fit for that particular pattern; the best fit became the *detected word*. When the output activation pattern demonstrated no clear-cut best fit, the network was assessed as not perceiving any word at all.

Network training used 60 repetitions of a set of 256 different sentences with degraded phonetic input to force reliance on working memory. Connection weights between different neuronal layers were adjusted using an online variant of back-propagation learning (Miikkulainen, 1993). This procedure caused learning to occur much more rapidly relative to more standard versions of back-propagation and more closely approximates actual live

TABLE 8.1
Phonetic Code for the 30 Words Belonging to the Network's Vocabulary

Word	Phonetic code
young	0001000101001110000001000
old	0100011101101011010100101
tell	1001000001100011000100000
omen	0100101100001000010010100
dog	0101001000000000111100000
Jane	1010000100000001110001001
run	0000001011000000000100111
ball	0110000001001000001011010
kick	0000010110011000000001010
give	1100010010000000110100010
boy	0000011000110110000100000
miss	0110010000000010000101011
large	1000001111001100100010001
small	1001101110001011000101100
story	0111000100101010001000100
frightens	0001001000011100010011000
girl	1010010000110000001000010
Bill	1001000011100000111000010
God	0101000001000001011100110
man	1101001001100000000000100
cop	0000001010011000011011100
Sam	0100010001001010000100000
think	0001010101000011001010000
kiss	1000010010011010001000000
won't	0000100101000010010000010
woman	1001000100000010000101110
chase	0001000000101000000010000
fear	1001000010000100001000100
love	0001100101010100010001000
warning	1001110100010010111000000

Note. Patterns of 1s and 0s were generated arbitrarily using a random number generator.

TABLE 8.2

Examples of the Output Semantic Feature Code for Representative Words
Belonging to the Network's Vocabulary

Output neurons ($n = 43$)	Semantic feature code	Word							
		boy	Jane	cop	kiss	miss	run	small	large
1	Noun	•	•	•					
3	Human	•	•	•					
12	Person-Jane		•						
14	Cop			•					
20	Verb				•	•	•		
21	Verb-complement-animate				•	•			
25	Verb-complement-null						•		
27	Verb-kiss				•				
28	Verb-miss					•			
39	Adjective							•	•
40	Age-attribute	•		•					
41	Size-attribute	•						•	•
42	Diminutive	•						•	
43	Superlative			•					•

Note. Examples of how the "meanings" of particular words were represented by the output layer of the network. Activation of Neuron 1 indicated that the input being processed was a noun. Conversely, activation of Neuron 20 signaled that the network had detected a verb. Activation of Neuron 21 signaled that the network detected a verb requiring a complement that ordinarily requires an animate agent (e.g., "kiss Jane," "chase boy"). Dots in cells mean that some of the neurons were skipped in the table.

learning rates. The learning process caused the working memory component of the network to store and make predictions based on prior information-processing steps, which aided translation of phonetic information into words.

After the network was trained, it was retested with a set of 23 sentences not used in training but incorporating the same vocabulary. During testing, each test sentence was separated from the next by a pause consisting of five null inputs (activation of all input neurons set to zero). The percentage of words successfully detected by the network was counted as well as the total number of misidentifications (when the network confused one word for another). Hallucinations were scored when output layer activation patterns yielded word percepts during pauses when phonetic inputs were absent. Assessment of network performance was undertaken with full phonetic information for each word and then repeated with degraded phonetic information. The latter condition was created by randomly selected two input neurons ordinarily turned on for each word and resetting them to zero. This

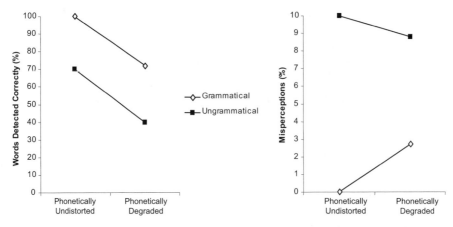

Figure 8.2. Word detection and misidentification rates for the standard network before pruning. Effects of reducing phonetic information and randomization of input word sequences are represented. These data demonstrate that the network uses meaning intrinsic to grammatical sequences of words to facilitate translating phonetic inputs into lexical percepts. From "Synaptic Elimination, Neurodevelopment, and the Mechanism of Hallucinated 'Voices' in Schizophrenia," by R. E. Hoffman and T. H. McGlashan, 1997, *American Journal of Psychiatry, 154,* p. 1896. Copyright 1997 by the American Psychiatric Association; http://ajp.psychiatryonline.org. Reprinted by permission.

manipulation forced the network to rely more on working memory and linguistic expectations based on previous inputs to fill in the blanks and produce the correct word percept.

An example of how network performance was assessed is given below. Suppose the input consisted of phonemes presented in a sequence corresponding to the following words:

cop—chase—old—man—#—#—#—#—#—Jane—kiss—girl,

where the # symbols are null inputs corresponding to a pause. Assume that the output of the network was

cop—chase—■—dog—■—■—■—fear—■—Jane—kiss—girl,

where ■ denotes the absence of any output produced by the network. The number of words correctly identified would be 5 out of 7. One word (*man*) would be scored as a misidentification, and *fear* would be scored as a hallucination. In assessing the simulation, sentences were presented with no phonetic degradation, and then the process was repeated where two of the "on" phonetic features for a given word were turned off.

Before any neuroanatomic manipulation, we tested the network's ability to detect words, first when words were presented in grammatical sentences and second when the same words were presented in random order. The results are illustrated in Figure 8.2. Successful word detection was shown to be highly dependent on grammatically meaningful word order when inputs were fully represented and when phonetic information was degraded. These data provide strong evidence that a specialized verbal working memory dependent on sequential word order was operative.

A neuroanatomic pruning procedure was then applied that was guided by the concept of "neurodevelopmental Darwinism" (Edelman, 1987). In mathematical terms, if the absolute value of a connection weight linking the temporary and hidden layer was below a certain threshold, it was reset to zero. We assumed that the number of synapses required to maintain a projection was directly correlated with the absolute value of the strength of that projection, an ordinate number with either positive or negative values. The total strength of connections lost (as an absolute number) was calculated as a percentage of the sum of connection strengths summed across all connections in the unpruned network. This fraction was used to estimate the percentage of synapses lost based on the assumption that the synaptic density of a connection will covary in a roughly linear fashion with the computational strength of that connection. This calculation is of interest insofar as many of the connections pruned in the model were weak in absolute terms and hence assumed to correspond to a relatively low number of synapses. It is only when relatively robust connections were eliminated that the network performance began to shift—initially for the better, but subsequently for the worse. We assumed that such connections were mediated by higher numbers of synapses.

As a comparison pathology, the consequences of loss of neurons themselves were also studied. Animal studies have indicated that neuronal loss accompanies normal neurodevelopment (Margolis et al., 1995). Along these lines, Huttenlocher (1979) described postmortem data strongly suggestive of frontal neuron cell loss in humans during early childhood. Also intriguing is an etiologic explanation of schizophrenia based on pharmacological studies of N–methyl-D-aspartate antagonists. Insofar as these drugs have been found to be psychotomimetic in humans and productive of excitotoxic cell death in animals, Olney and Farber (1995) have proposed that schizophrenia itself is due to an excitotoxic process where neurons are lost. Therefore, our neural network model included an "excitotoxic cell death" condition in which those neurons most consistently activated were functionally eliminated. Other methods of cell death, such as working memory neurons knocked out at random or because they are the least activated (i.e., disuse atrophy), also were studied.

The effects of pruning connections in the working memory component of the system are illustrated in Figure 8.3. The initial detection rate in response to phonetically degraded inputs improved when up to 30% of synapses were eliminated. In parallel, the number of misperceptions dropped considerably (see Figure 8.4). However, as pruning progressed to more

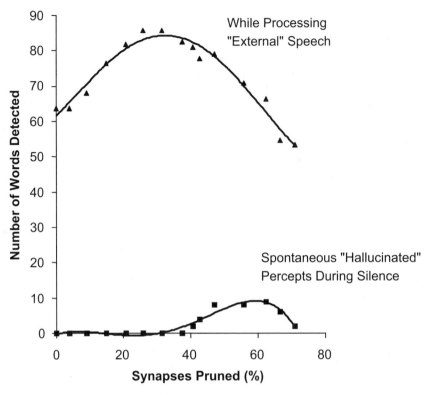

extensive levels, word detection dropped off, and misperceptions again rose. Moreover, spontaneous percepts during silent pauses began to emerge in the absence of any input, thereby simulating hallucinated, spoken speech (see Figure 8.3). These "hallucinations" consisted of a single word, *won't,* that tended to follow sentences ending in a noun. Thus, the hallucination tended to follow certain "normal" word sequence expectations, namely, that the word *won't* follows nouns (e.g., *girl won't run*). At very high pruning levels, hallucination rates again dropped back to near-zero levels (see Figure 8.3).

A comparison study of simulated pathology examining effects of neuronal death in the working memory system was also studied. Different types of neuron loss (neurotoxic cell loss, disuse atrophy, random neuronal

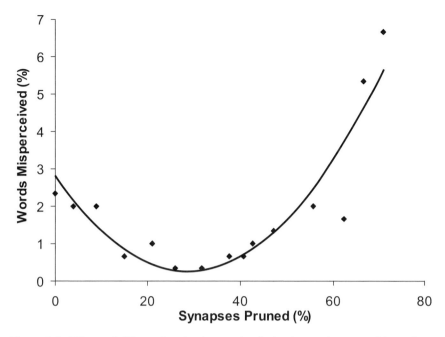

Figure 8.4. Effects of different levels of synaptic elimination on the network's tendency to misperceive words (i.e., to "hear" a word substituting for another word). From "Neural Network Models of Schizophrenia," by R. E. Hoffman and T. H. McGlashan, 2001, *The Neuroscientist, 7,* p. 450. Copyright 2001 by Sage Publications. Reprinted with permission.

dropout) produced impairments in translating inputs into word percepts but never significant enhancements of network function, as in the case of Darwinian pruning of connections. Moreover, no form of neuronal dropout led to spontaneous, "hallucinated" percepts occurring in the absence of phonetic input.

DISCUSSION

In terms of schizophrenia, the simulation demonstrates how overpruning connections in neural networks can induce hallucinations. This mechanism can be understood intuitively as reflecting the fact that pruning in our model appeared to enhance the ability of the network to fill in the gaps secondary to phonetic ambiguity using linguistic knowledge activated by means of a specialized working memory. When pruning was extended, this tendency to fill in gaps became so hypertrophied that word detection became disrupted, misperceptions increased, and "hallucinated" speech percepts emerged in the absence of any acoustic input whatsoever.

The behavior of the overpruned, hallucinogenic network helps us understand certain clinical aspects of actual patients with schizophrenia who experience "voices." Most important, the simulation demonstrates how hallucination-prone speech perception systems are also prone to misperceiving actual external speech, especially when phonetic information is degraded. This finding provides an explanation for a phenomenon commonly reported by patients with schizophrenia, namely, that they tend to hear personalized messages from television or radio or when they hear background speech, such as in a crowded room or on the street. Our simulation suggests that a key factor producing these experiences is speech (or song) that is produced rapidly or is otherwise unclear in terms of acoustic information that then results in misperceptions. These substituted words or phrases have personalized meaning—they are not random percepts. Thus, it can be readily appreciated how these patients develop enduring paranoia—believing that people are talking about them behind their backs or that they are the focus of some conspiracy or plot as evidenced by the bizarre messages they are receiving from television or radio.

Second, the simulation demonstrates why there is a characteristic age of onset for schizophrenia. If overpruning of corticocortical connections is central to the pathophysiology of this disorder as suggested by these findings, then one would predict that the age of onset of this disorder would be at the end of adolescence, which is when neurodevelopmentally induced pruning has run its course. This age of onset is roughly what is observed in actual cases, although the range of age can be considerably extended.

Third, the simulation produced an unexpected finding that was not part of the original study plan—at lower, prepsychotic levels of pruning, a distinct improvement in perceptual processing was demonstrated by the network. One advantage of corticocortical pruning is a conservation of energy requirements in the brain (Hoffman & Dobscha, 1989). Here we also have demonstrated a clear-cut information-processing advantage favoring pruned networks as well. These findings expand on another simulation study of artificial networks by Le Cun, Denker, and Solla (1990), who found that pruning promoted better generalization capacities. Our study also suggests that pruning promoted generalization—in particular regarding those sequences of words that produce meaningful sentences. Moreover, these generalizations were put into the service of decoding sequences of sensory inputs over time so that a specific "perceptual" capacity was itself enhanced.

These simulation findings can furthermore be used to generate some rough estimates of the percentage of synapses eliminated in order to optimize network functioning during development. As noted earlier, estimations of the fraction of synapses lost from the total pool of synapses following elimination of a particular connection were based on the absolute value of the weight of that connection. This analytic strategy predicted that optimal network function would be achieved after a reduction of synaptic density of approximately 30%. This estimate is relatively close to the observed 35% to 40% reduction in frontal cortex synaptic density in adulthood levels relative to peak childhood levels reported by Huttenlocher (1979). Moreover, our graphs can be used to estimate synaptic density reductions relative to optimized adult levels that are predicted to induce psychosis. These data predict that induction of hallucinations occurs at a pruning level of 15% to 20% beyond optimum synaptic density, a range not far removed from neuropil reductions of 17% to 21% detected in prefrontal brain regions in the brains of actual patients with schizophrenia (Selemon et al., 1995, 1998). However, this approach underestimates the loss of dendritic spines reported by Glantz and Lewis (2000) and Garey et al. (1998). However, these reductions were noted only for layer III neurons, not for neurons distributed across all layers of cortex. If this less selective method of counting dendritic spines were used, it is likely that reductions observed in the schizophrenic brains would be much smaller than that reported. It is worth noting also that neuropil volume and dendritic spines counts are variables that are distinct from synaptic density per se.

There are no data whatsoever directly assessing the synaptic density in speech perception neurocircuitry of the human brain across age ranges—the functional capacity emulated by the simulation. However, a study of song acquisition in songbirds demonstrated a reduction of synapses over time in brain areas responsible for this communication function (Scheich, Wallhäusseer-Franke, & Braun, 1991). Birdsong is not speech per se, but it is, like speech, a highly structured communication system involving sound sequences. It is at least plausible that a parallel developmental process occurs in humans where cortical pruning of synapses results in enhanced efficiency in processing sequential linguistic behavior.

As noted in the beginning of this chapter, females appear to have a somewhat later onset of schizophrenia than males. Our neurodevelopmental model of psychosis provides a potential explanation. Animal studies have found that higher levels of female hormones, such as estrogen, are associated with delayed developmental pruning of cortical connections and higher levels of connectivity and neuritic proliferation (Muñoz-Cueto, Garcia-Segura, & Ruiz-Marcos, 1990; Naftolin et al., 1990; Woolley, Wenzel, & Schwartzkroin, 1996). Our model predicts that a reduced rate of pruning associated with higher levels of female hormones during puberty could also determine the epidemiological differences in age of onset for men and women.

We have undertaken other studies that appear at least consistent with the simulation findings described above. First, the simulation predicted that schizophrenic patients would demonstrate subtle alterations of speech perception—namely, a reduced ability to correctly perceive continuous, narrative speech when speech sounds were phonetically degraded. Hoffman et al. (1999) tested this prediction in a group of 21 schizophrenic patients with auditory hallucinations, a group of 24 schizophrenic patients without a history of auditory hallucinations, and 26 normal control participants. Participants in the three groups were closely matched for level of education, age, and gender. The two patient groups were closely matched for overall level of illness. Narrative speech perception capacity was tested at different decibel levels of superimposed multispeaker babble, which varied phonetic ambiguity. As predicted by neural network simulations, patients with auditory hallucinations demonstrated a reduced word detection rate and an increased number of misperceptions compared with nonhallucinating patients and normal control participants. Using data from a higher noise condition in a two-variable discriminant analysis enabled us to correctly classify hallucinating versus nonhallucinating patients with 82.2% accuracy ($p < .002$, based on a discriminant function applied to the same data used to derive the discriminant equation).

We also have used repetitive transcranial magnetic stimulation (rTMS) to directly probe speech-processing neurocircuitry in hallucinating patients. This approach has allowed us to test the prediction made by the network simulation that auditory hallucinations of speech arise from activation of these neurocircuitry components. One-hertz rTMS was administered to the left temporoparietal cortex, a brain region known to play a critical role in semantic processing and verbal memory during speech perception (Fiez, Raichle, Balota, Tallal, & Petersen, 1996; Ojemann, 1978). Other studies have demonstrated that 1-Hz rTMS given over approximately 15 minutes produces sustained reductions in activation in the brain area directly stimulated as well as in other brain areas functionally connected to the former (for a review, see Hoffman & Cavus, 2002). Effects of active stimulation were compared with sham stimulation, using a double-blind design, that induced similar scalp sensations but minimized brain stimulation (Hoffman et al., 2000, 2003). These studies found robust statistical evidence of reduced hallucinations following active rTMS but not sham rTMS and provide further support for the hypothesis that speech-processing neurocircuitry plays a critical role in the genesis of auditory hallucinations.

CONCLUSION

Considerable data now support the hypothesis that schizophrenia is associated with reduced corticocortical connectivity. Our speech perception neural network simulation has provided a potentially useful model linking curtailed network connectivity to the genesis of auditory hallucinations. These neural network models do not precisely characterize the underlying etiology of connectivity disturbances. However, an unexpected finding aris-ing from the model was that connectivity reductions at a lower level were observed to enhance information processing. This finding provides an inter-esting explanation for synaptic pruning observed during the postnatal period in mammals that appears to be especially prolonged in the association cortex in humans—extending well into adolescence. Moreover, a specific causal factor leading to schizophrenia—namely, a failure to turn off neurodevelop-mental pruning at the end of adolescence—is suggested (McGlashan & Hoffman, 2000). This explanatory model provides a rationale for the charac-teristic age of onset of schizophrenia and the difference in age of onset between men and women, and it provides a detailed account of the mecha-nisms of auditory hallucinations, an important symptom in schizophrenia. Regardless of the ultimate validity of this claim, we hope that this line of research demonstrates the usefulness of neural network simulations in linking outward manifestations of neuropsychiatric disorders to underlying neuro-biological processes. Future advances in our understanding of psychiatric disorders, we believe, will require computational methods to delineate princi-ples of normal and abnormal neural system information processing. These insights will, we hope, yield new, more specific methods for treating schizo-phrenia and other mental illnesses that have remained so enigmatic in terms of their origins and so resistant to therapeutic intervention.

CLOSING COMMENTS

The simulations described in this chapter were derived from concepts and simulation methods described in a seminal article written Jeffery Elman (1990), which is highly recommended reading. A book-length review of computer simulations of neural network simulations and their usefulness in studying neuropsychiatric disorders was written by Manfred Spitzer (2000) and is also highly recommended. More technical discussions of different neural network methodologies and their conceptual underpinnings can be found in Rumelhart and McClelland (1986).

REFERENCES

Akil, M., Edgar, C. L., Pierri, J. N., Casali, S., & Lewis, D. A. (2000). Decreased density of tyrosine hydroxylase-immunoreactive axons in the entorhinal cortex of schizophrenic subjects. *Biological Psychiatry, 47*, 361–370.

Andreasen, N. C., & Flaum, M. (1991). Schizophrenia: The characteristic symp-toms. *Schizophrenia Bulletin, 17*, 27–49.

Arnold, S. E. (2000). Cellular and molecular neuropathology of the parahippo-campal region in schizophrenia. In *Annals of the New York Academy of Sciences: Vol. 911. The parahippocampal region: Implications for neurological and psychiatric diseases* (pp. 275–292). New York: New York Academy of Sciences.

Blennow, K., Bogdanovic, N., Gottfries, C. G., & Davidsson P. (1999). The growth-associated protein GAP-43 is increased in the hippocampus and in the gyrus cinguli in schizophrenia. *Journal of Molecular Neuroscience, 13,* 101–109.

Braff, D. L., Swerdlow, N. R., & Geyer, M. A. (1999). Symptom correlates of prepulse inhibition deficits in male schizophrenic patients. *American Journal of Psychiatry, 156,* 596–602.

Buchanan, R. W., Vladar, K., Barta, P. E., & Pearlson, G. D. (1998). Structural evaluation of the prefrontal cortex in schizophrenia. *American Journal of Psychiatry, 155,* 1049–1055.

Chaturvedi, S., & Sinha, V. D. (1990). Recurrence of hallucinations in consecutive episodes of schizophrenia and affective disorder. *Schizophrenia Research, 3,* 103–106.

Dierks, T., Linden, D. E. J., Jandl, M., Formisano, E., Goebel, R., Lanfermann, H., & Singer, W. (1999). Activation of Heschl's gyrus during auditory hallucinations. *Neuron, 22,* 615–621.

Eastwood, S. L., & Harrison, P. J. (1995). Decreased synaptophysin in the medial temporal lobe in schizophrenia demonstrated using immunoautoradiography. *Neuroscience, 69,* 339–343.

Edelman, G. M. (1987). *Neural Darwinism: The theory of neural group selection.* New York: Basic Books.

Elman, J. L. (1990). Finding structure in time. *Cognitive Science, 14,* 179–211.

Feinberg, I. (1982–1983). Schizophrenia: Caused by a fault in programmed synaptic elimination during adolescence? *Journal of Psychiatric Research, 17,* 319–334.

Fiez, J. A., Raichle, M. E., Balota, D. A., Tallal, P., & Petersen, S. E. (1996). PET activation of posterior temporal regions during auditory word presentation and verb generation. *Cerebral Cortex, 6,* 1–10.

Friston, K. J., & Frith, C. D. (1995). Schizophrenia: A disconnection syndrome? *Clinical Neuroscience, 3,* 89–97.

Frith, C. D., & Done, D. J. (1989). Experiences of alien control in schizophrenia reflect a disorder in the central monitoring of action. *Psychological Medicine, 19,* 359–363.

Garey, L. J., Ong, W. Y., Patel, T. S., Kanani, M., Davis, A., Mortimer, A. M., et al. (1998). Reduced dendritic spine density on cerebral cortical pyramidal neurons in schizophrenia. *Journal of Neurology, Neurosurgery and Psychiatry, 65,* 446–453.

Glantz, L. A., & Lewis, D. A. (1997). Reduction of synaptophysin immunoreactivity in the prefrontal cortex of subjects with schizophrenia: Regional and diagnostic specificity. *Archives of General Psychiatry, 54,* 943–952.

Glantz, L. A., & Lewis, D. A. (2000). Decreased dendritic spine density on prefrontal cortical pyramidal neurons in schizophrenia. *Archives of General Psychiatry, 57,* 65–73.

Gold, J. M., Carpenter, C., Randolph, C., Goldberg, T. E., & Weinberger, D. R. (1997). Auditory working memory and Wisconsin Card Sorting Test Performance in schizophrenia. *Archives of General Psychiatry, 54,* 159–165.

Goldman-Rakic, P. S., & Friedman, H. R. (1991). The circuitry of working memory revealed by anatomy and metabolic imaging. In H. S. Levin, H. M. Eisenberg, & A. L. Benton (Eds.), *Frontal lobe function and dysfunction* (pp. 72–91). New York: Oxford University Press.

Gur, R. E., Cowell, P. E., Latshaw, A., Turetsky, B. I., Grossman, R. I., Arnold, S. E., et al. (2000). Reduced dorsal and orbital prefrontal gray matter volumes in schizophrenia. *Archives of General Psychiatry, 57,* 761–768.

Gur, R. E., Turetsky, B. I., Cowell, P. E., Finkelman, C., Maany, V., Grossman, R. I., et al. (2000). Temporolimbic volume reductions in schizophrenia. *Archives of General Psychiatry, 57,* 769–775.

Heckers, S., Rauch, S. L., Goff, D., Savage, C. R., Schacter, D. L., Fischman, A. J., & Alpert, N. M. (1998). Impaired recruitment of the hippocampus during conscious recollection in schizophrenia. *Nature Neuroscience, 1,* 318–323.

Hoffman, R. E. (1986). Verbal hallucinations and language production processes in schizophrenia. *Behavioral and Brain Sciences, 9,* 503–517.

Hoffman, R. E., Boutros, N. N., Hu, S., Berman, R. M., Krystal, J. H., & Charney, D. S. (2000). Transcranial magnetic stimulation and auditory hallucinations in schizophrenia. *The Lancet, 355,* 1073–1075.

Hoffman, R. E., & Cavus, I. (2002). Slow transcranial magnetic stimulation, long-term depotentiation, and brain hyperexcitability disorders. *American Journal of Psychiatry, 159,* 1093–1102.

Hoffman, R. E., & Dobscha, S. K. (1989). Cortical pruning and the development of schizophrenia: A computer model. *Schizophrenia Bulletin, 15,* 477–490.

Hoffman, R. E., Hawkins, K. A., Gueorguieva, R., Boutros, N. N., Rachid, F., Carroll, K., & Krystal J. H. (2003). Transcranial magnetic stimulation of left temporoparietal cortex and medication-resistant auditory hallucinations. *Archives of General Psychiatry, 60,* 49–56.

Hoffman, R. E., & McGlashan, T. H. (1997). Synaptic elimination, neurodevelopment, and the mechanism of hallucinated "voices" in schizophrenia. *American Journal of Psychiatry, 154,* 1683–1689.

Hoffman, R. E., & McGlashan, T. H. (2001). Neural networks models of schizophrenia. *The Neuroscientist, 7,* 441–454.

Hoffman, R. E., Rapaport, J., Ameli, R., McGlashan, T. H., Harcherik, D., & Servan-Schreiber, D. (1995). A neural network model of hallucinated "voices" and associated speech perception impairments in schizophrenic patients. *Journal of Cognitive Neuroscience, 7,* 479–496.

Hoffman, R. E., Rapaport, J., Mazure, C., & Quinlan, D. (1999). Schizophrenic patients reporting hallucinated "voices" demonstrate selective speech perception alterations. *American Journal of Psychiatry, 56,* 393–399.

Honer, W. G., Falkai, P., Chen, C., Arango, V., Mann, J. J., & Dwork, A. J. (1999). Synaptic and plasticity-associated proteins in anterior frontal cortex in severe mental illness. *Neuroscience, 9,* 1247–1255.

Huttenlocher, P. R. (1979). Synaptic density in the human frontal cortex—Developmental changes and effects of aging. *Brain Research, 163,* 195–205.

Huttenlocher, P. R., & Dabholkar, A. S. (1997). Regional differences in synaptogenesis in human cerebral cortex. *Journal of Comparative Neurology, 387,* 167–178.

Hyde, T. M., Ziegler, J. C., & Weinberger, D. R. (1992). Psychiatric disturbances in metachromatic leukodystrophy: Insights into the neurobiology of psychosis. *Archives of Neurology, 49,* 401–406.

Johns, L. C., & McGuire, P. K. (1999). Verbal self-monitoring and auditory hallucinations in schizophrenia. *The Lancet, 353,* 469–470.

Judd, L. L., McAdams, L., Budnick, B., & Braff, D. L. (1992). Sensory gating deficits in schizophrenia: New results. *American Journal of Psychiatry, 149,* 488–493.

Kalikow, D. N., & Stevens, K. N. (1977). Development of a test of speech intelligibility in noise using sentence materials with controlled word predictability. *Journal of the Acoustic Society of America, 5,* 1337–1351.

Karson, C. N., Mrak, R. E., Schluterman, K. O., Sturner, W. Q., Sheng, J. G., & Griffin, W. S. (1999). Alterations in synaptic proteins and their encoding mRNAs in prefrontal cortex in schizophrenia: A possible neurochemical basis for "hypofrontality." *Molecular Psychiatry, 4,* 39–45.

Le Cun, Y., Denker, J. S., & Solla, S. A. (1990). Optimal brain damage. In D. S. Touretsky (Ed.,) *Advances in neural information processing systems* (Vol. 2, pp. 598–605). San Francisco: Morgan Kauffmann.

Lim, K. O., Hedehus, M., Moseley, M., de Crespigny, A., Sullivan, E. V., & Pfefferbaum, A. (1999). Compromised white matter tract integrity in schizophrenia inferred diffusion tensor imaging. *Archives of General Psychiatry, 56,* 367–374.

Margolis, R. L., Chuang, D.-M., & Post, R. M. (1995). Programmed cell death: Implications for neuropsychiatric disorders. *Biological Psychiatry, 35,* 946–956.

McGlashan, T. H., & Hoffman, R. E. (2000). Schizophrenia as a disorder of developmentally reduced synaptic connectivity. *Archives of General Psychiatry, 57,* 637–648.

McGuire, P. K., Silbersweig, D. A., Wright, I., Murray, R. M., David, A. S., Frackowiak, R. S., & Frith, C. D. (1995). Abnormal monitoring of inner speech: A physiological basis for auditory hallucinations. *The Lancet, 346,* 596–600.

Miikkulainen, R. (1993). *Subsymbolic natural language processing: An integrated model of scripts, lexicon and memory.* Cambridge, MA: MIT Press.

Muñoz-Cueto, A., Garcia-Segura, M., & Ruiz-Marcos, A. (1990). Developmental sex differences and effect of ovariectomy on the number of cortical pyramidal cell dendritic spines. *Brain Research, 515*, 64–68.

Naftolin, F., Garcia-Segura, L. M., Keefe, D., Leranth, C., Maclusky, N. J., & Brawer, J. R. (1990). Estrogen effects on the synaptology and neural membranes of the rat hypothalamic arcuate nucleus. *Biological Reproduction, 42*, 21–28.

Ojemann, G. A. (1978). Organization of short-term verbal memory of human cortex: Evidence from electrical stimulation. *Brain and Language, 5*, 331–340.

Olney, J. W., & Farber, N. B. (1995). Glutamate receptor dysfunction and schizophrenia. *Archives of General Psychiatry, 52*, 998–1007.

Pakkenberg, B. (1993). Total nerve cell number in neocortex in chronic schizophrenics and controls estimated using optical disectors. *Biological Psychiatry, 34*, 768–772.

Park, S., & Holzman, P. S. (1992). Schizophrenics show spatial working memory deficits. *Archives of General Psychiatry, 49*, 975–982.

Rumelhart, D. E., & McClelland, J. L. (Eds.). (1986). *Parallel distributed processing: Explorations in the microsctructure of cognition* (Vols. 1–2). Cambridge, MA: MIT Press.

Sartorious, N., Shapiro, R., & Jablonsky, A. (1974). The International Pilot Study of Schizophrenia. *Schizophrenia Bulletin, 1*, 21–35.

Scheich, H., Wallhäusseer-Franke, E., & Braun, K. (1991). Does synaptic selection explain auditory imprinting? In L. R. Squire, N. M. Weinberger, G. Lynch, & J. L. McGaugh (Eds.), *Memory: Organization and locus of change* (pp. 114–159). New York: Oxford University Press.

Selemon, L. D., & Goldman-Rakic, P. S. (1999). The reduced neuropil hypothesis: A circuit-based model of schizophrenia. *Biological Psychiatry, 45*, 17–25.

Selemon, L. D., Rajkowski, G., & Goldman-Rakic, P. S. (1995). Abnormally high neuronal density in schizophrenic cortex: A morphometric analysis of prefrontal area 9 and occipital cortex area 17. *Archives of General Psychiatry, 52*, 805–818.

Selemon, L. D., Rajkowski, G., & Goldman-Rakic, P. S. (1998). Abnormally high neuronal density in prefrontal area 46 in brains from schizophrenic patients: Application of 3-dimensional stereologic counting method. *Journal of Comparative Neurology, 392*, 402–412.

Shergill, S. S., Brammer, M. J., Williams, S. C. R., Murray, R. M., & McGuire, P. K. (2000). Mapping auditory hallucinations in schizophrenia using functional magnetic resonance imaging. *Archives of General Psychiatry, 57*, 1033–1038.

Shergill, S. S., Cameron, L. A., Brammer, M. J., Williams, S. C., Murray, R. M., & McGuire, P. K. (2001). Modality specific neural correlates of auditory and somatic hallucinations. *Journal of Neurology, Neurosurgery & Psychiatry, 71*, 688–690.

Spence, S. A., Liddle, P. F., Stefan, M. D., Hellewell, J. S., Sharma, T., Friston, K. J., et al. (2000). Functional anatomy of verbal fluency in people with schizophrenia and those at genetic risk: Focal dysfunction and distributed disconnectivity reappraised. *British Journal of Psychiatry, 176*, 52–60.

Spitzer, M. (2000). *The mind within the net: Models of learning, thinking, and acting.* Cambridge, MA: MIT Press.

Tamminga, C. A., Vogel, M., Gao, X., Lahti, A. C., & Holcomb H. H. (2000). The limbic cortex in schizophrenia: Focus on the anterior cingulate. *Brain Research Reviews, 31*, 364–370.

Tiihonen, J., Hari, R., Naukkarinen, H., Rimon, R., Jousmaki, V., & Kajoli, M. (1992). Modified activity of the human auditory cortex during auditory hallucinations. *American Journal of Psychiatry, 149*, 255–257.

Velakoulis, D., Pantelis, C., McGorry, P. D., Dudgeon, P., Brewer, W., Cook, M., et al. (1999). Hippocampal volume in first-episode psychoses and chronic schizophrenia: A high-resolution magnetic resonance imaging study. *Archives of General Psychiatry, 56*, 133–141.

Warren, R. M., & Warren, R. P. (1970). Auditory illusions and confusions. *Scientific American, 223*, 30–36.

Weinberger, D. R. (1987). Implications of normal brain development for the pathogenesis of schizophrenia. *Archives of General Psychiatry, 44*, 660–669.

Weinberger, D. R., Aloia, M. S., Goldberg, T. E., & Berman, K. F. (1994). The frontal lobes and schizophrenia. *Journal of Neuropsychiatry and Clinical Neuroscience, 6*, 419–427.

Weinberger, D. R., Berman, K. F., Suddath, R., & Torrey, E. F. (1992). Evidence of dysfunction of a prefrontal-limbic network in schizophrenia: A magnetic resonance imaging and regional cerebral blood flow study of discordant monozygotic twins. *American Journal of Psychiatry, 149*, 890–897.

Woolley, C. S., Wenzel, H. J., & Schwartzkroin, P. A. (1996). Estradiol increases the frequency of multiple synapse boutons in the hippocampal CA1 region of the adult female rat. *Journal of Comparative Neurology, 373*, 108–117.

Young, C. E., Arima, K., Xie, J., Hu, L., Beach, T. G., Falkai, P., & Honer W. G. (1998). SNAP-25 deficit and hippocampal connectivity in schizophrenia. *Cerebral Cortex, 8*, 261–268.

9

COMPLEX DYNAMICS IN DEPRESSION: AN APPLICATION TO LONG-TERM, MOOD-RATING TIME SERIES

RACHEL A. HEATH, ELAINE M. HEIBY, AND IAN S. PAGANO

Mood disorders are dynamical behaviors with temporal structures that have not yet been widely explored. A detailed knowledge of the temporal structure of mood disorders would inform assessment approaches, diagnostic criteria, and etiology as well as prevention and treatment strategies. One reason for the paucity of time-series research is that many assessment devices commonly used to diagnose mood disorders and their potential determinants are not conducive to repeated measurements. Another reason is the need for mathematical modeling procedures that accommodate the restrictions of the at best ordinal data yielded by current assessment methods.

One purpose of this chapter is to encourage mood disorder research that uses measures feasible for time-series assessment, such as self-monitoring, so that the dynamic structure of such measures can be investigated. Another purpose is to offer a method of dynamic time-series modeling of ordinal data and provide empirical support for the method. Numerical diagnostics from the arsenal supplied by nonlinear dynamics are applied to empirical time-series trajectories of self-monitored dysphoric affect associated with 1 individual with a unipolar mood disorder and 1 control participant. Unveiled

263

are selected pathognomonic signatures of mood disturbance indicated by an in-depth analysis of symptom time course for the depressed and non-depressed participants.

Previous analyses of these same depressed and nondepressed partici-pants had revealed that mood fluctuations exhibit nonlinear dynamics with clear power-law dynamics, as indicated by spectral analysis of the mood-rating time series (Heiby, Pagano, Blaine, Nelson, & Heath, 2003). Nonline-arity for a stationary time series, that is, one with its parameters remaining constant over time, is presumed to occur whenever the characteristic proper-ties of a linear time series do not apply, such as a constant covariance structure with possible linear trend.

Herein, we report a more refined analysis of the same time-series data analyzed by Heiby et al. (2003) on the basis of a new measure of dynamics, monotonic multiscale entropy. Although the ordinal data, when analyzed in this way, could not reveal nonlinearity in the mood fluctuations produced by a depressed participant and a nondepressed participant, there were clear differences in the temporal profiles of the mood dynamics for the 2 partici-pants, with the depressed participant indicating less complexity than that observed for the nondepressed participant. The implications of such a result for the mathematical modeling of the inherent mood–environment interac-tion processes involving the interplay between noise and determinism are considered. In the sections to follow, we briefly describe first emotional states, mood disorders, current methods of assessment, and the dynamic nature of mood disorders. We then indicate various techniques for dynamic modeling, and then we offer and empirically test a method for dealing with ordinal data yielded by most measures of mood disorders. Finally, we suggest implications for both the diagnosis and treatment and delineate data analy-sis issues.

EMOTIONAL STATES AND MOOD DISORDERS

Emotional states such as sadness change in nature and intensity over time. Transient sadness over a loss, happiness over a gain, and anger toward an obstruction are generally considered to be adaptive. In response to what are often seemingly random environmental changes, these emotional states can serve as discriminative stimuli and reinforcements for cognitive, other emotional, and sensorimotor behaviors that in turn restore euthymia (Staats, 1996).

When euthymia is not restored, and the negative emotion and accom-panying behaviors perseverate over a week or two, the condition is often considered to be a mood disorder. Sadness becomes depression, happiness becomes manic euphoria, and anger becomes manic irritability. Because emotional states fluctuate over time, it is not surprising that the course of major mood disorders is recurrent in most cases. About 70% of individuals with unipolar depression and about 90% of individuals with bipolar disorder exhibit more than one episode within various monitored time periods (Coryell & Winokur, 1992).

Prediction of initial and subsequent episodes of mood disorders has eluded clinical scientists. This is partly because most attempts to inspect the course of mood disorders have been based on time-invariant methods that are more useful for understanding fairly static behaviors (e.g., IQ scores among persons with severe mental retardation). To capture the dynamic nature of unstable behavior, such as emotional states and mood disorders, ongoing assessment is necessary. Adequate assessment of such unstable behaviors requires regular monitoring leading to data, such as mood ratings, that arise from multiple successive observations from individual participants. These observations constitute a time series and ideally consist of measurements conducted at fixed time intervals over the period of psychological assessment and treatment. We now review the use of time-series measurements in clinical observations in the context of current assessment practices.

MEASUREMENT OF MOOD DISORDERS

Time-series measurement is one of the hallmarks of behavioral assessment (Haynes & O'Brien, 2000). For some behaviors, time-series assessment can be conducted by well-validated physiological (e.g., heart rate as an index of anxiety) or direct observation (e.g., frequency of hitting someone in a classroom as an index of conduct disorder) devices. For mood disorders, however, no accepted physiological index exists. Direct observation by others is not feasible in most outpatient settings and is not possible for the covert symptoms experienced by patients.

Assessment of mood disorders and consideration of theoretical causal variables have been conducted primarily by structured interviews, self-report questionnaires, and self-monitoring devices. These instruments generally contain items based on nominal or ordinal scaling (including Likert-like scaling that presumes equality of intervals, when conventional descriptive statistics are applied). Instruments measuring mood disorders and their etiologic factors that are designed with true interval scaling await development. Nominal and ordinal data place restrictions on numerical diagnostic methods. Later in this chapter, we offer a dynamic modeling procedure designed to accommodate ordinal data derived from self-report measures. Meanwhile, a brief review of current assessment devices for mood disorders underscores the challenge of identifying their temporal structure.

Structured interviews have become the psychometric gold standard for assessment of mood disorders (Summerfeldt & Antony, 2002). Interview schedules yield nominal data that categorize the presence or absence of symptoms that meet the criteria of the *Diagnostic and Statistical Manual of Mental Disorders* (American Psychiatric Association, 2000). Structured interviews are expensive to conduct. Their administration involves extensive interviewer training to ensure sufficiently high interrater reliability. Interviews are administered on an individual basis and require 1 to 2 hours to complete. In both research and clinical settings, structured interviews are usually administered only once or twice, precluding inspection of the frequency and duration of recurrent episodes of mood disorders. The nominal data from such interviews, however, could generate diagnostic validity indicators for comparison with cost-efficient measurement methods that use more precise scaling. Structured interview schedules could also be converted from nominal to ordinal, or perhaps even interval, scaling to capture a wider range of scores.

Self-report is a common behavioral assessment method to measure not only the symptoms of mood disorders but also a range of theoretical factors, including those based on environmental, cognitive, emotional, sensorimotor, and organic causes (Heiby & Staats, 1990; Riedel, Heiby, & Kopetskie, 2001). Self-report instruments are subject to numerous sources of measurement error, such as response bias, memory, response set, fatigue, and practice effects. Therefore, validity estimates for self-report measures are at best moderate. However, questionnaires are easy, quick, and economical to administer.

There are dozens of commonly used brief self-report questionnaires designed to assess mood disorders and etiologic factors (Nezu, Ronan, Meadows, & McClure, 2000). These questionnaires often contain Likert scale items. Despite being more conducive to time series measurement than interviews, most clinical and research applications of these questionnaires involve infrequent assessment. They fail to yield data needed to mathematically model the temporal structure of mood disorders (Haynes, Blaine, & Meyer, 1995; Heiby, 1995; McFall & Townsend, 1998).

Self-monitoring has been the primary behavioral assessment method for obtaining frequent measurements of mood and other temporally variable behavior. Self-monitoring data can be collected using paper-and-pencil forms, cell phones that connect to either an answering machine or a link to a Web page, and hand-held computers. Self-monitoring instruments contain items that are generally measured on either a nominal or a Likert-like ordinal scale. Self-monitoring of mood disorders is inexpensive and reduces the memory error inherent in retrospective measures. However, self-monitoring procedures are difficult to implement, because they require compliance by the participant. Several methods of enhancing compliance to self-monitoring, such as accuracy checks and the provision of prompts and reinforcements, have been demonstrated (Korotitsch & Nelson-Gray, 1999). Nevertheless, only a few studies have investigated the dynamic structure of self-monitored mood data (e.g., Gottschalk, Bauer, & Whybrow, 1995; Heiby et al., 2003; Woyshville, Lackamp, Eisengart, & Gilliland, 1999).

Time-series assessment of mood can assist in the diagnosis of a mood disorder. The *Diagnostic and Statistical Manual of Mental Disorders* (American Psychiatric Association, 2000) defined a major depressive episode as involving "a depressed mood most of the day, nearly every day" (p. 356) for at least 2 weeks of consecutive days, which is temporally somewhat vague. From an inspection of hourly mood data reported over a 6-month period, Nelson and Heiby (2001) found that the number of depressive episodes exhibited by a participant with a history of depression ranged from zero to five, depending on how "most of the day" was defined. The use of time-series assessment and inspection of the dynamic temporal structure of mood data revealed by such an assessment can assist in refining both the definition and identification of the onset of mood disorders.

DYNAMIC MOOD DISORDERS

Dynamic disorders such as depression exhibit temporal variability without any obvious cause in each individual case (Bélair, Glass, an der Heiden, & Milton, 1995). Because many disorders present as abrupt changes in their underlying dynamics, such as when a depressed person suddenly becomes dysfunctional in social and occupational roles and requires hospitalization, the most likely representation of the temporal fluctuations is in terms of nonlinear, rather than linear, dynamics. Even when the depressive episode is apparently random, closer scrutiny may reveal a mixture of chaos and stochastic noise, or "stochaos," following an idea originally proposed by Freeman (2000). The balance between chaos, or nonlinearity, and noise is important, because it is reasonable to assume that any imbalance, such as too little noise, might produce mood fluctuations, for example, that are both too regular for adequate adaptation and insufficiently responsive to environmental stressors. This imbalance between noise and nonlinearity may be the precursor to a person's transition to a chronic depressed mood.

A depressed individual's inadequate adjustment to environmental demands might result from a mismatch between his or her lower than normal level of adaptive resources and the resources needed to adequately function in a challenging environment (e.g., social skills needed to replace the loss of a friend). We refer to the current level of adaptive resources as the *degrees of freedom*, or *complexity*, exhibited by the individual's behavioral fluctuations.

Low degrees of freedom correspond to regular behavior fluctuations, whereas higher degrees of freedom occur when the fluctuations become more irregular, or even noisy.

When considered in terms of complexity theory, a general conceptualization of real-world processes that includes nonlinear dynamics as a special case, the notion that depressed individuals exhibit insufficient degrees of freedom in their behavior fluctuations has been referred to as the maladaptive determinism hypothesis (MDH; Heiby et al., 2003; Pagano, Barkhoff, Heiby, & Schlicht, 2006). *Determinism* in this instance refers to processes, possibly nonlinear, that can be distinguished from those that are purely stochastic. This hypothesis posits coherence between the temporal structure of mood disorders and mood regulation skills but not between transient sadness and mood regulation skills. The MDH applies only to relatively stable mood states.

Adaptive transient sadness in response to seemingly random environmental events is posited to require flexibility in mood regulation skills. In other words, transient adaptive sadness is characterized by a dominant random component because it adjusts to possibly unexpected exogenous factors that occur over relatively short time periods. In contrast, perseveration of mood regulation skills regardless of environmental events is posited to characterize mood disorders. Perhaps maladaptive mood is characterized by greater determinism because it responds relatively more to endogenous factors that do occur as a function of time and perseverate even in the presence of environmental change.

To summarize, it has been suggested by us and others, such as Gottschalk et al. (1995), that any stable mood state, such as sadness, is determined by an interplay of endogenous and exogenous influences. The endogenous influences are primarily deterministic, possibly nonlinear or even chaotic, and the exogenous influences influence the mood state by superimposing stochastic noise upon mood dynamics. During ill health, endogenous processes dominate, leading to greater determinism or regularity in mood dynamics, whereas in healthy people there is a greater influence of exogenous influences, leading to more irregular and complex mood fluctuations. Time-series analysis is required to detect these subtle effects on mood dynamics in both healthy and ill people.

The MDH can be evaluated using time-series data of symptoms of mood disorders and etiologic factors, analyzed using sophisticated nonlinear data analysis procedures. If this hypothesis is supported, a corollary suggests that whereas healthy individuals interact with their environments using established and somewhat automatic mood regulating skills, people with a history of a mood disorder must be more aware of environmental influences in order to exhibit a greater level of adjustive behavior and euthymia. The analogy here is with the progressive automaticity of skilled behavior resulting from controlled, or attended, practice (Shiffrin & Schneider, 1977; for elaboration of a similar proposal, see chap. 7, this volume). The practical significance of the MDH is that low-complexity mood fluctuation is diagnostic of a mood disorder as distinguished from transient sadness, with therapy being implemented at the onset of any symptom and designed to gradually increase the complexity of mood fluctuations over time.

Applications of complexity ideas have become more prevalent in medicine, with additional insight being gained about disease dynamics. In heart disease, for example, a certain complexity of physiological function is required for health. Once the complexity of heart function decreases, the risk of fatal heart disease increases markedly. A similar phenomenon occurs in neurology, where the electroencephalograph response in epilepsy and coma is characterized by a sudden decrease in complexity during, and just before, a seizure (Heath, 2004). Aging, that terminal condition from which we all suffer to varying degrees, might also be associated with less complex behavioral and physiological systems. However, a relative increase in neural noise might also contribute to the decline in cognitive function with increasing age (Vaillancourt & Newell, 2002). As we demonstrate further below, a loss of complexity might accompany mood disorders.

Complex systems involve a large number of interacting units. Even when their processing mechanisms are governed by simple rules, the emergent behavior of such a system is often complex, so complexity at a macroscopic level arises from simplicity at a microscopic level. Self-organized criticality is a special feature of some complex systems when they are at their most adaptive. In this state, excitation of the system by just a small input is sufficient to cause a considerable change in the system's response.

Chaos occurs when a complex system becomes sensitively dependent on its initial conditions. If the game of golf were chaotic, then the following fictitious scenario might occur. The first author of this chapter, Rachel A. Heath, has always aspired to play golf as proficiently as Laura Davies, but instead she hits the ball just slightly later than Laura and just to the side of the ideal spot on the ball. This minuscule difference in golfing abilities causes Rachel to hit the ball a short distance into the rough, whereas, quite unfairly, Laura hits hers a long way up the fairway! Chaotic systems have relatively low degrees of freedom, especially compared with stochastic processes that have infinite degrees of freedom, at least theoretically.

We now summarize nonlinear data analysis methods. Most of these techniques arise from physical applications for which the time series consists of many thousands of observations. Psychological applications, on the other hand, are constrained by the relative paucity of data as well as by the possibility that the time-series observations are measured on scales that do not adhere to the ratio and interval properties of physical scales such as length and temperature.

NONLINEAR ANALYSIS TECHNIQUES

Perhaps the most useful indicator of a nonlinear system's function is its complexity, a rather difficult concept to define precisely. In behavioral data, measures such as mood ratings do not lend themselves to analysis by the nonlinear techniques developed initially by physicists (e.g., Kantz & Schreiber, 1997) because of their limited range and the complex measurement properties of self-report devices. Frequently, insufficient data militate against the direct application of the nonlinear diagnostic methods that have been successfully applied in the physical sciences. Even when measurement properties do permit a meaningful analysis, rapid fluctuation in the parameters generating the nonlinear process leads frequently to nonstationary outcomes for which there is little consensus about the most appropriate data analysis procedure. Although time-varying parameters are expected in mood-rating time series that change in response to therapeutic agents, including behavioral therapies, such temporal variations can lead to spurious and unpredictable outcomes if the data analysis method requires time invariance for its proper application.

Useful indexes for quantifying the complexity of sequential data include the correlation dimension, D2, and the maximum Lyapunov exponent. Both measures require large amounts of stable data for their accurate estimation, a problem for the analysis of psychological data in particular (Heath, 2000). D2 quantifies a lower bound on the number of degrees of freedom required to represent data fluctuations geometrically. The maximum Lyapunov exponent measures how rapidly nearby data points in this geometric space change their relative position over time. A positive Lyapunov exponent is a necessary, but not sufficient, condition for chaos. Without further investigation, D2 and the maximum Lyapunov exponent do not provide unequivocal evidence for nonlinearity. For example, low D2 estimates suggesting a low-dimensional geometric data representation can also arise from analyzing linearly transformed white noise (Shen, Olbrich, Achermann, & Meier, 2003). Thus, more appropriate data analysis methods, such as those based on the irregularity of fluctuations in a time series, are needed.

Approximate entropy (ApEn; Pincus, 1995), a measure of irregularity in a time series, was designed for analyzing short series such as those commonly observed in the social sciences. ApEn measures the likelihood that runs of successive time-series values maintain a similar pattern when the runs are expanded to include the next point in time. Regular or highly predictable data produce low ApEn values, whereas randomness is associated with large ApEn values because there is minimal similarity in successive runs of erratically changing time-series values.

A disadvantage of ApEn is that estimates from different conditions can be compared only when the number of data points is similar. ApEn changes when data are transformed, even when the means and variances are equated using normalization. Nevertheless, when there are at least 1,000 observations, the standard error of the ApEn estimate remains relatively small, facilitating statistical comparisons across conditions. Another advantage lies in its robustness, ApEn being relatively unaffected by extreme data values.

Torres and Gamero (2000) observed that alternative entropy measures are more sensitive to changes in the complexity of a time series than is ApEn. An additional advantage is that such measures can be computed more efficiently. Other entropy measures are superior to ApEn in tracking changes in complexity in a physiological time series and, unlike ApEn, are relatively unaffected by superimposed noise. We now describe in some detail these new entropy measures.

To overcome the cross-sample comparison and scaling problems with ApEn, and to compensate for the effects of time scale differences, Richman and Moorman (2000) developed sample entropy. Consider the time series $\{u(1), u(2), ..., u(N)\}$. Similarly to ApEn, sample entropy measures the extent to which the dynamics occurring within a time window of length m, that is, $[i, i + 1, i + 2, ..., i + m - 1]$, for $i = 1, N - (m + 1)$, remain similar when the time window length is increased to $m + 1$.

For a deterministic process with no measurement uncertainty, the prediction of future dynamics is determined precisely by the past, whereas for a random process the dynamics during one time period is unrelated to that occurring in previous time periods. For most temporal processes intermediate values of predictability might be expected. So, sample entropy, as a measure of relative uncertainty, is large for unpredictable data but small for completely predictable data.

Sample entropy is computed from a normalized data sequence, that is, one with a mean of zero and a variance of 1, by completing the following three steps:

1. Representing successive m-tuples of data values as vectors, that is, points, in an m-dimensional space.
2. Computing all interpoint distances using the max distance metric defined below.
3. Counting the number of pairs of points lying within a distance r from each other. This count is defined as $B(r)$.

This process—Steps 1, 2, and 3—is repeated for $(m + 1)$-tuples of data values in an $(m + 1)$-dimensional space to yield a count $A(r)$. Sample entropy is then defined by $-\text{Log}[A(r)/B(r)]$, where $A(r)/B(r)$ represents the conditional probability that successive subsequences of $(m + 1)$ observations have a similar dynamic progression as subsequences of m observations.

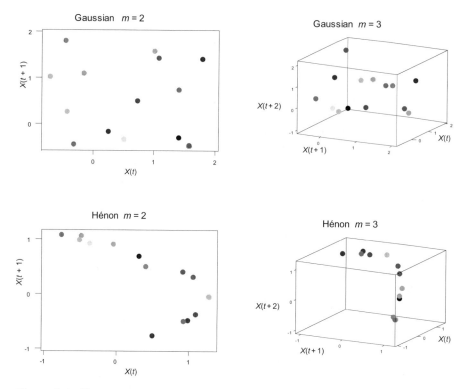

Figure 9.1. Changes in the relative location of nearby points in two dimensions when the space becomes three dimensional. Examples are provided for random, or Gaussian, points (upper graphs) and points produced by a chaotic Hénon process (lower graphs).

More specifically, for a time series containing N data points, $\{u(i), i = 1, N\}$, we first form all of the successive m-dimensional vectors leading to the embedded vector time series, $x(i) = \{u(i + k), 0 \leq k \leq m - 1\}$. For example, if $m = 2$, then the time series $\{1,2,4,8\}$ is transformed into the two-dimensional vectors $x(1) = \{1,2\}$, $x(2) = \{2,4\}$, and $x(3) = \{4,8\}$. The distance between any two vectors is defined most conveniently by the max distance metric, $d[x(i), x(j)] = \max\{|u(i + k) - u(j + k)|, 0 \leq k \leq m - 1$. So, the distance between any two vectors equals the maximum of their intercomponent differences; for example,

$$d[x(1), x(2)] = \max\{|1 - 2|, |2 - 4|\} = 2. \qquad (9.1)$$

Using this metric, sample entropy is then defined as explained in the previous paragraph (Richman & Moorman, 2000).

The computation of sample entropy is illustrated graphically for both chaotic and Gaussian sequences in Figure 9.1. The clustered points in two dimensions tend to remain more clustered in three dimensions for the chaotic series than is the case for the Gaussian series. This tendency is quantified by the estimate of sample entropy being larger for the Gaussian series.

COMPUTING SAMPLE ENTROPY FROM ORDINAL DATA

In Heiby et al. (2003), the data obtained from the 2 participants consisted of ratings on a 7-point Likert scale. Without further information on the psychological representation of each of the rating categories, an analysis in terms of ordinal data scaling is preferable. Because the sample entropy calculation assumes continuous interval-scale data, we need to modify the computational procedure to encompass the less detailed information obtained in ordinal measurement.

We now present a new method for computing the complexity of ordinal data time series using logic similar to that employed in calculating sample entropy. We determine the direction of change—increasing, decreasing, or constant—for successive time-series values using both triples and quadruples of successive rating scale values. Next, we compute the relative frequencies of all possible such transitions, leading to transition probability tables, or matrices, that are computed separately for both successive triples and quadruples. Using the two transition matrices obtained for successive triples and successive quadruples of rating scale values allows us to compute the Shannon information index in both cases. By analogy with the method used to compute sample entropy, the difference in information for quadruples and triples provides a complexity index for the ordinal-scale time-series data.

More specifically, the following method takes into consideration the monotonic invariance of the ordinal scale. By analogy with the sample entropy method, it takes successive triples and quadruples of data values and examines the number of changes in direction of the time series over these three and four values, respectively. So, for three successive time-series values, $u(i)$, $u(i + 1)$, and $u(i + 2)$, nine possible ordinal relationships exist. The summed directions of change in time-series values are shown in square brackets, where an increase from one time period to the next, irrespective of size, is represented by +1, a decrease is represented by −1, and no change is represented by 0.

For example, if $u(i) < u(i + 1) < u(i + 2)$, then there are two successive monotonic increases in time series values, leading to the index [+ 2]. If $u(i) < u(i + 1) = u(i + 2)$, then there is just the one monotonic increase leading to an index of [+ 1]. If $u(i) < u(i + 1) > u(i + 2)$, then the initial monotonic increase is canceled by the following monotonic decrease, leading to an index of [0]. The other possible monotonic changes in series values, together with their corresponding index values, are $u(i) = u(i + 1) < u(i + 2)$ [+1],

$u(i) = u(i + 1) = u(i + 2)$ [0], $u(i) = u(i + 1) > u(i + 2)$ [–1], $u(i) > u(i + 1) < u(i + 2)$ [0], $u(i) > u(i + 1) = u(i + 2)$ [–1], and $u(i) > u(i + 1) > u(i + 2)$ [–2].

Using only the change sums, there are five categories by which we can classify the ordinal progression of the time series over three successive time points, {–2,–1,0,+1,+2}. Let $h2(s,t)$ represent the transition probability for all transitions from state s to state t, where such states can be any pair of the set {–2,–1,0,+1,+2}. The Shannon information for two-step progressions, $I2$, is then given by

$$I2 = - \sum_{s=-2}^{+2} \sum_{t=-2}^{+2} h2(s,t)\log[h2(s,t)]. \qquad (9.2)$$

If there is no change in the time-series, then all of the transition probability will be concentrated at $s = t = 0$, so that $I2 = 0$. When there is a monotonic increase in the time-series values, the nonzero transition values occur only at $s = t = +2$, so that once again $I2 = 0$. A similar outcome occurs when the time series is monotonic decreasing. Thus, $I2$ is unaffected by monotonic trends in the data. The more changes in direction the time series takes, the more widely the transition probabilities are distributed in $h2(s,t)$, and the higher will be the $I2$ value. So, $I2$ measures the fluctuations of monotonic persistence in an ordinal-scale time series.

$I2$ will be largest when all types of monotonic trends are equally likely. This means that two-step persistence should be as likely as one-step persistence in both increasing and decreasing directions. This pattern is more likely to arise from time series that have moderate levels of persistence rather than no persistence, like Gaussian noise, or in time series with *antipersistence*, that is, alternations of increases and decreases of time-series values that minimize the likelihood of changes being categorized as [+2] or [–2].

We now compute a similar information index for monotonic progressions of the time series through four successive values. In a straightforward extension of the above method, we obtain seven monotonic progression categories, {–3, –2, –1, 0, +1, +2, +3}. Let $h3(s,t)$ represent the transition probability for all transitions from state s to state t, where such states can be any pair of the set {–3,–2,–1,0,+1,+2,+3}. The Shannon information for three-step progressions, $I3$, is then given by

$$I3 = - \sum_{s=-3}^{+3} \sum_{t=-3}^{+3} h3(s,t)\log[h3(s,t)]. \qquad (9.3)$$

By analogy with the basic principle underlying the computation of sample entropy, we compute the change in monotonic persistence information when the series progresses over a fourth successive value compared with that contained in progressions over three successive series values. This change in information is given by $I3 - I2$, which is then an estimate of a new measure known as *monotonic sample entropy*. A large change in direction information suggests that the time series has a large number of ordered fluctuations, including some sequential dependencies, whereas lower non-zero values suggest that the series is more random with a larger number of alternations.

So, zero values of monotonic sample entropy signal either no change in a time series or a monotonic trend. Small positive values represent a time series with fairly rapid fluctuations, such as Gaussian noise, whereas larger values of monotonic sample entropy indicate a series with larger, more regular fluctuations. This relationship between monotonic sample entropy and fluctuation regularity is somewhat different from that obtained using the original version of sample entropy. The latter index bases its information change on proximity measures, whereas the monotonic version measures variability in persistence, there being no distance metric for ordinal data equivalent to that used to compute sample entropy.

Recent research has demonstrated the usefulness of rescaling versions of sample entropy in which the time scale of the time series is contracted by averaging successive time-series values and applying sample entropy to the resulting time series. In the next section, we explain how this is done for continuous data and how a similar rescaling procedure can be devised for ordinal data.

MULTISCALE ENTROPY

Multiscale entropy (MSE) is a quantitative index originally proposed as an effective diagnostic procedure for heart pathology (Costa, Goldberger, & Peng, 2002). One of the very few published applications in other fields is an analysis of gait dynamics in young and elderly people by Costa, Peng, Goldberger, and Hausdorff (2003). To our knowledge, there have been no applications of MSE in psychology.

The MSE method computes sample entropy for increasingly coarser time scales, S. When $S = 1$, sample entropy is computed for the original time series. When $S = 2$, a new time series is computed by averaging successive pairs of observations to yield a time series that is half as long, that is, the interobservation time is doubled compared with the original time series. When $S = 3$, a new time series is computed by averaging successive triples of observations to yield a time series that is one third as long, that is, the interobservation time is trebled compared with the original time series. For values of S greater than 3, the original time series is correspondingly further compacted using progressively coarser time scales. In the

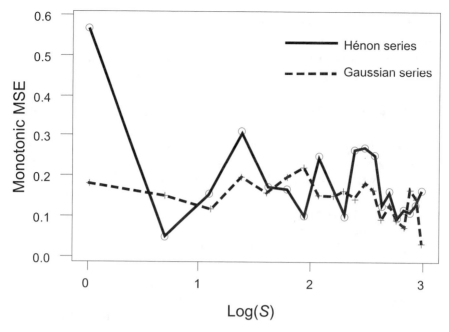

Figure 9.2. Comparison of chaotic Hénon and Gaussian series. Monotonic multiscale entropy (MSE) for the chaotic Hénon series and a Gaussian series as the time scale (*S*) increases.

following data analyses, *S* is converted to a logarithmic value to highlight the changes at low time scales.

In applications to ordinal-scale measures, the successive time-series values are added, rather than averaged, because the latter operation is not defined for ordinal scales of measurement. By doing this, new time series can be obtained for various values of *S*, ranging from 1 to 20 in the following application to mood-rating time-series data.[1] Using this rescaling of the original time series, one can compute a multiscale version of monotonic sample entropy, monotonic MSE.

As shown in Figure 9.2, the monotonic MSE when Log(*S*) equals zero is substantially less for the more complex Gaussian series (dashed line) than for the chaotic Hénon series (solid line). So the more complex the series, the lower the monotonic MSE, but only when Log(*S*) equals zero, that is, for the original time series.

Detecting nonlinearity in ordinal time series is difficult, because ordinal measurement does not change with a monotonic transformation of the original time-series values. For example, we could square each number in

---

[1]Software for computing monotonic MSE written in the *R* statistical language can be obtained from Rachel A. Heath (rachel.heath@newcastle.edu.au).

a series of positive values and still maintain the same ordinal relationship between numbers in the series. Indeed, a measure such as monotonic sample entropy remains the same for any monotonic—that is, nonincreasing or nondecreasing—transformation of the original time series. However, we can assess the ability of monotonic sample entropy to detect the presence of nonlinearity in time series derived from continuous physical processes that have suitable properties so that surrogate time series can be computed. In the next section, we explain the computation of surrogate time series from the original time series and describe their application in hypothesis testing.

USING SURROGATE SERIES TO DETECT NONLINEAR DYNAMICS IN TIME SERIES

Traditional statistical hypothesis testing assumes a null hypothesis that specifies the value of a population parameter such as, for example, the mean being equal to 100. The research hypothesis then specifies an alternative, such as the population mean being greater than 100. When the null hypothesis is true, a test statistic for sample data will have a known probability distribution that can be used to determine how likely the sample estimate of the population parameter is when the null hypothesis is true. Alternatively, when the probability of a Type I error equals α, a $(1 - \alpha) \times 100\%$ confidence interval for the population parameter can be estimated from a known distribution of the sample estimate when the null hypothesis is true. If the sample estimate lies outside this confidence interval, then the null hypothesis can be rejected with a maximum Type I error probability, α. If the distribution of sample estimates when the null hypothesis is true cannot be estimated mathematically, then a distribution of estimates from a number of random samples of the available data can be obtained using resampling. This procedure is used in the following analyses.

The null hypothesis for any assessment of nonlinearity in a time series is the assumption that the series is linear. Time series that satisfy the null hypothesis with respect to any given data series are known as *surrogate time series*, or just *surrogates*. With respect to any experimental time series, the criterion for linearity requires that both first-order properties, such as the mean, and second-order properties, such as the variance and autocovariances of the surrogate time series, match those of the data. This can be achieved by computing the power spectrum of the experimental time series and then using it plus different random permutations of the phase spectrum to create as many surrogate time series as are needed. In the following analyses, surrogate time series were computed using the *surrogates* command in the TISEAN nonlinear time-series analysis package (Hegger, Kantz, & Schreiber, 1999; Schreiber & Schmitz, 2000).

The nonlinear index is then computed for the experimental time series and for all of the surrogate time series, the frequency distribution of the latter being essentially a resampled distribution under the null hypothesis. If the experimental time-series index lies outside, say, a 95% confidence interval based on the surrogate nonlinear index distribution, then we can reject the null hypothesis and claim nonlinearity at the 5% level of statistical significance. In the following analyses, 19 surrogates are computed for each experimental series to represent an approximate 95% confidence interval centered at the average nonlinear index. Further details of this procedure are contained in Heath (2000), with applications being illustrated by Heath, Kelly, and Longstaff (2000). We now apply this hypothesis-testing procedure based on surrogate data when the null hypothesis is true to detect departures from linearity in the continuous Hénon chaotic time series using monotonic MSE measures.

DETECTING NONLINEARITY USING MONOTONIC MULTISCALE ENTROPY

When any new nonlinear data analysis technique is developed, the question arises as to whether the technique is sensitive to the nonlinearity contained in a known nonlinear time series. For this purpose, the chaotic Hénon time series that passes all known tests for nonlinearity was used. Figure 9.3 shows the monotonic MSE results for the Hénon time series (solid line) compared with the 95% confidence interval for surrogate series computed from the same Hénon series. Because the value for the Hénon series lies outside the 95% confidence interval computed under the null hypothesis that the time series is linear, we conclude that monotonic MSE provides a sensitive index of nonlinearity, but only for the original time series, that is, when $S = 1$. The averaging of successive data values in the Hénon time series probably removes the nonlinearity present in the original series. Before applying monotonic sample entropy, we first discuss applications of traditional nonlinear procedures to understand the dynamics evident in mood rating time series.

APPLICATION TO MOOD TIME SERIES

As noted earlier, mood disorders are often recurrent. These disorders can be controlled, but not prevented or cured, by medical and psychological interventions. For such dynamic disorders, a possible investigative strategy involves devising a mathematical or computer model of the underlying dynamic mechanisms; evaluating the model's behavior when psychologically

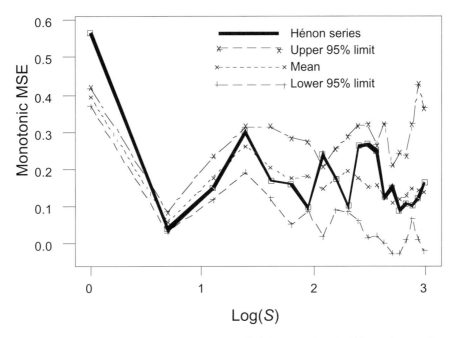

Figure 9.3. Monotonic multiscale entropy (MSE) for the chaotic Hénon time series compared with the 95% confidence interval for monotonic MSE computed from the corresponding surrogate time series as the time scale *S* increases.

meaningful parameters are manipulated; and, finally, comparing the model's predictions of both normal and pathological behavior. An adequate candidate model based on these tests can then be used for both the initial diagnosis and the continuous evaluation of a person's response to treatment.

At present, this diagnostic and therapeutic process is not universally available, in part because of the convention of measuring mood disorders with infrequent administration of interviews and self-report questionnaires. However, a small number of studies have applied nonlinear dynamical analyses to depressive disorders by measuring mood with frequently reported self-monitoring devices. The pioneering study in this area was conducted by Gottschalk et al. (1995), who examined mood fluctuations in a group of people with rapid-cycling bipolar disorder who had experienced at least four mood-changing episodes in the previous 12 months. Each participant, and his or her age- and gender-matched control who had no mood disorder symptoms, maintained a daily mood diary over a period ranging from 1 year to 2.5 years. Each diary entry represented a numerical estimate of how they felt (from *best* to *worst*; see Gottschalk et al., 1995, p. 948) on a high-resolution (100-millimeter) rating scale. The diary entries yielded time series with approximately 700 observations, enough to compute some of the commonly used nonlinear dynamical indices but with severe limitations unless the time series has low complexity.

The *log–log power spectrum* is a linear measure that relates the logarithm of the relative predominance (power) of each mood fluctuation frequency to the logarithm of mood frequency. For mood-rating data, the log–log power spectrum was linear, with a negative slope of −1.29 for the bipolar participants and a slope of −0.69 for the healthy participants.

In a similar study, Woyshville et al. (1999) obtained 90 daily mood ratings from 36 participants who had been diagnosed with an affective disorder as well as from 27 healthy clients. The log–log spectrum slope was −0.43 for participants with an affective disorder and −0.22 for the healthy participants, a slope ratio for disordered compared with healthy clients similar to that obtained by Gottschalk et al. (1995).

Because a zero-slope log–log power spectrum is produced by Gaussian noise, the greater absolute slope produced by the bipolar participants indicates insufficient noise in their mood fluctuations compared with the control participants' data. So less noisiness is a dynamic indicator of ill health. Linear log–log spectra also suggest that mood fluctuations are possibly time-scale invariant, implying that similar mood dynamics might be measured using a more frequent, and less time-consuming, sampling strategy for acquiring mood-rating data. For example, analyzing time series consisting of daily, or even hourly (during the waking hours), mood ratings might provide useful information on the effects of various therapeutic strategies on depression.

By plotting successive mood ratings against each other, the resulting phase plots for bipolar clients in Gottschalk et al.'s (1995) study were more highly structured than those for the healthy clients, except for one bipolar client who had responded well to treatment. The minimum number of degrees of freedom required to represent mood fluctuations for bipolar patients was 4, based on a fractal dimensionality, or D_2, estimate of 3.2. For the healthy participants, the fractal dimensionality was essentially unbounded, suggesting a high noise component. Such a result indicated that the mood control system for bipolar clients generated less complex fluctuations compared with that of the healthy participants. Gottschalk et al. proposed that the different dynamics exhibited by bipolar and healthy clients result from differences in how endogenous and environmental processes interact to influence mood dynamics.

Heiby et al. (2003) studied mood fluctuations in 2 young women, one with a history of recurrent unipolar depression and the other with no history of depression. The participants rated their mood every hour for 10 hours a day for 6 months, using prompts from an hourly beep on a watch alarm as well as periodic telephone calls from an investigator to minimize the likelihood of a missed rating and to reinforce compliance.

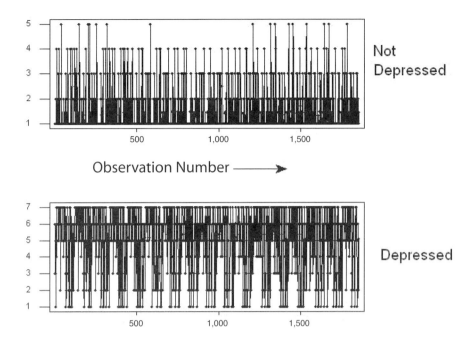

Figure 9.4. Mood-rating time series for the nondepressed participant (top panel) and depressed participant (bottom panel; data from Heiby et al., 2003).

Mood ratings were regularly calibrated using a telephone version of the Beck Depression Inventory (Beck, 1967), yielding 80% agreement between ratings and the Beck Depression Inventory depression score. Supportive psychotherapy over the previous 3 years had had no major effect on depressive episode frequency for the depressed participant, leading to relatively stable mood fluctuations over the 6-month rating period. An examination of ratings suggested that both time series were reasonably stationary in terms of their median.

The nondepressed participant provided 1,840 ratings, with just 2.0% missing values. A similar number of ratings, with 4.4% missing values, was obtained for the depressed participant. Approximately 2,000 data points are sufficient to apply basic methods for nonlinear data analysis, provided the system has less than 4 degrees of freedom (Heath et al., 2000), as was confirmed by Gottschalk et al.'s (1995) analyses for bipolar clients.

Figure 9.4 shows the time series of mood ratings for the 2 participants. The higher the rating, the greater the level of depressive mood. The depression ratings, made on a 7-point scale, were higher for the depressed participant (bottom panel of figure), there being some evidence for both persistence and a regular cycling of mood. The nondepressed participant (top panel of figure) displayed less persistent mood fluctuations, resulting in greater mood variability than was observed for the depressed participant.

Because spectral analysis of the two participants' data revealed significant periodicities, possibly resulting from menstrual cycle effects, of 26 days for the depressed participant and 23 days for the nondepressed participant, fluctuations at these frequencies were removed from each mood-rating time series before computing further analyses. The log–log power spectrum slope was −1.95 for the nondepressed participant and −2.15 for the depressed participant. Although these values are in the same direction as those observed by Gottschalk et al. (1995), they are almost twice as large and exhibit *brown noise*, a process characterized by an additive Gaussian process, or random walk. Furthermore, there is scarcely any difference in the slopes compared with the values obtained in the earlier studies.

The estimated fractal dimensionality was 2.7 for the depressed participant and essentially unbounded for the nondepressed participant. The estimated dimensionality of a surrogate time series with the same linear properties as the data, but no nonlinearity, was 4.0, a value significantly larger than that observed for the depressed participant's mood fluctuations. This result supported the idea that mood ratings for the depressed participant exhibited low-complexity nonlinear dynamics.

To account for these findings, Heiby et al. (2003) proposed the MDH, discussed earlier in this chapter, which states in this instance that the depressed state exhibits more deterministic (i.e., more predictable) behavior than is observed for healthy people. Because more predictable behavior is associated with endogenous resources of low complexity, such individuals might find it difficult to cope with complex exogenous demands.

Because it is difficult for raters to maintain consistent mood estimates over extended time periods, self-monitored mood ratings suffer from subjective influences and measurement difficulties. It is important to note that ordinal-scale mood ratings cannot always be analyzed legitimately using the available nonlinear quantitative techniques. The following analysis examined the presence of nonlinearity in mood-rating time series when ordinal data are available. We assume that a possibly continuous nonlinear process underlies the data obtained in mood-rating tasks even when the ratings themselves have ordinal measurement properties. This nonlinear process can be revealed by surrogate analysis of the mood-rating time series.

ANALYSIS OF MOOD-RATING DATA USING THE MONOTONIC MULTISCALE ENTROPY METHOD

We analyzed the data collected in Heiby et al. (2003) using the monotonic MSE method. No preprocessing to remove significant periodicities

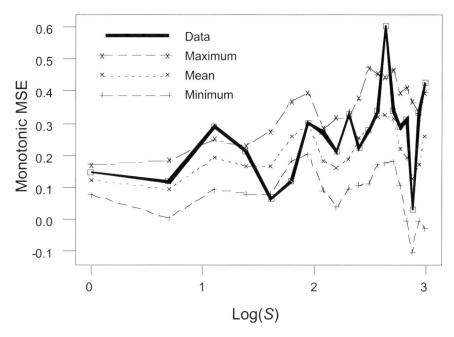

Figure 9.5. Comparison of Heiby et al. (2003) experimental data with Gaussian and chaos (Hénon): monotonic multiscale entropy for the nondepressed participant as the time scale *S* increases. Maximum, mean, and minimum refer to values for surrogate series.

from the mood-rating time series was used, because a reanalysis of the filtered data did not reveal any major differences in outcome. The results are shown in Figures 9.5 and 9.6 for the nondepressed and depressed participants, respectively, and for $S = 1, 20$. The solid line in each figure plots the results for the experimental data. The three dashed lines show the maximum, mean, and minimum values of monotonic MSE for the 19 surrogate series, representing a pseudo 95% confidence interval under the null hypothesis that the experimental data are linear.

Because the solid lines in both Figures 9.5 and 9.6 lie mostly between the maximum and minimum values of monotonic MSE values for the surrogate data, there is no substantial evidence for nonlinearity in either data set. However, there are a couple of points in Figure 9.6 that lie below the 95% confidence interval, suggesting some slight nonlinearity in the system generating the mood ratings when data are pooled over two and three successive observations. It is worth noting that the monotonic MSE value for the depressed participant, 0.26, is greater than that for the nondepressed participant, 0.15, when $S = 0$, and for small values of S thereafter. This finding suggests that the change in monotonic MSE as the mood ratings progress from three successive values to four successive values is greater for

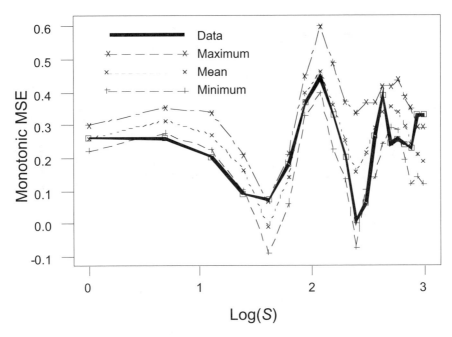

Figure 9.6. Comparison of Heiby et al. (2003) experimental data with surrogate series: monotonic multiscale entropy (MSE) for the depressed participant as the time scale *S* increases. Maximum, mean, and minimum refer to values for surrogate series.

the depressed participant. Hence, the rate of generation of persistent mood fluctuations is greater, reflecting generally more highly structured mood ratings for the depressed participant.

Figure 9.7 shows the comparison between the monotonic MSE results for the nondepressed and depressed participants with those of two benchmark time series, one a Gaussian series and the other a chaotic Hénon series. The nondepressed participant's data are more closely related to that for Gaussian data, whereas the depressed participant's data are not so close to a Gaussian series. Because there is no overlap between the 95% confidence intervals for both surrogate series in Figures 9.5 and 9.6, we can be confident that the depressed participant's data have a greater value than that for Gaussian noise for Log(S) = 0, just as is the case for the Hénon series. However, the previous analysis using surrogate series provides no evidence for chaos, or nonlinearity, in the system producing this series.

Thus, we are left with the suggestion that there is a substantial qualitative difference in the dynamics of mood fluctuations for the depressed and nondepressed participants' data, but there is no clear evidence for nonlinearity in the underlying dynamic mood-generating system. The greater proximity of the depressed participant's data to that of the chaotic series and,

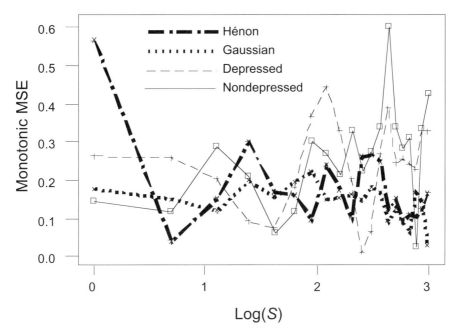

Figure 9.7. Monotonic multiscale entropy (MSE) for comparing the nondepressed and depressed participants' mood ratings from the Heiby et al. (2003) experimental data with Gaussian and chaotic Hénon benchmark time series as the time scale *S* increases.

likewise, the tendency for the nondepressed participant's data to be similar to that of a Gaussian process, suggests that depression is associated with a less complex mood state. A comparison with the data analysis methods used by Heiby et al. (2003) suggests that detecting nonlinearity depends on the measurement scale assumptions of the applied data analysis method.

Of course, the calculations involved in computing monotonic sample entropy are rather different from those used to compute conventional nonlinear indices such as fractal dimensionality. In the case of ordinal time series, it is not possible to compute nonlinearity indexes from the raw data because the rankings remain unaltered when a monotonic transformation is applied to the data. Nevertheless, we can still use monotonic sample entropy to detect nonlinearity in known continuous nonlinear time series by using the surrogate time-series method, so evidence against nonlinearity for the mood rating time series is undoubtedly a valid outcome. In practical terms, however, it is more constructive to view monotonic sample entropy as a complexity index and compare the data from depressed and nondepressed participants using this criterion. By doing this, we can still evaluate the validity of the MDH in this context. In the following section, we summarize the outcomes of the analyses and consider practical applications of this new method.

IMPLICATIONS FOR THE DIAGNOSIS AND TREATMENT OF MOOD DISORDERS

Monotonic MSE analyses of sequential mood data obtained from 2 individuals suggest that their mood fluctuations are not nonlinear. However, mood fluctuations for the depressed participant indicate lower complexity than that occurring for the nondepressed participant. Analyzing the time course of mood disorders and their etiologic factors using modern nonlinear techniques may provide new insight into a fundamental characteristic of human behavior, our need to adjust to environmental challenges. Such analyses illustrate the importance of considering individual participants' time-series data. They provide a detailed account of idiographic differences between adaptive transient emotional states and mood disorders. Such information is not so readily available from conventional statistical techniques, such as analysis of variance. The innovative application of monotonic MSE in psychology reported in this chapter suggests how revealing such technologies can be for diagnosis, prevention, and treatment programming. For example, lower complexity of mood ratings could be an indicator of a pending depressive episode that might be prevented.

The most common effective treatments for mood disorders involve pharmacotherapy targeting neurotransmitters (Paykel, 1992) and cognitive–behavioral psychotherapy targeting mood regulation skills (Chambless et al., 1996). The analyses of time-series mood data presented in this chapter suggest that effective treatments could involve stochastic infusion and learning to adjust to seemingly random environmental events. For example, a cognitive–behavioral technique that has been successfully applied to depression called *cognitive defusion* involves replacing perseverative depressogenic thoughts with a variety of hypotheses related to one's ongoing, changing situation (Luoma & Hayes, 2003). The temporal structure of mood disorders also suggests that prevention and treatment interventions may be most effective if they are implemented on the onset of dysphoric or manic indicators, due to expected perseveration, rather than waiting until the individual meets clinical diagnostic criteria.

The difference between the current analysis and the more conventional nonlinear analyses performed by Heiby et al. (2003) relates primarily to the recognition that the numerical operations required in the conventional analyses are not directly applicable to ordinal data, unless of course we consider ratings as interval-scale measures. Because interpoint distances cannot be unambiguously defined for ordinal data, we used measures based on the extent and direction of changes over time in the time-series values. Despite a loss of measurement precision, the new method can detect nonlinearity when it is known to exist. Furthermore, we could readily compare the results of monotonic MSE with benchmark Gaussian and chaotic series and by so doing interpret the results in a more meaningful way.

CONCLUSION

Applications of nonlinear dynamical concepts and techniques in quantitative psychology are still in their infancy. Advances in measurement technology, such as hand-held computers, can assist in the acquisition of time-series self-monitored data of complex human behavior and some etiologic factors (Haynes et al., 1995). However, much research needs to be completed before the following important issues can be resolved:

- the appropriate choice of nonlinear data analysis procedures, as well as efficient diagnostic methods;
- the development of a measurement theory for nonlinear dynamical psychological processes, especially for ordinal data; and
- the development of mathematical and computer models that successfully predict the available data from a variety of psychological fields and offer insights for future research.

The analyses reported here have provided an initial attempt at evaluating evidence for nonlinearity in ordinal rating scale time-series data. Although further research needs to be done, there is at least some promise of future success given that the results for the depressed and nondepressed participants' data could be contrasted meaningfully with benchmark Gaussian and chaotic series. Other promising techniques for analyzing such time series include those based on symbolic dynamics and generalized entropy ideas (Gregson, 2002; Gregson & Leahan, 2003).

The complex interaction between environmental influences and endogenous processes in dynamic behavioral disorders ensures that identification of causality is virtually impossible. Moreover, any qualitative change in dynamic disorders can result from the effects of both exogenous and endogenous control processes. In depression, the loss in complexity observed in mood fluctuations is perhaps a sign of endogenous physiological processes that are decoupled from the environmental as well as the cognitive, emotional, and sensorimotor behavioral mood-regulating resources available to healthy people. An interesting possibility is that those who have been diagnosed with mood disorders need to relearn the automaticity that normally accompanies any environmental effects on mood in healthy people. During the disease and therapeutic phase of the illness, the mood regulation system will exhibit fewer degrees of freedom, and lower complexity, compared with the highly complex mood control system used by healthy people. By analogy with the work of Shiffrin and Schneider (1977) in human cognition and that of the authors of chapter 7 in this book, such automaticity can occur only once the disrupted mood control system is retrained using both pharmacological and cognitive–behavioral therapies.

Clinical applications of the methods described in this chapter require a greater emphasis on quantitative monitoring of client progress than is common in current clinical practice. However, such monitoring occurs at the informal and more formal clinical evaluation levels, and there is no reason why clients should not be requested to monitor their own subjective experience as part of the therapeutic process. Indeed, those diagnosed with borderline personality disorder who are undergoing dialectical behavior therapy (DBT) are required to monitor their urges and feelings on a daily basis on diary cards using Likert rating scales. Such data are surely the grist for the new data analysis mill described herein. Our current research involves assessing how well ordinal time-series analysis of diary card time series can monitor each client's progress using DBT. This is a valuable application of the method, because DBT is both time consuming and expensive.

The advantage of obtaining a large amount of sequential behavioral data in clinical psychology has been clearly demonstrated. Interesting differences between the behavioral characteristics of those with, and those without, a mental disorder were revealed using a novel quantitative procedure. Although there was no evidence for nonlinearity in the mood time series, the ratings provided by the depressed participant were clearly less complex than those from the nondepressed participant. A speculative interpretation of this finding suggests that those with a mental disorder exhibit a behavioral repertoire that is inadequate for efficient functioning in a challenging environment. Similar findings replicated across other mental disorders and with many more participants demonstrate the practical and theoretical benefits of applying tools developed by cognitive scientists in the challenging field of clinical psychology.

REFERENCES

American Psychiatric Association. (2000). *Diagnostic and statistical manual of mental disorders* (4th ed., text revision). Washington, DC: Author.

Beck, A. T. (1967). *Depression: Clinical, experimental, and theoretical aspects.* New York: Hoeber.

Bélair, J., Glass, L., an der Heiden, U., & Milton, J. (1995). *Dynamical disease: Mathematical analysis of human illness.* Woodbury, NY: American Institute of Physics.

Chambless, D. L., Sanderson, W. C., Shoham, V., Bennett Johnson, S., Pope, K. S., Crits-Christoph, P., et al. (1996). An update on empirically validated therapies. *Clinical Psychologist, 49*, 5–18.

Coryell, W., & Winokur, G. (1992). Course and outcome. In E. S. Paykel (Ed.), *Handbook of affective disorders* (pp. 89–108). New York: Guilford Press.

Costa, M., Goldberger, A. L., Peng, C.-K. (2002). Multiscale entropy analysis of complex physiologic time series [Electronic version]. *Physical Review Letters, 89*, 68102.

Costa, M., Peng, C.-K., Goldberger, A. L., & Hausdorff, J. M. (2003). Multiscale entropy analysis of human gait dynamics. *Physica A: Statistical Mechanics and Its Applications, 330*, 53–60.

Freeman, W. J. (2000). A proposed name for aperiodic brain activity: Stochastic chaos. *Neural Networks, 13*, 11–13.

Gottschalk, A., Bauer, M. S., & Whybrow, P. C. (1995). Evidence of chaotic mood variation in bipolar disorder. *Archives of General Psychiatry, 52*, 947–959.

Gregson, R. A. M. (2002). Scaling quasi-periodic psychological functions. *Behaviormetrika, 29*, 41–57.

Gregson, R. A. M., & Leahan, K. (2003). Forcing function effects on nonlinear trajectories: Identifying very local brain dynamics. *Nonlinear Dynamics, Psychology, and Life Sciences, 7*, 139–159.

Haynes, S. N., Blaine, D., & Meyer, K. (1995). Dynamical models for psychological assessment: Phase space functions. *Psychological Assessment, 7*, 17–24.

Haynes, S. N., & O'Brien, W. H. (2000). *Principles and practice of behavioral assessment.* New York: Kluwer Academic/Plenum Publishers.

Heath, R. A. (2000). *Nonlinear dynamics: Techniques and applications in psychology.* Mahwah, NJ: Erlbaum.

Heath, R. A. (2004). Complexity and mental health. In T. Holt (Ed.), *Complexity for clinicians* (pp. 83–94). Oxford, England: Radcliffe Medical Press.

Heath, R. A., Kelly, A., & Longstaff, M. (2000). Detecting nonlinearity in psychological data: Techniques and applications. *Behavior Research Methods, Instrumentation & Computers, 32*, 280–289.

Hegger, R., Kantz, H., & Schreiber, T. (1999). Practical implementation of nonlinear time series methods: The TISEAN package. *Chaos, 9*, 413–435.

Heiby, E. M. (1995). Assessment of behavioral chaos with a focus on transitions in depression. *Psychological Assessment, 7*, 10–16.

Heiby, E. M., Pagano, I. S., Blaine, D. D., Nelson, K., & Heath, R. A. (2003). Modeling unipolar depression as a chaotic process. *Psychological Assessment, 15*, 426–434.

Heiby, E. M., & Staats, A. (1990). Depression and its classification. In G. Eifert & I. Evans (Eds.), *Unifying behavior therapy: Contributions of paradigmatic behaviorism* (pp. 220–246). New York: Springer Publishing Company.

Kantz, H., & Schreiber, T. (1997). *Nonlinear time series analysis.* Cambridge, England: Cambridge University Press.

Korotitsch, W. J., & Nelson-Gray, R. O. (1999). An overview of self-monitoring research in assessment and treatment. *Psychological Assessment, 11*, 415–425.

Luoma, J. B., & Hayes, S. C. (2003). Cognitive defusion. In W. O'Donohue, J. E. Fisher, & S. C. Hayes (Eds.), *Cognitive behavior therapy: Applying empirically supported techniques in your practice* (pp. 71–78). Hoboken, NJ: Wiley.

McFall, R. M., & Townsend, J. T. (1998). Foundations of psychological assessment: Implications for cognitive assessment in clinical science. *Psychological Assessment, 10*, 316–330.

Nelson, K., & Heiby, E. M. (2001, November). *Self-monitoring and identification of depression.* Poster presented at the annual convention of the Association for the Advancement of Behavior Therapy, Philadelphia.

Nezu, A. M., Ronan, G. F., Meadows, E. A., & McClure, K. S. (2000). *Practitioner's guide to empirically based measures of depression.* New York: Kluwer Academic/Plenum.

Pagano, I. S., Barkhoff, H., Heiby, E. M., & Schlicht, W. (2006). Dynamical modeling of the relations between leisure activities and health indicators in a cross-national sample. *Journal of Leisure Research, 38*, 61–77.

Paykel, E. S. (1992). *Handbook of affective disorders.* New York: Guilford Press.

Pincus, S. (1995). Approximate entropy (ApEn) as a complexity measure. *Chaos, 5,* 110–117.

Richman, J. S., & Moorman, J. R. (2000). Physiological time-series analysis using approximate entropy and sample entropy. *American Journal of Physiology: Heart Circulation Physiology, 278*, H2039–H2049.

Riedel, H. P. R., Heiby, E. M., & Kopetskie, S. (2001). Psychological behaviorism theory of bipolar disorder. *Psychological Record, 51*, 507–532.

Schreiber, T., & Schmitz, A. (2000). Surrogate time series. *Physica D, 142,* 346–382.

Shen, Y., Olbrich, E., Achermann, P., & Meier, P. F. (2003). Dimensional complexity and spectral properties of the human sleep EEG. *Clinical Neurophysiology, 114*, 199–209.

Shiffrin, R. M., & Schneider, W. (1977). Controlled and automatic human information processing: II. Perceptual learning, automatic attending, and a general theory. *Psychological Review, 84*, 127–190.

Staats, A. W. (1996). *Behavior and personality: Psychological behaviorism.* New York: Springer Publishing Company.

Summerfeldt, L. J., & Antony, M. (2002). Structured and semistructured diagnostic interviews. In M. Antony & D. H. Barlow (Eds.), *Handbook of assessment and treatment planning for psychological disorders* (pp. 3–37). New York: Guilford Press.

Torres, M. E., & Gamero, L. G. (2000). Relative complexity changes in time series using information measures. *Physica A: Statistical Mechanics and Its Applications, 286*, 457–473.

Vaillancourt, D. E., & Newell, K. M. (2002). Changing complexity in human behavior and physiology through aging and disease. *Neurobiology of Aging, 23,* 1–11.

Woyshville, M. J., Lackamp, J. M., Eisengart, J. A., & Gilliland, J. A. M. (1999). On the meaning and measurement of affective instability: Clues from chaos theory. *Biological Psychiatry, 45,* 261–269.

GLOSSARY

additivity: A data pattern from a factorial experiment in which the magnitude and direction of differences across the levels of one factor remain constant despite changes in the prevailing levels of the other factor(s).

amnesia: Condition resulting in a profound impairment in acquiring new information in the face of relatively preserved functioning in other cognitive domains, often due to damage in the medial temporal lobe or diencephalon.

attractor: A stable state exhibited by a dynamically changing system that tends to re-create itself when the system is in another state that partially resembles the attractor state. Attractors occur naturally in complex biological and physical systems and are commonly produced by connectionist models of neural networks involving complex interactions of large numbers of neuronal units.

auditory hallucinations: For patients with schizophrenia and affective disorder, these hallucinations generally consist of audible speech with timbre characteristics that become well recognized by the patient and that suggest particular speakers. The content of these hallucinations occasionally consists of single words but more often reflects phrases or extended, discursive language.

back-propagation: A statistical method for training simulated multilayered networks to produce specific outputs when presented with specific inputs. The training method allows the network to represent generalization derived during training as shifts in the weights of connections linking neurons in one layer to neurons in an adjacent layer.

base distribution: An account of task performance whose properties, such as parameters, are randomly distributed according to a mixing distribution. (See also **Bayesian statistics, mixture model.**)

Bayesian information criterion: A criterion for the fit of model predictions to empirical observations that imposes a penalty for models that have more free parameters than others.

Bayesian statistics: A general system for conducting statistical inference by treating the population parameter as a random variable having a probability distribution and using Bayes's theorem to revise that distribution after new data are obtained. (See also **prior and posterior distribution.**)

capacity index: A quantification of cognitive work accomplished by a system since t time units after commencement of processing. The quantity is $-\ln[S(t)]$, where $S(t)$ is the survivor function of the distribution of process-completion latencies.

categorical data: A sequence of data observations, each of which falls into one and only one category of a well-defined set of categories. Thus, a sequence of observations results in a pattern of counts over the categories, where a category count is the number of observations that fall into that category.

category learning: Placing stimuli into categories with feedback about the accuracy of classification, although experimenter instruction as to the stimulus characteristics on which to base classifications typically remains absent.

caudate nucleus: Basal ganglia structure receiving input from multiple cortical regions and projecting to other basal ganglia nuclei and ultimately back to cortical structures to form cortical–striatal loops; involved in a variety of cognitive and motor processes.

cerebellum: Large portion of the brain located between the brain stem and the cerebral cortex; implicated in both motor and cognitive functions.

choice consistency: The degree to which choice behavior is dictated by expectancies. (See also **expectancy-valence model**.)

cognitive models: Quantitative summaries of cognitive processes and representations that are used to explain intelligent (human or animal) behavior.

coherence probability: A part of the population-parameter mapping method for estimating the latent scientific parameters; a measure ascertaining whether a random Monte Carlo sample from the Bayesian posterior distribution for the observational categories is consistent with the scientific model. (See also **population-parameter mapping, Bayesian statistics, prior and posterior distribution**.)

complexity: The number of unrelated variables required to represent a system's dynamics. The larger the number of variables, or degrees of freedom, the larger the complexity.

confidence ratings: Participants' explicit ratings of their confidence about their judgments in a cognitive task, typically a recognition memory task.

connection weight: A number assigned to a simulated anatomic projection from one neuron to another that determines the degree that activation in the former influences the input registered by the second neuron.

decision boundary: In a classification problem with two classes (or categories), a hypersurface that partitions the underlying space into one of two response regions, with items on one side of the hypersurface belonging in one class and items on the other side belonging to the other class.

deterministic: A system whose temporal evolution can be predicted without error provided both the initial state and the system's parameters are known precisely.

Dirichlet–multinomial distribution: A particular hierarchical statistical model for the multinomial distribution. Each data observation in the sequence is governed by the multinomial distribution; however, the category probability parameters of the distribution vary independently from observation to observation governed by a special hyperdistribution called the *Dirichlet distribution*. (See also **mixture model**.)

distribution function: The probability of a process being completed at or before t time units after commencement. Denoted $F(t)$, it is the complement of the survivor function, or $1 - S(t)$.

e: Approximately 2.72, it is a constant analogous to π; it is fundamental in science and mathematics. e^x is sometimes written $\exp(x)$, whereby $\exp(1)$ is approximately 2.72.

Erlang distribution: A process whose subprocesses are k' in number, each being exponentially distributed and each having the same rate parameter v. Its probability density function, proportional to the relative frequency of process completion at t time units since commencement, is $(vt)^{k'-1}/(k'-1)!\ ve^{-vt}$; its mean is k'/v, and its variance is k'/v^2.

expectancy: Predicted consequence of selecting a choice alternative. (See also **expectancy-valence model.**)

expectancy-valence model: A computational modeling analysis that includes the components of **choice consistency** and **expectancy** (see entries).

excitotoxicity: A form of neuronal death that is caused by excessive excitation or activation. This form of neurotoxicity can be induced by certain drugs as well as disease states, such as epilepsy.

exponential distribution: A one-parameter distribution of process latencies. Its probability density function, proportional to the relative frequency of process completion at t time units since process commencement, is ve^{-vt}, its mean being $1/v$ and its variance being $1/v^2$. An Erlang distribution with only one subprocess reduces to the exponential distribution.

exponentiate: To raise a value to a power; for example, x^y is x exponentiated by y.

hierarchical statistical model: A model designed for the case in which a sequence of data observation is governed by a fixed parametric statistical model, with the proviso that the parameters of the model vary independently from observation to observation. The sequence of parameters is drawn from a distribution called the *hyperdistribution*, and it has its own parameters, called *hyperparameters*. Thus, the sequence of parameters itself can be regarded as a sequence of independent and identically distributed observations from a parametric statistical model, and this two-level structure is why these models are called *hierarchical*. Sometimes such models are called *random effects models*. (See also **Bayesian statistics, mixture model, Dirichlet–multinomial distribution.**)

Huntington's disease: A progressive neurological movement disorder that is genetically determined and is due to cell death in the caudate nucleus. It invariably results in cognitive deficits in executive functions, memory, and attention and eventually dementia.

implicit classification: Placing stimuli into categories without experimenter instruction as to the stimulus characteristics on which to base classifications or feedback about the accuracy of classifications.

independent and identically distributed: A sequence of data observations is said to be independent and identically distributed if it arises from a series of independent random variables, each governed by the same (identical) distribution.

Kolmogorov–Smirnov test: A test for the departure of data from a specified distribution, such as normal.

likelihood distribution: The probability of outcomes (or data) given a probabilistic model with specified values for the parameters of the model. (See also **likelihood function**.)

likelihood function: A mathematical expression that indicates the probability or density of any particular observed data set as a function of the parameters of the model. (See also **Bayesian statistics, likelihood distribution, prior and posterior distribution**.)

maladaptive determinism hypothesis: The idea that highly predictable and regular fluctuations in some variable, such as heart rate or mood rating, are associated with illness, that is, a lower level of adaptation to environmental stressors.

maximum-likelihood estimation: Estimation of the value of a parameter whereby the likelihood for outcomes (or data) is maximized given the model.

mixing distribution: A distribution governing the probabilities, or probability densities, of properties such as parameters of a base distribution. (See also **Bayesian statistics, hierarchical statistical model, mixture model**.)

mixture model: A model whose account of task performance, expressed in terms of the base distribution of a response parameter, has properties (e.g., parameters) that are randomly distributed according to a mixing distribution. (See also **Bayesian statistics, hierarchical statistical model**.)

moment matching: A method of parameter estimation whereby modeled moments of response distributions, such as means and variances of response latencies, are combined so as to isolate their parameters. The parameter k' of the Erlang distribution, for example, is estimated as $\text{mean}^2/\text{variance} = (k'^2/v^2)/(k'/v^2)$. Empirical moments are substituted in the estimation procedure.

Monte Carlo simulation: A method of generating data from a parametric statistical model by using a random number generator. One selects a particular probability distribution from the model and then, using a random number generator, samples a series of independent and identically distributed observations from the selected distribution.

mood disorder: A condition in which fluctuations in a person's feelings are inappropriate, leading to maladaptive behavior and distress.

multidimensional scaling: A mathematical model that provides a spatial representation of participants' psychological organization of stimuli, in which the perceived similarity between two stimuli is modeled as a decreasing function of the distance between the two stimuli.

multinomial distribution: A parametric statistical model for categorical data. It assumes that the sequence of observations is independent and identically distributed over the categories, and it specifies the probabilities of various patterns of counts in the categories as a function of category probability parameters and the total number of observations. In the special case of two categories, the multinomial distribution becomes the familiar binomial distribution.

multinomial processing tree models: Specially designed parametric statistical models for categorical data in information-processing tasks. In a multinomial processing tree model of a particular task, the category probabilities are defined in terms of parameters that have substantive interpretations that arise from an information processing tree account of the task. Such an account assumes that each observed response category is the result of one or more unobserved (latent) sequences of processing events represented in a probabilistic branching tree structure.

nonlinear dynamics: Fluctuations in a sequence of observations that cannot be represented by a linear system, that is, one for which the values can be transformed by multiplying them by a constant and adding a constant without changing the system's properties.

nonstationary series: A series that has at least one time-varying parameter. The mean and possibly the variance change with time.

normal distribution: A family of probability distributions that differ in their location (the mean) and spread (the variance–covariance). It is often called a *bell-shaped distribution* because its probability density function resembles a bell. (Also called a *Gaussian distribution*; see also **parametric statistical model**.)

one-step-ahead predictions: Predictions of the choice made on the next trial following any given trial in a repeated choice task.

parameter: "An arbitrary constant whose value affects the specific nature but not the formal properties of a mathematical expression" (Borowski & Borwein, 1989, p. 435). In modeling, a parameter value affects model predictions but not model structure (i.e., the model's mathematical organization).

parametric statistical model: A family of probability distributions for a particular data structure. They are indexed by the parameters of the model in the sense that a particular model distribution on the data structure is specified as a function of the numerical values of the parameters. The parameters are defined by specifying a set of all possible parameter values called the *parameter space*. A familiar example of a parametric statistical model is the family of (normal) Gaussian distributions defined for continuous numerical data. The distributions are given by $f(x) = \dfrac{1}{\sqrt{2\pi\sigma^2}} \exp\left(-\dfrac{1}{2}\left(\dfrac{x-\mu}{\sigma}\right)^2\right)$, and they are indexed by two parameters, μ and σ, that reside in the parameter space $\Lambda = \{(\mu,\sigma) \mid -\infty < \mu < \infty; 0 < \sigma < \infty\}$.

Parkinson's disease: A progressive neurological disorder caused by the death of dopamine-producing cells in the pars compacta of the substantia nigra. Although primarily considered a movement disorder, it often results in deficits in memory, attention, and executive functions.

perceptual organization: See **psychological space**.

phase plot: A graphical representation of a time-series trajectory obtained by plotting successive values of the series.

Poisson distribution: A distribution of discrete values, such as number of subprocesses of an Erlang distribution k', whose probability function is $m^k/k'! \ e^{-m}$ and whose mean and variance are both m.

population parameter mapping: A method developed by Chechile (1998) for estimating the latent parameters of a scientific model that account for the experimental observations. In population parameter mapping estimation, random vectors are repeatedly sampled from the Bayesian posterior distribution of a purely statistical representation for the data that does not assume the scientific model. Each vector is then mapped (if possible) to the corresponding vector for the parameters of the scientific model.

power law: A relationship between power and frequency in a spectral analysis of time series data that is not linear. The relationship can be made linear by applying a logarithmic transformation to both the power and frequency.

prior and posterior distribution: In the Bayesian framework, there is a probability distribution used to represent the knowledge about the population parameter. The *prior distribution* is the probability distribution before data are collected; the *posterior distribution* is the corresponding distribution after data are collected. Bayes's theorem is used to revise the prior distribution to the posterior distribution. The key agent of this revision is the likelihood function. (See also **Bayesian statistics**.)

process model: An analytic model that specifies mathematically the theorized links between the operation of a cognitive process and task performance. (See also **stochastic model**.)

psychological space: Participants' spatial representation of stimuli in terms of their perceived similarity and dissimilarity; also called **perceptual organization**.

psychotomimetic drugs: Drugs that induce or mimic psychotic states, such as hallucinations and paranoia, when ingested.

recency: The degree to which a decision maker weighs recent events in the choice history compared with events that occurred in the more distant past.

recognition memory: Explicit classification of stimuli as previously viewed or not.

repeated choice task: A task in which a person has to choose repetitively between multiple alternatives and where each choice is followed by feedback.

response parameter: A property of task performance, such as response latency or response category (e.g., accuracy, item recognition, or item recall).

signal detection theory: A theory that provides a framework for quantifying the ability to discern "signal" from "noise," or one category of items from another. According to the theory, there are a number of perceptual and decisional factors that determine how well one performs.

spectral analysis: A transformation of a time series from the time domain to the frequency domain so that the amplitudes and phases of its frequency components can be determined.

stochastic model: "The mathematical abstraction of an empirical process whose development is governed by probabilistic laws" (Doob, 1953, p. v). (See also **process model**.)

striatum: Subcortical nuclei, including the caudate and the putamen, which have extended efferent and afferent connections with the cortex; implicated in both motor and cognitive functions.

substantia nigra pars compacta: A subdivision of the substantia nigra within the midbrain that provides the main source of dopamine to the basal ganglia; an important area of pathology in Parkinson's disease believed to underlie motor symptoms.

survivor function: The probability of a process remaining incomplete at t time units following commencement. Denoted $S(t)$, it is the complement of the distribution function, or $1 - F(t)$.

time series: A sequence of observations on the same variable measured at possibly but not necessarily equal intervals of time.

valence: An affective reaction to stimuli that are of significance to the organism.

REFERENCES

Borowski, E. J., & Borwein, J. M. (1989). *The HarperCollins dictionary of mathematics* (2nd ed.). New York: HarperCollins.

Chechile, R. A. (1998). A new method for estimating model parameters for multinomial data. *Journal of Mathematical Psychology, 42,* 432–471.

Doob, J. L. (1953). *Stochastic processes.* New York: Wiley.

AUTHOR INDEX

Numbers in italics refer to listings in the references.

Bradley, B. P., 223, *235*
Braff, D. L., 244, *258, 260*
Braithwaite, R. B., 9, *16*, 171, *174, 233*
Brammer, M. J., 244, *261*
Braun, K., 255, *261*
Brawer, J. R., *261*
Brewer, W., *262*
Brewin, C. R., 208, *233*
Bricolo, E., 216, *234*
Brinkley, C. A., 82, *110*
Broadbent, D. E., 93, *108*, 215, 218, *234*
Broga, M. I., 10, *16*, 231, 232, *236*
Brown, R. G., 123, *144*
Browne, M. W., 4, *17*, 148, *175*
Bryan, T. H., 62, *76*
Bryant, R. A., 31, *48*
Buchanan, R. W., 208, *234*, 241, *258*
Buchner, A., 31, *46, 47*
Buckely, J., 85, *109*
Budnick, B., 244, *260*
Bundesen, C., 216, *234*
Buschke, H., 54, *76*
Busemeyer, J. R., 5, 6, *16*, 83, 87–89, 92,
    98, 99, 102, 104, 105, 107, *108–*
    111, 202, *203*
Butterfield, E. C., 54, *76*

Cagigas, X. E., *145*
Cameron, L. A., *261*
Capetillo-Cunliffe, L., 208, *236*
Carlin, J. B., 41, *47*
Carlsson, A., 142, *144*
Carpenter, C., 245, *259*
Carroll, J. C., 184, *203*
Carroll, K., *259*
Carter, C. S., 208, *234*
Carter, J. R., 6, 8, 10, *16, 17*, 151, 158,
    160, 161, 169, 172, *174, 176*,
    181, *204*, 217, 225, 229, 232,
    234, 236
Carver, C. S., 106, *108*
Casali, S., 242, *257*
Cavedini, P., 81, 86, *108*
Cavus, I., 256, *259*
Celaya, L. J., 208, *234*
Ceschi, G., 32, *47*
Chaderjian, M. R., 208, *234*
Chajczyk, D., 208, *235*
Chambless, D. L., 286, *289*
Chandler, J. P., *174*

Chang, J. J., 184, *203*
Chapman, J. P., 71, *76*
Chapman, L. J., 71, *76*
Charnallet, A., *45*
Chaturvedi, S., 243, *258*
Chechile, R. A., 26, 46, 52, 55–57, 59–61,
    63–67, 69, 70–72, 74, 75, 76, 298,
    299
Chelazzi, L., 216, *234*
Chen, C., *260*
Chosak-Reiter, J., 20, 26–27, *46*
Chuang, D.-M., 240, *260*
Cisima, M., *108*
Clark, L., 81, 86, *108*
Clay, R., 4, *16*
Cohen, J., 224n, *234*
Cohen, M. M., 189, *203*
Coles, M., 85, *109*
Colledge, E., 86, *108*
Collette, F., 31, *45*
Congdon, P., 60, *76*
Contoreggi, C., 86, *109*
Cook, M., *262*
Coryell, W., 265, *289*
Costa, M., 275, *289*
Costello, G. G., 148, *174*
Cowell, P. E., 241, *259*
Creelman, C. D., 193, *203*
Cressie, N. A. C., 23, *49*
Crits-Christoph, P., *289*
Cronbach, L. J., 8, 9, *16*
Curran, T., 31, *46*
Curtiss, S., 63, 73, *79*

Dabholkar, A. S., 240, *260*
Dalgleish, T., 208, *233*
Damasio, A. R., 81, 82, 85, 103, *107, 108*
Damasio, H. C., 81, 82, *107, 108*
Danion, J.-M., *47*
D'Annucci, A., *108*
David, A. S., *260*
Davidson, P. O., 148, *174*
Davidsson, P., 242, *258*
Davis, A., *258*
Davis, J. D., 133, *145*
Davison, M., 173, *177*
Davison, M. L., 184, *203*
Dawson, M. E., 208, 213, *237*
de Crespigny, A., *260*
De Finetti, B., 60, *77*

de Haan, E. H. F., 29, *45*
Delis, D. C., 123, *144*, *146*
Del Vecchio, N., 32, *46*
Demadura, T. L., *144*
Denburg, N., *108*
Denby, C., *45*
Denker, J. S., 254, *260*
Densmore, M., *174*
Dick, M. B., 20, *46*
Dierks, T., 244, *258*
Di Lollo, V., 72, *77*
Dobbins, I., 31, *50*
Dobscha, S. K., 245, 254, *259*
Doering, D. G., 62, *77*
Dolan, S., 104, *108*
Donchin, E., 85, *109*
Done, D. J., 244, *258*
Doob, J. L., 298, *299*
Dowling, E. T., *16*
Drislane, F., 72, 73, *77*
Drost, D., *174*
Dubois, B., 124, *144*
Dudgeon, P., *262*
Dwork, A. J., *260*
Dykman, B., 208, *234*

Eastwood, S. L., 242, *258*
Edelman, G. M., 251, *258*
Edgar, C. L., 242, *257*
Edwards, J. M., 216, *234*
Edwards, W., 221, *234*
Efron, B., 98, *108*
Eisengart, J. A., 267, *291*
Ell, S. W., 131, *143*, *144*
Elman, J. L., 246, 257, *258*
Elwood, K. D., 57, *77*
Embretson, W. S., 210, *234*
Endler, N. S., 215, 216, *234*
Entwisle, D. R., 64, *77*
Erdfelder, E., 31, *46*, *47*
Erev, I., 93, 97, *108*, *110*
Ernst, M., 106, *109*
Eslinger, P. J., 85, *108*
Essex, C., 173, *177*
Estes, W. K., 4, 6, *16*, 123, *144*
Evans, M., 7, 12, *16*, 33, *47*, 153, 155, 157, 165, 168, *174*, 214, *234*

Fabiani, M., 85, *109*
Falkai, P., *260*, *262*

Fanini, A., 216, *234*
Farber, N. B., 251, *261*
Farmer, M. E., 63, 72, *77*
Fay, G., 72, *77*
Feijen, J., 31, *48*
Feinberg, I., 240, 241, *258*
Feltovich, N., 97, *109*
Fienberg, S. E., 23, *46*
Fiez, J. A., 256, *258*
Fific, M., 148, *177*, 209, *238*
Fillenbaum, G., *48*
Filoteo, J. V., 123, 124, 130, 131, 133, 138, 140, 142, *144–146*, 202, *203*
Finkelman, C., *259*
Finn, P. R., 82, *109*
Fischman, A. J., *259*
Flanagan, O., 10, *16*
Flanery, M. A., 134n, *146*
Flaum, M., 243, *257*
Folstein, M. F., 27, *47*
Folstein, S. E., 27, *47*
Formisano, E., *258*
Forster, M. R., 4, *17*, 148, *175*
Forster, P. M., 215, *234*
Frackowiak, R. S., *260*
Freeman, W. J., 267, *289*
Friedman, H. R., 246, *259*
Friedrich, F. J., 123, *146*
Friston, K. J., 242, *258*, *261*
Frith, C. D., 242, 244, *258*, *260*
Frost, R. O., 106, *109*

Galaburda, A. M., 62, 72, 73, *77*
Galbraith, K., 171, *177*
Galton, C. J., *49*
Galway, T. M., 171, *175*
Gamero, L. G., 271, *290*
Gao, X., 242, *262*
Garcia-Segura, M., 255, *261*
Gardner, R. C., 172, 176, 213, *236*
Garey, L. J., 241, *258*
Garzia, R., 63, *77*
Gelman, A., 41, 44, *47*
George, L., 149, 150, *175*, 213, 224, *234*
Geyer, M. A., 244, *258*
Gianesini, T., 216, *234*
Gilden, D. L., 7, *17*
Gill, J., 41, 44, *47*
Gilliland, J. A. M., 267, *291*

SUBJECT INDEX

Chi square, 165, 166
Chi-square contingency test, 7–8
Choice, decision making and, 87
Choice consistency parameter, 91–92
Cingulate gyrus, 242
$C_o(t)$. *See* Capacity OR Coefficient
Cocaine abusers, 104–106
Cognition-intensive coping, 173
Cognitive capacity, 170–171
Cognitive defusion, 286
Cognitive-processing capacity, 207–233
   and distribution properties, 210–214
   quantifying, 209–210
   and schizophrenia, 223–232
   stress-susceptibility effects on,
      214–223
Cognitive science, 179–203
   category learning in, 198–202
   implicit classification in, 188–192
   perceptual organization in, 183–188
   recognition memory in, 192–198
   stimulus set development in,
      181–183
Coherence, 6, 62, 70
Competition between Verbal and
      Implicit Systems (COVIS),
      131–132
Complexity, 267–269, 282
Complex tasks, 85n
Compound multinomial distribution, 37
Compound Poisson, 163
Computer modeling, 12
Conditional joint probability density,
      164
Conjunctive rule, 132
Conservation of energy, 254
Consortium to Establish a Registry for
      Alzheimer's Disease (CERAD),
      26–27
Construct validity, 8–9
Controlled processing, 208
Correlation dimension, 270
Cortical connectivity, 242
CR. *See* Capacity Ratio
Criterial noise, 121, 128

DBT (dialectical behavior therapy), 288
Decay models, 93
Decision bound, 115, 116, 126, 127
Decision bound theory, 121

Decision maker (DM), 86
Decision-making models, 81–107
   baseline, 94
   and cocaine abusers, 104–106
   evaluation of, 95–101
   expectancy-valence, 87–92
   future studies of, 106–107
   and Huntington's/Parkinson's
      disease, 102–104
   independent attention to gains/
      losses, 94
   inference vs. decay, 93
   and Iowa gambling task, 83–87
Decision processes, 115–116
Degrees of freedom, 267–268
Delta learning rule, 89
Dendritic spines, 255
Density function ($f(t)$), 211, 212
Depression
   source monitoring in, 29–30
   time-series application to, 280–282
Descriptive model, 221, 222
Detected words, 247
Detection failure, 221–223
Determinism, 268
Deterministic models, 187–188
Dialectical behavior therapy (DBT), 288
*Dictionary and Bibliography of Discrete
      Distributions* (Patil and Joshi), 12
Diffusion tensor imaging, 242
Dirichlet distribution, 37
Dirichlet–multinomial (D-M)
      distribution, 36–38
Disease dynamics, 269
Distribution properties, 210–214
DM (decision maker), 86
D-M distribution. *See* Dirichlet–
      multinomial distribution
Dopamine, 131–132, 142
Dopamine-mediated reward signal,
      131–132
Double factorial technology, 229
Drug abusers, 86, 104–106
Dynamic mood disorders, 267–269
Dyslexia, 62–73
   and analysis of 6P model, 64–70
   cognitive processes underlying,
      62–63
   and discussion of 6P model, 70–73
   prevalence of, 62
   as term, 62

Independent attention to gains and
losses, 94
Independent parallel model with
moderately limited capacity
(IPMLC), 226–232
Independent parallel processing with
fixed capacity (IPFC), 230, 231
Independent-parallel unlimited capacity
(IPUC), 226–233
Individual differences in MPT modeling,
32–44
assessing individual participants,
38–40
calibrating Hu's simulation
subroutine, 36–38
hierarchical modeling, 41–44
testing for, 35–36
Individual differences scaling
(INDSCAL) model, 184
Information integration, 130, 132, 136
Information-integration category
learning, 132, 137–142
Input layer, 247
Interaction effect, 71
Interference models, 93
Interviews, 266
Iowa gambling task, 81–87
IPFC. *See* Independent parallel processing
with fixed capacity
IPMLC. *See* Independent parallel model
with moderately limited capacity
IPUC. *See* Independent-parallel
unlimited capacity

Latent class MPTs, 43–44
Lateral geniculate nucleus, 72
Lexical decision task, 53
Limited capacity, 209
Linear information-integration learning,
140, 141
Linear integration, 124, 126–130
Log-likelihood criterion, 95
Log–log power spectrum, 280

Magnocellular system, 72
Major depressive episodes, 267
Maladaptive determinism hypothesis
(MDH), 268–269, 282
Mathematical modeling, 12

Mathematical psychology, 4, 51–52, 54
Maximum likelihood estimate (MLE), 34,
220
Maximum likelihood procedures, 122
Maximum Lyapunov exponent, 270
MDH. *See* Maladaptive determinism
hypothesis
MDS study. *See* Multidimensional scaling
study
Mean latency, 155, 157, 160
Medial temporal area, 136, 246
Memory
and decision making, 87
deficits in elderly adults, 25
for recent outcomes, 89–91
Memory-search facilitative stimulus
encoding, 147–174
cognitive–behavioral correlates of
additional encoding
subprocesses g, 171–172
data-predicting model, 153, 155–160
discussion overview, 169–170
distribution of aggregate data,
160–161
elongated encoding/cognitive
capacity, 170–171
exigencies of application, 172–173
extensions, 173
model-predicted performance data,
153, 154
overall interpretation, 152–153
paradigm, 149–151
predictions of group performance
data, 161–163
predictions of individual performance data, 164–169
results, 151–152
tests of model fit/competing model
fit, 160
Memory search in schizophrenia,
223–232
application of $C_o(t)$ to results of
paradigm, 229–231
clinical inferences, 231–232
$C_o(t)$ in light of paradigm, 225–229
paradigm, 224–225
Memory set, 210
Memory-set size, 224
Metachromatic leukodystrophy, 242
Metric scaling, 184
Miller inequality, 229

Mixing distributions, 153, 155, 157, 158
Mixture models, 148, 153, 155–160
    base distribution of, 153, 155, 156
    expected encoding latency in, 158, 159
    mixing distributions of, 153, 155, 157, 158
    prediction of individual performance data, 164–169
    prediction of mean latency in, 157, 158
    predictions of group performance data, 161–163
    schematic of, 159
    selection of parametric distributions in, 156, 157
MLE. *See* Maximum likelihood estimate
Model 4, 65
Model 7A, 59
Model 7B, 59
Model-based analyses, 126–128
Model evaluation, 95–101
    bootstrapping, 98
    example using simulated data, 98–101
    prediction, 95–96
    simulation, 96–97
Models for Behavior (Wickens), 12
Moment matching, 168
Monotonic MSE
    detecting nonlinearity using, 278, 279
    and diagnosis/treatment of mood disorders, 286, 287
    for mood disorder analysis, 282–285
Monotonic sample entropy, 275
Monte Carlo simulations, 8
Mood disorders, 263–269, 278–288
    diagnostic/treatment implications for, 286–287
    dynamic, 267–269
    and emotional states, 264–265
    measurement of, 265–267
    monotonic MSE method for analyzing, 282–285
    time-series applications to, 278–282
Motivational parameter, 88–89
MPT models. *See* Multinomial processing tree models
M stimulus, 184

Multidimensional scaling (MDS) study, 182, 184–188, 202
Multinomial distribution, 23
Multinomial processing tree (MPT) models, 19–45, 52, 55, 56
    binary tree structure of, 21–22
    identification of, 23
    individual differences in. *See* Individual differences in MPT modeling
    for neuropsychological test battery results, 26–27
    for process dissociation, 30–32
    software for analyzing, 23–24
    for source monitoring, 27–30
    for storage–retrieval measurement, 24–26
    structure of, 20–24
Multiple-systems approach to category learning, 136n, 137n
Multiscale entropy (MSE)
    description of, 275–277
    monotonic. *See* Monotonic MSE

Naperian logarithm, 213
Natural logarithm, 213
NC (normal control) participants, 128
Negative-priming deficit, 171–172
Network architecture for simulation, 245–253
    components of, 246–247
    learning process used in, 247, 249
    performance assessment of, 249–251
    phonetic codes for, 247, 248
    pruning procedure used in, 251–253
Neural connectivity, 240
Neuroanatomic pruning, 251–253
Neurodevelopmental Darwinism, 251
Neurology, 269
Neuronal density, 241
Neuronal loss, 251
Neuropil volume, 241, 255
Neuropsychological test batteries, 26–27
New recognition, 57–59
N–methyl-D-aspartate antagonists, 251
Nobel Prize, 4
Noise, 6–8, 267, 280, 282
Nonlinear analysis techniques, 270–273
Nonlinear dynamical system, 173

Nonlinear information-integration learning, 140, 141
Nonlinear information-integration rule, 133, 134
Normal control (NC) participants, 128
Normative model, 221–223
Nosofsky's model, 196
Novelty excess, 171

Obsessive–compulsive disorder, 86
Old recognition, 57–59
Optimal classifier, 115–116
Optimal decision bound model, 121, 126
Ordinal data, 273–275
Orthographic encoding, 72
Output codes, 247, 249
Output layer, 247, 249
Overdispersion, 8, 41

Pair-clustering model, 22, 24–26
Paranoid-schizophrenia patients, 154, 155, 166, 167
Parkinson's disease (PD) patients, 114
    attentional processes in, 123–125, 128–131
    category rule learning in, 133–138
    and expectancy-valence model, 102–104
    information integration in, 138–142
Percepts, 246
Perceptual categorization task, 114, 116–120
Perceptual noise, 121
Perceptual organization (PO), 183–188
Perceptual processes, 115
Pharmacotherapy targeting neurotransmitters, 286
Phonetic code, 247, 248
Phonetic inputs, 246, 249
Phonological processing, 63
PO. See Perceptual organization
Poisson distributions, 156, 158
Pooling, issues with, 32–33
Population-parameter mapping (PPM), 60, 62, 65, 66, 69, 74–75
Posterior probability, 66
Posterior probability density function, 164
PPM. See Population-parameter mapping

Prediction, 95–96
Prefrontal cortex, 241
Priming, 171–172
Probabilistic scaling, 187–188
Probability density function, 155, 210
Probability distribution, 22
Probability distribution function, 211
Probability of detection failure, 221
Probe item, 210
Probe-item encoding, 152, 210
Process dissociation, 30–32
Processing-tree theory, 82
Pruning procedure, 251–255
Psychological measurement, 52–55
Psychological space, 184
Psychometrics, 4, 51, 52, 54
Psychopathic individuals, 86
Putamen of basal ganglia, 102

Quantitative Methods in Psychology (Lewis), 11
Questionnaires, 266

Ramping up, 171
Random-walk models, 53–54
Rapid attention shifts 'n' learning (RASHNL) model, 199–201
Rapid temporal processing, 63
RASHNL model. See Rapid attention shifts 'n' learning model
Reading aloud, 63
Reading disorder. See Dyslexia
Reality monitoring, 28
Recall, 54, 56, 57, 70
Recency parameter, 89–91
Recognition, 62, 192–198
Recognition test, 56, 57
Reinforcement learning model, 87–92
    baseline, 94
    independent attention to gains/losses, 94
    interference vs. decay, 93
Relative judgment random-walk model, 54
Reliability of choice behavior, 91–92
Repetitive transcranial magnetic stimulation (rTMS), 256
Response bias, 29
Response time, 53–54

Response Times (Luce), 12
Retrieval, 54, 67, 69
Rewards, 131
RTMS (repetitive transcranial magnetic
    stimulation), 256
Rule application variability, 122, 128,
    133–137
Rule-based category learning, 132–137

Sample entropy, 271–275
Schizophrenia, 239–257
    age of onset, 240
    assessing individual participants in
        study of, 39–40
    and auditory hallucinations of
        speech simulation, 243–245
    memory problems in, 25, 26
    memory search analysis in. *See*
        Memory search in schizophrenia
    as neurodevelopmental disturbances,
        240–242
    prevalence of, 239
    and pruning of neural connections,
        253–255
    and simulation network architecture,
        245–253
    source monitoring in study of, 28–
        29
    and speech perception, 255–256
SDT. *See* Signal-detection theory
Selective attention, 123–131
Self-monitoring, 266–267
Self-organized criticality, 269
Self-report, 266
Self-terminating processing, 208
Semantic dementia, 30
Seven-parameter models, 59
Sexual-aggression research, 186–189, 192,
    197, 199–202
Shadowing, 61
Shannon information index, 273, 274
Short-term memory, 63
Shrinkage, 168
Signal detection, 53
Signal-detection theory (SDT), 193, 195,
    196
Simplex search, 95
Simulation, 96–101
Single-systems approach to category
    learning, 136n, 137n

6P model, 57–62, 64–71
    analysis of, 65–70
    discussion of, 70–71
    estimating model parameters for,
        60–62
    modeling error for, 75
    and PPM, 74–75
    recognition trials for, 57–59
    and seven-parameter models, 59
    test procedures in, 64–65
SNAP-25, 242
Songbirds, 255
Source monitoring, 27–30
Speech perception, 243–245, 254–256
Spine density, 241
Spoken language comprehension, 72
Statistical advantage, 170, 227
*Statistical Decision Theory and Bayesian
    Analysis* (Berger), 12
Statistical Distributions (Evans, Hastings,
    and Peacock), 12
Stimulus set development, 181–183
Stochaos, 267
*Stochastic Modeling of Elementary
    Psychological Processes* (Townsend
    and Ashby), 12
Stochastic models, 7
Stochastic Processes (Ross), 12
Storage, 67
Storage–retrieval measurement models,
    55–59
    differences in, 55–56
    MPT, 24–26
    recall test in, 56
    recognition test in, 56, 57
Stress-negotiation deficit, 173
Stress-susceptibility effects on cognitive
    processing, 214–223
    capacity ratio application, 218–220
    hypotheses, 217
    normative/descriptive models,
        220–223
    paradigm, 214–217
    parametric extension, 220
Striatal damage, 136, 137, 141, 142
Striatal pattern classifier, 140
Structured interviews, 266
Subcortical dopamine levels, 142
Subjective probability framework, 60
Sum of strength formula, 91
Super capacity, 209

Surrogate time series, 277–278
Survivor function, 170, 211–213
Synaptic density, 240–241, 255
Synaptophysin, 241, 242

Tail of caudate nucleus. *See under*
    Caudate nucleus
Temporary storage layer, 247
Testing for individual differences, 35–36
Theory and Problems of Advanced Calculus
    (Spiegel), 11
Theory and Problems of Laplace Transforms
    (Spiegel), 11
Theory and Problems of Mathematics for
    Economists (Dowling), 11
Time series, 265–286
    and dynamic mood disorders,
        267–269
    with monotonic MSE, 278, 279,
        282–285
    and mood disorders, 265–267,
        278–282
    multiscale entropy, 275–277
    nonlinear, 270–273
    sample entropy computed from
        ordinal data, 273–275
    surrogate, 277–278
Time-series research, 263

Tukey's test for nonadditivity, 8
Two-dimensional, conjunctive rule
    strategies, 138

Unconditional joint probability density,
    164
Unidimensional rule-based category
    structure, 119, 138
Unlimited capacity, 209
Utility function, 88

Valence, 87–88
Vascular dementia (VD), 27
Ventromedial damage, 81
Ventromedial prefrontal cortex (VMPFC)
    damage, 83, 85, 86, 92, 102
Visual encodings, 72–73
Visual Field × Stimulus Type interaction,
    151–152
Visual transient system, 63
VMPFC damage. *See* Ventromedial
    prefrontal cortex damage
"Voices," 243

Weighted MDS (WMDS) model, 184,
    186–187
Working memory, 245, 246, 249–251

ABOUT THE EDITOR

Richard W. J. (Jim) Neufeld, PhD, is professor in both the Department of Psychology and the Department of Psychiatry, University of Western Ontario, London, Ontario, Canada, where he also is a core faculty member of the Graduate Program in Neuroscience. He has received the Joey and Toby Tannenbaum Schizophrenia-Research Distinguished Scientist Award (being the first psychologist recipient), the Ontario Mental Health Foundation Senior Research Fellowship, and the University of Western Ontario Faculty of Social Science Research Professorship. Dr. Neufeld is a past associate editor of the *Canadian Journal of Behavioral Science* and of the journal *Psychological Assessment*. He has served as a member of the Association of State and Provincial Psychology Boards' Examinations Committee and was chairman of its Academic Standards Subcommittee. He was the first clinical scientist to be chairman of the board of the Ontario Mental Health Foundation and is a past director of the American Psychological Association/Canadian Psychological Association–approved doctoral program in clinical psychology at his university. Dr. Neufeld has authored or edited 7 books and journal special sections. His 150 publications and 20 technical reports have appeared in journals ranging from the *Journal of Mathematical Psychology* and the *British Journal of Mathematical and Statistical Psychology* to the *Journal of Abnormal Psychology* and the *Journal of Consulting and Clinical Psychology*.